MASSACRES OF THE MOUNTAINS

VOLUME II

"NO HORSES TO SPARE."

MASSACRES OF THE MOUNTAINS

A HISTORY OF

THE INDIAN WARS OF THE FAR WEST
VOLUME II

By J. P. DUNN, Jr., M.S., L.L.B.

𝕵𝖑𝖑𝖚𝖘𝖙𝖗𝖆𝖙𝖊𝖉

NEW YORK
HARPER & BROTHERS, FRANKLIN SQUARE
1886

Copyright, 1886, by HARPER & BROTHERS.

All rights reserved.

MASSACRES OF THE MOUNTAINS
A HISTORY OF THE INDIAN WARS
OF THE FAR WEST

By J.P. Dunn, Jr. M.S., L.L.B.

As Published in 1886
VOLUME II

Trade Paperback ISBN: 1-58218-204-3
Hardcover ISBN: 1-58218-276-0
eBook ISBN: 1-58218-205-1

All rights reserved, which includes the right to reproduce this book or portions thereof in any form whatsoever except as provided by the U. S. Copyright Law. For information address Digital Scanning, Inc.

Digital Scanning and Publishing is a leader in the electronic republication of historical books and documents. We publish many of our titles as eBooks, as well as traditional hardcover and trade paper editions. DSI is committed to bringing many traditional and little known books back to life, retaining the look and feel of the original work.

©2001 DSI Digital Reproduction
First DSI Printing: September 2001

Published by DIGITAL SCANNING, INC.
Scituate, MA 02066
www.digitalscanning.com

CONTENTS

VOLUME II

	CHAPTER XII.	PAGE
DEATH TO THE APACHE!		356
	CHAPTER XIII.	
SAND CREEK		396
	CHAPTER XIV.	
CAÑON DE CHELLY AND BOSQUE REDONDO		447
	CHAPTER XV.	
FORT PHIL KEARNEY		477
	CHAPTER XVI.	
PUNISHING THE PIEGANS		509
	CHAPTER XVII.	
THE TRAGEDY OF THE LAVA BEDS		543
	CHAPTER XVIII.	
THE LITTLE BIG HORN		584
	CHAPTER XIX.	
JOSEPH'S NEZ PERCÉS		629
	CHAPTER XX.	
WHITE RIVER AGENCY		675
	CHAPTER XXI.	
CRUELTY, PITY, AND JUSTICE		716
LIST OF AUTHORITIES		757
INDEX TO VOLUME I AND II		765

ILLUSTRATIONS

	PAGE
"No horses to Spare"	*Fronticepiece*
An Apache Warrior	360
Black Knife	363
Silver Mines of Santa Rita	375
A Record of Mangas Colorado	382
Papago Chief	384
Apache Crucified by Papagos	387
Apaches Watching a Train	390
Tubac	393
Apache Boot, Head-dress, etc.	395
Texan Rangers	399
Old Fort Union	405
Standing off the Cheyennes	409
Which Tribe Did It?	413
Little Raven	418
Friday – A Good Arapahoe	421
George Bent	425

ILLUSTRATIONS

	PAGE
One the Little Blue	428
Indians Attacking Stage	432
Indian Scouts Celebrating	435
The Charge on Black Kettle's Camp	441
Giant's Arm-chair	449
Canon de Chelly	454
Cliff House in Canon de Chelly	459
Colonel Kit Carson	463
Near the Head-waters of the Navaho	469
Moqui Pueblo	473
Prospectors in the Mountains	478
Spotted Tail	*faces* 482
On the Bozeman Trail	485
Torture by Prairie Indians	489
Fort Phil Kearney and Vicinity	493
The Last Stand	497
Red Cloud	501
Sioux Village in Winter	505
Blackfeet and Trappers	512
Trader's Camp	515
"No Horses to Spare"	519
Edmonton House	525
Fort Benton	529
Lieut.-General P.H. Sheridan	533

ILLUSTRATIONS

	PAGE
Summer Camp on Marias River	539
Map of the Modoc Country	544
Modoc Squaws	547
Major-general E.R. S. Canby	551
A View of the Caves	555
View of Camp and Lake	557
The Rev. Dr. Thomas	560
General Alvin Gillem	566
Donald McKay, Leader of the Scouts	572
General Jefferson C. Davis	575
Captain Jack and Companions	579
The Bad Lands	586
Sitting Bull's First Adventure	592
Sitting Bull Storms a Crow Encampment and Takes Thirty Scalps	593
Sitting Bull Scalps a Teamster	594
Sitting Bull Steals a Drove of Horses	595
Old Fort Reno - Crook's Supply Camp	599
Rosebud River	605
Plan of Custer's Fight on the Little Big Horn	613
Massacre Monument	619
Major-general George A. Custer	622
Sitting Bull	625
Young Joseph	630
Ollacut	635

ILLUSTRATIONS

	PAGE
General O. O. Howard	638
Lapwai	643
Plain of the Geysers	653
The Stinking Water	656
General S. D. Sturgis	657
Joseph's Last Battle	661
General N. A. Miles	669
The Snowy Range	677
Ouray	683
Henry M. Teller	686
Captain Billy	689
Southern Utes	693
Jack	696
Colorow	700
Antelope	703
Plan of White River Agency	707
J. Douglas	710
Major T. T. Thornburgh	713
Haunts of the Apaches	718
Effect of Extermination Policy on Arizona Settler	720
General George Crook	728
General Pope	741
San Xavier del Bac	745
Crook's Battle-field in the Sierra Madre	751
Alcatraz Island	753

MASSACRES OF THE MOUNTAINS
VOLUME II

MASSACRES OF THE MOUNTAINS
VOLUME II

CHAPTER XII.
DEATH TO THE APACHE!

No more serious phase of the Indian problem has presented itself to the American people than that offered by the Apache tribes. Aided by the desert nature of their country, they have resisted the advance of the whites longer than any other Indian nation. They have fought with bravery and inconceivable cunning. They have committed atrocities that devils alone would seem capable of, and have been subjected to atrocities that devils might blush to commit. They have made their name a terror and a thing of execration to a section of country five times larger than all New England. They have kept miners for years from treasure deposits that have been regarded as of fabulous richness. They have gained the reputation of being the most treacherous, cruel, and inhuman savages that have been known in the United States. People who have been willing to extend sympathy and assistance to other Indians, have stood aghast at the murderous work of the Apaches, and given their opinions that nothing but the extermination of the tribe could ever rid Arizona and New Mexico of a constant liability to outrage and devastation. In noteworthy connection with this reputation is the fact that the Apaches are among the least known of the Indian tribes. Not only has their hostile attitude prevented white men from associating with them, but even when brought in contact with the whites they maintain a jealous reserve as to their habits, particularly those of a religious character. By way of example, it is commonly believed that they do not bury their dead, and never touch a dead body except in case of necessity; yet Colonel Cremony, who had excellent opportunity for knowing, insists that they bury their more prominent men, at least, with great ceremony, though he was unable to learn exactly what the formalities were.

The Apaches, as has been previously mentioned, speak the same language as the Navahos and Lipans; and all Southern Indians using this common tongue are often called Apaches. The Apaches proper call themselves "Shis Inday," or People of the Woods, a rather strange name for a tribe living in a country where three trees constitute a *bosque* or forest, but taken by them probably because the principal timber growth of the region is on the mountains which have long afforded them safe retreats. They were in nine tolerably distinct tribes through the earlier part of the present century, though by confederations and factional separations, in the course of their long warfare, some of this identity has been lost. At the beginning of our intercourse with them they were best divided as follows: Chiricahuas (Chiricagüis), Gileños, Mimbreños, Mescaleros, Jicarillas (Xicarillas, Hickorias), Pinaleños, Mogollons, Coyotéros, and Tontos. These names refer chiefly to their geographical positions. The Chiricahuas lived in South-eastern Arizona, about the Chiricahua Mountains. They are sometimes called Cochees, from their noted chief Cochise or Cheis, who was gathered to his fathers several years since, much to the relief of neighboring settlers. East of these, in the mountains about the headwaters of the Gila, was a small band of about two hundred warriors, known as the Gileños or Gila Apaches. The name Gileños is also sometimes used generically, including two or three additional tribes. North-east of these, in South-western New Mexico, lived the Mimbreños or Mimbres (Miembres —Willows) Apaches, otherwise known as the Copper Mine Apaches, from the fact that they infested the celebrated copper mines of Santa Rita del Cobré. To the east, beyond the Rio Grande, and west of the Pecos, dwelt the Mescaleros, who derived their appellation from their extensive use of the mescal (maguey, American aloe, or century-plant) for food, and in the manufacture of the intoxicating drink known by the same name. The Jicarillas lived in the mountains of Northern New Mexico, above Taos, and were closely associated with the Southern Utes. North-west of the Chiricahuas was a tribe sometimes called the Pinaleños or Pinal (Penole) Apaches, and sometimes the Arivapas (Aribaipais), from the Rio Arivapa which flows on the south-west of the Pinal range to the Gila. The Mogollons (Mogayones) lived directly north of these in the Mogollon Mountains and the deserts about them. Westward along the Gila River, and through the country north of it, roamed the Coyotéros, the most considerable of the tribes, who are said to have their name from their habit of eating the coyote or prairie wolf. It is possible, however, that the name is a corruption of Garrotéros (club men) which was formerly applied to some of the western tribes. The Tontos, who lived chiefly in the rough country south and west of Bill Williams Mountain, say that they broke off from the Coyotéros many years ago, and that their Indian name, which means "unruly," has been corrupted into the Spanish word *tonto*, which means "stupid."

No little confusion has arisen from the numerous names, of different languages, given to these and kindred tribes. The Indians east of the Pecos, called Llaneros or Apaches, are properly Lipans. They have always been confederated with the Comanches and Kiowas in our dealings with them, and are now located in Indian Territory with those tribes. The Faraones or Taracones, mentioned in old Spanish books, were probably Navahos; the word *Yutajenne* is given as the Apache synonym of the name, and *Yutajenne* or *Yutakah* is the Apache name for the Navahos. The Yampais or Yavipais are now known as Apache Mohaves. The Cajuenches were probably the same as the Cuchanos or Yumas. The Hualapais (Hualpies, Wallapais) have been called Apache Yumas since 1868, when that name was given them by General Gregg, who was then commanding in Arizona.

The Apaches were always known as wild Indians. It is doubtful if the Spaniards ever obtained any control over them, and certain that the Mexicans never retained any. Between these two peoples there was almost continuous war. The condition of the people of the Northern Mexican settlements was such that there was little chance of successful opposition to the Apaches. They were poor, and hardly more advanced in knowledge than their Indian enemies.

The central government exacted heavy taxes from them, but did nothing for their protection. The supreme power in their settlements was in the hands of the *ricos* or wealthy men, who often resisted the government and often contended among themselves. Some of the *ricos* were of quite pure Spanish blood, but the great mass of the people were the mongrel Mexicans, and these were nearly all in the state of peonage or bondage for debt. As a general rule it was found cheaper and more consonant with the warlike spirit of the Mexicans to buy peace of the Apaches than to fight them. Instead of uniting and making an effort for common defence, it was usually the case that when the State of Chihuahua was at war with the Indians, the State of Sonora would be at peace, and vice versa. The property and even the captives taken in the one State would be purchased in the other. General Carasco, military governor of Sonora after the Mexican war, on one occasion broke into this system. Sonora was at war with the Apaches, and Chihuahua was not only at peace but also was issuing rations to them quarterly at the village of Janos, near our border. Carasco advanced on this place by night marches, and succeeded in surprising them during the feasting that ensued upon the issue of rations. He killed a number and took ninety prisoners. Medina, the governor of Chihuahua, made complaint to the general government of this breach of inter-state customs, but the authorities sustained Carasco. This was a fortunate decision for the Northern Mexicans, for Carasco did more to protect their frontier than any ruler they had for years. He impressed the poor as soldiers, and forced the rich to supply the means for keeping them in the field. His methods were unpopular, however, and he was poisoned.

Many anecdotes are related by travellers of the poltroonery of the Mexicans in their contests with the Apaches. It is not strange that they appeared cowardly. They were poor, without organization, and with nothing in life to stimulate them to bravery. They were obliged to support themselves mainly by agriculture and stock-raising, and these pursuits put them continually on the defensive, while they scattered the people so as to make defence difficult. The Americans who went into the Apache country prior to our conquest were on a different footing from the Mexicans. They were chiefly trappers or traders, and though many of them had Mexican wives or mistresses, quite as many had their marital companions from among the Indians, while their business interests were quite diverse. The traders had more cause for sympathy with the Mexicans than the trappers, and yet the traders were so seldom attacked that the Mexicans accused them of having treated secretly with the Apaches. Their immunity was really due to constant preparation for attack; the Apaches never attack except by surprise. The trappers acted with one side or the other, or remained neutral, as their temporary interests demanded.

AN APACHE WARRIOR.

In 1837 the Mexicans of both Sonora and Chihuahua were at war with the Apaches, and both were becoming desperate over the successful incursions of the enemy. Chihuahua promulgated a law called the *Proyecto de Guerra*, or project for war, by which the State offered one hundred dollars for the scalp of an Apache warrior, fifty for the scalp of a squaw, and twenty-five for that of a child. Sonora was also paying a bounty for scalps, and both gave to the captor any booty he might take from the Indians. This liberality was produced mainly by the many atrocities of Juan José, a Mimbres chief, who had been educated among the Mexicans, and used his knowledge of their customs to great advantage in his warfare. One favorite scheme of his was robbing the mails, for the purpose of obtaining information as to the plans of the Mexicans. At this time there were several parties of trappers on the head-waters of the Gila, and the captain of one of these, a man named Johnson, undertook to secure a number of Apache scalps. It is said that in addition to the scalp bounty he was induced to this by pay from the owners of the Santa Rita copper mines. At any rate he made a feast and invited to it a number of Mimbreño warriors, who accepted his hospitable bidding. To one side of the ground where his feast was spread he placed a howitzer, loaded to the muzzle with slugs, nails, and bullets, and concealed under sacks of flour and other goods. In good range he placed a sack of flour, which he told the Indians to divide among themselves. Unsuspicious of wrong, they gathered about it. Johnson touched his lighted cigarrito to the vent of the howitzer, and the charge was poured into the crowd, killing and wounding many. The party of trappers at once followed up the attack with their rifles and knives. A goodly number of scalps were secured, that of Juan José among others, but the treachery was terribly repaid. Another party of fifteen trappers was camped on a stream a few miles distant. The surviving Mimbreños went to these unsuspecting men and murdered every one of them. Their vengeance did not stop at this. The copper mines of Santa Rita were furnished with supplies from the city of Chihuahua by guarded wagon-trains (*conductas*) that brought in provisions and hauled back ore. The time for the arrival of the train came and passed, but no train appeared. Days slipped away; provisions were almost exhausted; the supply of ammunition was nearly gone. Some of the miners climbed to the top of Ben Moore, which rises back of the mines, but from its lofty summit no sign of an approaching *conducta* was visible. Starvation was imminent.

The only hope of escape for the miners and their families was in making their way across the desert expanse that lies between the mines and the settlements. They started, but the Apaches, who had destroyed the train, hung about them, and attacked them so persistently that only four or five succeeded in reaching their destination.

The scalp bounty was not always so effective in procuring the death of Apaches as in this case. A few years after our conquest, when the vigilance committees of California had filled Arizona with the most villainous collection of white men that ever breathed, there was enacted a comic tragedy in which the principal performer was John Gallantin. He was a desperate scoundrel, and had gathered about him a band of cut-throats whose infamous characters were excelled only by his own. The governor of Chihuahua undertook to make these men useful to the State by paying them thirty dollars for each Apache scalp they secured. They brought scalps in profusion, but the Apache raids were nowise diminished. On the contrary, large numbers of Mexicans and friendly Indians were assassinated and scalped in the midst of the settlements. The suspicions of the Chihnahuans were excited, and Gallantin was at length discovered taking the scalps of some Mexicans whom his people had murdered. This accounted for the extraordinary activity of "the Apaches," and Gallantin and his band left the country. They gathered up some twenty-five hundred sheep as they went along, and with these made their way to the Colorado at the mouth of the Gila. They were met with professions of great friendship by the Yumas, who were then (1851) commanded by Caballo en Pelo (Naked Horse), a chief of great prowess. Having placed themselves in favorable positions in the camp of the desperadoes, the Yumas suddenly fell upon them and murdered the entire party. The scalp-bounty system was not given up by the Mexicans, and, what is more remarkable, man-hunters were allowed to pursue their occupation on our side of the line for the scalp markets of Chihuahua and Sonora. In 1870 Lieutenant Drew was visited by such a party from Janos, Chihuahua, who coolly proposed to massacre the Indians who were then under his protection, preparatory to going on a reservation. He said,

BLACK KNIFE. (FROM THE PAINTING BY STANLEY.)

"These people do not care a straw for the depredations committed in this or any other country; they work for the money a scalp brings, and one from a friendly Indian is worth as much as one of any other." Orders were soon after issued which lessened this business as an international commerce.

When the Americans invaded the country during the Mexican war, the Apaches welcomed them as allies, though their professions of friendship were not much believed. At San Lucia Springs, near the Santa Rita mines, General Kearny was met by Mangas Colorado (Red Sleeves—in defective Spanish), chief of the Mimbreños, who vowed eternal friendship to the Americans. It was noticed, however, that they kept shy of howitzers, and that one of them wore a shirt made of a Henry Clay campaign flag, which doubtless signified a dead American somewhere. The Apaches were overwhelmed with admiration of our soldiers and their weapons. Said one of their chiefs to General Kearny, as they prepared to leave, "You have taken New Mexico and will soon take California; go, then, and take Chihuahua, Durango, and Sonora. We will help you. You fight for land; we care nothing for land; we fight for the laws of Montezuma and for food. The Mexicans are rascals; we hate and will kill them all." This feeling, though somewhat advantageous to us during war, was a disadvantage as soon as peace was made. We were bound by the treaty of Guadalupe Hidalgo to protect our newly-acquired Mexican citizens, and also to prevent our Indians from depredating in Mexico. Americans who settled in New Mexico lived, of course, in the Mexican settlements, and had interests much in common with the Mexicans. The Apaches in the neighborhood of these settlements were not very troublesome for several years, but the western bands pursued their old vocation of plunder with unabated vigor. The settlers below the Gila, and the emigrants who passed over the southern road, retained their lives and property only by eternal vigilance.

After the massacre of the miners, the Mimbreños held possession of the Santa Rita mines for a dozen years undisturbed. The place became known as their great stronghold, and no white men were able to break through its surrounding wilds.

In 1850 there came an invasion. The American half of the Mexican Boundary Commission, under charge of Mr. J. R. Bartlett, decided to make the copper mines their head-quarters for a time, and a force of three hundred men took possession of the place. The Mimbreños, under the leadership of their great war-chief Cuchillo Negro, or Black Knife, were disposed to resist at first, but thought better of it, and received the Americans with professions of friendship. A short time after the commission was established in these quarters, there came along three Mexican traders, who had been among the Pinal Apaches, and purchased of them a young Mexican girl named Inez Gonzales. This girl, who was about fifteen years old, had been a captive for nine months. Her parents lived at the town of Santa Cruz, whence she had started in company with her aunt and others, with an escort of soldiers, to attend the feast of San Francisco at Magdalena. They were ambushed by the Pinaleños; the men were killed, and the women and children carried away. The Mexicans were taking her to Santa Fé, probably to sell her or to keep her for immoral purposes, as was the common practice with female slaves. Mr. Bartlett had no hesitancy as to releasing her, inasmuch as the United States had expressly agreed, in the treaty of Guadalupe Hidalgo, to release all such captives and to suppress the traffic in them. Inez was returned to her parents by the commissioner when he arrived in Santa Cruz. She subsequently became the mistress of Captain Gomez, who commanded the troops in Northern Sonora. He married her on the death of his wife, and after his death Inez married the Alcalde of Santa Cruz, her social standing not having been at all affected by her romantic adventures.

The release of this captive did not directly affect the Indians, but a few days later two Mexican boys, who were held as slaves by the Mimbreños, took refuge in the tent of Colonel Cremony, with the commission, and appealed to him to save them from their masters. These children, Saverro Aredia and José Trinfan, had heard the Indians speaking of the release of Inez, and determined to seek the same protection. Protection was given to them. There were some indications that the Apaches, thwarted in recovering them, might murder them, and on account of this Mr. Bartlett sent them away at night, under guard, to the camp of General Condé, the Mexican commissioner. Condé at once forwarded them into Mexico. The Mimbreños were very indignant at this summary release of their property—a rather inconsistent interference, too, at a time when the Fugitive Slave Law had just gone into operation—but after holding a council, and being informed that they could not help themselves, they concluded to accept about two hundred and fifty dollars' worth of goods for the two boys.

As this institution of slavery in the West has been the cause of much trouble with the Indians, a glance at its features and extent will be advantageous in considering the difficulties between the two races. The system obtained with all the tribes of the Rocky Mountains, and also with the Kiowas and Comanches who sprang from mountain stocks. Instead of dooming their captives to death, or adopting them into their tribes, as the Eastern Indians did, they held them for barter and the performance of menial duties. The slave was the property of his immediate captor, but in case he was taken by a band he was the property of the tribe. Ownership was frequently changed by sale or gambling. The slave was wholly subject to the caprices of his owner, even to his life. "Women," says Captain Johnson, speaking of the Apaches, "when captured, are taken as wives by those who capture them, but they are treated by the Indian wives of the capturers as slaves, and made to carry wood and water; if they chance to be pretty, or receive too much attention from their lords and masters, they are, in the absence of the latter, unmercifully beaten and otherwise maltreated. The most unfortunate thing which can befall a captive woman is to be claimed by two persons. In this case she is either shot or delivered up for indiscriminate violence." This latter abrupt method of deciding controversies was adhered to by the Apaches to prevent quarrels among themselves. Other property was treated similarly. If a horse were claimed as booty by two warriors, they must adjust their differences speedily or the animal was shot.

The case of Inez Gonzales was not an exceptional one,

wherein Mexicans who had been captured by Indians were bought and held as slaves by Mexicans. It was the almost universal rule. In the preceding summer, Indian agent Calhoun released four Mexicans, three boys and a woman, all of whom had been bought by Mexicans from the Apaches. He reported: "The trading in captives has been so long tolerated in this Territory that it has ceased to be regarded as a wrong; and purchasers are not prepared willingly to release captives without an adequate ransom. In legislating upon this subject it should be distinctly set forth under what circumstances captives shall be released, and limiting the expenditures that may be incurred thereby. Unless the Mexicans are paid for such captives as they have purchased, and have now in possession, but very few of them will be released; nor will it answer well to allow captives to make their election as to a release, for their submission to their masters is most perfect, and they are well instructed as to proper replies to interrogatories. . . . I may, in conclusion, mention that there are a number of Indian captives held as slaves in this Territory, and Congressional action may be necessary in relation to them, and I respectfully submit the question for appropriate consideration." The Mexicans could never see any great evil in slavery. Their system of peonage, or bondage for debt, amounts to life servitude in most cases, for wages are so low that a peon ordinarily earns only enough for his subsistence. There was no public sentiment against the subjection of women to the pleasures of their owners, for virtue is almost unknown among them. It is the common mode, to this day, for one who desires a Mexican mistress, to select the girl and make arrangements with her parents by the payment of a small sum monthly.

The Americans who settled in the country held very similar ideas in regard to Mexicans and Indians, both of whom were considered as inferior races. The trapper or trader who desired a squaw purchased one, and the settler who wanted servants very commonly purchased them. They took to the system so naturally that legislation was made necessary to prohibit it. Many of the more reckless characters engaged in the business of catching and selling slaves, as is illustrated in the following extract from the journal of Colonel Cooke: "I had lately a conversation with old Weaver, which was not official. He said, 'The Tontos live in that range over there; I never see them with more than one or two lodges together; they are a band of the Coyoteros, and are called fools for their ignorance. When I went over once, from the Pimas to the Cochanos and Mochabas [Mohaves], I met some lodges and had a fuss with them.'—'What sort?'—'Oh, we killed two or three and burned their lodges, and took all the women and children and sold them.'—'What!'—'Yes, I have often caught the women and children of Digger Indians and sold them in New Mexico and Sonora. Mr.— of Tucson told me a squaw I sold him ran off, and was found dead, famished for water I s'pose, going over from the Pimas to the Colorado.'—'What! have you no feeling for her death, trying to return to her father and mother you tore her from?'—'I killed her father and mother, as like as not; they stole all our traps; as fast as we could stick a trap in the river, they'd come and steal it, and shoot arrows into our horses; they thought we would leave them for them to eat, but we built a big fire and burned them up.' " The weaker tribes of course suffered most in this business. The wretched Diggers of the Salt Lake Basin were especially the victims of it, in an early day, as was often testified to by travellers. Farnham says, "These poor creatures are hunted in the spring, when weak and helpless, by a certain class of men, and when taken are fattened, and carried to Santa Fé and sold as slaves. A 'likely girl,' in her teens, often brings three or four hundred dollars. The men are valued less."

The Diggers fell under the control of the Mormons, and to their honor be it said that they made an effort to ameliorate the condition of these captives. The evil to be remedied is thus set forth in the preamble of an act passed in January, 1852:

"*Whereas*, from time immemorial, the practice of purchasing Indian women and children of the Utah tribe of Indians by Mexican traders has been indulged in and carried on by those respective people until the Indians consider it an allowable traffic, and frequently offer their prisoners or children for sale; and

"*Whereas* it is a common practice among these Indians to gamble away their own children and women; and it is a well-established fact that women and children thus obtained, or obtained by war, or theft, or in any other manner, are by them frequently carried from place to place, packed upon horses or mules, lariated out to subsist upon grass, roots, or starve, and are frequently bound with thongs made of rawhide, until their hands and feet become swollen, mutilated, inflamed with pain, and wounded; and when with suffering, cold, hunger, and abuse they fall sick, so as to become troublesome, are frequently slain by their masters to get rid of them; and

"*Whereas* they do frequently kill their women and children taken prisoners, either in revenge, or for amusement, or through the influence of tradition, unless they are tempted to exchange them for trade, which they usually do if they have an opportunity; and

"*Whereas* one family frequently steals the children and women of another family, and such robberies and murders are continually committed in times of their greatest peace and amity, thus dragging free Indian women and children into Mexican servitude and slavery, or death, to the almost entire extirpation of the whole Indian race; and

"*Whereas* these inhuman practices are being daily enacted before our eyes in the midst of the white settlements, and within the organized counties of the Territory; and when the inhabitants do not purchase or trade for those so offered for sale, they are generally doomed to the most miserable existence, suffering the tortures of every species of cruelty, until death kindly relieves them and closes the revolting severity:

"Wherefore, when all these facts are taken into consideration, it becomes the duty of all humane and Christian people to extend unto this degraded and down-trodden race such relief as can be awarded to them," etc.

The act following this argumentative recital provides that any white person having a captive in his possession, shall go with it before the select-men, or the probate judge, and bind the captive to some proper person, in the discretion of the select-men, for a term of not over twenty years. The person to whom he is bound is required to send him to school three months in the year, from the age of seven to sixteen, and to clothe him in a suitable manner. The select-men are also empowered to obtain such captives from the Indians for the purpose of binding them out.

In the North slavery prevailed everywhere, and was abetted and encouraged by the Hudson's Bay Company. Said Mr. Slocum, of slavery in Oregon, "The price of a slave varies from five to fifteen blankets. Women are valued higher than men. If a slave dies within six months of the purchase, the seller returns one-half the purchase-money.

... Many instances have occurred where a man has sold his own child. ... The slaves are generally employed to cut wood, hunt and fish for the families of the men employed by the Hudson's Bay Company, and are ready for any extra work. Each man of the trapping parties has from two to three slaves, who assist to hunt and take care of the horses and camp. They thereby save the Company the expense of employing at least double the number of men that would otherwise be required on these excursions. ... As long as the Hudson's Bay Company permit their servants to hold slaves, the institution of slavery will be perpetuated." Slavery was, in fact, more extensive in Oregon than anywhere else in the West, and more similar to the African and Oriental systems. Stanley says of Casino, the celebrated Klickitat chief, "In the plenitude of his power he travelled in great state, and was often accompanied by a hundred slaves, obedient to his slightest caprice." The same authority says, "It is a very common practice of the Shaste, Umpqua, and Rogue River Indians; to sell their children in slavery to the tribes inhabiting the banks of the Columbia River. During my tour through the Willamette Valley in 1848, I met a party of Tlickitats (Klickitats) returning from one of these trading excursions, having about twenty little boys, whom they had purchased from the Umpqua tribe." The Oregon Indians also preyed upon the degraded tribes of California in this trade, and the Modocs, Klamaths, and Pitt River Indians obtained the reputation of fierce and cruel slave-drivers in procuring captives for sale to their Northern neighbors.

All through the Rocky Mountains, except in what we have called the north-eastern triangle, this system of human slavery extended, and it had obtained such a root that it was very hard to extirpate. In Colorado it was brought to a summary end, so far as white slave-holders were concerned, in 1865, through the efforts of the government. Indian Agent Head, accompanied by Deputy Marshall E. R. Harris, visited all owners of Indian slaves and informed them that they must be released. Says Mr. Head, "I have notified all the people here that in future no more captives are to be purchased or sold, as I shall immediately arrest both parties caught in the transaction. This step, I think, will at once put an end to the most barbarous and inhuman practice which has been in existence with the Mexicans for generations. There are captives who know not their own parents, nor can they speak their mother tongue, and who recognize no one but those who rescued [!] them from their merciless captors." In New Mexico and Arizona the slaves have not yet been fully emancipated. There were twenty Mexican slaves released from among the Navahos in 1883. In 1866 the number of Indians held as slaves and peons by the whites was estimated officially at two thousand. There are undoubtedly many Indian slaves held among the Mexicans in those Territories now, but the system of peonage, and the fact that they are kept in fear of expressing discontent, makes it difficult to release them. In Northern Mexico there are numbers of Indians, of our tribes, still held in slavery, and the officials of Arizona reservations are continually besieged with appeals to restore to our Indians their captive kindred.

The condition of these slaves was as shocking as proclaimed in the Mormon document quoted above. The female captives were nearly always subjected to indignities, both among the Indians and the whites, and among the latter they were frequently made public prostitutes for the gain of their owners. Among the Indians there was also the constant liability of sacrifice for religious purposes. At the death of any person of prominence it was customary to kill one or more captives, who should serve as slaves to the deceased in the spirit world, as has been recounted herein, in the narrative of the captivity of Olive Oatman. Walker (Wacca), the noted Ute chief, who died in 1855, and was buried on a high mountain about twelve miles south-east of Fillmore, Utah, was accorded full honors of this kind. Four Pi-ede slaves, three children and one woman, were buried in the grave with him. Three of them were killed and thrown into the grave; the other was thrown in alive. Among the Chinooks the burial custom was to bind a slave hand and foot and tie him to the corpse, after which they were deposited together in the place of sepulture; after three days the victim was strangled by another slave. The particulars of the treatment that might be anticipated by captives were known to both races, and, as may be imagined, the whole system tended to make their hatred intense. When people are killed, and out of the way, warfare may to some extent be forgotten, but when relatives and friends are held in slavery, there is a constant pressure to rescue them or be revenged. This was a feeling common to both sides, and in regard to women it was perhaps more strong with the Apaches than with the Mexicans. The Apache women were noted for their chastity. In this respect they were far superior to the Mexicans, and equal, if not superior, to any Indians on the continent. The fate to which their captive wives and daughters was doomed often caused poignant sorrow among them. Of course there was not the same effort made by the whites to restore Indian slaves to their tribes that there was to recover Mexican or American slaves. The "axiom" of Aristotle, that "Barbarians are designed by Nature to be slaves," is one that has always been adopted by superior races when thrown in contact with inferior ones.

The forcible purchase of the Mexican boys by the Boundary Commission, was not forgotten by the Mimbreños, who considered it an invasion of their rights. The relations of the parties were soon further complicated through the killing of an Apache by Jesus Lopez, a Mexican teamster. The Apaches insisted that the Americans should hang this man, who undoubtedly deserved hanging. Mr. Bartlett objected to performing such summary justice, but promised to have the offender tried at Santa Fé. The Indians contended, with much show of reason, that he ought to be hung there, where the crime was committed. After a lengthy discussion, in which it was urged that the Apaches had recently killed an American on the road between Janos and the mines, for which they had made no reparation, the matter was arranged by paying the mother of the murdered man thirty dollars, and twenty dollars per month thereafter, being the amount of the murderer's wages. Three weeks later the Indians began stealing the horses and mules belonging to the Commission. They vehemently denied that they were guilty, at first, but soon a pursuing force overtook one of the bands of thieves, and found it commanded by Delgadito (the Slender), a Mimbreños chief, who had slept in the Commissioner's camp only two nights before. In the course of a month nearly two hundred horses and mules were taken, and at the end of that period the advancement of the work caused Mr. Bartlett to move on with his almost dismounted command. The Mimbreños considered his departure as a victory for them, and always thought that they drove the Americans away.

During the stay of the Commissioner's party, a number of miners had settled at the Pino Alto gold mines, north-west of the Santa Rita mines, and these remained there when the copper mines were abandoned. They grew in numbers, and the Mimbreños were unable to dislodge them. After several years Mangas Colorado tried to accomplish this end by deceit. He would approach a miner and tell him in a confidential way of wonderful gold mines to which he would escort him, out of personal friendship, only they two must go alone. No one risked a trip with the kind-hearted chief, but after several weeks some of the miners happened to compare notes, and the probable treachery was revealed. The next time Mangas appeared at the mines, he was tied up and soundly whipped. It would have been far more politic to have killed him. He never forgave this injury—the greatest that could be inflicted on an Indian—and he certainly avenged it on a royal scale. For years he was the greatest and most vindictive leader of the Apaches. He united himself by marriage with Cochise (Cheis), the principal chief of the Chiricahuas, and also made a marital alliance with the Navahos that gave him great influence in that tribe. Murders and robberies innumerable were committed under his leadership. He succeeded for a long time in keeping together larger bodies of warriors than had ever been known among the Apaches, and in devastating all the regions through which they roamed.

During all this time the Jicarillas were disturbing the peace on the northern side of the Rio Grande settlements. In October, 1849, they committed the massacre of the White party which attracted wide-spread attention at the time. Mr. White, with his wife and child, was coming to Santa Fé, where he had formerly been a merchant, in company with a wagon

SILVER MINES OF SANTA RITA.

train belonging to Mr. Aubrey. They had passed the country considered dangerous, and the Whites started ahead, accompanied by a German named Lawberger, an unknown American, a Mexican, and a negro. While camped between Rock Creek and Whetstone branch, a party of Jicarillas approached them and demanded presents. White refused, and drove them out of camp. Presently they returned, and were again refused and ordered out. Instead of going they opened fire, killing the negro and Mexican. The others tried to fly, but were killed, excepting Mrs. White and the child, who were taken prisoners. The dead bodies were laid along the road, but were not scalped or stripped, and the Indians concealed themselves. A party of Mexicans soon came along, and began plundering the wagons. The Indians fired on them, but succeeded only in wounding one boy, who was left for dead. He lay quiet until the Indians went away, and then came to Santa Fé and reported the occurrence. A company of dragoons, with Kit Carson as guide, followed the Indians for three or four days before they found them. They made an attack and killed several, but the Indians murdered Mrs. White and the child before they fled. A severe snow-storm came on, from which both sides suffered severely, and rendered farther pursuit impossible. In 1851 these Indians murdered a party of eleven persons who were carrying the mail. After some further hostilities they entered into a treaty with Agent Calhoun, and went on reservations near Fort Webster and Abiquiu, but the treaty was not ratified. Mr. Meriwether, who succeeded Mr. Calhoun in August, 1853, found the Jicarillas on his hands, with no money to provide for them. He told them he could do nothing for them, and turned them out. As they had made no provision for winter, they proceeded to support themselves by theft. In a few months their depredations became so insufferable that the troops were sent after them. Lieutenant Bell had a successful skirmish with them on March 5th, but on March 30th Lieutenant Davidson's command of sixty men was attacked by two hundred Jicarillas and Utes, and only nineteen men escaped, most of them wounded. A large force of regulars and volunteers was then put in the field, and, on July 30th General Garland reported that the Jicarillas had been subdued and had sued for peace. There was one band, however, that escaped and took refuge among the Utes; these renegades with their allies destroyed the settlement on the Arkansas, and were punished as recorded in the sketch of the Utes hereafter.

The Mescaleros, to the south-east of the Rio Grande settlements, were the Apaches for whose civilization there seemed the best prospect. They were more devoted to agriculture than the others, and consequently had more to lose by war. They exercised the ancient prerogative of thieving to a limited extent for some years, but in the winter of 1854–55 their depredations became so extensive that they could not be tolerated. Captain Ewell, of the 1st Dragoons, was sent against them with one hundred and eighty men. The Mescaleros met them on the Peñasco, on the night of January 17th, and fought them all the next day as they advanced. The troops lost three killed, and the Indians were seen to bear away fifteen dead bodies. The Mescaleros retreated in the direction of the Guadalupe Mountains. On February 23d a party of fifteen warriors attacked a grazing camp of four soldiers, surprising them and pulling their tent down upon them, but the soldiers extricated themselves and drove the Indians off with heavy loss. The Mescaleros then concluded that their mission was not fighting the Americans. They came to Agent Steck at Fort Thorne, and begged for peace. Peace was granted, and a reservation was given them in their own country, between the Pecos River and the Sacramento Mountains. The Mescaleros thereafter behaved quite well until the Texan invasion, early in the civil war, but the Mexicans gained in blood-thirstiness what the Indians had lost. In February, 1858, a militia party from Messila, known as the "Messila Guard," attacked a peaceful Mescalero camp close by the village of Doña Ana, and pursued the Indians into the houses of the Doña Anans, where they fled for refuge. Eight or nine Indians were killed and one child taken captive. The citizens of Doña Ana denounced this affair as a riotous and wanton outrage, though they seemed to object more to the disturbance of themselves than to the wrong done the Indians. In April these same *valientes* attacked the Mescalero camp on the reservation near Fort Thorne, killed seven and took several prisoners. The garrison was promptly called to arms, and after a brief chase captured thirty-five of the attacking party, including Juan Ortega, their leader. The military authorities were now thoroughly indignant. The officers at the fort knew that these Indians had been peaceable and well-behaved, so that Mexican affidavits of outrages committed by them were not effective; and the prisoners were held, notwithstanding the writs of habeas corpus that were issued for their release. General Garland also determined to withdraw his troops from Fort Thorne and let the valiant Messilans have their fill of Indian fighting. This called forth a petition from the people, in which assertions of their own valor and prayers for protection are ludicrously blended. General Garland left two companies to protect settlers innocent of outrage, but informed others that they "have no claims to the protection of the military, and will receive none."

The eastern Apaches remained at peace until the beginning of the war of the rebellion. They were not making any material progress towards civilization, except in the matter of becoming drunkards. The intercourse laws could not be enforced in New Mexico because there were no "Indian lands." The Mexicans had treated the Indian title as extinct, and we had taken the Mexican title, in consequence of which our legislators assumed that the Indians, who actually held the country, and had held it from the "time when the memory of man runneth not to the contrary," had no title whatever. To make this absurdity more serious in its results, none of the treaties made with the Apaches were ratified, and therefore the reservations designated for them did not come within the protection of the intercourse laws. The result was that the most of the property that the Jicarillas and Mescaleros got hold of went for *aguardiente*. The Western tribes continued their piratical warfare. Several expeditions were sent against them, but none resulted in any permanent advantage or any material punishment to the Indians.

At the opening of the war a Pandora's box of evils was opened over every square mile of New Mexico and Arizona. Among the officers of the army were many Southerners, and these did not hesitate to return to the South. Some tried to take their soldiers with them, but these attempts were generally unsuccessful. Immediately after came an order withdrawing the troops from the frontier posts. This meant a desertion of nearly all the country, for life in it had only been made possible by the presence of the soldiers. The overland mail company abandoned its line through the two territories (one at that time), thus putting an end to all communication. The Western Apaches seemed to have awakened to new life. They pursued their work of murder and robbery with such daring that no safety was possible. Men were killed and ranches plundered in the midst of well-settled districts. The Indians seemed to be everywhere.

This activity was occasioned in the first place by a military blunder. In the spring of 1861 some Apaches stole a cow and a child from the Mexican mistress of an American, and, on complaint of the latter at Fort Buchanan, seventy-five men were sent to demand the property of the Chiricahuas, who were accused of the theft. The party went to Apache Pass and camped, with a white flag flying over the tent of the commander. Under its protection Cochise and five other chiefs came in to talk. They professed absolute ignorance of the theft, and stuck to it, on account of which obduracy orders were given to seize them. Cochise seized a knife, slit the canvas, and escaped, carrying with him three bullets. One chief was knocked down and spitted on a bayonet while attempting to follow. The other four were bound. The Indians at once began hostilities by killing some prisoners. The captive chiefs were hung in retaliation, and the Apaches attacked the troops. The latter were badly whipped, and obliged to return to the fort. The abandonment of the posts by the troops soon after on the order of recall was believed by the Indians to have resulted from their hostilities, and they were satisfied that they need only fight if they desired to rid themselves of the Americans. The Arizona settlements, which were at that time all within the Gadsden Purchase, and chiefly in the Santa Cruz Valley, were made desolate. At first ranches were destroyed one after another, and travellers waylaid and murdered. Having accomplished this work thoroughly, the Apaches began operations against the strongholds of their enemies. The silver mines east of Tubac were held for a few weeks; but it was necessary to arm the peons to accomplish this, and arming them forced the Americans in charge to stand guard constantly, to preserve their lives from their employés. The mines were abandoned as soon as their business affairs could be arranged. Tubac was deserted soon afterwards. Tucson dwindled away to a village of two hundred souls.

What was lacking in the desperate nature of the situation was added by the invasion of the Texans. They occupied all of the southern part of New Mexico, and all of what is now Arizona that was occupied by the whites. On the southeast they occupied Fort Stanton, the only post in the Mescalero country. All the Apache tribes except the Jicarillas were within the region held by them, and the Jicarillas were the only Apaches that remained at peace. It is worth remembering that but for the friendly attitude of the Jicarillas and the Utes, New Mexico must almost certainly have fallen into the hands of the Texans. The Mescaleros, who had been behaving well previously, became involved in a quarrel with the Confederate soldiers, and a fight resulted in which several were killed on both sides. The Mescaleros then began an Ishmaelitish war, sparing no one. The settlements which had grown up on the Rio Bonito were quickly devastated, and the war was carried to the villages of the Rio Grande country. On the south-west Mangas Colorado prevented the settlers from suffering the pangs of ennui. Most of the Mimbres went to war immediately after he was flogged by the miners, and the Chiricahuas and Gileños made common cause with them. On the morning of September 27, 1861, a force of over two hundred warriors attacked the mining village of Pino Alto, but fortunately for the people Captain Martin had arrived the night before with a detachment of the Arizona Guards, a volunteer organization, and after several hours' hard fighting the Indians were driven off with considerable loss. Soon after one hundred and fifty warriors attacked a large wagon train, one day out from Pino Alto, and besieged it for fourteen hours. The train escaped destruction by the timely arrival of the Arizona Guards, who escorted it to the Mimbres River.

Any long continuance of this state of affairs must have been ruinous to New Mexico; but aid was at hand. The Colorado Volunteers marched down from the North, turned back the Texans, and joined Canby in driving them from the Rio Grande. At the same time General Carleton, with a column of three thousand Californians, was advancing by way of Fort Yuma, driving all hostiles before him, and opening communication through to the coast. The combined forces of Mangas Colorado and Cochise made a desperate resistance to his advance at Apache Pass, in the Chiricahua Mountains, but the Californians were supplied with howitzers and shells, and the Apaches found that their positions, which they had made almost impregnable to direct attack, afforded them no protection from these new missiles of their white foes. They fled with a loss of sixty-six killed; the Californians had two killed and three wounded.

A RECORD OF MANGAS COLORADO.

Just after this engagement Mangas Colorado was seriously wounded while trying to cut off a messenger that was carrying back news of the fight at the pass. He was taken to the village of Janos, in Northern New Mexico, by his warriors, and put under charge of a physician there, with notice that if he did not recover, every one in the place would be killed. He recovered. A short time after his recovery, early in 1863, he was captured by Captain Shirland of the California Volunteers, and killed while attempting to escape. It is said that the sentinel stirred him up with a heated bayonet and then shot him. It was time for him to die. He was about seventy years old, and had secured all the revenge to which one man is entitled. His skull is said to ornament the phrenological museum of Prof. O. S. Fowler.

General Carleton arrived at the Rio Grande settlements in September, 1862, and relieved Canby, who went to take a glorious part in the great struggle in the South. Carleton, being rid of white enemies, devoted his attention to the subjugation of the Indians. He first sent Col. Kit Carson, with five companies of New Mexican volunteers, to occupy Fort Stanton, from which he was to operate against the Mescaleros and any Navahos that were in that region. Captain McCleave, with two companies of California Volunteers, was sent into the Mescalero country by way of Dog Cañon (Cañon del Perro), from the south-west. Captain Roberts, with two companies of Californians, was sent into the same region from the south, by way of the Hueco (Wacco) tanks. The orders to each command were: "The men are to be slain whenever and wherever they can be found. The women and children may be taken prisoners, but, of course, they are not to be killed." Carson took possession of Fort Stanton with no material hinderance. McCleave encountered the Apaches at Dog Cañon, which was one of their greatest strongholds. There were about five hundred of them—over a hundred warriors—and they were completely routed by the Californians. They fled to Fort Stanton and surrendered to Carson, who took them under his protection, rather against the sanguinary instructions of Carleton, and sent five of their chiefs to Santa Fé to treat for peace. General Carleton required them to go on a reservation at the Bosque Redondo, on the Pecos River. The spokesman of the Mescaleros was Gian-nah-tah (Always Ready), known to the Mexicans as Cadéte, or the Volunteer. He was a son of Palanquito, their former head chief, who died soon after they were first treated with, in 1855. Gian-nah-tah said, "You are stronger than we. We have fought you so long as we had rifles and powder; but your weapons are better than ours. Give us like weapons and turn us loose, we will fight you again; but we are worn out; we have no more heart; we have no provisions, no means to live; your troops are everywhere; our springs and water-holes are either occupied or overlooked by your young men. You have driven us from our last and best stronghold, and we have no more heart. Do with us as may seem good to you, but do not forget we are men and braves."

The Mescaleros were sent to the Bosque Redondo with the promise that if they should remain there peaceably until the war was finished, so that they would not be confused with the hostiles, they should be given a reservation in their own country. At the Bosque they came under charge of Colonel Cremony, formerly with the Boundary Commission, to whose intelligent labor the world is indebted for much of its knowledge of Apache customs. It may be mentioned, by-the-way, that he collected a valuable vocabulary of the Apache language and forwarded it to the Smithsonian Institution over twenty years ago, but it has not yet been published. The Indians came to the Bosque rapidly; by spring four hundred Mescaleros were on the reservation, and the remainder were reported as having fled into Mexico or joined the Gila tribes. The disposal of the Mescaleros gave some opportunity for proceedings against the Mimbreños. An expedition was sent into their country in January, 1863, which resulted in the defeat and capture of Mangas Colorado, with a loss of twenty of his warriors. Fort West was established in the Pino Alto country, and scouting parties were kept in the field. By the latter part of April, forty of the band had been killed, includ-

PAPAGO CHIEF.

ing a brother and one of the sons of Mangas. The attention of the greater part of the troops was turned to the Navahos during the year 1863 and the early part of the next year. By March, 1864, there were 3600 Navahos and 450 Apaches at the Bosque. By the twentieth of that month 2600 more Navahos were reported captured and on their way. Events were occurring in Arizona, however, that soon carried the seat of active operations to that territory. In 1862 Pauline Weaver, the pioneer prospector of Arizona, discovered the placers on the Colorado near La Paz, and in 1863 he found the district that bears his name, south-west of Prescott, and the remarkable mines of Antelope Peak. In the spring of 1863 a party of prospectors under Captain Walker, an old California mining celebrity, left the Rio Grande settlements and went into the same region. The new mines attracted many people, to whom General Carleton gave all the protection and assistance in his power.

In the summer of 1864, his hands were comparatively free in New Mexico, and the troops were centred on the western Apaches. The extermination policy then received as full and fair a trial as could possibly be given to it. The forces were adequate, for every one joined in the movement. On April 20th General Carleton detailed his plans to Don Ignacio Pesquira, Governor of Sonora, saying, "If your excellency will put a few hundred men into the field on the first day of next June, and keep them in hot pursuit of the Apaches of Sonora, say for sixty or ninety days, we will either exterminate the Indians or so diminish their numbers that they will cease their murdering and robbing propensities and live at peace." To Don Luis Perrazas, Governor of Chihuahua, a similar request was forwarded. The miners in the new districts of Arizona agreed to keep a force in the field if the government would furnish provisions, and this General Carleton did. The Pimas and Maricopas were furnished with American leaders, and given over two hundred muskets, with ammunition. The governors of Arizona and New Mexico were requested to aid, and did so. To Governor Goodwin, of Arizona, Carleton wrote: "Pray see the Papagos, Pimas, and Maricopas, and have that part of the programme well and effectually executed.

You will be able to secure the efforts of the miners without trouble. Let us work earnestly and hard, and before next Christmas your Apaches are whipped. Unless we do this, you will have a twenty years' war." For his own part Carleton located a force of five hundred men on the Gila, north of the Chiricahua Mountains, to operate from that point. Could a plan be more perfect? Here was a combination of the military, citizens, and friendly Indians of two nations against the Apaches. They all went into it heartily, with a sincere hatred of the enemy, and with many old scores to pay off. The oft-repeated orders were to kill every male Indian capable of bearing arms, and capture the women and children. It is not possible to give here even a synopsis of the fights that occurred. The brief mention of the encounters with Indians in the general orders for the year covers six such pages as these, in fine print. The results of the year's work, so far as they could be obtained, were officially summed up thus: Indians killed, 363—wounded, 140; soldiers killed, 7—wounded, 25; citizens killed, 18—wounded, 13; recovered from Indians 12,284 sheep, 2742 horses, 35 mules, 31 cattle, and 18 burros; taken by Indians, 4250 sheep, 26 horses, 154 mules, and 32 cattle. The greater part of the damage done was to the Navahos, who, to the number of over two thousand, were sent to the Bosque Rodondo, taking with them most of the sheep that were reported as captured. For the Apaches alone the returns sum up, 216 Indians and 16 whites killed; 146 horses captured by Indians, and 54 recovered; 17 cattle taken by Indians, and 21 taken from them; 3000 sheep taken by Indians, and 175 recovered. The loss to the whites was not fully reported, and the Indians were much damaged in addition to this by the destruction of their crops. Nearly all the Apaches planted to some extent in the sheltered valleys of their wildernesses.

This war was conducted on strictly extermination principles. It is true that removal to the Bosque was named as an alternative, but only thirty western Apaches ever reached the Bosque, from all sources. The troops were constantly stimulated to activity. Failure was the only offence that could be committed, and success was approved, no matter how obtained.

APACHE CRUCIFIED BY PAPAGOS.

By way of example, the general orders for 1864 contain the following: "January 24th.—A party of thirty Americans and fourteen Pima and Maricopa Indians under Col. King S. Woolsey, aid to the governor of Arizona, attacked a band of Gila Apaches, sixty or seventy miles north-east of the Pima villages, and killed nineteen of them and wounded others. Mr. Cyrus Lennon, of Woolsey's party, was killed by a wounded Indian." That does not read badly, but it is not the whole truth. This party started out to hunt for stock supposed to have been stolen by the Indians. They were signalled by a party of Coyotéros and Pinals, who dared them to come and fight. Woolsey sent an interpreter to them to tell them that he did not wish to fight, but to make peace. On his invitation thirty-five of them came into the camp with their arms. The chief, Par-a-muck-a, insolently ordered Woolsey to clear a place for him to sit upon, as he was a great chief. Woolsey calmly folded up a blanket and handed it to him. He then told the Apaches that he would make a treaty with them and give them certificates of good conduct such that no white man would ever molest them. His men were gathered about in preparation for the treaty. Woolsey drew his revolver and gave Par-a-muck-a the Arizona certificate of a "good Indian" at the first shot. His men signed on the bodies of the others. Only one Indian—a lame man who could not run away—affixed his signature. He did it with his lance, on the person of Mr. Lennon. This is historically known as "the Pinal treaty," and the place is appropriately called "Bloody Tanks."

This occurrence is not mentioned in any spirit of "mawkish sentimentality," but merely to show that the extermination policy had a fair trial. These Indians would undoubtedly have murdered their new white friends if they had obtained the opportunity. They are entitled to no compassion on the ground of treachery used against them. The Apache makes war by treachery. His object is to harm his enemy but to escape uninjured, and he thinks that a man who walks up to open danger is a fool. He will go into dangerous places himself, but he goes by stealth. He never attacks except by surprise. He is brave, but he has no ambition to die a soldier's death. Apache glory consists strictly in killing the enemy. A wounded or helpless Apache will fight like a demon to protect his friends, but a sound Apache would never take such risks to bear away a wounded compatriot as a Sioux or Cheyenne warrior would. Of necessity, this warfare had its effects on the Apaches, in the way of making peace seem more endurable, but they were neither exterminated nor conquered. In April, 1865, Inspector-general Davis held a parley with Victoria, Acosta, and other chiefs, among whom were Pasquin, Cassari, and Salvador, the sons of Mangas Colorado. The Indians were very destitute, and wanted peace, but they did not wish to leave their coun-

APACHES WATCHING A TRAIN.

try. The iron rule, of removal to the Bosque, staggered them. They agreed to send four chiefs to inspect the reservation and report to the tribe, but none of them came back, as they promised, and the war went on as before.

At the close of the war of the rebellion the United States was divided into five Military Divisions, and these were subdivided in nineteen Departments. New Mexico was put in the Department of the Missouri, commanded by Major-general Pope, which was a part of the Military Division of the Mississippi, commanded by General Sherman. Arizona was in the Department of California, commanded by Major-general McDowell, which was a part of the Military Division of the Pacific, commanded by Maj.-gen. H. W. Halleck. The extermination theory was believed in by General Halleck, so far at least as the Apaches were concerned. He said, "It is useless to negotiate with these Apache Indians. They will observe no treaties, agreements, or truces. With them there is no alternative but active and vigorous war, till they are completely destroyed, or forced to surrender as prisoners of war." The hostile Apaches were nearly all in Arizona, which was commanded by Brigadier-general Mason, and the war there was prosecuted much as before, or, if possible, more bitterly. Both sides were becoming more and more exasperated, and vented their spleen in ways that only served to make matters worse. The Indians were adopting the practice of mutilating the dead, which was formerly contrary to their customs. The whites frequently killed inoffensive Indians on general principles. In 1868 a man named Mitchell causelessly killed Waba Yuma, head chief of the Hualapais, and that tribe, which had been peaceable, went to war. They had been looked upon with the contempt that frontiersmen commonly feel for peaceable Indians, but they proved vicious enemies. General McDowell reported that, "the officers from Prescott say they would prefer fighting five Apaches to one Hualapais."

In the mean time trouble had come at the Bosque. The question of a permanent reservation at that point became a political one, and everything connected with it passed into the realms of misrepresentation, so that the truth is hard to reach. It is clear, however, that the reservation crops failed, or were destroyed by insects, year after year. It is also clear that the Navahos and Apaches did not get along well together. The Navahos were the stronger in numbers, and appeared to have the ear of the commanding officer. After the Mescaleros had been at the Bosque for two years, the land which they had been cultivating was taken from them and given to the Navahos, while they were assigned to another location. This was done to prevent quarrelling, but to the Mescaleros it appeared an act of favoritism. There could be no harmony between them and the Navahos. They had long been at war, and their customs were totally different. The Mescaleros claimed the fulfilment of General Carleton's promise that they should have a reservation in their own country; indeed, Agent Labodie testifies that they had looked forward to this all the time, and had used their influence in bringing in their own hostiles solely for that purpose. They were not removed. The Bosque reservation for all Apaches and Navahos had become General Carleton's pet scheme. On November 3, 1865, the entire tribe of Mescaleros left the Bosque and went to their own country. They went to war because they knew that leaving the reservation would be considered an act of war, and that they must fight or go back. One of their leading men, Ojo Blanco (White Eye*), had left several weeks prior to this time with a small party. After several years of desultory warfare, during which the anti-Bosque party had gained their point, and the tribes were returned to their former homes, the Mescaleros were settled on a reservation in their own country.

The military operations of the '60's were not devoid of results. New Mexico had a season of comparative quiet, in the better settled parts, and Arizona was yielding to the progress of civilization. The valley of Santa Cruz was again filled with ranchemen. Tubac was reoccupied, and Tucson

---

* The Apache words for "white eye" are *Pin-dah Lick-o-yee*, and this is the name they use to designate Americans, in their own language. We are "white eyes," not "pale faces," to them. They also use the word Americano in common with other tribes who are more or less versed in Spanish.

TUBAC

regained its lost population. The mining regions on the Colorado and about Prescott were held by the whites. Yet, in fact, there was merely a change in the seat of war. The Apaches held mountain fastnesses, as yet unknown, from which they sallied forth to raid into the very heart of the settlements. No one dared to travel the roads unarmed, and small parties were not safe when they had arms. Horses were run off in broad day from within half a mile of Prescott. Men who were not vigilant were liable to be killed anywhere. No Apache tribe was subdued. The later years of this period found them at war from the Pecos to the Colorado. The bitterness and want of confidence which had been instilled into the Indians by this system of warfare are results which are not subject to measurement, but it must, in fairness, be admitted that they did follow in some degree. On the whole the policy of extermination in Arizona, coupled with concentration in New Mexico, proved a dismal failure, after a full and fair trial. The army officers began to realize this, and Indians who were willing to make peace were permitted to gather about Fort Goodwin, Camp Grant, and in the White Mountains. This marked the beginning of a new era in Arizona, which will be considered in a subsequent chapter.

APACHE BOOT, HEAD-DRESS, ETC.

CHAPTER XIII.
SAND CREEK.

ON the night of November 28, 1864, about seven hundred and fifty men, cavalry and artillery, were marching eastward across the plains below Fort Lyon. There was a bitter, determined look on their hard-set features that betokened ill for some one. For five days they had been marching, from Bijou Basin, about one hundred and fifty miles to the northwest, as the crow flies, but some fifty miles farther by their route. When they started the snow was two to three feet deep on the ground, but, as they progressed, it had become lighter, and now the ground was clear. The night was bitter cold; Jim Beckwith, the old trapper who had been guiding them, had become so stiffened that he was unable longer to distinguish the course, and they were obliged to rely on a half-breed Indian. About one third of the men had the appearance of soldiers who had seen service; the remainder had a diversity of arms and equipments as well as of uniforms, and marched with the air of raw recruits. About half a mile in advance were three men, the half-breed guide and two officers, one of the latter of such gigantic proportions that the others seemed pygmies beside him. Near daybreak the half-breed turned to the white men and said: "Wolf he howl. Injun dog he hear wolf, he howl too. Injun he hear dog and listen; hear something, and run off." The big man tapped the butt of his revolver in an ominous way, and replied: "Jack, I haven't had an Indian to eat for a long time. If you fool with me, and don't lead us to that camp, I'll have you for breakfast." They found the camp. There were one hundred and twenty Cheyenne and eight Arapahoe lodges in it, stretched along the bank of a shallow stream, which crept sluggishly down a broad bed of sand. On each side of the camp, ranging out perhaps a mile, was a herd of ponies, the two numbering about eleven hundred. It was between daybreak and sunrise; the Indians were just beginning to move. A squaw heard the noise of the approaching horses, and reported that a herd of buffalo was coming. Others ran out, who quickly discovered that the rumbling was the tread of horses, and that a large body of troops was approaching. In a moment all was confusion. Men, women, and children ran here and there, getting their arms in readiness or preparing for flight. The principal Cheyenne chief hastily ran up an American flag over his teepee, with a white flag above it. A white trader, who was in one of the teepees, came out and hastened towards the soldiers. At the same time two detachments of cavalry were galloping towards the herds, and some of the Indians were running in the same directions.

Firing began between these parties. The white trader seemed confused, and stopped. A cavalryman said: "Let me bring him in, major," and, starting from the ranks, galloped towards him, but a bullet from the camp tumbled him from his horse, and the trader turned and ran back. The herd of ponies on the farther side of the camp became alarmed and ran towards the camp, the soldiers cutting off only about half of them. The main body of troops pressed forward, firing as they came, led by their giant commander, who rode through the ranks, calling out: "Remember our wives and children, murdered on the Platte and the Arkansas." The Indians were beginning to fall rapidly under the deadly fire. Part of them caught the straggling ponies which had reached the camp, and fled. The remainder, warriors and squaws, with some children, retired slowly up the creek, fighting as they went. 'They continued thus for about three quarters of a mile, to a point where the banks rose from three to ten feet, on either side of a level expanse of sand, some three hundred yards wide. Along the banks the Indians made their stand, protected by them on one side, and on the other by heaps of loose sand which they had scraped up. Most of the troops were now in confusion, each doing about as he liked. About one half of them were firing on the line of Indians in the creek bed, and squads were riding about, killing stragglers, scalping the dead, and pursuing the flying. No prisoners were being taken, and no one was allowed to escape if escape could be prevented. A child of about three years, perfectly naked, was toddling along over the trail where the Indians had fled. A soldier saw it, fired at about seventy-five yards distance, and missed it. Another dismounted and said: "Let me try the little — —; I can hit him." He missed too, but a third dismounted, with a similar remark, and at his shot the child fell. At the creek bed the fight was at long range and stubborn. A private was firing at an Indian who climbed up on the bank from time to time, and made derisive gestures at the soldier's fruitless efforts. "Let me take that gun of yours for a minute, colonel," said the soldier. The colonel handed him his rifle, an elegant silver-mounted one, presented him by the citizens of Denver; the Indian showed himself again; the rifle cracked and he dropped dead. The squaws were fighting along with the men. One had just wounded a soldier with an arrow, and a comrade put his rifle in rest, remarking, "If that squaw shows her head above the bank again, I'll blow the whole top of it off." An officer, standing by him, said: "I wouldn't make a heathen of myself by shooting a woman." The words had hardly dropped from his lips when the same squaw sent an arrow through the officer's arm, and his philanthropic remark changed to a howl of "Shoot the — —," and the soldier did it. The Indians could not be dislodged by the small arms, but towards noon two howitzers were brought into action and they broke the line. The Indians fell back from one position to another, the combat becoming gradually a running fight, which was kept up for five miles or more, and abandoned by the pursuers a short time before dusk. The soldiers then gathered at the Indian camp, where they remained until the second day following. Most of the corpses were scalped, and a number were mutilated as bodies are usually mutilated by Indians, with all that implies. Near evening, on the day after the battle, Jack Smith, the half-breed who had guided the soldiers to the camp, and a son of the white trader who was in the camp, was shot by one of the men. He had tried to run away during the fight, but had been brought back. The

TEXAN RANGERS

colonel commanding was warned that he would probably be killed if the men were not ordered to let him live. He replied: "I have given my orders, and have no further instructions to give." There were, at the time, seven other prisoners in the camp, two squaws and five children, who were taken to Fort Lyon and left there. They were the only prisoners taken. When the camp was broken, the buffalo-robes were confiscated for the sick, the soldiers took what they wanted for trophies, and the remainder was burned. The Indians lost three hundred, all killed, of whom about one half were warriors and the remainder women and children. The whites lost seven killed and forty-seven wounded, of whom seven afterwards died.

This was "the massacre of the friendly Cheyenne Indians at Sand Creek, by the Colorado troops, under Colonel John M. Chivington," or "the battle on the Big Sandy, with the hostile Cheyennes and Arapahoes," as you may be pleased to consider it. That is to say, it is a statement of what occurred there, as nearly as the truth can be arrived at, without favor or reservation. It is but just to add that the great majority of the troops who participated in it say it was not so bad as here represented, and that the witnesses of the action and events connected with it, who subsequently denounced it, make it no worse, notwithstanding the fact that many, who knew nothing of the facts in the case, have added much to the statement above given. The number killed was the point most in controversy in the investigations of the matter, ranging from about seventy, in Major Wynkoop's estimate, to six hundred, in Colonel Chivington's original report. The Indians conceded a loss of one hundred and forty, of whom sixty were warriors, and the testimony of all who counted bodies, after the battle, indicates the number stated above. Concerning this affair there has been much of exaggeration, much of invective, much of misunderstanding, and much of wholly unfounded statement. Indeed, so much has been said in regard to it that the controversy is far more extensive than the original trouble, and the historical shape that it has assumed is the creation of the controversy, not the fight. Now that twenty years have passed away—that the Indian is only a memory where he then roamed—that a new generation has taken the place of the old—let us try calmly to unravel the thread of truth from the fantastic fabric which has so long concealed it; and to do this we must first know something of the actors on that field.

Who was Colonel Chivington? In 1840 he was a rough, uncouth, profane child of nature, just stepped across the threshold of manhood. He lived in Warren County, Ohio, about two miles south of the line of Clinton. At a log-rolling in the neighborhood a good old Methodist brother reproved him, one day, for profanity, and the sturdy youth answered defiantly: "I will swear when I please and where I please." But he brooded over the rebuke, and a few days later he went to his reprover's house, determined to swear there, before his family. He did not do as he intended. Some unknown power beat down his resolution, and the curse died trembling on his tongue. He went away, but the mysterious influence followed him; his eyes were turned inward on his guilty soul; he could not rest. He struggled against it, but in vain, and soon he sought at the altar the pardon for his sins. Scoffers may smile at the change of heart by divine grace, but sure it was there was a change in him. He became an industrious, orderly man; he joined the Methodist Church and lived consistently with its discipline; he apprenticed himself to a carpenter and thoroughly learned the trade. Towards 1850 he determined to move West and enter the ministry, and this he did, working meantime at his trade. At the end of the second year of his clerical service he was transferred to the Missouri Conference and continued his labors there. It was a troubled field for him, for he was peculiarly a Northern man. Mobs collected at various times to hinder his preaching, but his apparent abundance of "muscular Christianity" kept him from serious trouble, and his intended disturbers often remained to hear him preach.

His kindly nature helped him to preserve peaceful relations, also. One day he met an old planter, hauling logs, with his team mired down. Chivington dismounted, tied his horse, waded into the mud, and helped him out. The planter desired to know to whom he was indebted, and, on being told, exclaimed: "Come right home with me. A preacher that will get off in the mud to help a stranger won't steal niggers." They were good friends thereafter. A few years later Chivington was in Kansas, taking an active part with Lane and his friends in the border war. After the Kansas troubles were settled, we find him serving acceptably, for two years, as a missionary to the Wyandot Indians, and afterwards, as interpreter and guide, travelling through the West with the Methodist bishops who were establishing missions among the Indian tribes. Soon after the beginning of the war he went to a quarterly meeting at Denver, being then a Presiding Elder in Western Kansas and Colorado, and, while there, preached to the soldiers at their barracks. They liked his style and urged him to stay with them. Governor Gilpin offered him a chaplaincy, but he said that if he went with the soldiers he wanted to fight, so he was made a major instead. There is one point in his character that must not be lost sight of, if his history is to be understood. He was, like other Kansas free-soilers, an uncompromising Union man, and had no use for a rebel, white or red. His dislike to anything savoring of treason got him into trouble time and again, but he never held back on that account. On one occasion, after the war, he seriously disturbed his domestic peace by peremptorily shutting off some reminiscences from his brother-in-law, an ex-confederate.

And what of the Colorado troops? They included men from all ranks and classes in life; many of them are prominent and respected citizens of Colorado now. About two thirds of those at Sand Creek were one-hundred-days' men, of the 3d regiment; the remainder were veterans, mostly of the 1st regiment. These last had established a military reputation beyond all cavil, and, without referring to other services, a brief sketch of their work in New Mexico will satisfy the reader that no equal body of men ever did greater or more gallant service for the Union. In the early part of 1862 General Sibley invaded New Mexico with an army of twenty-five hundred, including a large number of Texan Rangers, having evidently in view the conquest of the entire mountain country. Our government had been paying little or no attention to the Far West; its hands were full in the East. Even the official communications in some departments had not been replied to in a year past. The Confederacy was more watchful. Full information of the situation in the West had been given to its leaders by officials, civil and military, who had been located at various Western points, and had hastened to the South as soon as the war opened. The United States troops in the country were few in number. The Indians were ready for war whenever an opportunity presented itself. The Mexicans were supposed to be friendly to the South, and the lower classes were known to be ready for rapine and pillage, at any time and against anybody. The Mormons were in ecstasy over the apparent fulfilment of their late Prophet's war prophecy, and were willing to help on the "Kilkenny-cat fight." Besides, they were still sore over the troubles of 1857, and had no love for the national government. The Secession element in California was quite strong, especially in the southern part, which was to have been a slave state under the Calhoun plan. These facts at once determined the policy of the South, and the invasion was begun. If it had been successful—what an awful possibility!—The South would have had a coast-line impossible of blockade, the entire line of Mexico for external communication, the mines to fill her depleted treasury, and an extensive country which could have been reconquered only at immense cost of life and money. The Texans entered New Mexico from the south. They took Fort Fillmore without resistance, and marched up the Rio Grande unchecked, until they reached Fort Craig, where General Canby awaited them. They decided not to attack the fort, and were flanking it, to go forward, when Canby came out and attacked them at Valverde. They rather worsted him, and he retired to the fort, while they pursued their march up the river. They occupied Santa Fé, and found that the Mexicans were not nearly so glad to see them as they had anticipated; still, little discouraged, they pushed on towards Fort Union, some sixty-five miles northeast, on the edge of the plains, the arsenal and supply depot for that section.

Governor Gilpin, all this time, had been moving in the mining camps of Colorado, and, on February 22, the 1st Colorado regiment, under Colonel Slough, left Denver through

OLD FORT UNION.

snow a foot deep. They reached Fort Union on March 11, after a journey of great hardship, and were there armed and equipped. They pressed forward, and, on the 23d, reached the month of Apaché Cañon, the location of "Pigeon's Ranch," or, more properly, the ranch of M. Alexandre Vallé; the Texans had by this time reached the opposite end of the cañon. In this cañon, where Armijo had failed to meet Kearny, the Greek miner met the Greek cowboy. It was a contest the like of which never occurred elsewhere. The Southerners had adopted as their favorite name, "Baylor's Babes;" the Coloradoans gloried in their chosen title of "Pet Lambs" —grim satires these, as well on the plainsmen who charged McRae's Battery with revolvers and bowie-knives, as on the mountaineers who never learned what it was to be whipped. On the 26th the advance of the Texans met two hundred and ten cavalry and one hundred and eighty infantry under Major Chivington, and, in the words of a local writer, it "was more like the shock of lightning than of battalions." Said M. Vallé, who witnessed the fight, "Zat Chivington, he poot down 'is 'ead, and foight loike mahd bull." Both detachments reeled back from this hard bump, and on the 28th, the main forces having arrived, they went at it again. The Texans surprised the Coloradoans' camp, but the Lambs stood their ground, and, after a desperate fight, the Babes were forced to retire, and they retired to a little surprise-party at home. While they had been making their attack, Chivington had led a force of one hundred men up the precipitous side of the cañon, along a rugged and dangerous path, and down on the Texan rear-guard of some six hundred men. It was a desperate charge to make, but it resulted in a brilliant success, and the Texan train of sixty-four wagons and two hundred mules, with all their supplies and ammunition, were destroyed. The Texan invasion was ruined. Sibley began his retreat, and Slough fell back on Fort Union for his supplies, but only for a breathing space. On April 13 the Coloradoans had joined General Canby and begun a pursuit of the retiring Texans, which was kept up for one hundred and fifty miles; a pursuit so disastrous to the pursued that one half of their original force was left behind, dead, wounded, and prisoners, together with all their stores, public and private. So much for the Colorado troops.

The Cheyennes we know something of already. The village attacked was that of Black Kettle (Make-ta-ve-to), the principal chief of the southern Cheyennes, and the few lodges of Arapahoes were under Left Hand (Na-watk), second in rank of the southern chiefs. There had been trouble in these tribes ever since the treaty of Fort Wise, in 1861. The warriors denounced the chiefs for making the treaty, and were particularly opposed to the construction of the Kansas Pacific Railroad through their lands, as they knew it would drive away the buffalo. The chiefs were threatened with death if they undertook to carry out its provisions, and so the intense desire of the Cheyennes and Arapahoes for an agricultural life, which is recited as the cause of the treaty, had to go ungratified. The first serious troubles, after Sumner's campaign, occurred after this treaty was made, and all the succeeding troubles grew out of it. The Cheyennes began committing minor offences in 1861, and, as they were unpunished, they gradually grew bolder, until, in 1863, Agent Lorey reported that the Cheyennes were dissatisfied, and that the Sioux were urging them to open war. In other words, the war feeling had grown so strong that it was necessary to treat with them anew. Governor Evans went out, by agreement, to treat with them, on the head-waters of the Republican, but they failed to come as agreed. The governor sent his guide, a squaw-man named Elbridge Gerry (a grandson of the signer of the Declaration of Independence, of the same name), in search of them. He returned after an absence of two weeks, and reported that they had held a council and decided not to treat. One chief, Bull Bear (O-to-ah-nac-co), the leader of the "Dog-soldiers," had offered to come in, but his warriors would not allow him to do so. The Cheyennes afterwards confirmed this statement fully; they said they were going to remain at peace, but would make no treaty that they had to sign; that they were going to have their lands; and even if a railroad was built through their country, they would not allow any one to settle along it. The chiefs who had signed the treaty of Fort Wise said they were obliged to repudiate it or their warriors would kill them. Minor depredations were committed during the remainder of 1863 and the early part of

1864, and, during the winter, word was received, from spies among them, that a coalition was being formed among all the plains tribes, to drive the whites out of the country. This information proved true, for in the spring and summer of 1864, the Sioux, Comanches, Kiowas, Cheyennes, and Arapahoes were engaged in active hostilities. The reader will note here, that no one has ever pretended that any of the eighteen hundred Southern Cheyennes, except the six hundred at Sand Creek, were not open enemies at the time.

The effect of this warfare on the whites was distressing. Nearly every stage was attacked, emigrants were cut off, and the settlements were raided continually. The overland trains, on which the entire settlements depended for supplies, were deterred from moving by fear of attack. On June 14 Governor Evans applied for authority to call the militia into the United States service, or to call out one-hundred-days' men, which was not granted. Matters became worse. All the set-

STANDING OFF THE CHEYENNES.

tlements from the Purgatoire to the Cache la Poudre, and for two hundred miles on the Platte, were in consternation. The settlers left their crops and built block-houses for mutual protection. Those near Denver fled to that place. The governor was besieged with petitions for arms and authority to organize for protection. On August 8 all the stage lines were attacked. On August 11 Governor Evans issued a proclamation, calling the people to organize for self-protection, and under this several companies were formed which were considered sufficient for the defence of the settlements. But they could not protect the settlements from famine. On August 18 Governor Evans despatched Secretary Stanton: "Extensive Indian depredations, with murder of families, occurred yesterday thirty miles south of Denver. Our lines of communication are cut, and our crops, our sole dependence, are all in exposed localities, and cannot be gathered by our scattered population. Large bodies of Indians are undoubtedly near to Denver, and we are in danger of destruction both from the attack of Indians and starvation. I earnestly request that Colonel Ford's regiment of 2d Colorado Volunteers be immediately sent to our relief. It is impossible to exaggerate our danger. We are doing all we can for our defence." There was no favorable answer received to this, and, on September 7, a second despatch followed: "Pray give positive orders for our 2d Colorado Cavalry to come out. Have notice published that they will come in detachments to escort trains up the Platte on certain days. Unless escorts are sent thus we will inevitably have a famine in addition to this gigantic Indian war. Flour is forty-five dollars a barrel, and the supply growing scarce, with none on the way. Through spies we got knowledge of the plan of about one thousand warriors in camp to strike our frontier settlements, in small bands, simultaneously in the night, for an extent of three hundred miles. It was frustrated at the time, but we have to fear another such attempt soon. Pray give the order for our troops to come, as requested, at once, or it will be too late for trains to come this season." The troops were not sent, but, in the mean time, authority had been given by the War Department to raise a regiment of one-hundred-days' men, and the 3d Colorado was organized and impatiently waiting for arms and equipments, which they did not get until a short time before their march to Sand Creek.

But were the Cheyennes responsible for all this? Quite as much so as any of the tribes. They began stealing stock early in the spring, and, on April 13, a herdsman for Irving, Jackmann, & Co. reported that the Cheyennes and Arapahoes had run off sixty head of oxen and a dozen mules and horses from their camp, thirty miles south of Denver. Lieutenant Clark Dunn was sent after them with a small party of soldiers. He overtook them as they were crossing the Platte, during a heavy snow-storm. A parley was commenced, but was interrupted by part of the Indians running off the stock, and the soldiers attempting to disarm the others. A fight ensued, in which the soldiers, who were greatly outnumbered, were defeated, with a loss of four men, the Indians still holding the cattle. After this fight, there was not a word nor an act from any member of the Southern Cheyennes indicative of peace, until the 1st of September, when the Indian agent at Fort Lyon received the following:

"CHEYENNE VILLAGE, *Aug.* 29, 1864.

"MAJOR COLLEY,—We received a letter from Bent, wishing us to make peace. We held a council in regard to it. All come to the conclusion to make peace with you, providing you make peace with the Kiowas, Comanches, Arapahoes, Apaches, and Sioux. We are going to send a messenger to the Kiowas and to the other nations about our going to make peace with you. We heard that you have some [Indian prisoners] in Denver. We have seven prisoners of yours which we are willing to give up, providing you give up yours. There are three war-parties out yet, and two of Arapahoes. They have been out for some time, and are expected in soon. When we held this council there were few Arapahoes and Sioux present. We want true news from you in return. That is a letter.

"BLACK KETTLE, *and other chiefs.*"

This letter was written for the chiefs by Edmond Guerrier and George Bent, Cheyenne half-breeds. Black Kettle was head chief of all the Southern Cheyennes, and conceded by all to be the most friendly of the chiefs towards the whites, with, possibly, the exception of Bull Bear. Yet, by this letter, he and the other chiefs admit fully that they were hostiles; that three Cheyenne war-parties were then out; that they were in coalition with the other tribes, and would consult them before treating; that they would treat only if all the other tribes treated. Indeed, why should the Cheyennes deny that they were hostile? They had been raiding in every direction; had run off stock repeatedly; had attacked stages and emigrant trains; had killed settlers; had carried off women and children; had fought the troops under Major Downing; had defeated those under Lieutenant Dunn and Lieutenant Ayres; and had been evading other bodies of troops all summer. They attacked the settlements on the Little Blue, and, after killing the men, they carried off Mrs. Ewbanks, Miss Roper, and three children. It was almost certainly they who killed Mr. and Mrs. Hungate and their two babies at Running Creek. They carried off Mrs. Martin and a little boy from a ranch on Plum Creek. General Curtis prepared two or three times to march against them, but was diverted from his purpose by rebel raiders from Arkansas. He sent General Blunt after them, and they ambushed his advance-guard at Pawnee Fork and almost annihilated it. On November 12, after Black Kettle had gone to Sand Creek, a party of Cheyennes and Arapahoes approached a government train on Walnut Creek, east of Fort Larned, and, after protesting friendship and shaking hands, suddenly fell upon the teamsters and killed fourteen of them, the only person who escaped alive being a boy who was scalped and left for dead. He recovered, but became imbecile, and died from the effects of the injury.

The Cheyennes never denied that they were hostiles; that they were was a discovery of the Indian ring, perpetuated by Indian worshippers. When they sent in the letter quoted above Major Wynkoop went out to them, and brought in Black Kettle, his brother White Antelope, and Bull Bear, of the Cheyennes, and Neva and other Arapahoes, representing Left Hand, for a talk with Governor Evans. They said then: "It was like going through a strong fire or blast for Major Wynkoop's men to come to our camp; it was the same for us to come to see you." From this talk I quote the following: "GOV. EVANS. 'Who committed the murder of the Hungate family on Running Creek?' NEVA. 'The Arapahoes; a party of the northern band who were passing

WHICH TRIBE DID IT?

north. It was Medicine Man or Roman Nose and three others. I am satisfied, from the time he left a certain camp for the North, that it was this party of four persons.' AGENT WHITELY. 'That cannot be true.' GOV. E. 'Where is Roman Nose?' NEVA. 'You ought to know better than me; you have been nearer to him.' GOV. E. 'Who killed the man and the boy at the head of Cherry Creek?' NEVA (after consultation). 'Kiowas and Comanches.' GOV. E. 'Who stole soldiers' horses and mules from Jimmy's camp twenty-seven days ago?' NEVA. 'Fourteen Cheyennes and Arapahoes together.' GOV E. "What were their names?" NEVA. "Powder Face and Whirlwind, who are now in our camp, were the leaders.' COL. SHOUP. 'I counted twenty Indians on that occasion.' GOV. E. 'Who stole Charley Autobee's horses?' NEVA. 'Raven's son.' GOV. E. 'Who took the stock from Fremont's orchard and had the first fight with the soldiers this spring north of there?' WHITE ANTELOPE. 'Before answering this question I would like for you to know that this was the beginning of the war, and I should like to know what it was for. A soldier fired first.' Gov. E. 'The Indians had stolen about forty horses; the soldiers went to recover them, and the Indians fired a volley into their ranks.' WHITE ANTELOPE. 'That is all a mistake; they were coming down the Bijou and found one horse and one mule. They returned one horse, before they got to Gerry's, to a man, then went to Gerry's expecting to turn the other one over to some one. They then heard that the soldiers and Indians were fighting somewhere down the Platte; then they took fright and all fled.' GOV. E. 'Who were the Indians who had the fight?' WHITE ANTELOPE. 'They were headed by the Fool Badger's son, a young man, one of the greatest of the Cheyenne warriors, who was wounded, and though still alive he will never recover.' NEVA. 'I want to say something; it makes me feel bad to be talking about these things and opening old sores. . . . The Comanches, Kiowas, and Sioux have done much more injury than we have. We will tell what we know, but cannot speak for others.' GOV. E. 'I suppose you acknowledge the depredations on the Little Blue, as you have the prisoners then taken in your possession.' WHITE

ANTELOPE. 'We [the Cheyennes] took two prisoners west of Fort Kearney, and destroyed the trains.' . . . NEVA. 'I know the value of the presents which we receive from Washington; we cannot live without them. That is why I try so hard to keep peace with the whites.' Gov. E. 'I cannot say anything about those things now.' NEVA. 'I can speak for all the Arapahoes under Left Hand. Raven has sent no one here to speak for him; Raven has fought the whites.' " Little Raven (Oh-has-tee) was head chief of the Southern Arapahoes, and was notoriously hostile. Even Major Wynkoop conceded that he had, during the summer, killed three men and carried off a woman.

But even if most of the Cheyennes had been hostile, were not the Indians at Sand Creek friendly? It is usually difficult to disprove an Indian's protestations of friendship in a satisfactory way, but if ever it was done it was here. Black Kettle had admitted his hostility, as shown above. So had his brother, White Antelope. War Bonnet, a chief who was killed there, was identified as one of the most active hostiles in the attack on General Blunt at Pawnee Fork. The testimony shows, without contradiction, that there were at least two hundred warriors in the camp, and it would be very difficult to point out a Cheyenne warrior who had been friendly. It had been the plea of the chiefs, all along, that they desired to carry out the treaty of Fort Wise, but were deterred by fear of their warriors. But more satisfactory than the established reputation of these Indians was the testimony of scalps, women's and children's dresses, and stolen goods, which were found in profusion in the teepees. Perhaps medical testimony will be most convincing as to the condition of the scalps. Dr. Caleb S. Birtsell, Assistant Surgeon, testified, "While in one of the lodges dressing wounded soldiers a soldier came to the opening of the lodge and called my attention to some white scalps he held in his hand; my impression, after examination, was that two or three of them were quite fresh; I saw, in the hands of soldiers, silk dresses and other garments belonging to women." Major Anthony, commanding at Fort Lyon, considered that there were three Indians in the camp who were friendly, Black Kettle, Left

Hand, and One Eye, and these he desired to be spared. Black Kettle escaped unhurt; Left Hand received a wound from the effect of which he afterwards died; and One Eye was killed. He was in the camp as a spy; placed there, on a salary of $125 per month and a ration, by Major Wynkoop, to watch these "friendly" Cheyennes, and continued in the same position by Major Anthony.

And this brings us to another equally serious question. Although these Cheyennes at Sand Creek had been hostile, were they not at Sand Creek under a promise of protection by the military? To this the testimony answers clearly, "No." That is a rather startling statement to one who is familiar only with the current version of Sand Creek, but it is true, nevertheless. Both the congressional and departmental investigations were peculiar. The former was conducted by a committee of men whose minds were made up before they began; the style of their questions, the inaccuracy of their findings, and the fact that they condemned every one for prevarication who differed from what they expected in testimony, prove this. The latter was conducted by Major Wynkoop, who had been displaced by Major Anthony at Fort Lyon but a short time previous to the fight, who was one of the leading prosecuting witnesses, and who was, immediately after the investigation, appointed to the Agency, a position which is very rarely forced on men against their wishes. There was also a military commission appointed, which took testimony at Denver and Fort Lyon; it was presided over by Colonel Tappan, of the 1st Colorado Cavalry, who was recognized as a personal enemy of Chivington. This was the only one of the tribunals before which Chivington appeared and was given opportunity to cross-examine or produce witnesses. The reports of the other investigations were made without any knowledge of its proceedings; in fact, its proceedings were not published for two years after the reports were made. In the testimony at both of the earlier investigations, scheming and jealousy crop out at many points. The prosecuting witnesses who were out of office charged the prosecuting witnesses who were in office with stealing from the Indians, and selling them their own goods. The fullest latitude was given to hearsay, and expressions of opinion were courted. But the most striking thing in all that testimony was the adroit manner in which several witnesses confused the relations of Black Kettle's Cheyennes, to Fort Lyon, with those of Little Raven's Arapahoes. Their real relations were explained to the Committee on the Conduct of the War, clearly enough to have been understood by men who were not blinded by prejudice, but the committee only carried on to perfection the work which the witnesses had begun. The testimony of all

LITTLE RAVEN.

the witnesses, taken together, shows that the Indians who came to the fort and were subsisted by Major Wynkoop were six hundred and fifty-two of the Southern Arapahoes, under their head chief, Little Raven. That this chief had been hostile is not questioned; Major Wynkoop himself blames him and his warriors for all the depredations committed by the Arapahoes. On November 2 Major Anthony arrived and assumed command; he found these Arapahoes camped two miles from Fort Lyon, with all their arms, and coming daily to the fort for provisions; he told them they must surrender their arms, and they gave up a lot of old and worn-out weapons, which, they said, were all they had. After ten days he concluded that he was exceeding his authority in this, returned their arms to them, and told them to go away. They went; Major Wynkoop says that Little Raven's band went to Camp Wynkoop, and Left Hand's joined the Cheyennes. The Arapahoes who went with Left Hand numbered about forty.

The most satisfactory evidence in regard to this is not in the testimony of any one, but in the official report of Major Anthony, made at the time, when there was no "Sand Creek" to attack or defend. On November 6, in a letter to headquarters, after recounting his disarming the Arapahoes, he says: " Nine Cheyenne Indians to-day sent in, wishing to see me. They state that six hundred of that tribe are now thirty-five miles north of here, coming towards the post, and two thousand about seventy-five miles away, waiting for better weather to enable them to come in. I shall not permit them to come in, even as prisoners, for the reason that if I do I shall have to subsist them upon a prisoner's rations. I shall, however, demand their arms, all stolen stock, and the perpetrators of all depredations. I am of the opinion that they will not accept this proposition, but that they will return to the Smoky Hill. They pretend that they want peace, and I think they do now, as they cannot fight during the winter, except where a small band of them can find an unprotected train or frontier settlement. I do not think it is policy to make peace with them now, until all perpetrators of depredations are surrendered up, to be dealt with as we may propose." This, then, was the true state of affairs; on November 6 there was not a Cheyenne at Fort Lyon; there were six hundred and fifty-two Arapahoes under the hostile chief Little Raven, who was then playing friend; there were six hundred Cheyennes under Black Kettle, thirty-five miles north, proposing to come in. And what was done in regard to the Cheyennes? They came on down after some further parleying; they were not allowed to come into the fort at all, or camp in the vicinity of the post. They were told that they might go over on Sand Creek, forty miles away, and camp, and if the commandant received any authority to treat with them he would let them know. They were not in the camp two miles from Fort Lyon at any time; they were never disarmed; and they were never held as prisoners.

Neither did these Indians have any promise of immunity from Governor Evans or Colonel Chivington, as is intimated by the committee. They met but once, at the council in Denver, on September 28. It has been stated over and over that the Cheyennes came to Sand Creek, in response to Governor Evans's circular, calling on the friendly Indians to take refuge at the forts—friendly Cheyennes and Arapahoes at Fort Lyon. This statement is absolutely and unqualifiedly untrue. The circular was dated June 27. Three months later the chiefs appeared in Denver to talk peace, in consequence of the circular, but were plainly told it was too late for any treaty. Governor Evans said to them: "Whatever peace they make must be with the soldiers, and not with me;" and the entire talk was on that basis. I quote again: "WHITE ANTELOPE. 'How can we be protected from the soldiers on the plains?' GOV. E. 'You must make that arrangement with the military chief.' WHITE ANTELOPE. 'I fear that these new soldiers who have gone out may kill some of my people while I am here.' GOV. E. 'There is great danger of it.'" Again, Governor Evans said: "I hand you over to the military, one of the chiefs of which is here to-day, and can speak for himself to them if he chooses." The chief referred to was Colonel Chivington, Commander of the District—it should be noted, however, that Fort Lyon was not in Chivington's district. He said: "I am not a big war chief, but all the soldiers in this country are at my command. My rule of fighting white men or Indians is to fight them until they lay down their arms and submit to military authority. They are nearer Major Wynkoop than any one else, and they can go to him when they get ready to do that." If any one can torture those utterances into promises of immunity he is welcome to do so.

Some five weeks later the messengers of the Cheyennes arrived at Fort Lyon and were turned away, as above stated. They did not arrive there until after Major Wynkoop was superseded by Major Anthony. They did not make any arrangement with Major Wynkoop; it was impossible for them to do so, as he was not in command. More than that, Major Wynkoop never, at any time, had any authority to make any treaty with them, and the Indians knew it. White Antelope said, in the council: "When Major Wynkoop came, we proposed to make peace. He said he had no power to make a peace, except to bring them here and return them safe." The Cheyennes went over to Sand Creek and camped, not anticipating any trouble, because there were no soldiers near them, except the garrison, and it was too small to risk an attack. Indeed, they were ready for an attack from it, and sent word that, "If that little — — red-eyed chief wants a fight, we will give him all he wants." The chief referred to was Major Anthony, who was afflicted with sore eyes at the time. The Indians were not allowed to visit the fort, and none of their friends or supposed allies, except on first being blindfolded. This was under general orders which were adopted a few weeks previously, after a Sunday-morning performance by friendly Indians at Fort Larned. On that occasion the Indians had drawn supplies for the week, and some squaws were executing a dance

FRIDAY—A GOOD ARAPAHOE.

for the edification of a part of the officers and men, when the braves stampeded the cattle belonging to the post, with all the horses and mules, and succeeded in getting away with them. At the first whoop of the stampede the dancers jumped on their ponies and scampered away, demonstrating that the affair had been planned in cold blood. Major Anthony testified that he had no friendly relations with these Cheyennes; that he should have attacked them before Chivington came if his force had not been too small; that he told Chivington it was only a question of policy whether they should be attacked or not, as it would probably cause an attack by the large band, which was not far distant. So far as the propriety of attacking these Indians was concerned, there is not the least question but that Chivington was justified in his attack, under all the rules of civilized warfare. They were hostiles, and there was no truce with them. There is another matter—it seems almost absurd to mention it, but it were well to prevent any further misunderstanding—and that is the display of flags by Black Kettle, which some persons have seemed to lay much stress upon. The uniform testimony of the soldiers was that they saw nothing of the kind, but that is immaterial. No one of common understanding would profess that the display of a flag of any kind was cause for stopping troops in the midst of a charge, and especially in the midst of a surprise of an enemy's camp.

Having now shown the propriety of the attack, we arrive at the question of the propriety of the manner in which it was made, a question much more difficult of solution. One point is certain—every one in authority felt that the Indians ought to be punished. Major Wynkoop testifies that Governor Evans at first objected to seeing the chiefs at all, but finally consented to hold the council which has been mentioned. His feelings on the subject were exposed to the Indians at the council in these words: "The time when you can make war best is in the summer time; when I can make war best is in the winter. You, so far, have had the advantage; my time is just coming." He told them, as before stated, that they would have to talk to the military authorities, and his action was approved by the Indian Bureau. The military had no desire, for peace at the time. It is quite true that the field orders of General Curtis directed hostilities only against hostile Indians, and expressly stated that "women and children must be spared," but "hostile Indians" meant Indians who had been hostile, and neither he nor any other commander in the West was in favor of treating till the Indians had been punished. On the day of Governor Evans's council with the chiefs, General Curtis telegraphed the District Commander: "I fear agent of the Interior Department will be ready to make presents too soon. It is better to chastise before giving anything but a little tobacco to talk over. No peace must be made without my directions." The last telegram Chivington received from him, before marching, was: "Pursue everywhere and punish the Cheyennes and Arapahoes; pay no attention to district lines. No presents must be made and no peace concluded without my consent." The reader will observe that General Curtis is not by these directions made responsible for killing the women and children, or deciding that the Sand Creek camp was hostile, but his desire to punish the Indians was clear and decided. And it was so all through the West. A few weeks later, when Colonel Ford wanted to make peace with the Kiowas and Comanches, General Dodge, his Department Commander, telegraphed him: "The military have no authority to treat with Indians. Our duty is to make them keep the peace by punishing them for their hostility. Keep posted as to their location, so that as soon as ready we can strike them." So, in New Mexico, General Carleton had instructed Colonel Kit Carson: "If the Indians send in a flag and desire to treat for peace, say to the bearer that when the people of New Mexico were attacked by the Texans, the Mescaleros broke their treaty of peace, and murdered innocent people, and ran off their stock; that now our hands are untied, and you have been sent to punish them for their treachery and their crimes; that you have no power to make peace; that you are there to kill them wherever you can find them; that if they beg for peace, their chiefs and twenty of their principal men must come to Santa Fé to have a talk here; but tell them fairly and frankly that you will keep after their people and slay them until you receive orders to desist from these head-quarters." On September 19 Curtis writes to Carleton: "General Blunt is at or near Fort Larned looking out for Indians, and may co-operate with you in crushing out some of the vile hordes that now harass our lines of communication." On October 22 Carleton writes to Blunt, hoping he will effect a union with Carson, "so that a blow may be struck which those two treacherous tribes will remember." On January 30, 1865, Curtis writes to Governor Evans: "I protest my desire to pursue and punish the enemy everywhere, in his lodges especially; but I do not believe in killing women and children who can be taken."

It is equally certain that the desire of punishing these Indians was increased, with loyal people, by the belief that their hostility was produced by Southern emissaries. How far their hostility was so produced will never be definitely known, but there was reason for the belief, without doubt. Soon after the beginning of the war the insurgents had occupied Indian territory and enrolled many Indians in Confederate regiments. The loyal Indians tried to resist, but, after two or three engagements, about seven thousand of them were driven into Kansas. From the men among them three regiments were organized, and the women and children were subsisted out of the annuities of the hostiles. In the latter part of 1862, John Ross, head chief of the Cherokees, announced officially that the Cherokee nation had treated with the Confederate States, and, as is well known, there were several regiments of Indians in the regular Confederate service, besides numbers in irregular relations, among whom were Cherokees, Creeks, Choctaws, Chickasaws, Osages, Seminoles, Senecas, Shawnees, Quapaws, Comanches, Wachitas, Kiowas, and Pottamattamies, and none of them regained friendly relations with the United States until the treaty of September 21, 1865. On the south of Colorado the Comanches and Kiowas were at war, with Southern sympathies. The Mescaleros had taken the war-path on the advance of the Texans. To the north it was the same. The Sioux troubles all originated in Minnesota, and concerning them our Consul-general in Canada, Mr. Giddings, wrote at the time: "There is little doubt that the recent outbreak in the Northwest has resulted from the efforts of secession agents operating through Canadian Indians and fur-traders." The war feeling was so strong among the Sioux that the friendly Yanktons, in 1862, refused to receive their annuities unless a force of soldiers was brought, to protect them from the other Sioux, who insisted on their becoming hostile. As the Minnesota Sioux were driven west the feeling spread everywhere, and in the winter of 1863–64 ripened into the coalition "to clean out all this country," while the government had its hands full with the South. With the Indians on all sides of them moved to war by Southern emissaries, the natural supposition is that the Cheyennes and Arapahoes were at war from the same reason, and especially as the Sioux, Comanches, Kiowas, and Apaches were their friends and allies, while the Pawnees, Kaws, and Osages, their hereditary enemies, were in the service of the United States. It was certain that the South had hopes of opening hostility in this region, for, in 1863, nineteen rebel officers were killed by friendly Osages, and on their persons were found papers authorizing them to organize the sympathetic in Colorado and Dakota. White Wolf, a friendly Arapahoe, informed Agent Whitely, in the latter part of August, that the Cheyennes had "declared their intention to take all the forts on the Arkansas when joined by the Texan soldiers," and this indicated that some one had told them a move in that direction was contemplated. Finally, George Bent, half-breed Cheyenne, son of Colonel Bent, had served under Price in Missouri, had been captured, and, after being paroled, had joined the Cheyennes. He had taken part in their depredations, and helped write their letter to Colley, and was reported and believed to be a rebel emissary to them. Chivington spoke of them as "red rebels" in official correspondence, long before the Sand Creek fight, and to men of

GEORGE BENT.

his feelings there was just this one crime of treason that could add anything to the atrocity of Indian warfare.

There are two reasons given for killing women and children, and for mutilation, which are worthy of consideration. First, as a matter of policy, it is believed by frontiersmen that Indians should be fought just as they fight. They look contemptuously on the policy of treating them according to the rules of civilized warfare. They believe that the only way to make Indians sign a treaty which they will keep, is, when at war with them, to kill them at every opportunity, destroy their property, and make their homes desolate; in short, to make them suffer. The plains Indians have given more cause for this belief than other tribes. They have repeatedly shown a disposition to go to war in the spring, when their ponies were getting fat, and subsistence was easily had, but as winter came on, and hardship began, they were ready to treat. They have had cause, too, to laugh at the silly whites, who bought their friendship with presents, while the blood of slaughtered innocents was hardly dried. They took advantage of the white man by killing his helpless people, while, for the safety of their own, they relied on the white man's ideas of warfare. Their women took advantage of him by fighting, as they did at Sand Creek, Ash Hollow, and many other places, along with the men, and, when the battle went against them, proclaiming their sex and claiming immunity. There is not a bit of doubt that killing women and children has a very dampening effect on the ardor of the Indian. In this very case of Sand Creek they said "they had always heard that the whites did not kill women and children, but now they had lost all confidence in them." Their "loss of confidence" grows a trifle amusing, when it is remembered that they had been killing women and children all summer themselves. Scalping and mutilation also strike terror to the Indian heart. Their religious belief is that the spirit in the next world has the same injuries that are inflicted on the body here. For this reason they almost invariably mutilate corpses, besides taking the scalp, which is almost an essential for entrance to the happy hunting-grounds. The greatest acts of daring ever shown by plains Indians have been in carrying off the bodies of their dead to prevent these misfortunes. That the Sand Creek affair inspired them with terror is beyond question. The Cheyennes and Arapahoes got over into Kansas and Indian Territory as quickly as possible, and stayed there. A party of Sioux raided down into Colorado once afterwards, but when they heard that the Colorado troops were after them they scampered off as though the evil spirit were at their heels.

Secondly, is the matter of vengeance. There is a certain amount of justice in the theory of meting to a man in his own measure, and the people of Colorado had old scores to pay in the accounts of murder, robbery, and rape. The treatment of women, by any Indians, is usually bad, but by the plains Indians especially so. When a woman is captured by a war-party she is the common property of all of them, each night, till they reach their village, when she becomes the special property of her individual captor, who may sell or gamble her away when he likes. If she resists she is "staked out," that is to say, four pegs are driven into the ground and a hand or foot tied to each, to prevent struggling. She is also beaten, mutilated, or even killed, for resistance. If a woman gives out under this treatment, she is either tied so as to prevent escape, or maimed so as to insure death in case of rescue, and left to die slowly. That there may be no question of the guilt of these Sand Creek Cheyennes, I quote the statement of Mrs. Ewbanks, who was captured at the same time as the prisoners surrendered by them, as taken down by Lieutenant Triggs, of the 7th Iowa Cavalry, and Judge-advocate Zabriskie, of the 1st Nevada Cavalry. "Mrs. Lucinda Ewbanks states that she was born in Pennsylvania; is twenty-four years of age; she resided on the Little Blue, at or near the Narrows. She says that on the 8th day of August, 1864, the house was attacked, robbed, burned, and herself and two children, with her nephew and Miss Roper, were captured by Cheyenne Indians. Her eldest child, at the time, was three years old; her youngest was one year old; her nephew was six years old. When taken from her home was, by the Indians, taken south across the Republican, and west to a creek, the name of which she does not remember. Here, for a short

ON THE LITTLE BLUE.

time, was their village or camping-place. They were travelling all winter. When first taken by the Cheyennes she was taken to the lodge of an old chief, whose name she does not remember. He forced me, by the most terrible threats and menaces, to yield my person to him. He treated me as his wife. He then traded me to Two Face, a Sioux, who did not treat me as a wife, but forced me to do all menial labor done by squaws, and he beat me terribly. Two Face traded me to Black Foot (a Sioux) who treated me as his wife, and because I resisted him his squaws abused and ill-used me. Black Foot also beat me unmercifully, and the Indians generally treated me as though I was a dog, on account of my showing so much detestation towards Black Foot. Two Face traded for me again. I then received a little better treatment. I was better treated among the Sioux than the Cheyennes; that is, the Sioux gave me more to eat. When with the Cheyennes I was often hungry. Her purchase from the Cheyennes was made early last fall (1864), and she remained with them (the Sioux) until May, 1865. During the winter the Cheyennes came to buy me and the child, for the purpose of burning us, but Two Face would not let them have me. During the winter we were on the North Platte the Indians were killing the whites all the time and running off their stock. They would bring in the scalps of the whites and show them to me and laugh about it. They ordered me frequently to wean my baby, but I always refused; for I felt convinced if he was weaned they would take him from me, and I should never see him again."

Mrs. Ewbanks's daughter died in Denver, from injuries received among the Indians, before her mother was released. Her nephew also died from his injuries, at the same place. Miss Roper, who was surrendered with the children, had experienced the same treatment that no white woman was ever known to escape at the hands of the plains Indians. Mrs. Martin, another prisoner surrendered by them, was taken by the Cheyennes on Plum Creek, "west of Kearney," as testified by herself and admitted by White Antelope in the council. Mrs. Snyder, another captive, had grown weary of the friendship of these Cheyennes, and hung herself before Major Wynkoop arrived. These things were known to the people of Colorado, and two thirds of the troops who went there were citizen-soldiers, raised for the express purpose of fighting Indians. Be it known, also, that these offenses were committed without any provocation from settlers, beyond occupying the lands which the chiefs of the Cheyennes had relinquished in treaty. There is absolutely not on record, from any source, a single charge, let alone an instance, of aggression or injury to any Cheyenne or Arapahoe, by any settler of Colorado, prior to Sand Creek. The sole troubles had been with the soldiers in chastising the Indians for past offences. The people of Colorado did want revenge, and these men, who had been cooped up all summer in towns and blockhouses, whose crops were ruined, whose stock had been run off, whose houses had been burned, who had been eating bread made of forty-five- dollar flour, who had buried the mutilated bodies of their neighbors, in helpless wrath, who had heard the stories of the women captives-these men marched to Sand Creek, with the fire of vengeance in their hearts, and quenched it in blood.

Let us now look for a moment at the report of the Joint Committee on the Conduct of the War. It states, first, that these Indians wished "to deliver up some white captives they had purchased of other Indians." The Indians did not pretend to have purchased them. They admitted in the council that they had captured them, and the captives themselves testified to the same, as shown above. It states that after the council these Indians went to Fort Lyon, where they "were treated somewhat as prisoners of war, receiving rations and being obliged to remain within certain bounds." As has been shown, the Cheyennes were never treated as prisoners of war, received no rations, and did not remain within any bounds. The Indians who did so were Little Raven's Arapahoes, who were hostile, by the declarations of the Arapahoe chiefs in the council, and the testimony of Major Wynkoop. These Indians went away before the Cheyennes came, but eight lodges of them, under Left Hand, who was friendly, went to the Cheyennes and camped with them at Sand Creek. This wrongful and unjust confusion is kept up all through the report. It states that "all the testimony goes to show that the Indians under the immediate control of Black Kettle and White Antelope, of the Cheyennes, and Left Hand, of the Arapahoes, were and had been friendly to the whites, and had not been guilty of any acts of hostility or depredation." Not only does the testimony show the opposite to be true, but also there is no testimony whatever to that effect. There was testimony to the friendly character of these chiefs, but not to that of their Indians, and, in fact, no Indians could be separated out as theirs, for at the time of their letter, and the council, and afterwards, the Cheyennes were all together, and all under their "immediate control." Even when the party at Sand Creek came in ahead, it was reported by them that the remainder of the tribe was a short distance back, waiting for good weather.

It states that "a northern band of the Cheyennes, known

as the Dog Soldiers, had been guilty of acts of hostility; but all the testimony goes to prove that they had no connection with Black Kettle's band," and that "Black Kettle and his band denied all connection with or responsibility for the Dog Soldiers." As shown in a former chapter, the Dog Soldiers were not a separate band, but were a department in the tribal government. Black Kettle and his band did not deny connection with them or responsibility for them; many of the band at Sand Creek were Dog Soldiers. Bull Bear, the leader of the Dog Soldiers, was at the council in Denver as one of Black Kettle's sub-chiefs. The only time that any of the Indians had an opportunity to make a statement which could go to the committee, was at the council in Denver, and there the Dog Soldiers were mentioned but once, and in this passage: "BLACK KETTLE. 'We will return with Major Wynkoop to Fort Lyon; we will then proceed to our village and take back word to my young men, every word you say. I cannot answer for all of them, but think there will be but little difficulty in getting them to assent to help the soldiers.' MAJOR WYNKOOP. 'Did not the Dog Soldiers agree, when I had my council with you, to do whatever you said, after you had been here?' BLACK KETTLE. 'Yes.'" The committee is far more kind to Black Kettle than he is to himself. It had determined that he should not be connected with them. Senator Doolittle pressed this question on John S. Smith, one of the most bitter of the prosecuting witnesses: "Is the northern band the same that are commonly called the Dog Soldiers?" Smith, who had been among them twenty-seven years, answered: "No, sir; the Dog Soldiers are mixed up promiscuously; this is a band that has preferred the North Platte and north of the North Platte, and lives over in what is called the bad land, *mauvais terre.*" The same fact was shown by Major Wynkoop in his cross-examination, by Chivington, before the Military Commission, as follows: "Q. Will you explain what the Dog Soldiers are and how they are controlled? A. I understand that the Dog Soldiers are a portion of the warriors of the Cheyenne tribe, and presume that they are controlled by the head men."

It states that " these Indians, at the suggestion of Governor

Evans and Colonel Chivington, repaired to Fort Lyon and placed themselves under the protection of Major Wynkoop." Enough of the council proceedings has been quoted to show the falsity of this. They told the Indians that they could not treat with them, but that they must go to the military, and when they got ready to lay down their arms and surrender as prisoners of war they might go to Major Wynkoop. But, in fact, the Cheyennes did not even send in their messengers until after Major Wynkoop was suspended. They

INDIANS ATTACKING STAGE.

were never under his protection at all. It states that Jack Smith, the half-breed son of John S. Smith, was in Black Kettle's camp, at the time of the attack, as a spy, employed by the government. As shown above, he guided the troops to the camp to make the attack. This man was the only prisoner killed after the fight, and it was in evidence before the committee that he had led an attack on a stage a short time previously. That he was present he did not deny, but said he approached the stage for some information, and, on being fired on, fired back in self-defence. But it is not necessary to particularize further. The report abuses every one who, in telling the truth, happened to differ from the preconceived judgment of the committee; it distorts and colors every matter of fact involved so as to injure Chivington and his men; it omits or glosses over all the injuries to the people of Colorado; and, having arrived at a proper pitch of indignation and misrepresentation, it assails Colonel Chivington in a gush of sanguinary rhetoric, that reads more like the reputed address of Spartacus, to the gladiators than the impartial judgment of rational men.

But, outrageous as was the report of the committee, it was dignified, just, and proper by the side of the ornamental misrepresentation that outsiders have added. It has been said that Sand Creek "brought on the general war of 1865, which cost the government $35,000,000 and much loss of life," and this statement has become a part of the "history" of the affair. Sand Creek brought on that war just about as much as the battle of Gettysburg brought on the late civil war. It was an event in the war, and no amount of. misrepresentation can make it anything else. Leaving the Cheyennes out of consideration altogether, the general war had been in progress since the early spring of 1864. But, as a matter of fact, it did not even aggravate the war. It has already been shown that the Cheyennes had been at war all summer, and no other tribe went to war on account of it. On January 12, 1865, on receipt of orders to investigate Chivington's action, General Curtis despatched to Washington: "Although the colonel may have transgressed my field orders concerning Indian warfare, and otherwise acted very much against my views of propriety in his assault at Sand Creek, still it is not true, as Indian agents and Indian traders are representing, that such extra severity is increasing Indian war. On the contrary, it tends to reduce their numbers and bring them to terms. . . . I will be glad to save the few honest and kindly disposed, and, protest against the slaughter of women and children; although, since General Harney's attack of the Sioux many years ago at Ash Hollow, the popular cry of settlers and soldiers on the frontier favors an indiscriminate slaughter which is very difficult to restrain. I abhor this style, but so it goes, from Minnesota to Texas. . . . There is no doubt a portion of this tribe assembled were occupied in making assaults on our stages and trains, and the tribes well know that we have to hold the whole community responsible for acts they could restrain, if they would properly exert their efforts in that way." Again, on January 30, he wrote to Governor Evans: "Let me say, too, that I see nothing new in all this Indian movement since the Chivington affair, except that Indians are more frightened and keep farther away. By pushing them hard this next month, before grass recruits their ponies, they will be better satisfied with making war and robbery a business." On the same day he wrote Major-general Halleek: "There is no new feature in these Indian troubles except that Indians seem more frightened." General Curtis commanded the department; he had all the information as to the state of the hostilities that could be had; he evidently was not inclined to defend Chivington; and therefore his testimony on this point ought to be conclusive.

Said Hon. Mr. Loughridge to the House of Representatives: "Some of the few captured children, after they had been carried many miles by the troops, were taken from the wagons and their brains dashed out. I gather this from the records and official reports, and blush to say that its truth cannot be questioned." Mr. Loughridge might well blush for other reasons. There is not one word in all the testimony, records, and official reports, to substantiate this statement. The nearest and only approach to it, in the report of the Joint Committee, is this statement by Lieutenant Cannon, who accompanied the expedition: "I heard of one instance of a child, a few months old, being thrown into the feed-box of a wagon, and, after being carried some distance, left on the ground to perish." In the testimony taken by the Military Commission, Lieutenant Cramer and Private Louderback give similar hearsay evidence, in almost the same words. Only one witness was examined, at any time, who professed to have personal knowledge of this abandonment, and that was Sergeant Lucian Palmer, who was introduced by the prosecution, before the Military Commission. He said: "They [the two squaws] took care of it [the pappoose in question] the first

INDIAN SCOUTS CELEBRATING.

day after we left Sand Creek; they had it in bed with them the night we stopped this side of Sand Creek; they left it themselves, as no one else had anything to do with it, to my knowledge." Thus the prosecution disposed of the feed-box story, and left Mr. Loughridge without even that faint support for his slander. It was distinctly testified, by every witness who was questioned on the subject, that no one was killed after the fight except Jack Smith. It was also established, without contradiction, that the two squaws (wives of white men) and five children, who were said, by every witness except those mentioned, to have been the only prisoners taken, were conveyed to Fort Lyon and left there. These are but samples that show the extraordinary extent to which this delusion has been carried. The wealth of epithets and invectives that has been gathered to damn the reputation of this man Chivington, by people who have, at best, but superficially examined his case, constitutes a veritable treasury of vituperation. If everything that was said against him by the witnesses were true, and much of it, on its face, was not, he is still the colossal martyr to misrepresentation of this century.

The sequel to Sand Creek throws some valuable light on the character of the case. On October 14, 1865, a treaty was made with the Cheyenne chiefs on the Little Arkansas, on which occasion John S. Smith and Major Wynkoop were figuring prominently. The treaty, in its original draft, went out of the way to attack Chivington and the troops, and this feature the Senate omitted by amendment. The treaty was made on behalf of the entire tribe, but the majority of the Dog Soldiers were not present and never formally accepted its provisions. The most striking feature of it is that, while they were assigned a reservation with the privilege of roaming over their original territory, these friendly Indians were prohibited from camping within ten miles of a main travelled road, night or day, and were pledged not to go to any town or post without permission of the authorities there. Special remuneration was given to every one who had lost relatives or property at Sand Creek, and annuities of goods and money to the tribe in general, to the amount of $56,000 annually until they moved to the reservation, and $112,000 annually afterwards. Thefts, murders, and other offences were perpetrated by Indians in the following summer, and, so far as could be learned, they were committed by a party of Dog Soldiers, numbering some two hundred lodges, who had joined with about one hundred lodges of Sioux, under the chief Pawnee Killer. In the spring of 1867 General Hancock started with an expedition into the plains with the intent of making a peaceful demonstration of power, which would induce all doubtful and hostile Indians to go on reservations. Agents of the Indian bureau were invited to accompany the expedition, to assist in talks with the Indians, and did so.

They found the band of Dog Soldiers and Sioux on Pawnee Fork, about thirty miles above Fort Larned. After negotiating, and making several appointments for councils, which they did not keep, the Indians slipped away one dark night with all their property that they could carry. Spring was not their season for treating. The next heard of them was that they had burned several stage stations on the Smoky Hill route and killed, after torturing, three station keepers at Lookout Station, near Fort Hays. On receipt of information of this, General Hancock destroyed what was left of their village, and troops were kept in search of the Indians all summer, under command of General Custer. There were a number of engagements between them, and considerable loss of life, with no material advantage to either side. At the same time a severe pen-and-ink contest was being waged between war people and peace people in the East, and the peace people got the upper hand. The result of it all was that at the end of the season Custer was under arrest on a charge of leaving Fort Wallace without orders, while the Indians, who had had no opportunity to lay in supplies for the winter, made another treaty, in which the whole tribe, Dog Soldiers included, joined. This time they took a reservation wholly within Indian Territory, a triangular tract bounded by the Kansas line and the Cimarron and Arkansas rivers. They were to receive a suit of clothes for each Indian, and $20,000 annually, besides teachers, physicians, farmers, millers, carpenters, blacksmiths, and other guides to civilization. It was not agreed that they were to be given any arms or ammunition, and this the reader will remember. They agreed not to molest any coach or wagon, carry off any white woman or child, nor kill or scalp any white man; to surrender any wrongdoer for punishment, and not to interfere in any way with the building of the Kansas Pacific Railroad.

In the spring of 1868 it was learned that arms and ammunition were being issued to Indians, and a military order was made prohibiting it. The agents raised a cry that the Indians could not hunt the buffalo without arms and ammunition (they prefer the bow and arrow for this, and seldom used anything else); the peace people joined in the chorus that the Indians were being starved, and the order was revoked. On August 1 the Arapahoes received 100 pistols, 80 Lancaster rifles, 12 kegs of power, a keg and a half of lead, and 15,000 caps. On August 10 Colonel Wynkoop, our old acquaintance, who had been promoted, and appointed Indian Agent after the investigations, wrote: "I yesterday made the whole issue of annuity goods, arms, and ammunition to the Cheyenne chiefs and people of their nation; they were delighted at receiving the goods, particularly the arms and ammunition, and never before have I known them to be better satisfied, and express themselves as being so well contented previous to the issue. . . . They have now left for their hunting-grounds, and I am perfectly satisfied that there will be no trouble with them this season." What hunting-grounds had they left for? On September 10, just thirty days later, Colonel Wynkoop, in explaining that the Indians had gone to war because "their arms and ammunition" had not been issued promptly, writes: "But a short time before the issue was made a war-party had started north from the Cheyenne village, on the war-path against the Pawnees; and they, not knowing of the issue, and smarting under their supposed wrongs, committed the outrages on the Saline River which have led to the present unfortunate aspect of affairs." It was rather unfortunate. The inference from his letter is that it was all right for them to use their weapons, furnished for the purpose of hunting, in making war on the Pawnees, who had been, for several years, our most valuable allies and friends on the plains; but that they should attack the whites was unfortunate. Two hundred Cheyenne, four Arapahoe, and twenty Sioux warriors raided down the Saline and the Solomon, killing, ravishing, burning, and torturing. They carried off two young women, who were afterwards recovered from Black Kettle's band, if he can be said to have had any particular band, by threatening to hang some of their principal chiefs, who were captives. Much of the plundered property was found in Black Kettle's camp.

Wynkoop then proposed. to locate the friendly Indians near Fort Larned, in order to separate the good ones from the bad ones, Larned being about as near to the seat of war as they could be placed; but General Sherman would have nothing of that kind. He said the Indians who were peaceable should stay on their reservation, where they belonged. Never was a better opportunity for friendly Indians to separate themselves from the bad ones and let themselves be known: and they did it. After some hard fighting in the summer and fall, notably the eight days' fight between General Forsyth's party and four hundred and fifty Cheyennes, aided by Sioux and Arapahoes, on the Arickaree fork of the Republican, the bad Indians went into winter quarters, and a winter expedition was sent against them under Custer, who was reinstated for the occasion. The reservation was vacant. The good Cheyennes were not visible. The entire southern tribe was camped away south on the Wachita, on lands where they had not even the right to hunt, with the hostile Kiowas, Arapahoes, Comanches, and Apaches, forming an almost continuous camp for twelve miles. Custer followed the trail of a returning war-party into Black Kettle's camp, and, in the early dawn of November 27, surprised the Indians, while they were sleeping off the effects of the previous night's celebration over fresh scalps and plunder. Here, as at Sand Creek and Ash Hollow, women fought with the men, and a number of them were killed, but their fighting did no good. 103 Indians were killed, and 53 squaws and children were captured, together with 875 ponies, 1123 robes, 535 pounds of powder, 4000 arrows, and arms and goods

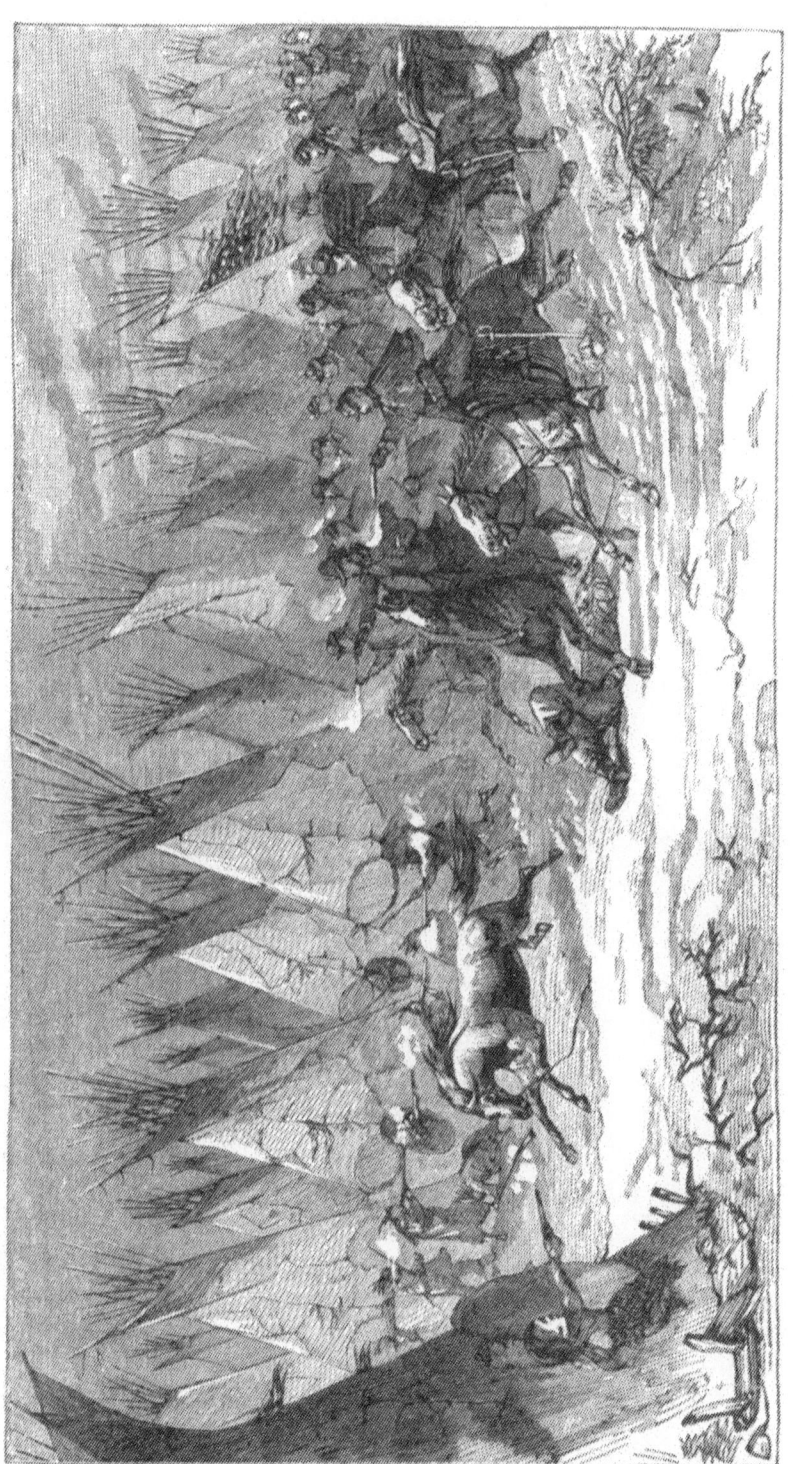

THE CHARGE ON BLACK KETTLE'S CAMP.

of all descriptions, constituting all their possessions. What could be advantageously kept was retained, and the remainder, including 700 ponies, was destroyed. The entire Indian force attacked Custer, but he succeeded in getting his troops and captives safely away. And what did the irrepressible Wynkoop after this affair? He affirmed that the Cheyennes were martyrs ever, and that on this occasion they were peaceably on their way to Fort Cobb to receive their annuities when attacked! He also resigned his position as Indian Agent, feeling, probably, that it would be forced on him again. But Hancock and Custer were bigger game than poor Chivington. Their brother officers and officials examined their cases more carefully than they did that of the volunteer colonel, and Custer himself ventilated the matter in a series of articles in the *Galaxy* that made some people open their eyes.

After the war, Chivington returned to his old home in Ohio and settled on a small farm. A few years later his house was burned, and he afterwards moved to Blanchester, Clinton County; where he purchased the Press, and edited it for two or three years. In 1883 he was nominated on the Republican ticket for Representative to the legislature, and in the campaign "Sand Creek" was used for all it was worth. It began in the contest for the nomination and was continued until Chivington withdrew from the race. It was believed, and still is, by. good judges of politics, that he would have been elected by a majority of five hundred or more, but there was a large Quaker population in Clinton, and, as is well known, the Society of Friends considers itself the special guardian of the Indian. He had an up-hill fight on his hands, and the opposition was very bitter. I can but think another thing influenced his determination. While this fight was being pressed upon him, he received an urgent letter from Colorado, asking him to attend and address a meeting of old settlers, on the twenty-fifth anniversary of the settlement of the state. There he would find old friends, who knew the true history of Sand Creek, and felt as he did. He went. There were hearty welcomes given to distinguished pioneers by the people assembled in Jewell Park on that day, but none so demonstrative as Colonel Chivington's. The chairman introduced him with these words: "We all remember the Indian wars of 1864 and '65, and with what joy we received the news that some of them at least had met the reward due to their treachery and cruelty. The man who can tell you all about those wars, who can tell you all you want to know of the Indians, and who can give you the true story of Sand Creek, is here. I have the honor, ladies and gentlemen, to introduce Colonel Chivington, one of Colorado's 'Pet Lambs.'"

He began his speech amid enthusiastic cheers, but as he proceeded the attention grew breathless. He told his story in a simple, straightforward way, and nods of assent and approval, from all parts of the pavilion, silently indicated that he need not prove the truth of his statements to the people gathered there. He did not reply to the thousand charges made against him, nor did he assume an argumentative style until he closed in these words: "But were not these Indians peaceable? Oh, yes, peaceable! Well, a few hundred of them have been peaceable for almost nineteen years, and none of them have been so troublesome as they were before Sand Creek. What are the facts? How about that treaty that Governor John Evans did not make with them in the summer of 1863? He, with Major Lorey and Major Whiteley, two of his Indian Agents, and the usual corps of attachés, under escort, went out to the Kiowa to treat. When he got there, they had gone a day's march farther out on the plains and would not meet him there, and so on, day after day, they moved out as he approached, until, wearied out, and suspicious of treachery, he returned without succeeding in his mission of peace. He told them by message that he had presents for them, but it was not peace and presents they wanted, but war and plunder. What of the peaceableness of their attack on General Blunt's advance-guard, north of Fort Larned, almost annihilating the advance before succor could reach them? What of the dove-like peace of their attack on the government train on Walnut Creek, east of Fort Larned, under the guise of friendship, till the drivers and attachés of the train were in their power, and at a signal struck down at once every man, only a boy of thirteen years barely escaping, and he, with the loss of his scalp, taken to his ears, finally died. What of the trains captured from Walnut Creek to Sand Creek on the Arkansas route, and from the Little Blue to the Kiowa on the Platte route, of supplies and wagons burned and carried off, and of the men killed? What of the Hungate family? Alas! what of the stock of articles of merchandise, fine silk dresses, infants' and youths' apparel, the embroidered night-gowns and chemises? Ay, what of the scalps of white men, women, and children, several of which they had not had time to dry and tan since taken? These, all these, and more, were taken from the belts of dead warriors on the battle-field of Sand Creek, and from their teepees which fell into our hands on the 29th day of November, 1864. What of the Indian blanket that was captured, fringed with white-women's scalps? What says the dust of the two hundred and eight men, women, and children, ranchers, emigrants, herders, and soldiers, who lost their lives at the hands of these Indians? Peaceable? Now we are peaceably disposed, but decline giving such testimonials of our peaceful proclivities, and I say here as I said in my own town, in the Quaker county of Clinton, State of Ohio, one night last week, I stand by Sand Creek."

Said the *Rocky Mountain News,* of the following day, "Colonel Chivington's speech was received with an applause from every pioneer which indicated that they, to a man, heartily approved the course of the colonel twenty years ago, in the famous affair in which many of them took part, and the man who applied the scalpel to the ulcer which bid fair to destroy the life of the new colony, in those critical times, was beyond a doubt the hero of the hour." This is the simple truth. Colorado stands by Sand Creek, and Colonel Chivington soon afterwards brought his family to the Queen City of the Plains, where his remaining days may be passed in peace.

What an eventful history! And how, through it all, his sturdy manhood has been manifest in every action. Through all the denunciation of that Indian fight, he has never wavered or trembled. Others have dodged and apologized and crawled, but Chivington never. He has not laid the blame upon superior officers, as he might do. He has not complained of misinformation from inferior officers, as he might do. He has not said that the soldiers committed excesses there which were in no manner directed by him, as he might do. He has simply stood up under a rain of abuse, heavier than the shower of missiles that fell on Cœur de Leon before the castle of Front de Bœuf, and answered back: "I stand by Sand Creek." And was it wrong? To the abstract question, whether or not it is right to kill women and children, there can be but one answer. But as a matter of retaliation, and a matter of policy, whether these people were justified in killing women and children at Sand Creek is a question to which the answer does not come so glibly. Just after the massacre at Fort Fetterman, General Sherman despatched to General Grant: "We must act with vindictive earnestness against the Sioux, even to their extermination, men, women, and children. Nothing less will reach the root of the case." Was it right for the English to shoot back the Sepoy ambassador from their cannon? Was it right for the North to refuse to exchange prisoners while our boys were dying by inches in Libby and Andersonville? I do not undertake to answer these questions, but I do say that Sand Creek is far from being "the climax of American outrages on the Indian," as it has been called. Lay not that flattering unction to your souls, people of the East, while the names of the Pequods and the Conestoga Indians exist in your books; nor you of the Mississippi Valley, while the blood of Logan's family and the Moravian Indians of the Muskingum stain your records; nor you of the South, while a Cherokee or a Seminole remains to tell the wrongs of his fathers; nor yet you of the Pacific slope, while the murdered family of Spencer or the victims of Bloody Point and Nome Cult have a place in the memory of men-your ancestors and predecessors were guilty of worse things than the Sand Creek massacre.

CHAPTER XIV.

CAÑON DE CHELLY AND BOSQUE REDONDO.

WE left the Navahos in their chronic state of war, that is to say, the state of robbing their neighbors and being robbed by them while the troops were absent, and of making peace when the troops marched against them. From the mass of conflicting testimony taken in 1865, in regard to the Indian history of New Mexico, and from other sources, it appears that one side made aggressions about as often as the other, the common opinion being that the Navahos captured the greater number of sheep, and the Mexicans the greater number of slaves. The Navahos were preferred to other Indians for slaves on account of their tractable nature, intelligence, light skins, and the voluptuousness of the females. Dr. Louis Kennon, whose opportunities for observation had been good, testified, "I think the number of Navajo captives held as slaves to be underestimated. I think there are from five to six thousand. I know of no family which can raise one hundred and fifty dollars but what purchases a Navajo slave, and many families own four or five-the trade in them being as regular as the trade in pigs or sheep. Previous to the war their price was from seventy-five to a hundred dollars, but now they are worth about four hundred dollars. But the other day some Mexican Indians from Chihuahua were for sale in Santa Fé. I have been conversant with the institution of slavery in Georgia, but the system is worse here, there being no obligation resting on the owner to care for the slave when he becomes old or worthless." Of course the Mexicans grumbled continually about the awful incursions of the savages, but there was little disposition on the part of the military to use any great violence against the Navaho nation. They understood the situation, having had the best of opportunities for hearing the Navaho side of the question; many of the officers had Navaho mistresses.

Occasionally there would be a rupture between the Indians and the soldiers, the most noted of these being the fight at Fort Fauntleroy, in September, 1861. This trouble arose over a horse-race, on which there had been very heavy betting. The soldiers backed a horse ridden by Lieutenant Ortiz, one of the post officers, and the Indians the other. The Indians' horse ran off the track after running about one hundred yards, the result, it was said, of a broken bridle, and they claimed a draw. The commanding officer, on the refusal of the winners to draw the race, gave orders that the Navahos should not be allowed to enter the post. The winners filed into the post, whooping and hallooing, with fifes screeching and drums beating, and as they did so a shot was fired, and an Indian killed. Who fired the shot is not certainly known, but it was said to be a sentinel, past whom the Indian was trying to make his way. The soldiers armed themselves, and attacked the Indians in a confused way, without any orders. Says Captain Hodt, of the 1st New Mexican Cavalry: "The Navahos, squaws, and children ran in all directions, and were shot and bayoneted. I tried my best to form the company I was first sergeant of, and succeeded in forming about twenty men—it being very hard work. I then marched out to the east side of the post; there I saw a soldier murdering two little children and a woman. I hallooed to the soldier to stop. He looked up, but did not obey my order. I ran up as quick as I could, but could not get there soon enough to prevent him from killing the two innocent children and wounding severely the squaw. I ordered his belts to be taken off and him taken prisoner to the post. On my arrival in the post I met Lieutenant Ortiz with a pistol at full cock, saying, 'Give back this soldier his arms, or else I'll shoot you, G—d d—n you,' which circumstances I reported to my company commander, he reporting the same to the colonel commanding, and the answer he received from the colonel was 'That Lieutenant Ortiz did perfectly right, and that he gave credit to the soldier who murdered the children and wounded the squaw.' Meantime the colonel had given orders to the offi-

GIANT'S ARM-CHAIR

cer of the day to have the artillery (mountain howitzers) brought out and to open upon the Indians. The sergeant in charge of the mountain howitzers pretended not to understand the order given, for he considered it as an unlawful order; but being cursed by the officer of the day, and threatened, he had to execute the order or else get himself in trouble. The Indians scattered all over the valley below the post, attacked the post herd, wounded the Mexican herder, but did not succeed in getting any stock; also attacked the expressman, some ten miles from the post, took his horse and mail-bag, and wounded him in the arm. After the massacre there were no more Indians to be seen about the post, with the exception of a few squaws, favorites of the officers. The commanding officer endeavored to make peace again with the Navahos by sending some of the favorite squaws to talk with the chiefs; but the only satisfaction the squaws received was a good flogging. An expressman was sent shortly after the affairs above mentioned happened, but private letters were not allowed to be sent, and letters that reached the post-office at Fauntleroy were found opened, but not forwarded. To the best of my knowledge the number of Navahos killed was twelve or fifteen; the number wounded could not be ascertained."

In the winter of 1860–61, Colonel E. R. S. Canby (soon afterwards General Canby) proceeded against the Navahos and inflicted severe punishment upon them until February, 1861, when an armistice of three months was agreed upon, and later this was extended to one year. In September Governor Connelly, Colonel Canby, and Superintendent Collins had a long talk with thirty of their leading men, in which the usual assurances of their peaceful intentions were given, but the peace was not lasting. They were not, in fact, in a condition that encouraged peace. Owing to constant hostilities, they had planted but little for three years, and much of what they had planted had been destroyed by the troops, as also many of their herds; they were obliged to steal or starve, and adopted the former alternative. In 1862 their agent reported that they had "driven off over one hundred thousand sheep, and not less than a thousand head of cattle, besides horses and mules to a large amount." In these depredations he said they had "murdered many persons, and carried off many women and children as captives." In consequence of this plundering, Governor Connelly made a call for militia in September, and some independent expeditions were also organized, but the latter were stopped by the authorities for the reason that these irresponsible companies invariably attacked friendly Indians and hostile ones indiscriminately. General Carleton assumed command of the district at this time, and took charge of all military operations. His forces were chiefly occupied with the Mescalero Apaches during the winter, but in the spring of 1863 he was ready for the Navahos.

General Carleton's plan was to remove all who would consent to the Bosque Redondo, on the Pecos River, in Eastern New Mexico, and to place the others with them as fast as they were captured. This plan had the merit of sparing the innocent the horrors of war, at least. That General Carleton was actuated by motives of humanity in adopting it can scarcely be questioned. He said: "They have no government to make treaties; they are a patriarchal people. One set of families may make promises, but the other set will not heed them. They understand the direct application of force as a law; if its application be removed, that moment they become lawless. This has been tried over and over again, and at great expense. The purpose now is, never to relax the application of force with a people that can no more be trusted than the wolves that run through the mountains. To collect them together, little by little, on to a reservation, away from the haunts and hills and hiding-places of their country; there be kind to them; there teach their children how to read and write; teach them the arts of peace; teach them the truths of Christianity." If there were any fault in this plan it was only in their removal from their native country, but for the purpose of separating the peaceful from the hostile during the war this could not very well be avoided. The Navahos were given ample warning of General Carleton's intentions. He notified part of the chiefs himself, and sent messengers among them to inform them that they might have until the 20th day of July, 1863, to come in, but that "after that day every Navaho that is seen will be considered as hostile, and treated accordingly."

Quite a number of Navahos accepted the proffered terms, and against the others the troops were kept operating from Forts Stanton, Craig, Canby, Defiance, and the post at Los Pinos; and the troops at all other posts were ordered to be constantly on the lookout for prowling bands of Navahos, which were liable to appear in any part of the country. They went everywhere in their expeditions. One band of a hundred and thirty warriors even penetrated the Mescalero country, southeast of the Rio Grande settlements, and, passing north, drove off cattle and sheep from the Basque Redondo; they were followed by a few troops and some Mescaleros, and the property was retaken, with other plundered goods. The orders to the soldiers, everywhere, were to kill every male Navaho capable of bearing arms, whenever and wherever he might be found; women and children were to be captured and held as prisoners. These orders were often repeated, and the officers were urged to the utmost activity by praise to the successful, and reproaches to the unsuccessful. The following, issued to Colonel Rigg, commanding at Fort Craig, on August 4, 1863, is a sample of the instructions: "I have been informed that there is a spring called *Ojo de Cibolo,* about fifteen miles west of Limitar, where the Navahos drive their stolen cattle and 'jerk' the flesh at their leisure. Cannot you make arrangements for a party of resolute men from your command to be stationed there for, say, thirty days, and kill every Navaho and Apache they can find? A cautious, wary commander, hiding his men and moving about at night, might kill off a good many Indians near that point." Such orders seem harsh, and yet they afforded the only means of bringing the Navahos to terms. The great difficulty was to get any opportunity to fight them. They were separated in small bands, under their patriarchal system, and, being constantly on the move through a country with which they were thoroughly acquainted, they were usually able to avoid the soldiers, for whom they kept a vigilant watch. After a few weeks of slight success, the soldiers were further stimulated to activity by a bounty of twenty dollars for each good horse turned over to the quartermaster's

CAÑON DE CHELLY.

department, and one dollar for each sheep. The principal offensive force was that operating from Fort Canby, under Colonel Kit Carson, but, notwithstanding the ability and activity of that noted Indian fighter, the results obtained during the summer and fall of 1863 were not important, and Carleton consoled the colonel with the hope: "As winter approaches you will have better luck." Still, as winter approached, success did not increase very materially, and the Navahos were still able to keep out of the way of the troops. It was therefore decided to strike them in the Cañon de Chelly, which was reputed to be their greatest stronghold, and Colonel Carson was ordered to prepare for this movement, which was to be made in January.

The Cañon de Chelly is one of the most remarkable works of nature in the United States. The Rio Chelly may be found, not very accurately traced, on any fair-sized map of Arizona, in the northeastern corner of that territory. Its headwaters are in the Sierra Tunicha, of Northwestern New Mexico, and it flows thence almost due west, for some thirty miles, then swings abruptly to the north, and empties into the Rio San Juan near the northern line of Arizona. The line of its western flow indicates the position of the cañon, which extends throughout that distance, the northward bend of the river being just beyond its mouth. The main cañon is counted as beginning at the union of three small streams, each of which has a cañon of its own. They are the Cienega Negra (Black Meadow), or Estrella (Star), on the southeast, the Palo Negro (Black Timber), or Chelly Creek, on the east, and the Cienega Juanica, or Juanita, on the northwest. The most easterly entrance used by the Indians is near the head of Chelly Creek; by it, the bottom of that stream is reached above the junction of the others. It is not accessible for animals. The Cienega Negra enters about three miles below the head of the Chelly proper, and the Juanica half a mile lower. At places above the entrance of the last-named stream the chasm is so narrow that one might almost leap across it, but the beholder involuntarily recoils from the dizzy view of over one thousand feet of unbroken descent to the yellow floor beneath. About half a mile below the Juanica there is another descent, where the wall of the cañon, there only seven hundred feet high, is broken and sufficiently sloping to permit a zigzag descent to pack-animals. Below this point the walls increase in height to fifteen hundred feet, and the width of the cañon from two hundred to three hundred and fifty yards. The next approach is by a side cañon that enters on the south side, about eleven miles below the Juanica; it is commonly known as Bat Cañon, but the Indians and Mexicans call it Cañon Alsada, or Cañon of the High Rock, from a natural obelisk, one thousand feet high, with a base of one hundred and fifty feet, that rises majestically at the mouth of the cañon, a hundred feet distant from the wall. This needle leans so much that it seems about to topple over. The Alsada entrance is the one commonly used in approaching from Fort Defiance, and the trail is cut deep in the sandstone by thousands of feet of men and animals that in past generations have followed it. The descent here is along ledges on the cañon wall, so narrow that animals are always driven ahead, for fear they may slip and carry the owner over. Occasionally, below this point, there are lateral openings in the cañon walls, but none of them extend more than a few hundred yards back, and there is no other entrance until about three miles above the mouth, where the Cañon del Trigo (Wheat Cañon) enters from the north. Below the Trigo the walls sink rapidly, and the cañon opens out into a rolling country, barren and unprepossessing.

The formation is all sandstone, which is the "country rock" for miles in every direction. From above, at almost any point, the traveller comes suddenly on this mighty chasm, without any warning of its presence in the rock plain over which he is passing. The sudden view of the awful depths is startling beyond description. From below, the stupendous height of the walls, which often project above the head of the beholder, cannot be fully comprehended. The floor of the cañon is comparatively smooth and very sandy, the general appearance being that of a river of sand flowing between the rock walls and circling around occasional islands of green. There is no detritus along the foot of either wall, as is common in other cañons. The rocks are apparently disintegrating and gradually filling the chasm, but the only agents in this work are the wind and the loose sand, and their progress is so slow as to be almost imperceptible. The particles of sand, whirled along in the air, are constantly eating away the walls and detached blocks of stone, and in the course of centuries have made a very wonder-land of weird shapes and fantastic sculpturing. The amount of water in the cañon depends wholly on the season. In years of drought there is none above the surface, but the sand is moist, and the Indians obtain what water they need by digging. In moderate seasons there is an occasional show of running water, which sinks again in the sand. In wet seasons there is a considerable stream, and about a mile below the Cañon Alsada there is seen a magnificent fall of water from the top of the cañon, sheer a thousand feet, swaying in the wind and breaking by the resistance of the air, until it is completely lost in a fine mist at the bottom. The Navahos say the stream has decreased of later years, and the remains of ancient acequias indicate the truth of their tradition. There is a slight growth of underbrush throughout the cañon, with grass at intervals, and now and then the corn-fields and peach-orchards of the Indians.

This place was inhabited long before Columbus set his sails to seek the Indies. Along its walls are perched the strange cliff-dwellings of that ancient and unknown race which once peopled the present deserts of Arizona. Some of them are on ledges only forty or fifty feet above the cañon floor, with parts on the floor, and others are six or seven hundred feet higher. How the higher ones were constructed is an unsolved problem, for there appears now no way of access to man but by ropes from above, or by broken flights of ladder-like steps cut in the rock at various places, and these houses are built of stone and heavy wooden beams. The timber in them is in excellent preservation, and the whitewash on the interior walls looks as though it had been put on within a year, yet the Navahos say that these buildings were there, just as they are now, when their forefathers came into the country. The architecture is that of the Pueblos, with similar masonry, the usual fragments of pottery, and the universal estufa. The Navahos have never used them, and, so far as is known, have never been able to reach some of them, to which, indeed, there appears no feasible approach, except possibly by balloon. The enterprising archæologist would probably find them just as the cliff-dweller left them when he departed on his last migration.

This cañon was not explored throughout until 1859, although the troops had often been in its vicinity, and the Navahos thought it afforded them an inaccessible retreat in time of war. Still it was not a place of retreat to which they all gathered, as was generally supposed, nor were there any fortifications in it, as rumor had declared. It is not probable that there were ever more than a thousand Indians living in it, for no large numbers were ever found there, and there was not the grass in it to support the large herds that they owned. Nine tenths, at least, of the Navaho nation made their homes at such other points in their extensive territory as afforded pasturage for their flocks; the Cañon de Chelly was merely the residence of a small portion of the tribe; but none of the whites knew just what was there, and the great chasm was regarded in all circles as the mysterious stronghold of the Navahos. The first recorded entrance into it by troops was made in September, 1849, by Lieutenant Simpson, of Colonel Washington's expedition, escorted by Major Kendrick, with sixty men. They entered at the mouth, went a short distance up the Cañon del Trigo, and then ascended the main cañon for nine and a half miles, in search of the fortifications of the Navahos. To confirm the stories of the guides about an impregnable fortress on a plateau so high that fifteen ladders were required to reach it, they found nothing but the cliff houses, and, on returning, announced that the mystery of the Cañon de Chelly was solved. In 1858, Colonel D. S. Miles entered it at the Cañon Alsada and marched to the mouth without any casualties, but he was so impressed with the advantages it afforded for attack from the summits of the walls that he reported: "No command should ever again enter it." In July, 1859, Captain Walker, commanding an expedition against the Navahos, entered the cañon half a mile below the entrance of the Juanica, and marched to the month. Two weeks later he returned to the head of the cañon and explored it to the point of his former descent. In view of these explorations it seems remarkable that General Carleton should have written, after Carson's expedition: "This is the first time any troops, whether when the country belonged to Mexico or since we acquired it, have been able to pass through the Cañon de Chelly, which, for its great depth, its length, its perpendicular walls, and its labyrinthine character, has been regarded by eminent geologists as the most remarkable of any 'fissure' (for such it is held to be) upon the face of the globe. It has been the great fortress of the tribe since time out of mind." In reality, however, this misinformation was uni-

CLIFF HOUSE IN CANON DE CHELLY.

versal. No officer who entered the cañon (judging from their reports) had any definite knowledge of what his predecessors had done. Carson surely should have been acquainted with the history of so famous a place, but, with an inaccuracy that is strikingly illustrative of the unreliability of traditional history, he reported that his troops had "accomplished an undertaking never before accomplished in war-time—that of passing through the Cañon de Chelly from east to west."*

Colonel Carson started from Fort Canby on January 6, 1864, with a force of three hundred and ninety officers and men, for the mouth of the cañon. Just before starting he sent Captain Pfeiffer, with one company, to operate from the eastern end. The depth of the snow on the divide between Fort Canby and the Pueblo Colorado was so great that his command was three days in reaching the latter place, a march that was usually made in one day. He had started his supply-train on the 3d, expecting that the oxen would be recuperated by the time of his arrival, but the train had taken five days in making the twenty-five miles, and had lost twenty-seven oxen. Reorganizing, and leaving part of the train, he pushed on to the cañon, which he struck on the 12th, about six miles above the mouth. On the night of the 11th he sent out Sergeant Andres Herrara, with fifty men, as scouts. In the morning this party found a fresh trail, and, following it rapidly, they overtook the Indians just as they were entering the cañon, and attacked them; they killed eleven and captured two women and two children, with one hundred and thirty sheep and goats. On the 13th Carson divided his force into two commands: one, under Captain Berney, was sent up the north side of the cañon, and the other, under Captain Carey, accompanied by Carson, moved up the south side, with the view of ascertaining the topography of the country and the position of the Navahos, if they had undertaken to make a stand. The latter party found and captured five wounded Indians at the scene of Herrara's fight. On the 14th they returned to the mouth of the cañon and found Pfeiffer there, he having come

---

* Carson's report has never been published. I quote from the manuscript copy on file in the office of the War Department, at Washington, to which the department has courteously afforded me access.

through the cañon successfully, without any casualty to his command; they had killed three Indians, and brought in nineteen women and children prisoners.

While returning to camp, Carson was approached by three Indians, under a flag of truce, who asked if they might come in with their families and surrender. He told them that they might if they came by ten o'clock the next morning, but not later. About sixty came in by the appointed time and acceded to the terms of surrender and removal to the Bosque. Says Carson: "They declared that, owing to the operations of my command, they are in a complete state of starvation, and that many of their women and children have already died from this cause. They also state that they would have come in long ago, but that they believed it was a war of extermination, and that they were equally surprised and delighted to learn the contrary from an old captive whom I had sent back to them for this purpose. I issued them some meat, and as they asked permission to return to their haunts and collect the remainder of their people, I directed them to meet me at this post [Fort Canby] in ten days. They have all arrived here according to promise, many of them, with others, joining and travelling in with Captain Carey's command. This command of seventy-five men I conferred upon Captain Carey at his own request, he being desirous of passing through this stupendous cañon. I sent the party to return through the cañon from west to east, that all the peach-orchards, of which there are many, might be destroyed, as well as the dwellings of the Indians." About three thousand peach-trees were destroyed in the cañon; and one hundred and ten Navahos came in with Carey's command. On January 23 Carson reported the results of the expedition as follows: "Killed, 23; captured, 34; voluntarily surrendered, 200; captured 200 head of sheep."

This expedition has passed into the realms of romance, like many other events in New Mexican history, and the facts have been lost sight of in the rosy coloring of imagination. Illustrative of this I quote the following from a popular biography of Kit Carson, that is introduced by what purport to be certificates to its accuracy by such well-known New Mexicans as Colonel Ceran St. Vrain and Judge Charles Beaubien:

COLONEL KIT CARSON.

"The Navajo Indians were very troublesome. For a whole decade they had defied the government, and now, enlisted as savage cohorts of the rebels, they were especially dangerous. They numbered several thousand warriors, and roamed over an immense tract of country. General Carleton selected Carson to command two thousand picked men, consisting of Californians, Mexicans, and mountaineers, to operate against these Indians. The campaign was a most brilliant one. After a succession of skirmishes, Carson succeeded in getting the enemy into a bed or ravine, and had his own forces so disposed as to command every approach, and in doing this compelled the surrender of ten thousand Indians, being the largest single capture of Indians ever known. The entire tribe, men, women, and children, was disposed of by this magnificent operation. This greatly increased the fame of the mountain leader, and the official reports to the War Department very justly sounded his praises in flattering terms, but none too extravagantly." This leads to the thought that if there be anything more unreliable than traditional history it is written history.

There is a generally prevailing impression, in regard to the results of Carson's expedition, similar to the above statement, and possibly derived from it. The great success of the expedition was not in immediate effect, but in the ulterior results of the campaign, which Carson, with his keen foresight, anticipated. He said, in his report of January 23, 1864: "But it is to the ulterior effects of the expedition that I look for the greatest results. We have shown the Indians that in no place, however formidable or inaccessible in their opinion, are they safe from the pursuit of the troops of this command, and have convinced a large portion of them that the struggle on their part is a hopeless one. We have also demonstrated that the intentions of the government towards them are eminently humane, and dictated by an earnest desire to promote their welfare; that the principle is not to destroy but to save them, if they are disposed to be saved. When all this is understood by the Navajoes, generally, as it soon will be, and when they become convinced that destruction will follow on resistance, they will gladly avail themselves of the opportunities afforded them of peace and plenty under the fostering care of the government, as do all those now with whom I have had any means of communicating. They are arriving almost hourly, and will, I believe, continue to arrive until the last Indian in this section of the country is *en route* to the Bosque Redondo." This prediction proved substantially a true one. The Navahos came in so fast that General Carleton's resources were taxed to the utmost to support them. By February 20, 750 had surrendered at Los Pinos and been forwarded to the Bosque. On February 24, 1650 were reported surrendered at Fort Canby. On February 24, 1300 more were reported from Los Pinos. By March 11, 1500 more had come in at Fort Canby, and Carleton notified Carson that he could not take care of more than one additional thousand. By July 8, there were 6321 at the Bosque, and 1000 more at Fort

Canby. The war was evidently ended; Fort Canby was ordered abandoned in August, and the troops sent into Arizona. Carson was sent to the plains to fight Kiowas and Comanches, with 200 Ute warriors, who had volunteered to go if allowed what they could capture.

The evil qualities of the removal and concentration began to show as soon as success had been attained. The number of Navahos had been underestimated by Carleton. Carson maintained that there were at least 12,000 of them, and, if any credit can be given to subsequent statistics, he was right, but Carleton insisted that there could not possibly be over 8000; there must not be; it would spoil the Bosque system if there were. The greatest number ever at the Bosque Redondo was between nine and ten thousand; the remainder of the nation lurked in their old haunts, or fell back to the desert regions of Arizona and Utah, to avoid the troops. Of course, under the system of voluntary surrender, the worst Indians, the ones whose surveillance was most desirable, did not come in; but the removal of the others left them plenty of room in their own country, and this, with the fear of the troops, kept them quiet. The troops attacked them whenever they met them, for several years afterwards. The expense of caring for the exiled Navahos was very great. The New Mexicans offered to relieve the government of a portion of this burden by a system of "binding out," but the offer was declined; and also all the Navahos who had been kept at the army posts, "for whatever purpose," were required to be sent to the Bosque. There was difficulty between the Navahos and the Mescaleros at their new home. They had been enemies of old, and there was nothing to bring about a reconciliation. Their customs differed. The Mescalero women were chaste, but had no part in the control of the tribe; the Navaho women were very dissolute, and exercised a strong influence in the tribal government. The Mescaleros were the bolder warriors, but they were far inferior in numbers. The tribal jealousies were aggravated by petty aggressions and hectoring. The Apaches accused the Navahos of trampling down their crops, and otherwise annoying them. The reservation authorities made the matter worse by removing the Mescaleros from the land they had been cultivating, and giving it to the Navahos. The Mescaleros then claimed the fulfilment of the promise to them of a reservation in their own country, and when this was refused they went without permission, and began hostilities.

Agriculture at the Bosque did not result successfully; the crops usually promised well enough, but something always spoiled them. One time it was drought, another cut-worms, another bad irrigation, or overflows, or hail-storms. The Indians were, of necessity, a great expense to the government. The cost of feeding them for seven months, March to September inclusive, in 1865, was $452,356.98. The cost for a year previous to this time averaged higher than this, but the exact figures cannot be given, on account of the large amount of stores transferred from other departments and not reported as to value. All this time it was well known that they could support themselves in their own country. The principal cause of their helplessness in their new homes was that they were a pastoral, not an agricultural, people. In their own country their chief food is goats' milk and the roots of certain herbs of wild growth. Their flocks had been largely destroyed during the war. Tradition puts the number of sheep killed by soldiers at fifty thousand, but the Navahos say that the Utes and Mexicans stole the greater part of them. The Bosque did not afford grazing facilities for the sheep and goats they still had, and these gradually decreased in number. It has been proven since then that they can and will take care of themselves, very easily, if they can get ample pasturage; and, unless stock-raising is to be considered a less civilized pursuit than agriculture, there is no reason why any forcible attempt should be made to change the natural bent of their industrial instincts.

The fitness of the Bosque Redondo for a reservation is something that has been the subject of great controversy and of misrepresentation on one or both sides. The following description of it, given by Captain Thomas Claiborne in 1859, when there was talk of establishing a military post there, may fairly be considered as impartial: "The Bosque Redondo is an elbow of the river [Pecos]; the molts of cottonwoods are mostly on the left bank of the Pecos, extending for perhaps six or seven miles, in clusters. The river is very crooked, and stretched from side to side of the valley, which, midway of the Bosque, is two miles or over wide. The appearance of the Bosque in that desert country is very agreeable. The lower half of the valley is tillable, the upper is filled with drift sand. A secondary mesa, twelve hundred yards wide and a mile and a quarter long, lies on the right bank of the river, about midway the Bosque, about thirty feet above the river-bottom, and is curtained by sand-hills about twenty-five feet higher than itself. A kind of red-top grass grows in the lower bottoms, mixed with bunch grass; the hills are covered with brown sedge grass; the mesa above spoken of is well covered with mesquite grass. The water of the river is bad and the surrounding country is most desolate. The place is altogether unfit for a post." That the water of the Pecos at this point is alkaline, and charged with certain salts, is unquestionable; this comes from the Aqua Negra, which debouches into the Pecos at Giddings's Ranch, above the Bosque. The water of the Aqua Negra, however, has always been used, more or less, at Giddings's Ranch, both by men and animals, without bad results, though it is somewhat diuretic. Dr. Warner, physician at Fort Sumner, testified that the water of the Pecos at the Bosque is wholesome. Cadéte (Gian-nah-tah), the Mescalero chief, testified: "It is not good, too much alkali, and is the cause of the sickness in the tribe and losing our animals." The Navahos sometimes said the water was all right, and sometimes that they thought it was bad, but they always unanimously expressed a preference for their old country.

The head of the opposition to the Bosque was Dr. Matthew Steck, a well-known settler in New Mexico, at that time Superintendent of Indian Affairs. He favored giving the Mescaleros a reservation in their own country, as had been promised them, and opposed the removal of the Navahos to the Bosque. He advocated his views in New Mexico, and, when he found he could do nothing there, he went to Washington to secure the same ends. Carleton complained bitterly of this attempted interference with his plans, and insisted on the enforcement of the ultra-humane policy; that is, on compelling the Indians to do what the white man in authority—in this case himself—may think to be best for them. He said: "Dr. Steck wants to hold councils with the Navajoes! It is mockery to hold councils with a people who are in our hands and have only to await our decisions. It will be bad policy to hold any councils. We should give them what they need, what is just, and take care of them as children until they can take care of themselves. The Navajoes should never leave the Bosque, and never shall if I can prevent it. I told them that that should be their home. They have gone there with that understanding. There is land enough there for themselves and the Apaches. The Navajoes themselves are Apaches, and talk the same language, and in a few years will be homogeneous with them." He was proven to be mistaken as to the two tribes becoming homogeneous; whether he was wrong in other regards is a question about which people will differ; in brief, it is simply the question whether the concentration policy is the right one—whether it is better to place Indians where they do not wish to be, oblige them to do things which they do not wish to do, and force them to abandon the pursuits by which they had formerly supported themselves. General Carleton also accused Mr. Steck of acting from interested motives, but he did not specify in what regard.

In the winter of 1864–65, the Navahos at the Bosque were reduced to terrible straits through the destruction of their crops by cut-worms. There was want all through that portion of the country from various causes. Neither the War nor the Indian Department was able to relieve them adequately. There was no relief from natural sources, for the acorns, cedar-berries, wild potatoes, palmillas and other roots, mescal and mesquite, on which they could rely in their old home in times of famine, were not found at the Bosque. Cattle and sheep were issued to them for food, "head and pluck," and the blood of the slaughtered animals was ordered to be saved to make "haggis and blood-puddings" for the orphan children. To add to their distress these people, who make the most serviceable blankets in the world and usually have plenty of them, were destitute, by the ravages of their enemies, of both blankets and clothing. They had no houses, and, as substitutes, holes were ordered to be dug, in which they might be sheltered from the wind. In spite of all his efforts and ingenuity, General Carleton knew that they must suffer, and, on October 31, 1864, he directed the commandant at Fort Sumner to explain his good intentions to the Indians. "Tell them," he said "to be too proud to murmur at what cannot be helped. We could not foresee the total destruction of their corn crop, nor could we foresee that the frost and hail would come and destroy the crop in the country; but not to be discouraged; to work hard, every man and woman, to put in

NEAR THE HEAD-WATERS OF THE NAVAHO.

large fields next year, when, if God smiles upon our efforts, they will, at one bound, be forever placed beyond want, and independent. Tell them not to believe ever that we are not their best friends; that their enemies have told them that we would destroy them; that we had sent big guns there to attack them; but that those guns are only to be used against their enemies, if they continue to behave as they have done."

With all his good intentions, General Carleton was inexcusable, under analogy of the laws that are daily administered in every state and territory of the Union. There is no excuse known for failure under such circumstances. When a man is restrained of his liberty, or deprived of any right, for the purpose of benefiting him, there is no extenuation except he be in fact benefited, or, at least, not injured. Good intentions never excuse a wrong; and though, as a war measure, placing the Navahos at the Bosque may be justified, keeping them there against their will, in time of peace, is clearly an infringement of natural right. Our government must actually benefit the Indians by the reservation system in order to justify itself. Still, General Carleton stuck to his theory, and said that if the Navahos were moved from the Bosque at all they ought to be sent to Kansas or the Indian Territory. In 1865 the worms destroyed the crops again, and on July 18, after giving directions for husbanding all food, Carleton instructed the officer in command: "You should tell the Indians what a dreadful year it is, and how they must save everything to eat which lies in their power, or starvation will come upon them." The Indians had been slipping away from the place in small parties since midwinter of 1864-65, and in July a large party, under Ganado Blanco (White Cattle), broke away forcibly, but they were pursued and driven back. In August Carleton concluded to let the few Coyotero Apaches on the reservation return to their own country, as they desired. In the summer of this year a commission, consisting of Senator Doolittle, Vice-President Foster, and Representative Ross, visited New Mexico, and made a full investigation of the Indian affairs there, but nothing resulted from it.

In 1865 Felipe Delgado succeeded Mr. Steck as Superintendent; he was in harmony with General Carleton, and reported that, "It is fair to presume that next year their [the Navahos'] facilities will be greater," etc. He had the good sense to recommend the purchase of sheep for them. In 1866 the crops failed again—this time, as Superintendent A. B. Norton and their agent reported, from bad seed, improper management, and overflows of the Pecos. There were reported to be 7000 Indians on the reservation, and the cost of keeping them was estimated at $1,500,000 annually. In 1867 the crops failed, from bad management and hail-storms, as reported; the Comanches attacked and robbed the Navahos several times; and many of their horses died from eating poisonous weeds. There were 7300 Indians reported as on the reservation, and their property had become reduced to 550 horses, 20 mules, 940 sheep, and 1025 goats. In 1868 Superintendent Davis reported: "The Navahos were located several years ago upon a reservation at the Bosque Redondo, by the military, and after expending vast sums of money, and after making every effort for more than four years to make it a success, it has proved a total failure. It was certainly a very unfortunate selection for a reserve; no wood, unproductive soil, and very unhealthy water, and the Indians were so much dissatisfied they planted no grain last spring, and I verily believe they were making preparations to leave as the Apaches did."

Fortunately for all concerned, General Sherman and Colonel Tappan, Peace Commissioners, reached New Mexico in May, 1868. They satisfied themselves that the Navahos would never become self-supporting or contented at the Bosque Redondo, and, on June 1, entered into an agreement with the tribe by which they were to be removed to their former country. The reservation then given them was included between parallel 37° of north latitude and a parallel drawn through Fort Defiance, for north and south lines, and parallel of longitude 109° 30' and a parallel drawn through Ojo del Oso, as east and west lines. The Indians were to receive five dollars annually, in clothing, for each member of the tribe, and ten dollars for each one engaged in farming or mechanical pursuits. Each head of a family was entitled to select one hundred and sixty acres of land, if he desired to hold in severalty, and in such case he was to receive one hundred dollars in seeds and implements the first year, and twenty-five dollars each for the second and third years. Buildings of the value of $11,500 were to be erected, and the Navahos pledged themselves to compel all their children between the ages of six and sixteen to attend school. A separate school-house and teacher was to be provided for every thirty pupils; $150,000 was to be appropriated at once to the Indians, part of which was to be expended in the purchase of 15,000 sheep and goats and 500 cattle, and the remainder to be used for the expenses of their removal and in such other ways as should appear most beneficial.

Under this liberal treaty the tribe was removed in 1868, and since then there has been a continuous improvement in their condition. They had very bad luck with their crops for several years, but their herds increased steadily. By 1873 they were reported to have 10,000 horses and 200,000 sheep and goats. In 1872 an Indian police force was organized at the agency, on recommendation of Captain Bennett, and placed under command of Manuelito, their war-chief, providing, for the first time in their history, for a control of offenders by tribal authority. It was discontinued in 1873 for a short time, but was soon put in force again, with beneficial results. A few years later the Indians abandoned it on account of the small pay given to the policemen. About fifteen men are now employed, and they appear to be all that are needed. In 1876 the Navahos were reported as self-supporting, notwithstanding they had lost 40,000 sheep by freezing during the past winter. In 1878 their agent said: "Within the ten years during which the present treaty with the Navahos has been in force they have grown from a band of paupers to a nation of prosperous, industrious, shrewd, and (for barbarians) intelligent people." They were reported at that time as numbering 11,800, and owning 20,000 horses, 1500 cattle, and 500,000 sheep; they were tilling 9192 acres of land, and obtained ninety-five per cent. of their subsistence from civilized pursuits.

In fact, they were increasing so rapidly that there was an urgent call for more room, and, as there was desert land to spare in all directions, it was given to them. By executive order of October 29, 1878, there was added to their reservation the land between the northern line of Arizona, parallel 110° of west longitude, parallel 36° of north latitude, and the western line of the reservation. Still there was a call for more land, and on January 6, 1880, they were given a strip fifteen miles wide along the eastern side of the reservation, and one six miles wide along the southern line. In the latter year three windmill pumps and fifty-two stock pumps were put in at different points on the reservation, which have stopped

MOQUI PUEBLO.

much of their wandering in search of water, and added greatly to the value of their grazing-lands. Their march of improvement has not stopped, and in 1884 the nation, estimated at 17,000, cultivated 15,000 acres of land and raised 220,000 bushels of corn and 21,000 bushels of wheat; they had 35,000 horses and 1,000,000 sheep. In 1884 the reservation was extended west to 111° 30', and the northern boundary was made the Colorado and San Juan rivers. By this addition the reservation encloses the Moqui Pueblo reservation on two sides, and the agencies for the two have been consolidated. This order, increasing the reservation by 1,769,600 acres in Arizona and Utah, was supplemented by one taking away 46,000 acres in New Mexico; the reservation as now established includes 8,159,360 acres, mostly desert land.

With their advancement in wealth the Navahos have made but little progress in civilization, and their condition is one that might well call for more extended mission work than has been done among them. The government is maintaining an industrial school at present, and the Presbyterian Church, to which they were assigned, has established a mission school two or three times, but it has been discontinued through the failure of Congress to furnish a suitable building. The Navahos, however, have repeatedly asked to have schools established, and the Presbyterian Board of Foreign Missions has recently decided to establish a school, whether the government complied with its promises or not. There were twenty-five reported, in 1884, as being able to read, but the report is not very reliable; only five were reported as able to speak English in 1883. Their manners, customs, and religion are practically unchanged, except that they have adopted civilized clothing to a large extent. They still plant with sharpened sticks, but this has been conceded by farmers to be the best way of planting in their country; seed must be planted deep in order to obtain moisture to insure growth, and ploughing only makes the ground dry. They never wash their sheep, and still chop the wool from them with case-knives, pieces of tin, or anything else that will cut, obtaining about one pound from each animal.* Their horses are seldom

---

* A large number of sheep-shears mere sent to them in 1885, and will probably be used.

used except, in travelling; three fourths of them are never broken, and are of no use whatever, except in the purchase of wives. Attempts have been made to introduce improved looms among them, but the women adhere tenaciously to their old modes. About fifty of the men were induced to build houses, in 1884, but the vast majority still adhere to their temporary *hogans*, and desert them when a death occurs. Their morals are as loose as ever, except that the consumption of liquor has decreased materially. These are the chief signs of advancement, and yet it has been said repeatedly that the Navahos afforded the best material for civilization among our Indian tribes. After forty years of our guardianship they are still barbarians—self-supporting while kept separate from the whites, but as helpless and as easily swindled as children, except in the most ordinary business dealings, and scarcely better fitted for the duties of citizenship than when we first knew them. They were always among thieves, and thus far Christianity and civilization have passed by on the other side. Possibly that is why they are now so prosperous.

CHAPTER XV.
FORT PHIL KEARNEY.

UNTIL the close of the War of the Rebellion, the great northeastern triangle of the mountain country, lying between the continental divide and the plains, had been subject to little encroachment from the white man, but civilization had been pressing up about it on all sides. On the east, the Sioux had been pushed back gradually until the great outbreak of 1862, in Minnesota, and then, by one stroke, forced into the confines of Dakota. At the south, the mining settlements of Colorado had grown populous and strong enough to entirely dispossess the Indian. On the southwest, the Saints had planted themselves immovably, and converted what hunting-grounds there were in that section into farms. On the west, the gold-hunters had crowded up to the continental divide and were moving down its eastern slope. They had advanced from the Pacific coast, passing from one point to another in wild stampedes, as new discoveries of the precious metal were made, but always growing in numbers and always pressing towards the east. The discovery of the Colville mines was followed in 1857–58–59 by the Frazer River excitement, which carried a large population into the Northwest. Then came the rush for the Salmon River mines in 1861–62, sending the adventurers into Southeastern Washington, to such an extent that in 1863 Idaho was organized as a territory, including the new settlements. The overflow from the Salmon River country, across the divide, began in 1861, and the prospectors soon found ground that was worthy their time and attention. In the following year the wonderful placers of this section became known, and there ensued a rush for the new Golconda that surpassed anything ever known in the Northwest. The richness of the mines justified the great immigration; it is estimated that the placers of Alder Gulch alone produced $50,000,000 of gold in the four years following their discovery. Helena, Virginia City, Bozeman, and other camps sprang up, with populations that produced nothing but gold, and which must be supplied with everything else from the outside.

There were two ways of reaching the Montana settlements from the East: one was by following the established

PROSPECTORS IN THE MOUNTAINS.

emigrant road through the South Pass, to Fort Hall, and thence north; the other was by boat, on the Missouri and Yellowstone rivers, to the head of navigation, and thence through the country of the Crows to the mines. Both these routes were very circuitous, being over five hundred miles longer than the direct road which was physically practicable, from Fort Laramie to Bozeman, along the eastern base of the

Big Horn Mountains. Several parties had gone into Montana by this route, which was at first called "Bozeman's Route," and afterwards, when definitely located, "the Montana Road." Besides the extra distance, the South Pass route, which was virtually the only road used by emigrants with teams, required crossing and recrossing the continental divide, a very considerable hardship to the way-worn emigrant. For these reasons it became desirable to open a direct road, and preparations for it were commenced in 1865, by negotiating with the Indians for the right of way.

The country through which the proposed road was projected belonged, when first known to the whites, to the Crows, or, as they call themselves, Absaroka or Upsaroka. It is sometimes called by the same name, which is then translated "the land, or home, of the Crows." The tribe is a branch of the Dakota family, numbering about three thousand five hundred, and is in three divisions; the Ki-kat-sa, or Crows proper, commonly known as the Mountain Crows; the Alla-ka-weah, and the Ah-nah-a-ways, who live farther to the east, and are termed the River Crows. These Indians are tall, well-formed, expert horsemen and good hunters. The fur traders had troubles with them at times, and gave them the reputation of rascals and thieves, but of later years they have been faithful and honorable friends of the whites. They had all the fighting they could attend to from their cousins, the Sioux, who waged relentless war upon them. On this account they cultivated the friendship of the whites, from whom they could procure arms and ammunition, and even had several reputable white chiefs, among whom were the celebrated Bridger and Beckwith. By the time that the early emigration to the mountains began, a large portion of the southern and eastern parts of the northeastern triangle had been deserted by the Crows as a habitation, though still held in common with the Sioux as a battle-ground and hunting-ground. By 1865 the Sioux, with their allies the Northern Cheyennes and Arapahoes, had gained control of these sections, and the Crows were virtually expelled from the country east and south of the Big Horn Mountains.

That part of the country, thus gained by the Sioux, which

lies between the Black Hills, the Big Horn Mountains, and the Yellowstone River, was known as the Powder River country, from its principal Stream, whose valleys, together with those of the Tongue River and the Rosebud, constituted the best hunting-ground remaining to the Sioux. For over thirty miles north from Fort Reno this country is much like the great plains, with little vegetable growth except sage-brush; north of that it is more fertile, covered with grass, and abounding in all the vegetable growth of the latitude. The monotony of evergreen forests is broken by groves of cottonwoods, willows, ashes, and red-birches. All kinds of berries, with grapes, cherries, and plums, grow wild, in profusion. The streams are clear and wholesome, instead of muddy and alkaline, as in the lower country. This beautiful region extends along the eastern and northeastern bases of the Big Horn Mountains, in a strip of varying width. Off to the northeast, at an average distance of perhaps twenty miles, begin the "bad lands," and the country takes on a dreary and desolate aspect. In this entire region large game was still abundant. The most extensive herds of buffalo yet remaining pastured there. Elk, deer, and antelope were to be met with everywhere. The terraced buttes were the favorite home of the big-horn. Bears rioted among the fruits and berries. Of small game, such as rabbits, grouse, and water-fowl, there was an abundance that can scarcely be imagined. Naturally enough, the Indians did not desire to lose this sportsman's paradise, but the government did not appear to know it.

It was the era of peace—in Washington. The Indians; in the annual reports, were doing nothing but defending themselves from the encroachments of lawless whites. They were ready and willing to do anything, if they could only secure schools and churches. Mr. Bogy, the Commissioner of Indian Affairs, sat back and smiled sarcastically at reports of hostilities. The peace people were busy, working themselves into a white heat over the wrongs of the Cheyennes. The entire country looked contemptuously on the strength of the red men. What! we, who had just put down the greatest rebellion the world ever knew, to be terrified by a few half-starved Indians? Oh, no! The army was cut down to its lowest possible figure, and much of it was employed in the late insurrectionary states. Its arms were chiefly old-fashioned muzzle-loaders, notwithstanding the wonderful improvements that had been made in weapons during the war. The Indians were better armed. On one occasion a cattle guard excused themselves for not firing on Indians who were attacking their herds, because the Indians had revolvers, while they had nothing but muzzle-loading muskets, and would be at the mercy of the Indians if they discharged them. "Judicious men" were sent out to treat with the Sioux for the right of way through to Montana. They met at Fort Sully, and, from October 10 to October 28, made treaties with the Minneconjous, Lower Brulés, Two Kettles, Blackfoot Sioux, Sans Arcs, Oncpapas, and Ogallallas, by which these Indians agreed to "withdraw from the routes overland already established or hereafter to be established through their country," and not to interfere "with the persons or property of citizens of the United States travelling thereon." The chief striking features about these treaties were the small number of signatures appended to them, and the absence of names of prominence among these. The Ogallalla treaty had but three signers—Long Bull, Charging Bear, and Man that Stands on a Hill—neither of whom, as was notorious, had any control over the tribe. In the mean time General Connor had marched into the Powder River country to chastise the Indians who declined to treat, but he had little success, and was forced to be content with establishing Fort Reno on the head-waters of Powder River.

The matter drifted on through the winter, the opposition growing somewhat less during that annual period of starvation, when the presents from the Great Father looked so much more enticing. The leader of the anti-cession party was Red Cloud (Mock-peah-lu-tah), who was at that time known only as the chief of the Bad Faces, one of the three bands into which the Ogallallas were divided. He was a warrior, not of hereditary rank, who was raised to the leadership on his merits, and was already exerting a wide influence. His influence was largely due to his medicine powers, which were not of the ordinary stripe. In common with many other Indians, he professed the power of seeing spirits, but, in excess of them, he claimed direct communication with the Great Spirit, who guided him in all matters of importance. Shrewd in all things, he was especially keen in his foresight. He realized that the building of the road meant the destruction of the game in their best hunting-ground, and the reduction of his people to the beggarly condition of the Indians who hung about the government posts. He bitterly opposed the treaties from the first. An able second was found in Ta-shun-kah-Ko-ke-pah (Man Afraid of his Horses), the warlike chief of the Honc-pah-te-lah band of Ogallallas. The name does not mean that he fears his horses, as it is often understood, but that he is fearful of losing them. It was given him because, on occasion of an attack by the Shoshonees, he abandoned his family in order to save his herd of ponies.

The most influential of the chiefs that favored the treaties was Spotted Tail (Sin-ta-Gal-les-sca), who, like Red Cloud, was not of hereditary rank, but a warrior who had risen by his courage and ability. He and his coadjutor Standing Elk (As-hah-kah-nah-zhe) will be remembered as among the Brulés who surrendered themselves, for the safety of their tribe, after the battle of Ash Hollow. When a young man of twenty, Spotted Tail quarrelled with one of the boldest and fiercest chiefs of his tribe, about a young girl, whom both admired. Meeting one day alone, outside the camp, the chief demanded of him that he should abandon his pretensions to the lady, on pain of instant death. The young brave did not stop to bandy words. Burning with rage and hatred, he snatched his knife from its sheath and defied his rival's prowess. The chief's keen blade had flashed in the air as quickly as his own; with a bound he was upon the presumptuous youth, and they were in the struggle for life or death. A few hours later an Indian, who passed that way, found them locked in each other's arms and covered with gaping wounds; the chief was dead, and Spotted Tail was senseless. He soon recovered from his wounds, and at once rose to prominence. It is pleasing to know, also, that he married the girl for whom he fought so well, and through life treated her with such kindness and affection as are rarely known among these In-

SPOTTED TAIL

dians. On the death of the head chief the tribe put aside the hereditary claimants, and elected Spotted Tail, by an almost unanimous vote, to the highest command. He had proved an able chief and remained friendly to the whites, but at the present juncture the sentiment against the road was so strong that his authority was reduced to a nominal control, even of his own tribe.

In the spring the commission located itself at Fort Laramie, being still engaged in efforts to get signers to its treaties, and especially to conciliate the Ogallallas. The idea prevalent among officials, both in the East and the West, was that there must be peace, and accordingly it was said with assurance that there would be. According to the statement of Special Agent Chandler, "Commissioner Taylor repeatedly asserted that he was sent there by the government for the purpose of making a treaty, and it should be accomplished, if made with but two Indians," as could be "proved by numerous officers and citizens at and near this post, who heard him." Every effort was made to induce the Indians who opposed the road to consent to it, but in vain. Colonel Taylor promised "that the travel on said road should be confined strictly to the line thereof, and that emigrants and travellers generally should not be allowed to molest or disturb the game in the country through which they passed;" but this offer, so evidently impossible of performance, did not deceive the Indians, and they still refused to treat. So certain, however, were all parties that the right of way would be granted, that the military occupation of the country began while the negotiations were pending. Colonel H. B. Carrington was ordered up from Fort Kearney, with about two thousand men, of whom eight companies were assigned to the new route. They numbered about seven hundred men, five hundred of them raw recruits. This command passed through Laramie in June, while the negotiations were going on, and marched directly for the Powder River country.

As soon as the destination of these troops was announced to the Indians, Red Cloud, Man Afraid, and their followers withdrew from the council and refused to return. The only ones of the Prairie Sioux who remained and agreed to abide by the treaties were the Lower Brulés, with a few stragglers from other tribes. At that time they numbered about two thousand five hundred, but a year later Spotted Tail, Standing Elk, and Swift Bear, the treaty chiefs, had with them only one hundred lodges, mostly of old women and squaws, the young men having gone to swell the ranks of Red Cloud. Included among the Indians that treated was the mixed band under Big Mouth and Blue Nose, which had lived about Fort Laramie so long that they were known as the "Laramie Loafers." They numbered about six hundred, but less than a hundred of them were men, and more than a hundred were half-breed children. So rapid was the defection of warriors to the hostile camps, that, within two weeks after the passage of the troops, Spotted Tail and Standing Elk told the whites that their young men had left them and gone to the Powder River country, and that parties who went far from home had best "go prepared, and look out for their hair."

The commissioners were right in insisting that a treaty should be made and the road opened. There was no existing treaty with the Sioux by which the United States relinquished the right of opening roads through their country, as has sometimes been stated. The United States does not often make treaties of that kind with Indians, and it is doubtful whether it ought at all. The reason for the law of eminent domain extends to the right of way over Indian lands, whether reserved or not, as it does to that over the property of the citizen, and the Indian should submit to it as the white man does. After land is reserved for the use of Indians, however, the law of eminent domain comes in conflict with another dogma of public policy, which is that the Indians should be kept separate from the whites until they become civilized. The damage done by the intrusion is held superior to the benefit resulting from the road, but in such cases right of way is almost invariably obtained by treaty. When a new railroad is to be built, it is pushed through the country with very little regard for the feelings of property owners. It may spoil the old spring, ruin the orchard, and wipe the beloved homestead out of existence, and this although in fact the road may be a mere speculation, and not a necessity at all. To this the white man must submit; why then should a much-needed road be left unmade for fear of spoiling the hunting-preserves of the red man? Certainly the Montana road ought to have been opened; the wrong done was in failing to report the actual feelings of the Indians to the government. If we may judge by the letters of Commissioner Bogy, he was in absolute ignorance of the condition of affairs. It was understood in Washington that the treaties were properly made and that everything was going on smoothly. The troops received assurances to that effect.

The detachment for the Powder River country was moving on. The soldiers were splendidly furnished with everything except arms, ammunition, and horses. Nearly all of them were armed with old, muzzle-loading, Springfield muskets; though the regimental band had Spencer breech-loading carbines, and a few of the officers had Henry rifles. Of ammunition only a small amount was taken from Fort Kearney,

ON THE BOZEMAN TRAIL.

in the expectation that a supply could be obtained at Fort Laramie, but unfortunately there was none there of proper make and calibre. There was no cavalry in the command, and only two hundred horses available for cavalry purposes. On these two hundred infantrymen, armed with muskets, were mounted. Verily this expedition was on a strictly peace basis. The Indians were proceeding on a different theory. On the morning after the command reached Fort Reno, one hundred and sixty-seven miles northwest of Fort Laramie, the peaceful Sioux ran off all the sutler's horses and mules. They were pursued, but none of the stock was recovered; the only thing the pursuers captured was a pony, so heavily laden with the presents recently distributed at Fort Laramie that he could not keep up in the chase. On July 14 the troops, who had then reached Piney Creek, received notice from the Indians that they must leave the country; that Fort Reno would not be disturbed, but that no new forts could be built. On the next morning the new fort was located at the mouth of Little Piney Creek. It was named Fort Phil Kearney, in honor of the distinguished cavalry officer, though the orthography does not indicate it.* Preparations for defence were at once begun by mowing the parade-ground and putting up signs to "Keep off the grass."

On the morning of the 17th, at daybreak, part of the post herd were stampeded, and the party that went in pursuit was surrounded by a large force of Indians, who killed two and wounded three of the soldiers. Later in the day, the same party of Indians came upon the travelling trading establishment of Louis Gazzous, commonly known as "French Pete," an old trader with a Sioux wife, and killed all the men, six in number. From that day until the 29th, five emigrant trains were attacked, fifteen men killed, and much stock run off, part of it from Fort Reno. On the 29th Carrington appears to have awakened to the fact that the hostile Indians were doing some damage. He telegraphed the Adjutant-general of the army, on that day, for Indian auxiliaries and additional force. On the 31st he requested reinforcements of General P. St.

---

* The family name is Kearny, but both the Nebraska post, which was named after Stephen W., and this one, are universally spelled Kearney.

George Cooke, commanding in that district. On August 3, Fort C. F. Smith was located on the Big Horn, ninety-two miles northwest of Phil Kearney, by two companies sent from the latter point. During August the hostilities were chiefly horse and cattle stealing. Only three men were killed on the line, one of them being Grover, the artist-correspondent. In the latter part of August General Hazen visited and inspected the post. He stated that two companies of regular cavalry had been ordered up from Fort Laramie, and a regiment of infantry was on the way from St. Louis. In September more than a dozen men were killed on the line, about five hundred horses, mules, and cattle were run off, and five mowing-machines, with much other property, were destroyed.

During all this time active work was continued on the fort, which was being constructed on an extensive and elaborate plan. Large parties of men were kept busy cutting timber and hauling it in; others were working on the stockades and buildings; saw-mills were running at full speed; hay was being cut and stored for the coming winter. The timber was cut about seven miles from the fort, and the men detailed to cut and bring it in were called "the wood train." It was used in such enormous quantities, and so much of their time was consumed in Indian attacks and alarms, that from seventy-five to one hundred men were employed almost constantly in this branch of the work. By the last of October the fort was enclosed. It stood on a little plateau, elevated fifty or sixty feet above the surrounding bottom lands, in the point at the mouth of the Little Piney. Its length was sixteen hundred feet, northwest and southeast, parallel to the Big Piney. The northwestern part of it, or fort proper, was eight hundred feet in length by six hundred in width, and surrounded by a stockade of heavy pine logs, which were eleven feet long and planted three feet in the ground. The logs were hewn to a touching surface of four inches, loop-holed, and pointed. At the eastern and western angles were block-houses. Enclosed in this stockade were quarters for the troops, cavalry stables, store-houses, and a few other buildings. The southeastern half of the fort was of the same length, and of nearly equal width, where the two parts joined, but narrowing to about four hundred feet at the southeastern end. It was enclosed in a rough cottonwood stockade, and was used for a corral, teamsters' quarters, stables, shops, and similar purposes. The amount of work in all this was very great, there being forty-two distinct buildings in the fort proper, while the stables and other buildings of the corral extended entirely around it, except at the gates, abutting on the stockade.

The country about the fort is hilly. Some six miles west of it the Big Piney comes down in a northeast course, till it passes Piney Island; then it turns to the southeast and flows in a direct line for over six miles, to the mouth of Little Piney, where it swerves and flows away almost due east. North of the fort, on the opposite side of the Big Piney, is Lodge Trail Ridge, trending northwest and southeast, and forming the divide between Piney and Peno creeks. The latter is a tributary of Goose Creek, which, in turn, flows into Tongue River. East of the fort is Little Piney Creek, then a few low hills, then Starling Creek, and beyond it Lake De Smet. Southeast of the fort is an island of seven or eight acres in Little Piney, and beyond the creek rises a high knoll called Pilot Hill, which was used for a lookout station. South of the fort are two or three hills, and then the Big Horn Mountains, rising in successive ridges till they culminate in Cloud Peak, miles to the south. To the west is Fort Ridge, seven hundred feet above the valley, separating the head-waters of the Big and Little Piney. It is so called from the supposed remains of an Indian fort on its summit. Just to the northwest of the fort begin the Sullivant Hills, which extend away in that direction to the Big Piney. Beyond them the creek is divided by the large island called Piney, which was the principal place for cutting timber. Beyond the creek in this direction are Peno Head and Rocky Face Ridge, two branches of a spur of the Big Horn. Between these and Lodge Trail Ridge are the head-waters of Peno Creek. The Montana road crosses the country described from southeast to northwest, running south of Lake De Smet, north of Pilot Hill and the fort, crossing the Big Piney just above the fort, swinging around the northeastern slopes of Lodge Trail Ridge, and down Peno Creek.

The amount of work done by the force at Phil Kearney

was astounding, but the Indian fighting was limited, and of a defensive nature. In one sense it was right enough that such should have been the case, for Carrington was sent out to build forts, and the work he did was in the line of his duty; but he might, at least, have kept scouts enough out to have known when thousands of warriors were in his immediate vicinity. The men were obliged always to go armed to their work, and accompanied by an escort guard. The wood trains

TORTURE BY PRAIRIE INDIANS.

were attacked repeatedly, in the woods and on the road, and several men were killed in these assaults. Private Johnson was cut off from his party and no trace of him found afterwards, which was almost conclusive evidence that he had been taken alive and reserved for torture. The Sioux have an unpleasant method of torture. They fasten a man, naked, to the ground, lying on his back, with arms and legs stretched out and fastened to pegs; then they build a fire on his stomach, and keep it up till he dies, occasionally touching a burning brand to other portions of his body, gouging out an eye, or otherwise adding to the agony of the victim. Private Smith was scalped and left for dead in the pinery, but recovered sufficiently to drag himself to the block-house, built for the protection of the axe-men, there to die. Two other private soldiers were cut off near the same place, and scalped before the eyes of their comrades. The men grew impatient, and longed for the time when they might quit carpenter-work, and seek revenge. The Indians grew bolder. Sometimes they contented themselves with attacking the wood train; sometimes they rode tantalizingly near the fort and challenged the soldiers to fight; two or three times they charged the picket that was kept on Pilot Hill to watch their movements. On these occasions a shell or a canister would be dropped among them, and the guard, which was on duty with horses saddled and bridled, would rush to the relief of the threatened watchmen. The simple expedient of placing a block-house or a small stockade on the hill, which would have made the picket perfectly secure, did not occur to any one. Carrington said he desired to assume the offensive, but wanted reinforcements, and these, though long-promised, were slow in coming. The only ones that reached the fort at all were sixty men of Company C, 2d cavalry, armed with Springfield muskets and old-fashioned Star carbines, who arrived in November.

Among those at the fort who were impatient for a fight was Brevet Lieutenant-colonel William J. Fetterman, a soldier by birth, instinct, and profession, who joined the command at the fort in November. He had his first opportunity on December 6. The wood train was attacked two miles from the fort, and forced to corral for defence. Fetterman was sent, with thirty-five cavalry and a few of the mounted infantry, to relieve the wood party, and drive the Indians across Lodge Trail Ridge, in which direction they usually withdrew, while Carrington, with twenty-five mounted infantry, crossed the Big Piney, to intercept the Indians on Peno Creek. Fetterman's party put the Indians to flight and chased them for about five miles, when they faced about and attacked the troops. Nearly all the cavalry fled, leaving Fetterman, assisted by

Captain Brown and Lieutenant Wands, with a dozen men, to face over a hundred warriors. They stood at bay until Carrington's force came in sight, when the Indians retired. In the mean while Lieutenant Bingham, joined by Lieutenant Grummond, with two or three men from Carrington's command, pursued a single dismounted Indian into an ambuscade, two miles from the remainder of the troops, where Bingham and Sergeant Bowers were killed. In this affair Red Cloud commanded in person. He had lookouts on all the neighboring hills, signalling the progress of affairs, and it is probable that he had planned a more extensive ambuscade, but that his plans miscarried.

The Indians made their arrangements better the next time. It was Friday, December 21, 1866. The morning was bright and pleasant, though there was snow on the hills. There was still little of the humdrum of army-post life about Fort Phil Kearney. The office building and one of the company quarters were not yet finished, and there were touches to be added at many points, before this chief architectural feature of the Powder River country was in condition to admit of Indian fighting. A force of some ninety men started to the pine woods for more material, little dreaming that the pine woods, the ravines, and the brush coverts all around were full of bloodthirsty warriors. About eleven o'clock an alarm was given, and the lookout signalled: "Many Indians on wood road; train corralled and fighting." A detachment was at once organized for their relief. At the same time Indian pickets were seen on the neighboring hills, and a score or more appeared at the crossing of the Big Piney, but these were quickly dispersed by a few shells. Colonel Fetterman asked permission to take command of the relief party, which was granted. Lieutenant Grummond volunteered, and was put in charge of the cavalry. Captain Fred H. Brown joined of his own motion. He had been at the post all summer, as regimental quartermaster, and was then engaged in closing up his business before going to Fort Laramie, whither he had been ordered. He was an enthusiastic Indian-fighter, and was particularly ambitious to get Red Cloud's scalp. Wheatley and Fisher, two frontiersmen who were at the post, went with Brown, making the entire party eighty-four men. The soldiers were of different companies; fifty of them had Spencer carbines and revolvers; the remainder carried Springfield muskets, except the two civilians and one of the officers, who had Henry rifles.

The corralled train, at which the fighting was going on, was south of the Sullivant Hills. Instead of proceeding directly to it, the command took a course back of these hills, across Big Piney Creek, on the southwestern slope of Lodge Trail Ridge, to cut off the Indians who were attacking the train. As they moved along, Indians appeared on their front and on their flanks, retiring before them, out of range, across Lodge Trail Ridge, whose crest Fetterman reached fifteen or twenty minutes before noon, and occupied, with his men deployed in skirmish line. At the same time the lookout signalled that the Indians had left the train, which had broken corral and moved on towards Piney Island. The train returned to the fort after dark without having been subjected to any further annoyance. Fetterman's halt on the crest of Lodge Trail Ridge was of very brief duration. His men disappeared over the summit and firing began soon after, which grew more and more rapid until, at noon, there was an almost continuous rattle of musketry. This was heard plainly at the fort, and conveyed the intelligence that a hard fight was in progress in Peno Creek Valley. The people at the fort grew anxious. Surgeon Hines, with one man, was sent to the wood train, with instructions, if it were safe, to join Fetterman. He found the wood train undisturbed, and started across the country to Peno Creek, but found many Indians on Lodge Trail Ridge, preventing him from further progress. He went back for reinforcements, and Captain Ten Eyck, with seventy-six men, all that were considered available, was sent out. The anxiety of all who were on the fort side of the ridge was intense. The relief party galloped on, but they seemed to crawl. Instead of taking the road they went straight to the ridge and ascended it. The firing was becoming less and less in volume. Who was giving way? What was silencing the guns? They knew at the fort which side had a small supply of ammunition. Just before Ten

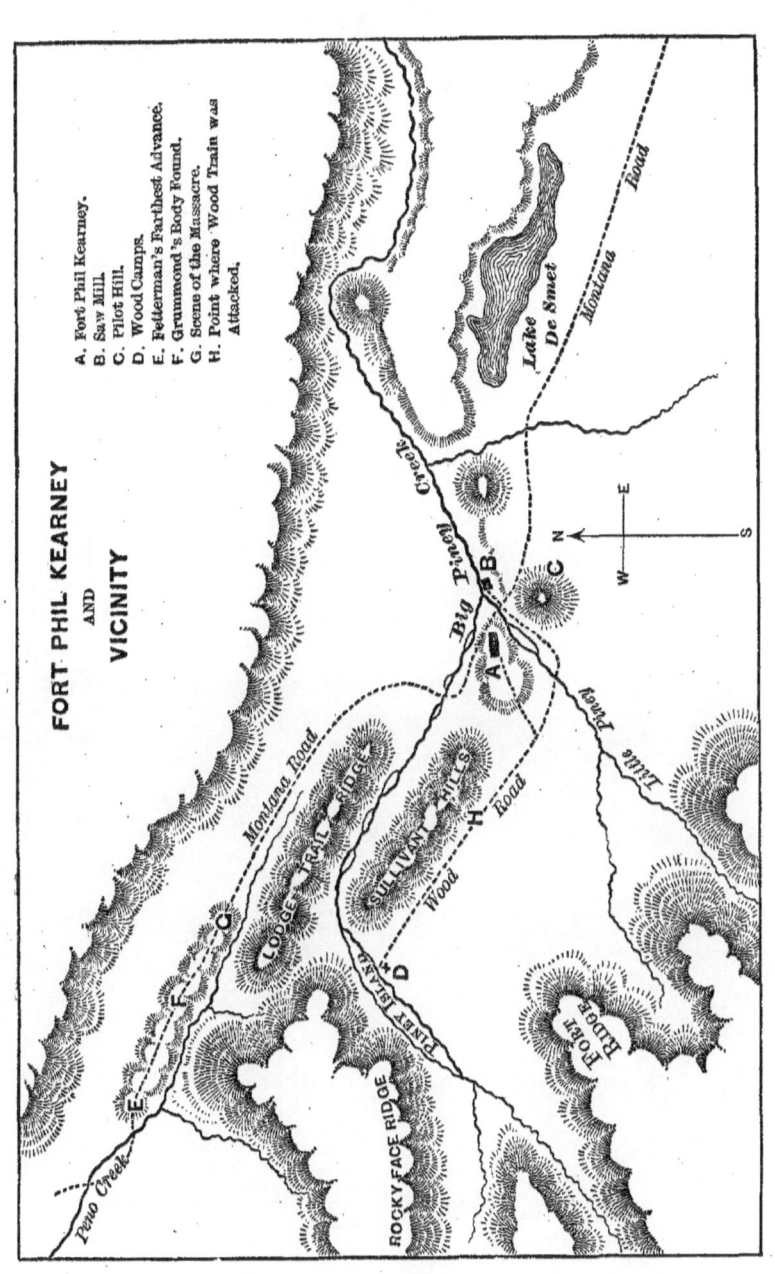

Eyck reached the summit of the ridge, at a quarter before one o'clock, two or three straggling shots were fired in the valley beyond; after that came silence. The struggle was evidently ended.

The relief party looked from the summit over the valley of Peno Creek. No soldiers were to be seen. The whole valley was filled with frenzied savages, who shook their weapons at the new arrivals, and challenged them to come down. A sergeant was despatched to the fort to report the situation and ask for a howitzer, which was not sent. For some cause, probably their losses, the Indians then began to withdraw from the valley of their own accord, and the relief party descended to the battle-field. The fight had taken place on a little ridge, three quarters of a mile in length, five to six miles from the fort, on the east side of Peno Creek, running parallel to it and to Lodge Trail Ridge, but beyond the latter. The road runs along its summit, rising to it opposite the northwestern extremity of Lodge Trail Ridge. Just beyond this point, on the road, a large number of Indians had been closely grouped when Ten Eyck's party first came in view, and here was the first intelligence of the ill-fated command which rode so gallantly from the fort but two hours before. Clustered on a space less than forty feet square were the bodies of Captain Brown, Colonel Fetterman, and sixty-five of the men. A more horrible sight could not be imagined. They were stripped naked, scalped, and so terribly gashed and mangled as to be almost unrecognizable. Years afterwards the Sioux showed a rough, knotty war-club of burr-oak, driven full of nails and spikes, which had been used to beat their brains out. It was still covered with brains and hair, glued to it in clotted blood. But with all the mutilation there were no signs of a struggle here. No empty cartridge shells were found around the bodies, though there were a few full cartridges. A few yards away the bodies of several of their horses were found, all heading towards the fort. All the appearances indicated that they had been suddenly overwhelmed by a rush of greatly superior numbers. Bulletholes through the left temples of Colonel Fetterman and Captain Brown, from weapons held so close that the powder had burned into their faces, showed that these officers had "saved a shot for themselves," as they had often said they would do, rather than fall into the hands of the Indians.

A messenger was sent to the fort for wagons, and his report, though meagre and indefinite, caused the hearts of the garrison to sink. After dark Ten Eyck's party returned, bringing forty-nine of the bodies, and the announcement that all were killed. No advance had been made, however, beyond the point where the bodies lay grouped, so that, while reasonably certain of the death of the others, there was no absolute assurance. The painfulness of the uncertainty was increased by the fact that among the bodies still unaccounted for was that of Lieutenant Grummond, the only married man of the detachment, whose wife was at the fort and in delicate health. The night of mourning and suspense passed away, and morning came. A party went out to learn the fate of the remaining members of Fetterman's command. They advanced cautiously to the point gained on the day before, and then on down the ridge. On the road, a quarter of a mile or more beyond the first pile of bodies, was found the corpse of Lieutenant Grummond. Still beyond, where the road made its abrupt descent to Peno Creek, were found the remains of half a dozen of the oldest and most experienced soldiers, with many empty cartridge shells scattered about them; and a little to one side, behind a pile of rocks, were the bodies of Wheatley and Fisher, with more than fifty empty shells by their sides, telling that they had not died tamely. Within a few hundred feet in front of this position were found ten dead ponies and sixty-five great gouts of blood, which had flowed from the death-wounds of as many Indians. No ponies and no blood-spots were found elsewhere. The bodies here were scalped and mutilated as the others, the mutilations being so shocking that they have never been made public, further than the general announcement that the bodies were gashed with knives, chopped with hatchets, and shot full of arrows; the rest is covered up in the statement that, "No such mutilation is on record." The bodies were brought in, and lay in ghastly array until the next Wednesday. The weather turned so intensely cold, on the night after the mas-

THE LAST STAND.

sacre, that the men who were digging the great grave for this heap of slain had to be relieved every half-hour, and the work went but slowly. On Wednesday they were laid away in their common resting-place, fifty feet long and seven feet deep, in the little cemetery at the foot of Pilot Hill.

Just what happened after Fetterman's command passed the top of Lodge Trail Ridge no one can say, for no man lived to tell it. The movement was in disobedience of orders, as directions were given, at least twice, not to pass the ridge. No one is left to tell why those orders were disobeyed, or how the snare was closed about the gallant band, or who attempted to fly, or who fought doggedly to the death. As read in the position of corpses, the record of cartridge shells, and the register of blood-stains, and confirmed by the Indians, it would seem that Fetterman moved down to the road with little resistance; that he advanced up the ridge beyond Peno Creek, leaving a part of his force at the crest to guard his rear, and followed down the road with the remainder; that at the farther end of the ridge the battle raged for almost an hour; that meantime a large force of the Indians, who numbered about two thousand, gathered in his rear at the other end of the ridge; that the ammunition of the majority of the soldiers became exhausted; that a retreat was determined on; that Wheatley, Fisher, and five or six of the older soldiers decided to remain where they were, either from the knowledge that retreat under such circumstances was certain death, or from a voluntary determination to stay behind and "stand off" the Indians until the others escaped; that the remainder, as they rode back, found themselves suddenly confronted by a force that made escape impossible; that Brown and Fetterman shot each other, and the rest were cut down by the savages. Only six of the entire command appeared to have been killed by bullets, a fact which indicates that their ammunition had been expended, and that the Indians could not be kept from coming to close quarters.

The Indians say that this massacre was accomplished by a special expedition, organized among the Minneconjous, under the direction of their head chief, High Back Bone. It was their intention to kill all of the garrison and destroy the fort, their hope being to decoy nearly all of the soldiers out, and, having massacred them, to attack the great stockade on all sides, as a small force would be unable to defend it. In addition to the Minneconjous, nearly all the warriors of the Upper Brulés, Ogallallas, Sans Arcs, Oncpapas, Two Kettles, Blackfoot Sioux, Northern Cheyennes, and Arapahoes, and stragglers from several other tribes, were on the war-path at the time, but only a part of them engaged in this affair. The party, as stated by the Indians, was composed of 350 lodges of Minneconjous, 100 lodges of Cheyennes, 100 of Arapahoes, 3 of Crows, and a part of the Ogallallas and Brulés, numbering in all about 2000 warriors. It will be observed that the percentage of warriors to a lodge, in a war-party, is much greater than under ordinary circumstances. When out for war the old men and women are left at home with the younger children. Only active squaws, and children old enough to be of service, accompany a war-party at any time, and very frequently only warriors go. The Indians say that Red Cloud was not in the attack, but had gone towards Fort Buford with his own band, the Oncpapas, and the others. They concede a loss of four Minneconjous, three Brulés, three Ogallallas, one Cheyenne, and one Arapaho, killed, and about sixty wounded, of whom several died and many were permanently maimed. They lost twelve horses killed, and fifty-six so severely wounded that they died within twenty-four hours. This estimate is unquestionably below the reality. There is scarcely a doubt that each of the sixty-five blood-spots on the field meant a dead Indian. Wounded Indians leave a battle-field with wonderful celerity, and one who cannot move, until he has bled freely, may safely be counted as dead or mortally wounded.

The tragedy was over, but who was to be blamed for it. There was a murmur from all the land, partly of rage against the Indians, and partly of disapproval of the military mismanagement that had made such a slaughter possible. A thorough investigation was ordered by General Grant. The off-hand impression was that the officer commanding at the post was in fault. He was at once superseded by Brevet Brigadier-general Wessels, then commanding at Fort Reno, who had orders to investigate. There was much said about Carrington at the time that was unjust and absurd—so much that it enabled him to pose as a martyr later on. The most remarkable statement was made by Indian Commissioner Bogy, who hastened to explain the affair without waiting to learn the facts. He demonstrated that the Indian force must have been small; that the only hostiles in that part of the country were a part of the Ogallallas, under Red Cloud, with a few individuals from other tribes; that the idea of the wood train being attacked by three hundred warriors, on December 6, was preposterous; that the statement that they challenged the troops to fight was a wild absurdity; that the only things that made the report credible at all were the corpses of the soldiers, which seemed to be in conflict with his theory. He accounted for them thus: "These Indians, being in absolute want of guns and ammunition to make their winter hunt, were on a friendly visit to the fort, desiring to communicate with the commanding officer, to get the order refusing them guns and ammunition rescinded, so that they might be enabled to procure their winter supply of buffalo. . . . I regret the unfortunate death of so many brave soldiers, yet there can be no doubt that it is owing to the foolish and rash management of the officer in command at that post."

RED CLOUD.

The matter of guns and ammunition was referred to because, in the preceding autumn, General Sherman had ordered Indian traders to discontinue the sale of weapons and ammunition to the Indians. This procedure raised the wrath of the Indian ring, for the greatest profit in the Indian trade is from this source. Commissioner Bogy explained how cruel and unnecessary the order was, as follows: "No Indian will buy two guns. One he absolutely needs; and as he has no means of taking care of powder, he necessarily will take, when offered to him, but a very limited quantity. It is true that formerly they hunted with bows and arrows, killing buffalo, antelope, and deer with the same; but to hunt successfully with bows and arrows requires horses, and as the valleys of that [the Powder River] country are now more or less filled with white men prospecting for gold and silver, their means of subsisting their horses have passed away, and they now have but few horses. I mention these facts so as to place before the country, as briefly as possible, the condition as well as the wants of the Indians." This statement, made so positively by Mr. Bogy, needs some correction. At that time, and for years before and afterwards, every plains Indian would buy as many guns and revolvers as possible, and would take all the ammunition he could get. Bows and arrows were still their favorite weapons for hunting buffalo, and were always carried, no matter how well armed they were otherwise. There were no white men prospecting in either the valleys or hills of the Powder River country, and the Indians had as many horses as ever, besides what they had stolen from the whites. Otherwise Mr. Bogy's statement appears proper enough. His theories about the Fetterman massacre are equally correct. His proposed remedy for any evil that might exist was to send out "a commission of judicious men."

The press, as usual, gave circulation to numerous wild stories concerning the affair, and made impossible pictures of the massacre. One even went so far as to report that the massacred men fell at the gates of the fort, begging for assistance, while the people on the inside dared not open the gates for fear the Indians would rush in. The commission which investigated the matter exonerated Carrington altogether, and the responsibility drifted over to his superior officer, General Cooke, commanding in the Department of the

Platte; at least, the latter was relieved by General Augur soon afterwards. Carrington was a good enough civil engineer, but he was a dress-parade style of officer, who would have been more in place as a teacher in a military school. He built a very nice fort, but every attack made on him and his men, during the building, was a surprise. There is nothing to indicate that he ever knew whether there were a thousand or only a hundred Indians within a mile of the fort. He seems to have disapproved of Indians. Perhaps he would have ostracized them socially, if he could have had his way. It is no excuse for this want of watchfulness to say that he had asked for reinforcements and not received them. He might have spared men enough from some of the ornamental work about the fort to have attended to that. Besides, he had been authorized, on August 11, to enlist fifty Indian scouts, on cavalry pay and allowances. The fact is, that reinforcements were not asked for the purpose of defending the fort and the work about it, but for an expedition of offence that had been instructed by General Cooke. There is nothing to show that Carrington apprehended any danger near the post. On December 19 he telegraphed Fort Laramie: "No special news since last report. Indians appeared to-day and fired on wood train, but were repulsed. They are accomplishing nothing, while I am perfecting all details of the post and preparing for active movements." That was all he said—no call for reinforcements; no worry about arms; all complacency and promise. Two days later he telegraphed: "Do send me reinforcements forthwith. Expedition now with my force impossible. . . . I hear nothing of my arms that left Leavenworth September 15. The additional cavalry ordered to join me has not reported. . . . I need prompt reinforcements and repeating arms. I am sure to have, as before reported, an active winter, and must have men and arms. Every officer of this battalion should join it. . . . Give me officers and men; only the new Spencer's arms should be sent; the Indians are desperate; I spare none (!) and they spare none." No more complacency; no more promise; only a recollection that he had asked for arms, ammunition, and reinforcements long before. It is but fair to say that no one fully realized and understood the feelings and intentions of the Indians; the news of the massacre came like a thunderbolt in the night, waking the whole nation from a sleep. But Carrington should have known more about the Indians in his immediate vicinity, and probably would, if he had paid more attention to them than firing shells into the woods to scare them away. There was fault everywhere. The Indian agents were wrong in misrepresenting the feeling of the Indians; so were the treaty commissioners. Carrington and Cooke were wrong in permitting the troops to go into a hostile country equipped as they were. Cooke, and officers higher up, were wrong in not seeing that arms, ammunition, and reinforcements were furnished when regularly called for.

After General Wessels took command at Phil Kearney, he undertook a winter campaign against the hostiles, but the weather was so intensely cold that it had to be abandoned. Neither side was able to make any movements of importance for several months. It was known that the Indians had attacked Fort Buford, at the mouth of the Yellowstone, five days after the massacre at Phil Kearney, and for two months it was commonly believed that the garrison had all been killed. Then messengers came through with the glad news that the one company of soldiers stationed there had beaten Red Cloud's army off, and held them back, until the cold drove them to their winter camps. In the spring a peace commission was sent out. It met Man Afraid of his Horses and others on June 12. They all said they had reformed, and were going to join Spotted Tail's Brulés; they wanted ammunition for hunting. They got no powder, and they fell from grace, if they had ever attained it. Hostilities were kept up all summer, with such vigor that the frontier was in continual alarm. The troops on the line of the Montana road had actually to fight for their wood and water, but they had one day of bloody revenge. On August 2 Major Powell, of Fort Phil Kearney, was guarding a wood train, on the road to the pinery, around the south side of the Sullivant Hills. He had divided his force, keeping thirty men in reserve in a little fortress, made of fourteen iron wagon-beds placed in a circle; the remainder were to retreat to this if attacked. Sud-

SIOUX VILLAGE IN WINTER

denly 800 Indian warriors swept down from the hills. The forces of the soldiers were separated; all fled to the fort except the reserve, in the corral of wagon-beds. At this the Indians rode, but the errors of 1866 had been remedied. The soldiers had breech-loading arms and plenty of ammunition. The Indians broke under their rapid and deadly fire, and drew off. Back in the hills were 1200 more of Red Cloud's warriors, who joined with the first attacking party and charged again, led by the great chief in person. The corral was a blaze of fire from the moment they came within five hundred yards, and the fire was far more effective than the Indians were used to, because they were massed together and hard to miss. Closer and closer they came, but there was no sign of giving way at the corral, and no cessation of that awful fire. The nerve of the Indians gave way, and they fled again. For three hours they kept at it, their courage always failing at the critical moment. Then they withdrew, and soon the little garrison was relieved by a party from the fort. They had lost but three killed and two wounded. The loss of the Indians was very heavy. A chief told Colonel Dodge that they had 1137 killed and wounded—but this is incredible. The Indians called it the "medicine fight," suspecting that their white friends had worked in some supernatural assistance.

In the fall the commission made up its report, and decided that the government had no right to put a road through the Powder River country. It cited Supreme Court decisions that have no bearing on the case, and made of importance ancient treaties that never existed. Nevertheless, their ideas prevailed. The country, and particularly the army, was anxious to have the Pacific Railroad completed, and the Indians would agree not to interfere with it, in consideration for our surrendering the Powder River country. With the railroad built, Montana would be more accessible from the south than from any other direction, and the Bozeman road would be of comparatively little use. Accordingly a treaty was made, at Fort Laramie, on April 29, 1868, relinquishing all claims to the country east of the Big Horn Mountains, in which all the chiefs joined, though the wary Red Cloud did not affix his name until November 6, when he had satisfactory assurance that the white man would keep his promises. In the summer of 1868 the troops abandoned the Montana road, whose opening had cost so much money and life, and the Sioux burned down the forts which had been planned with such mathematical nicety, and constructed in such architectural perfection. We gave up an unquestionable right, though perhaps not then worth asserting. A few years later we broke our faith and reasserted it. Then the work had to be done again.

CHAPTER XVI.

PUNISHING THE PIEGANS.

Of all the tribes within the Rocky Mountain region, the people of the Sakitapix or Blackfoot nation are most like the Eastern tribes, and this similarity is natural, for they are most probably an offshoot of the Algonquin family, and formerly lived much farther east. There are traces of their migration from above the sources of the Mississippi to the Upper Saskatchewan country, in which they lived when the era of credible history began with them. The two great branches of the Saskatchewan (Kisiskachewan—a Cree word, meaning swift current) rise in the Rocky Mountains, one about fifty miles and the other one hundred and eighty miles north of our line; they unite near longitude 105° West, and the main stream flows thence two hundred miles east to Lake Winnipeg. The home of the Blackfoot nation was between and about the two forks of the stream, when, before the whites had any acquaintance with them, the nation was separated by a great feud that arose on the death of their head chief, in battle with the Assinaboines. The older warriors followed the black banner of the hereditary claimant to the chieftaincy, but the younger ones generally ranged themselves under the red or bloody flag of a warrior who claimed succession by reason of prowess and ability. The supporters of the black-flag interest were defeated, and moved south to the Missouri. The migration was in the fall, after the prairies had burned over, and the black color received by their moccasins and leggings caused them to be called Satsika (Siksika), or Blackfeet, by the Crows. The victorious portion received the name of Kena (Kanaans) or Bloods. The Blackfeet were again divided through the ambition of a chief named Piegan (the Pheasant) who claimed the position of chief. He was defeated, and separated from the tribe, with his adherents, who were thereafter called Piegans (Peigans, Pagans, Pecaneaux). Later, the Gros Ventres of the North confederated with the Blackfeet. They were a band of Arapahoes who seceded from their tribe early in the current century, and after some ten years of wandering, during which they suffered severely at the hands of the Crows and Kootenays, they were relieved and taken into friendship by the Blackfeet.* In 1853 the numbers of these tribes were variously estimated as follows: Blackfeet, 250 to 500 lodges; Bloods, 350 to 400 lodges; Gros Ventres, 360 lodges; or a total of from 6500 to 12,000 souls. The lower estimates are probably more nearly correct. Their number at present is not definitely known, owing to the fact that they are partly in British America, but the most recent estimates are from 6000 to 7000. Those now in the United States are reported at 2300, and are consolidated under the name of Piegans; for comparison with the earlier population, 1100 Gros Ventres, who are now separated from the Piegans, must be added to this number.

These Indians were of high reputation as warriors, and esteemed themselves superior to the surrounding tribes, with whom they waged continual war. The men are tall Apollos, with large eyes and straight black hair. They pluck the beard from the face, and often remove the hair from the head, excepting the scalp-lock. Usually they were well clothed in garments made of dressed skins. The women are short and inclined to corpulency. The organization of the nation is quite complicated. Each tribe is divided into bands, and each band has a chief and a *mina maska,* or priest of the sun. Each tribe has a general council, called the Exkinoya, which meets once a year, when the tribe is assembled for the sun-dance and other religious ceremonies and festivities. The men are divided into seven ranks or degrees, according to their prowess, their skill, and their wisdom. Only members of the seventh or highest class are allowed in the Exkinoya, in which the legislative and judicial power of the tribe are centred.

---

* The Blackfoot Sioux have no connection with this nation. The similarity of name is purely accidental.

The sixth class includes the band chiefs, and entrance to it requires both valor and statesmanship. It is charged with the execution of the tribal laws. In enforcing orders, use is made of the entire police or "soldier" force of the tribe, including all unmarried warriors. The fifth class has charge of hunting and the moving of camps. The four lower classes mark merely the advancement of the warrior, as evinced by his deeds and ability. Four years is the ordinary time of probation required in each class, but this rule is sometimes broken over. Their chiefs are to some extent elective, but they have much regard for hereditary rank, especially if coupled with ability. In religion they are sun-worshippers, their deity being personified under the name of Napea. To this god they formerly offered annually a sacrifice of a young virgin, but this practice was long since abandoned, and of later years they have satisfied themselves with the mutilations of the sun-dance. Their religious nature is well developed, and their men have that peculiar dignity that is characteristic of the Indian in his wild state.

The Blackfeet have long had the reputation of being among the most treacherous and bloodthirsty of our savages, but it came chiefly from the statements of the tribes with whom they fought. This reputation has been widely extended through the "yellow-backed novel," that generally condemned, and more generally read, school-book of American youth, in which the Blackfeet are always at war and always very dangerous. As a matter of fact there was never any general or formal war between these people and the Americans. Their relations have been of a very friendly nature, Appleton's Encyclopædia to the contrary notwithstanding. In the early days of the fur trade they often fought with American trappers, but at that time they had no treaty with us, and considered the trapper an invader of their country, who was no better than a thief, for he came to take the furs which they were accustomed to gather and sell to the Hudson's Bay Company. In the struggle for supremacy between the rival fur companies, the Americans formed associations with the Nez Percés, Crows, and other enemies of the Blackfeet, and the latter, with other tribes, naturally fell under the influence

BLACKFEET AND TRAPPERS

of the British company, though there is little to show that they preferred the English personally to the Americans. The fight recounted by Irving, between them and Sublette's and other trappers, including Wyeth's party, which was brought on by the treachery of a Flathead and a half-breed, allies of the Americans, is a good example of the manner in which they were almost forced into a hostile attitude. Their early hostility to the trappers was also increased by the killing of one of their warriors by Mr. Lewis, of Lewis and Clarke's expedition. From similar causes, and from the fact that in stealing horses the Blackfeet made little distinction in owners, the unfriendly feeling became such that the American Fur Company was obliged to maintain a force of sixty or seventy men at its post on the Marias Driver.

The Blackfeet were cruel, in the manner of Indians, but not more so than their neighbors. An illustrative instance of this fact is recorded by Mr. Cox, who happened among the Flatheads at a time when they were torturing some Blackfoot prisoners. He says: "Having been informed that they were about putting one of their prisoners to death, I went to their camp to witness the spectacle. The man was tied to a tree; after which they heated an old barrel of a gun until it became red-hot, with which they burned him on the legs, thighs, neck, cheeks, and belly. They then commenced cutting the flesh from about the nails, which they pulled out, and next separated the fingers from the hand, joint by joint. During the performance of these cruelties the wretched captive never winced, and instead of suing for mercy, he added fresh stimulants to their barbarous ingenuity by the most irritating reproaches, part of which our interpreter translated as follows: 'My heart is strong. You do not hurt me. You can't hurt me. You are fools. You do not know how to torture. Try it again. I don't feel any pain yet. We torture your relations a great deal better, because we make them cry out loud, like little children. You are not brave; you have small hearts, and you are always afraid to fight.' Then, addressing himself to one in particular, he said, 'It was by my arrow you lost your eye;' upon which the Flathead darted at him, and with a knife in a moment scooped out one of his eyes; at the same time cutting the bridge of his nose nearly in two. This did not stop him; with the remaining eye he looked sternly at another, and said, 'I killed your brother, and I scalped your old fool of a father.' The warrior to whom this was addressed instantly sprang at him and separated the scalp from his head. He was then about plunging a knife in his heart, until he was told by the chief to desist. The raw skull, bloody socket, and mutilated nose now presented an horrific appearance, but by no means changed his tone of defiance. 'It was I,' said he to the chief, 'that made your wife a prisoner last fall; we put out her eyes; we tore out her tongue; we treated her like a dog. Forty of our young warriors—' The chieftain became incensed the moment his wife's name was mentioned; he seized his gun, and, before the last sentence was ended, a ball from it passed through the brave fellow's heart, and terminated his frightful sufferings. Shocking, however, as this dreadful exhibition was, it was far exceeded by the atrocious cruelties practised on the female prisoners; in which, I am sorry to say, the Flathead women assisted with more savage fury than the men."

On the other hand, while the Blackfeet were savages, they occasionally performed acts of unexpected generosity. Shortly before the arrival of Governor Stevens's party in the Blackfoot country, in 1853, a feud had arisen between the Blackfeet and Gros Ventres, on account of the murder of a Gros Ventre warrior by a member of the former tribe. The Gros Ventres retaliated, and open war resulted, during which several Gros Ventres were, captured by the enemy. They expected death by torture, but the Blackfeet fed them, treated them kindly, gave them horses, and sent them to their homes. This humane action paved the way for the reconciliation of these tribes, and a treaty between them and the tribes west of the main range, which Governor Stevens was desirous of effecting, and the Indians all agreed to meet him in council two years later. At this time, also, it was made apparent by the testimony of white men who had been among them, that the reports of their evil disposition had arisen from their hostile attitude towards the tribes with whom the Americans had been on terms of friendship. Mr. Doty summed up their feeling in 1853, thus: "Their present disposition towards the whites is unquestionably friendly. Undoubtedly a party of white men may travel through this country in perfect safety. The only danger would be that the Indians might take them for Indian enemies and rush upon them in the night. Their horses might be stolen, unless under the protection of a chief or an influential white man, one who is friendly and well known to them. The only white inhabitants of this country are the traders and employés at the American Fur Company's post, Fort Benton, and at Mr. Harvey's, or the opposition fort. These are on friendly terms with the Indians, as is evidenced by the fact that they are constantly sending traders with large quantities of goods to remote points in the Blackfoot country, who are not only permitted to go and come without molestation, bat are treated with much kindness and hospitality at the camps. The horses at this post [Benton] are always turned out to pasture without a guard, and are seldom or never stolen. So far as has been ascertained, their present relations with the Hudson's Bay Company are simply those of a limited trade, which is entirely confined to a portion of the Blackfeet and Blood bands. These Indians procure in the northern part of their territory a considerable number of small peltries, and in the summer-at which season they go farthest north—trade them at one of the Hudson's Bay Company's posts on the Saskatchewan River—'Chesterfield House,' I think. This trade is carried on for two reasons: First, because the Indians are paid there a higher price for their small peltries than is given by American traders. Secondly, they procure at that post an abundance of whiskey; and it is undoubtedly this latter consideration that induces them to go."

TRADER'S CAMP.

At this time the Bloods and Blackfeet occupied the country about the head-waters of the Marias and Milk rivers, as far north as latitude 50°; the Piegans were in the country between Milk River and the Missouri, on the Marias and Teton rivers; the Gros Ventres occupied the country between Milk River and the Missouri, from the mouth of the former to the country of the Piegans. All this region was well supplied with game, and the natural growth of grass afforded ample pasturage for the horses, of which these tribes owned many—about ten to each lodge. In character the land is much the same as the ordinary foot-hill country on the eastern slope of the Rockies, requiring irrigation for successful cultivation. The names given to its natural formations are usually Canadian French, instead of English or Spanish, as at the South. A divide or watershed is called a coteau; a table-land, or mesa, is always a plateau; a hill is a butte; a gulch, ravine, or arroyo is a coulie. The name teton (a breast) is also sometimes given to hills, and the probability is that the Teton tribes had their name from the French fur-traders.

In October, 1855, Governor Stevens met with the tribes on the Upper Missouri, near the mouth of Judith River. The Indians attended, as they had promised two years before. There were represented the Bloods, Blackfeet, Piegans, Gros Ventres, Flatheads, Pend d'Oreilles, Kootenays, and Nez Percés. Common amity was declared by the United States and these tribes, and the Indians also agreed not to make war against any other tribe except in self-defence. A great common hunting-ground was agreed upon, east of the main range, between the Mussel-shell and the Yellowstone, to which all the tribes were to have access, but in which none were to reside. White men were given the right of travelling unmolested everywhere, and the government was conceded the privilege of making roads of any description, through any part of the country. All the land north of the Mussel-shell and Missouri rivers, between the main range and a line drawn north from the mouth of Milk River, was declared to be "the territory of the Blackfoot nation, over which said nation shall exercise exclusive control." In consideration for the rights relinquished, the government was to pay the Blackfoot nation $20,000 annually for ten years; the further sum of $15,000 annually, for ten years, was to be expended "in establishing and instructing them in agricultural pursuits, and in educating their children, and in any other respect promoting their civilization and Christianization."

Under this treaty the Indians preserved a strict peace with the whites, though there was a disposition to carry on war with the Crows and Assinaboines. The Bloods were at first determined to pay no attention to their promises, as to these Indians; but on finding that the Piegans and Gros Ventres were standing firmly by the treaty, they abandoned their designs, and thereafter the only troubles between the tribes were occasioned by young men who would not listen to the advice of their chiefs and older warriors. These gradually decreased in frequency, and faith with the government was so admirably preserved that, in 1860, the Blackfeet were pronounced "the most peaceable nation on the Missouri River." Their annuities were brought up on boats each year, and distributed to them. Farming was tried by the agency people, but without success. The climate was too dry to permit successful farming without irrigation, and there was no money to be applied to making ditches. The money promised for schools might well have been used for that purpose, for they had no schools and no missions. It would be interesting to know what became of that $150,000. The Indians subsisted as before, wholly by the chase. One chief tried to cultivate eight or ten acres, but his crops failed, and he quit in disgust. This appears from the official records to have been the only step made towards that education for which $15,000 annually was agreed to be expended. Just at the close of the ten years, in October, 1865, the agent for the Blackfeet reported: "The moral condition of the Indians in this country is truly lamentable. Not one spark of civilization appears to have dawned upon their ignorant minds, and their capacity for improvement, if they ever had any, seems to have risen and set in total darkness." And yet he closes the same paragraph with the following sentence, which is one of the most touching expressions extant of the fervent, unconquerable faith of the average Indian agent: "Let us hope that success will yet crown our efforts to ameliorate the condition of these unfortunate and degraded savages, and place them and their children on the road to a better, brighter, and more glorious future." There has been a sorry crown for all the efforts made thus far.

During our civil war even the state of peaceful savagery into which the Blackfeet had lapsed was disturbed. The troubles with the Sioux prevented the Blackfoot annuities from reaching their destination. The tribes fell out among themselves and fought one another. The Sun River farm, as the agricultural experiment in their country was called, fell into decay, but the agency farmer made a comfortable living by keeping hotel and trading with the Indians. The gold discoveries of 1862-63 attracted a large white population to the southern borders of the Blackfoot country, and the newcomers furnished the Indians with all the whiskey they would pay for. There was still no war with the whites, who ran through the country at will, without molestation. In the spring of 1864 the Blackfeet showed their good-will by offering to aid General Sully in fighting the Sioux. In May of this year the white population had so increased that Montana was cut off from Idaho and organized as a separate territory. In December, 1864, trouble arose with the Bloods. A band of fourteen of them stole the horses of twenty white trappers, who were hunting near the Little Rocky Mountains. Nine of the trappers followed them, overtook them at daylight, killed two of them, and recovered the horses. From that time on, bad feeling increased among the Bloods. In April, 1865, they stole forty horses from Fort Benton. On May 10 they stole all the horses and mules from Sun River farm, and that school for agricultural instruction was abandoned. On May 22 a party of drunken white men at Fort Benton attacked a party of Bloods, who came there, and killed three of them. Three days later a large party of Bloods attacked ten white men, who were cutting logs on the Marias, and killed every one of them. These hostilities were all confined to a small portion of the Bloods, whose homes were properly in British America. The Blackfeet proper, the Gros Ventres, and the Piegans all retnained at peace, a matter of no little importance at that time, on account of the large amount of freighting that was being done from the month of Milk River to Fort Benton, there being two hundred and fifty wagons steadily engaged in this business.

In the fall of 1865 Agent Upson made a new treaty with the Sakitapix, which was never ratified: the Indians, it was claimed, having gone to war before the treaty reached Washington. There was not, in fact., any war, except one between the Piegans and Gros Ventres, resulting from reciprocal horse-

"NO HORSES TO SPARE."

stealing. There were no troops in the country to protect any one or enforce any order. The country contained many lawless white men. The better class of whites formed vigilance committees to protect themselves against both white and Indian marauders. The Gros Ventres had preserved a closer intimacy with the whites than the Piegans had, and in January two white men who happened to be in company with Gros Ventres were killed by Piegans. With horse-stealing, intertribal war, occasional raiding by the Bloods, and no troops, things went from bad to worse until the feeling of the white population was that the Blackfoot nation, excepting the Gros Ventres, was at war, but, in truth, the Blackfeet proper had gone into British America prior to the treaty, and had nothing to do either with the treaty or the subsequent troubles. A militia organization of five or six hundred men was made, for the protection of the settlements, but they never took the field against any of these Indians. In April, 1866, a party, supposed to be North Piegans, burned the buildings at the Sun River farm. In June, 1866, Little Dog, head chief of the Piegans, who had labored faithfully to preserve peace, returned to the Indian agent twelve horses that had been stolen from the whites. As he was returning to his camp he was ambushed by some of his own warriors, and he and his son were killed. There were several other acts of violence during the year, but hostilities were brought to a close by the orders stopping the sale and issue of ammunition, on account of the Sioux war over the Montana road, coupled with the nonissuance of supplies that had been expected under the new treaty. The Indians, with their usual improvidence, had made no adequate preparations for the winter of 1866–67, and they suffered much from want in that season, in consequence of which they were in a more peaceable condition in the following year. Both military and Indian authorities who investigated the situation in 1867 pronounced the apprehensions of war without foundation, which was true enough then. People were travelling the road from Helena to Fort Benton, and thence to Cow Island, without being troubled in the least. There was a party of ten emigrants killed in this year, but within the British line, and by Bloods. The fact is that no considerable portion of the Blackfoot nation had been hostile to the whites since 1853, nor were at any subsequent period. In 1867 the Gros Ventres were separated from the Blackfoot nation and placed with the River Crows, where they have since remained.

The years 1867 and 1868 passed with a peaceful condition of affairs in the Blackfoot nation. The whiskey-trade flourished at Fort Benton as it had never flourished before. Some of the Bloods and Blackfeet stole horses and sold them to the Hudson's Bay Company, but the southern bands returned many stolen horses to the whites, so that a reasonable balance was preserved. Three annual appropriations, of $7000 each, were made under the treaty of 1865, and in the fall of 1868 another treaty was made, which was not ratified, but for several years appropriations of $50,000 were made for the education and civilization of the nation. So far as subsistence was concerned, they were supposed to be taking care of themselves, but in reality what they did receive, which was not very much, was in supplies. The lawless part of the white population continued to act in a way that would bring on war if the Indians had any spirit. While the Piegans were at Fort Benton, in 1868, after signing the treaty, two white men assaulted and shot at Mountain Chief, the principal chief of the tribe, which produced a very angry feeling among them. Special Commissioner Cullen tried to have these men arrested, but, rather than take any part in such an unusual proceeding, the sheriff and justice of the peace at that point resigned their offices. The Indians soon after stole eighty horses from the whites at Diamond City, and other points, on account of which eighteen Piegans were seized by Cullen and held until the horses were returned. An attempt to enforce the intercourse laws was repressed in a most effective way. The principal witness who had been subpœnaed to testify in the matter of a seizure of two bales of buffalo robes, that had been purchased with whiskey, was followed by men from Fort Benton and hung until he was nearly dead, in consideration of which he agreed to leave the country in silence.

The year 1869 was ushered in with a bad state of feeling, which had been produced by the evil deeds of bad men on both sides, and this feeling grew worse during the summer. That part of the Indians were stealing horses was not even questioned by the tribes. The chiefs said it was done by men whom they could not control, and that they could not return the horses, because they were run off into British America and sold. Edmonton House and Mountain House, both on the Saskatchewan, were the two posts of the Hudson's Bay Company at which this traffic was carried on principally. It was shown by the affidavits of half a dozen white men, who had lived in the vicinity of these posts, that the trade was a regular and notorious one. It was shown that the factors of the company well knew that the horses were stolen, and that Hickland, the chief trader at the Mountain House, encouraged the thievery, and told the Indians what kind of horses he wanted them to get for him. All of the best of these horses were kept by the officers and employés of the company. Wells, Fargo, & Co. involuntarily supplied our neighbors over the line with seventy-three animals during 1868 and 1869. An officer of the company drove a fine pair of grays, bearing the "W., F., & Co." brand, and another pair was used in one of the company's grist-mills. From other parties there were reported stolen, during the summer and fall of 1869, two hundred and twenty-seven horses and mules, nearly all of which went into British America. It was also shown that the company sold the Indians arms and ammunition, in any quantity desired. The only way in which our government could reach this evil was by punishing the Indians, but there was another evil which might have been mitigated, at least, if proper attention had been given to it.

The misconduct of white men still continued, and gave the Indians a ready excuse for their misdeeds. In fact, nearly all of the horse-stealing occurred after barbarities which had been committed by these lawless people. All of the government authorities saw this wrong, and tried to have it righted, but the force which was authorized was directed against the Indians, and the settlements were left to purge themselves by natural progress. General Sully, Superintendent of Indian affairs, wrote, on August 3, 1869: "There is a white element in this country which, from its rowdy and lawless character, cannot be excelled in any section, and the traffic in whiskey with Indians in this territory is carried on to an alarming extent. This frequently causes altercations between whites and Indians, resulting often in bloodshed; and as they occur in sections where the civil authorities acknowledge themselves to be powerless to act, nothing but military force can at present put a stop to it. . . . From reliable reports, that increase daily, it is a wonder to me that open war with the Indians has not broken out already. . . . Nothing can be done to insure peace and order till there is a military force here strong enough to clear out the roughs and whiskey-sellers in the country." General Hardie, who was sent out by General Sheridan to investigate, testified to the same thing, in these words: "There are unprincipled and unscrupulous men of all classes who speak and act without reference to the truth and right, in pursuit of their private ends or the gratification of their passions. . . . There are plenty of lawless and unprincipled men upon the border who supply Indians with whiskey surreptitiously, if not openly, in defiance of the law." General De Trobriand, commanding in Montana, said: "There is in the territory a certain number of people whose pecuniary interest is intimately connected with the Indian trade, licit or illicit. Therefore they are averse to any Indian policy which can hurt their purse."

With these surroundings in view, the rise of the Piegan troubles of 1869 are simple of explanation. The Piegans of Mountain Chief's band, still smarting under the attack on him, were openly hostile; and they were aided and abetted by the bands of Bear Chief, Red Horn, and some others. On July 16, 1869, some of these Indians, while stealing horses, killed two white men near Fort Benton. In retaliation the whites there hung two suspected Piegans, and, a few days later, murdered an old man and his nephew, who were generally known to be innocent and inoffensive people. Depredations at once grew numerous. Horses were stolen everywhere. A freight train was attacked on Eagle Creek; one man and twenty oxen were killed before the Indians were driven off, with a loss of four of their warriors. On August 17 great excitement was caused by the murder of Malcolm Clarke, and the wounding of his son, at their ranch, twenty miles above Helena. It was re-

EDMONTON HOUSE.

ported that the place had been attacked by hostiles, and wild rumors of war prevailed for a time, but the opinion soon gained ground that the murder was due to a family quarrel. Clarke had married a Piegan woman, and was killed by a nephew of hers, named Peter, a notorious ruffian, of a very quarrelsome disposition. He was shunned by his own people on account of having killed his father-in-law, Bear's Head, a brother of the Chief, Heavy Runner. There were some twenty Piegans present at the time, among them Pal, a son of Mountain Chief, who, in the melée, shot one of Clarke's sons. Another son of Clarke escaped unharmed, as did also Miss Clarke, an estimable young woman, who leaped through a window and fled during the quarrel. Young Clarke, who was left for dead by the Indians, afterwards recovered. The excitement in the settlements cooled down for a time, but in September it was raised again by the murder of James Quail, near Silver City. It was reported at the time that he was scalped and mutilated, and no doubt was entertained that the Piegans were guilty of the crime. Later reports established the untruthfulness of the report of scalping, and mutilation. His horse was found near him, and, as it was known that he had a valuable watch and four or five hundred dollars with him, the presumption arose that he had been murdered by some white man. Still, many believed that Indians had committed the crime, and it was reported as talked among the Piegans that a warrior named Little Eagle was the murderer. There were two stage-robberies in the early fall, but it was definitely learned that they were the work of white bandits. The horse-stealing lessened perceptibly after the Clarke tragedy. It was learned later on that the hostile bands had left the vicinity of the settlements about September 1, part of them going to the Yellowstone, and part to the North. The friendly Piegans remained on the Marias.

The military authorities had been called on for assistance, by the Indian Bureau, in August, and again in October. They investigated carefully at the outset, and gave General Sully full opportunities to have the murderers surrendered, and stolen property given up, before taking any steps. It was determined to do nothing until the hostiles returned to the

Marias, which they were expected to do in January or February, but for some cause they came back about the middle of December. Within ten days after their return a party of ten hunters was attacked near the head of Sun River Valley, thirty mules were stolen from a government contractor at Dearborn, and the cabin of a wood-chopper, near Camp Cooke, was robbed, the last resulting in a fight. It was decided to strike, them at once, as this could be done without interfering with the peaceable Indians. The Blackfeet were all in British America. The Bloods were in two parties, one across the British line, and one above the Red Coulie, on the Marias. The Piegans were on the same stream, but lower down, and in separate bands, the hostiles being located at the Big Bend. The camps of Heavy Runner, Big Lake (Big Leg), Little Wolf, and The Boy were ordered to be left unmolested, as these chiefs had proven themselves friendly. Only the camps of Mountain Chief, Bear Chief, and Red Horn were to be struck. The expedition was put in charge of Colonel E. M. Baker, of the 2d Cavalry, at Fort Ellis. He left that post on January 6, with four companies of cavalry, and proceeded to Fort Shaw, at which point he was reinforced by two companies of mounted infantry, and departed thence to the north on the 19th.

The weather was intensely cold, and, as the success of the expedition depended largely on its secrecy, the marching was done at night after reaching the Teton River, on the 19th. On the night of the 20th the command proceeded to the mouth of Muddy Creek, a tributary of the Teton. On the night of the 21st they marched across the country towards the Big Bend of the Marias, but were unable to reach it. They lay all that day in a ravine, on the Dry Fork of the Marias, and at night marched on again. About eight o'clock on the morning of the 23d they reached the camp of Bear Chief and Red Horn, consisting of thirty-seven lodges, in the valley of the Marias. The attack was a complete surprise. Smallpox had broken out among the Indians, causing them to omit even the slight precautions that they would have naturally observed in a secure winter camp. The herd of ponies, over 300 in number, was cut off and secured. 173 In-

FORT BENTON.

dians, including Red Horn, were killed. Only 9 escaped from the place. All the rest, men, women, and children, were either killed or captured. Leaving Lieutenant Doane with a detachment to destroy the camp, Colonel Baker hastened down the river in search of Mountain Chief's camp, which was said to be four miles away, but he found nothing until he had gone sixteen miles, and then only seven deserted lodges. These were destroyed, and the command then marched to the post of the Northwest Fur Company, near the Red Coulie, where the Blood chiefs were summoned, and required to give up the stolen horses in their possession, after which the troops returned to their quarters. The captives that had been taken were released at once, on learning that the smallpox was among them, and found their way to other camps. Thus far the details of the "Piegan War" are as stated above, by the concession of all parties concerned, but beyond this there is some controversy, and the matter has been left in that undecided state which forces a recourse to the calculation of probabilities.

The principal point in dispute was the age and sex of the persons killed. The report from the Indians was first received, it having been collected from them by Lieutenant Pease, their agent, and was as follows: "Of the 173 killed on the 23d, 33 were men; of these, 15 only were such as are called by them young, or fighting, men; these were between the ages of twelve and thirty-seven; the remaining 18 were between the ages of thirty-seven and seventy; 8 of the latter were between the ages of sixty and seventy; 90 were women— 35 between the ages of twelve and thirty-seven, and 55 between the ages of thirty-seven and seventy; the remaining 50 were children, none older than twelve years, and many of them in their mothers' arms. Out of 219 belonging to Red Horn's camp, only 46 survived; among them are 9 young men who escaped during the attack, and 5 who were away hunting. The lives of 18 women and 19 children (none of them more than three years of age, and the majority of them much younger), some of whom were wounded, were spared by the soldiers. Red Horn himself was killed. At the time of the attack this camp was suffering severely with smallpox, having had it among them for two months, the average rate of deaths among them having been six daily." The original report of Colonel Baker was limited, in this regard, to the statement: "The result of the expedition is 173 Indians killed, over 100 prisoners, women and children." He never furnished a detailed report of the sex and age of the killed, such as General Sherman said was "proper and usual," any further than the following, by telegraph: "I am satisfied that the following numbers approximate as nearly to the exact truth as any estimate can possibly be made. That the number killed was 173. Of these there were 120 able men, 53 women and children; that of captives (afterwards released), there were of women and children 140." At least, no further report was submitted to the House of Representatives, which called on the War Department for all papers and correspondence connected with the affair. On February 3, General De Trobriand wrote, presumably from the information he had been able to acquire by that time: "The execution was made against 36 lodges, and there 173 were killed; about 100 squaws and pappooses were captured, and, after the action, turned loose unhurt."

It is apparent that both the first and second satements are exaggerated, and probable that the information on which the third was based was somewhat colored. As to the first, if the Indians had been dying at the rate of six a day, for two months, the camp would have been completely depopulated before the troops reached it. As to the second, the estimate of 120 able men, out of a total of 313, is a proportion that was never known to exist in any winter camp in the country. As established by all preceding and succeeding estimates and censuses of the Blackfoot nation, the ordinary proportion of warriors was two to each lodge, a lodge being estimated at seven people. The variations from this proportion in any recorded enumeration are very slight. We would therefore naturally expect, in a village of 37 lodges, 259 people; of whom 74 would be warriors. Smallpox might have decreased this total to 219, as stated by the Indians, but there is scarcely a possibility that there should have been only 29 fighting men belonging to the band, as stated by them, *i. e.,* 15 killed, 9 escaped, and 5 absent. The fair inference from all considerations, it being remembered that Colonel Baker's statement purports to be an estimate only, and that the examination of a camp in which there was smallpox would probably be brief, is that about 60 of the killed were warriors, and 113 women and children. The number of nominal captives was not probably more than 85.

The attack on the Piegans created a sensation in the East, or, more properly, a sensation was created by a letter of Vincent Colyer's, concerning it, which found its way into print. What Lieutenant Pease had reported merely as the statement of the Indians, this letter stated as fact, in these direct terms : "The facts were received to-day from Lieutenant W. B. Pease, United States Army, the agent of the Blackfeet, and is endorsed by General Sully, United States Army." This was a palpable misrepresentation. Lieutenant Pease expressly stated the sources of his information, and General

Sully's endorsement said: "The report that Lieutenant Pease sends is entirely what the Indians say of the affair, and of course it is natural to suppose it is prejudiced in their own favor. It is the Indians' side of the question, and, as I am here as their only representative, I consider it my duty to give them a hearing." On Mr. Colyer's letter the action of the troops was severely criticised in Congress, as it would probably have been also on the facts, for the criticism was addressed to the manner of making war which involved the killing of women and children. Said Mr. Voorhees: "When the Indians were a power in this land we made war on them according to civilized warfare. We struck them in manly battle. Now, when they are poor, broken, and miserable remnants, corrupted and demoralized, it is proposed to change our mode of warfare, and smite not merely the warrior, but the woman and the babe in her arms. I have thought much on this subject, and the more I think of it the more it fills me with horror. If, however, we are to change the policy of the government, let it go forth to the country now; . . . if the administration is to call home its peaceful agents who are endeavoring to civilize the Indians, and to send instead the sword and the fagot into their midst, when they are in their lodges, in the dead of winter; to strike them when dying of disease, sparing neither mother nor babe, till the scream of the last expiring infant shall be heard in its helpless agony on the gale, then avow it, avow it here, avow it boldly, and say that Indian warfare in these days means extermination—extermination without regard to age, sex, condition, or health, or anything else that usually protects non-combatants in war."

Mr. Mungen said: "In looking at the accounts of the inhuman sacrifices of those 'savages' who were women and children, I cannot see in it any mercy, or justice, or humanity, or Christianity, or any godlike attributes. As for the savages who murder and destroy our women and children, I would fight them to the last, but I would not torture even them; and I certainly would not jump upon a little Indian child, having the smallpox, and kill it." The debate, which was in Committee of the Whole, resulted in nothing but a call for the correspondence from the War and Interior departments, it having been shrewdly treated as a Democratic attack on General Sheridan, by the friends of the administration, although a Republican began the criticism and others aided in it. There was an attempt made also to interpose General Hancock, then commanding the Department of Dakota, as the responsible superior officer. In truth, General Sheridan was the responsible superior, he having sent Inspector-General Hardie to Montana to investigate, and, on receiving his report, having issued instructions to him, on January 15, in these words: "If the lives and property of citizens of Montana can best be protected by striking the Indians, I want them struck. Tell Baker to strike them hard."

LIEUTENANT-GENERAL P.H. SHERIDAN.

Neither General Sheridan nor any other officer advocated or defended any unnecessary killing of women and children, although they justified the attack. Colonel Baker reported: "I believe that every effort was made by officers and men to save non-combatants, and that such women and children as were killed were killed accidentally." General De Trobriand reported: "Quarter was given to all known in time as women and children." General Sheridan, after referring to women and children who save themselves during the bombardment of cities by hiding in cellars, said: "Should any of the women and children of the Piegans have lost their lives, I sincerely regret that they had not similar places of refuge, though I doubt if they would have availed themselves of them, for they fight with more fury than the men." General Sherman said: "There is no question at all of responsibility, save and except only as to whether Colonel Baker wantonly and cruelly killed women and children unresisting, and this I never believed." With all this unanimity of sentiment, and though Baker may not have directed it, it seems impossible that so many women and children should be necessarily killed, whether the number was 53, as estimated by the military, or 140, as claimed by the Indians, or a medium between these extremes, as is most probable. 173 Indians are too many to be necessarily killed out of thirty-seven lodges, especially when the only casualty to the attacking party was one man killed. Whether the results justified it is another question, but there is hardly room for doubt that but for the determined stand of all the officers in defence of the action, the attack on the Piegan village would have rested in the same category with Sand Creek.

To the conservative mind the justice of the criticisms made will depend largely on the question whether there was or was not existing a state of war. If there were, the military view that a single effective blow is the most humane way of ending a war, is certainly worthy of consideration. If not, the movement should have been confined to the arrest of criminals. As to this there was a difference of opinion. On August 18, when the first reports of the killing of Clarke reached him, General Sully telegraphed: "I fear we will have to consider the Blackfeet in a state of war." With subsequent reports his opinions changed, and on January 13 he thought that all difficulties might be ended by the seizure of Mountain Chief and half a dozen of his warriors. On October 6, General De Trobriand said: "The first fact, which I think must be admitted by all, is that there is actually *no Indian war* in the territory," and he then favored the arrest of a few men, as an adequate measure. With the depredations in December his opinions changed, and in January he favored chastising the hostile bands. General Hardie, at the latter period, thought a single severe blow "would be more sparing of blood, and better on all accounts," but he reported the facts and the opinions of both sides impartially, with the question: "Under all the circumstances, how far should the opinion of General Sully, as to scope of operations, govern the military?" To this General Sheridan replied by the telegraphic instructions above quoted, and the attack was made in pursuance of his order. In connection with the question as to the propriety of indiscriminate attack, it is to be remembered that Mountain Chief and the worst of the offenders, as conceded by all, escaped altogether. It is also noteworthy, as a probable result of the criticism, that there has not occurred since that time any such indiscriminate attack. However just may be the feeling of some that this method is the more effective, and therefore the more humane, the general sentiment of the country is against it. As Mr. Voorhees said: "It cannot be justified here or before the country; it cannot be justified before the civilization of the age, or in the sight of God or man."

Since the infliction of this severe punishment there has been no trouble reported from the Piegans, though they have had ample cause for it. While this result is to some extent attributable to that punishment, it is more largely explained by other things. Indians are usually obedient to their own laws; the lawlessness that white men object to arises from the fact that their laws differ from ours, and from the fact that our laws have not covered offences committed among them. The Indian tribes have been left to regulate their own behavior so long as they did not interfere with the whites. If a tribe had good laws the results were always beneficial, but with those whose laws were of a barbarous type there have occurred many crimes, from our stand, for which there was no redress. The Blackfeet, as has been mentioned, had a remarkably complete tribal organization, and when this was supplemented by a code of good laws, which they were induced to adopt in 1875, a most admirable state of quietude resulted. Their code prohibits intemperance, polygamy, sale of women, theft, and assault. Murder is punished by death. Their police force has executed these laws effectively. Not only this, but they have arrested a number of Indian and white criminals, who had committed crimes in the settlements and undertaken to escape across the reservation.

The Sakitapix have not advanced much in civilization, but what advance they have made has been due to their own efforts. They were assigned to the Methodist Church for missionary work, but none has been done among them. An alleged government school has been reported as being in operation at their agency for some fifteen years, at an expense of $1200 a year, paid out of their appropriations, and satisfactory results have been reported from year to year; but in 1884 comes the statement that sixteen of the Blackfoot nation—think of it, sixteen!—can actually read, and that fourteen of these have learned all of that during the past year. We have then, presumably, two children taught to read as the result of the work of the fourteen years previous, and an outlay of some $17,000. It is a great achievement to get $8500 worth of reading into one child's head. He ought to become an elocutionist of high degree—an ornament to any reservation. The chances are about one hundred to one that the Indians have been robbed by their agents, but it is also evident that the aid given them by the government has been inadequate. It is a fact that ought to be considered a reproach to the nation that peaceable tribes, as a rule, have received little assistance, no matter what their needs may be or their services have been. As to this nation, the statistical tables have furnished information which on its face is unreliable, but still is enough to show something of their sufferings from want. The deaths have repeatedly been in excess of the births, and in 1884 the terrible disproportion was reached of 247 deaths, chiefly from starvation and its concomitant ills, against 46 births. It has not needed statistical tables to prove their wretched lot; again and again the newspapers have published the item: "The Piegans are reported to be starving, notwithstanding the assistance furnished them by the government," and similar brevities. It is notorious that we have been starving these people, and it is true that Congress, which waxed so furious over the slaughter of a few dozens of women and children, is largely responsible for the death of a much greater number, by the more lingering and more cruel mode.

There has been no excuse for this neglect. The matter has been called to the attention of Congress several times, in the most urgent language, and Congress, in response, has cut down their appropriation. From 1871 to 1878 the appropriation was $50,000 annually; in the latter year it was cut to $40,000; in 1881 it was cut again to $35,000. All the expenses of the reservation, including the pay of from six to eight employés and teachers, were paid out of this sum. At the same time their other sources of support have been decreasing even more rapidly. The buffalo, which was formerly their main reliance, is entirely gone, and other game has so decreased that it can no longer be counted on for material support. The situation has been growing worse constantly until, in 1884, R. A. Allen, who took charge of the agency on April 1 of that year, reported as follows: "When I entered upon the duties of agent I found the Indians in a deplorable condition. Their supplies had been limited, and many of them were gradually dying of starvation. I visited a large number of their tents and cabins the second day after they had received their weekly rations, looked through them carefully, and found no provisions, except in two instances. All bore marks of suffering from lack of food, but the little children seemed to have suffered most; they were so emaciated that it did not seem possible for them to live long, and many of them have since passed away. To feed these Indians, about 2300 in number, from April 1 to June 30, I had 19,080 pounds bacon, 44,700 pounds beef, and 62,565 pounds flour, being only 1½ ounces bacon, 3½ ounces beef, and less than 5 ounces flour per day for each individual. I had no beans, rice, hominy, salt, nor any other articles of food, except sugar, tea, and coffee (of which I had only enough for the sick and infirm) to give them, the supply of such articles having been exhausted before this time, nor have I yet [August 14] received any. In the fore part of May I was reduced to such a strait that I was compelled to issue over 2000 pounds of bacon which had been condemned by a board of survey the past winter, but which I found not to be in as bad condition as had been supposed. In the latter part of June and fore part of July, so great was their destitution that the Indians stripped the bark from the saplings that grow along the creeks and ate the inner portion to appease their gnawing hunger." Do you grasp the dreadful import of these words? Here, in free America, in the year of grace 1884, when a surplus of so many millions had accumulated in the national treasury that financiers were frightened, this occurred, and nothing was done to relieve their sufferings. If the people had understood this, and had known how to reach the Piegans, they would doubtless have responded as cheerfully and as liberally to their cry of distress as they have to the calls of the famine-stricken elsewhere, but they did not. We have been trusting our authorized representatives to look after such things, and they have not done it. We ought to have known it, or rather it ought never to have occurred. There is something radically and horribly wrong in the management of Indian affairs to make such a thing possible. The Board of Indian Commissioners ought to assume the responsibility of calling on the people for aid in such a case, and it would be well if standing committees were appointed in each state and territory where Indians live, to see that such destitution is promptly reported to the Board.

An adequate relief of these Indians is not merely a matter of humanity and charity. We owe it to them to put a stop to this worse than inquisitorial cruelty. We confirmed to them by treaty, in 1855, all the land north of the Mussel-shell and Missouri rivers, from the mouth of Milk River to the main range of the Rockies, and to them, in common with other tribes, hunting-grounds between the Yellowstone and

SUMMER CAMP ON MARIAS RIVER.

the Mussel-shell, from the Rockies to Twenty-five Yard Creek. Under the unratified treaties of 1866 and 1868, and the executive orders of July 5, 1873, and August 19, 1874, we took from them all the land between the Mussel-shell and the Marias, as well as their hunting-grounds below—the best hunting-grounds they had—for which we gave them nothing but the annuities mentioned. By Act of Congress of April 15, 1874, the reservation was made to include only the land north of the Missouri and the Marias, from the western line of Dakota to the main range of the Rockies, and the eastern part of this was reserved for the Gros Ventres and River Crows, who are located there. It is true that the reservation was increased by executive order of April 13, 1875, but nearly all the increase was restored to the public domain by executive order of July 13, 1880. We took their land because we had power to do so; they were the wards of the nation, and the nation could do as it pleased. If an ordinary guardian should thus appropriate his ward's property the courts would not be slow in forcing him to disgorge, but there is no court, except the people, to supervise the doings of the Indians' guardian. Did the Blackfeet object to this? Certainly they did, but their protest availed them nothing. Not only did these orders take away their lands, but they left the reservation buildings outside the reservation, and new ones had to be built out of the miserable pittance—four cents a day to each individual—provided for their education, civilization, and support. Would not justice have been better here than the humanity that was exercised?

But, it may be asked, why do not these Indians do something for themselves? They have done all they could. In 1879, their agent reported: "Some of the most influential chiefs set an example to the rest by going into the field and working themselves, instead of simply standing by and seeing their squaws work." In 1882, he reported: "In all the work the agency requires the Indians are an efficient help, such as cutting and hauling firewood, also saw-logs from the mountains, and hauling in hay from the nearest hay-field, which is some ten miles from the agency. Our hay crop will be about one hundred tons. The Indians use their own ponies in hauling, and soon become fair teamsters." The trouble is that there is nothing for them to do by which they can support themselves. They are in an isolated position, where there is no call for unskilled labor from neighboring settlements. Farming has been tried on their reservation for over twenty years, and it has usually failed from drought or grasshoppers. In the few years that crops have looked hopeful, the Indians have been driven by starvation to eat them long before they matured, or the Indians from the British side of the line so preyed upon them that they were forced to abandon cultivation and come in to the agency, in order to protect their few remaining horses. Congress has been informed a number of times that farming in this country was hopeless without irrigation, and that no funds had been provided for making irrigation ditches or procuring implements, but Congress has just as often failed to do anything. How long is this to continue? There seems to be no help for it from the government. A deaf ear has been turned to the prayer of the living and the groan of the dying alike. The government too seldom moves until accumulated wrongs have brought on bloodshed. In this case we have been, and now are, writing one of the most damning pages in our Indian history. We are making either spectres to haunt our firesides, or demons to revenge their shameful wrongs. The time may come when they will light the frontier with the red torch of war. If it should, will any white man be able to say that their warfare "cannot be justified before the civilization of the age, or in the sight of God or man"?*

---

* Since the above was written, in August, 1885, it was reported that some of the Piegans (by which name the entire Blackfoot nation is now known) had been stealing horses, and had fought with white pursuers. Possibly the report was false. It is only surprising, however, that they have not stolen everything they could lay hold of.

CHAPTER XVII.
THE TRAGEDY OF THE LAVA BEDS.

No other tribe of American Indians ever leaped into notoriety so suddenly and unexpectedly as the Modocs, and no tribe has excited more interest since their appearance before the public. They were almost unknown in the East until 1873. There had never been more than four or five hundred of them since the whites knew them, and as they occupied a country which was not very desirable, and were known to be warriors who could not be bullied or intimidated, they were not much disturbed by adventurers. They were peculiar people; good-natured, as a rule, but high-tempered; industrious, and yet as haughty as the laziest Indians on the continent. They had more of that commendable pride which makes men desire to be independent and self-supporting than any of their neighbors. They were inclined to be exclusive in their social relations, but even among themselves there was little merry-making. They took a more serious view of life and its duties. Stubbornness and strong will were tribal characteristics. In feature they are rugged and strong, the cheek-bones large and prominent, the hair thick and coarse, the face heavy and not much wrinkled in old age. Their vitality is remarkable. The tribe lost about one hundred and fifty members by small-pox in 1847, and they were often at war with other tribes and with the whites, yet they number now about the same as when we first knew them, while other tribes, formerly stronger than they, have passed almost out of existence. There was no trouble with them, of any consequence, from 1856 to 1872. They lived in comparative peace, and the civilized world went on in its hurry and bustle, all unconscious of their existence. They hunted and trapped in their mountain wilds. They paddled their dug-out canoes over their lakes and streams, dragging their seines or seeking for water-fowl. In these same canoes they gathered the *wocus,* an aquatic plant peculiar to their lakes, with a pericarp like a poppy capsule, full of farinaceous seeds. This they threshed out and made into flour, or parched entire. They dug *kace* and *camas* and other roots. They dwelt in their curious conical houses, half underground and half covered with dirt, unmolested and unmolesting.

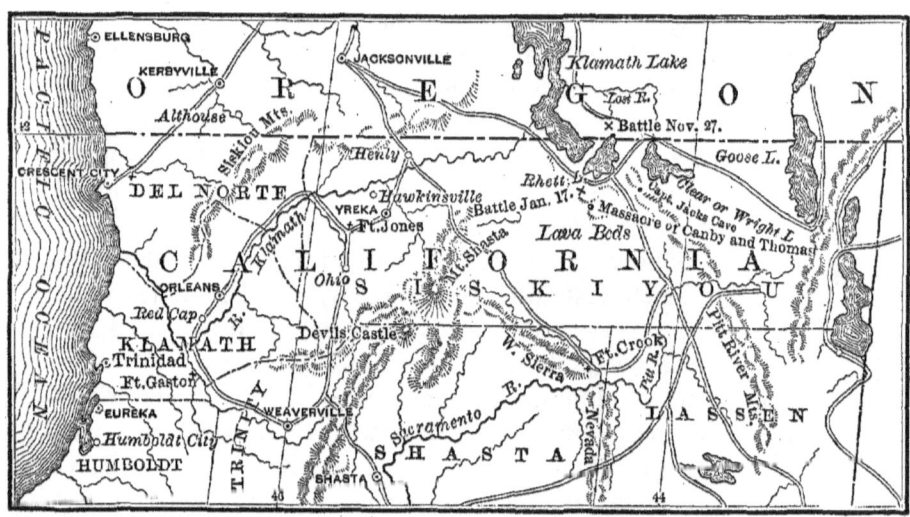

MAP OF THE MODOC COUNTRY.

On October 14, 1864, a treaty was made with the Klamaths, the Modocs, and the Ya-hoos-kin band of Snakes, by which they surrendered all their lands and accepted a reservation in Lake County, Oregon, in the military district known as the District of the Lakes. The Wohl-pa-pe Snakes and the O-che-o Pi-utes were afterwards placed on the same reservation. In the ordinary delay of Indian business, the Senate did not ratify the treaty until July 2, 1866. Two amendments were made to it which were simply grammatical corrections, not affecting the substance in any respect. It was then turned over to the active and vigilant Indian Bureau, in whose care it reposed for three years and a half. On December 10, 1869, it was submitted to the Indians for consent to the amendments. By that time trouble had arisen and a part of the Indians had become suspicious. Captain Jack, or Krentpoos (Kient-poos), thought that the treaty had been materially altered. The testimony of the other chiefs satisfied him, however, and it was accepted by all of them. On February 17, 1870, it was proclaimed—only five years and four months after it had been made. Thus do we attend to business of importance. The Indians, in the mean time, had all moved to the reservation, and settled down to work in good earnest, building cabins and enclosing plats for cultivation. Annuity goods were issued to them in the fall of 1867 and thereafter, though it appears that Captain Jack's band did not receive their portion. In a short time trouble arose. The Klamaths and Modocs were ancient enemies. The former were in two divisions, one under Captain George, and one under La-Lake, called respectively the Muck-a-lucks and the La-Lakes. The recognized head chief of the Modocs was Schonchin; but only a small portion of them acknowledged his authority, and his rank was contested by Captain Jack, on grounds of lineage and tribal choice. The reservation was on land which had formerly belonged to the Klamaths. The Klamaths began to devise and practise petty annoyances on the Modocs. They called them "strangers" and "beggars," who had come to the land of the Klamaths for support. They "hectored and bullied them, obstructed their fishing operations, insulted and beat their women whenever they could do it safely, and, in short, did everything that savages are so ingenious in doing to make another tribe miserable."

The Modocs complained to the agent, but the annoyance was not stopped. Schonchin endured the insults with the fortitude of a Stoic, but Jack's royal blood was not so tame. He left the reservation, taking a considerable number of the tribe with him. The agent then undertook to remedy the evil by moving the Modocs. He put up new reservation buildings in Sprague River Valley, in the eastern end of the reservation, and to this point, known as Yainax Agency, Schonchin's Indians removed. Jack and his Indians were also induced to return to the same place. They went to work on their new location, but they did not escape their tormentors.

By some blunder a band of Klamaths was located at the same place. After enduring the old annoyances for some time, they again complained to the agent that their treatment was unbearable. The agent, Captain Knapp, could see no better remedy than to move them again, and accordingly selected another location. The Modocs looked at it and declined to accept it, saying it was nothing but a trap to put them in the power of the Klamaths. They had lost their little crops, and failed to gather enough food for their support, on account of these annoyances and their removals, and were reduced almost to starvation. As no other relief was proposed, Jack announced his intention of leaving the reservation, and a majority of the tribe went with him. They went to their old homes on Lost River and about Tulé Lake, into which Lost River empties. The lake is also known as Rhett Lake and Modoc Lake. Once afterwards they were induced to return to Yainax Agency by Agent Meacham, but soon after a member of the tribe became sick and died. He was attended by a Klamath doctor, whom Jack either killed or caused to be killed, as is common with the Indians of the North-west. The Klamaths insisted that he should be arrested and tried for this offence, in consequence of which he again left the reservation, and was followed by two-thirds of the tribe. After some negotiation it was agreed that they might remain off the reservation so long as no complaints were made of them.

Besides Jack's Indians there was another band of Modocs off the reservation, living in Northern California, and known as the Hot Creek Indians, who had little to do with any of the others. They numbered about forty-five. There was also a little band of nine or ten warriors, with their women and children, led by the Curly-headed Doctor. They had broken off from Jack's band, but still fraternized with its members to some extent. They were the worst of the Modocs, and paid very little attention to the authority of any one. The conduct of the Modocs off the reservation has been a matter of some controversy, but it is pretty well established that whatever lawlessness can be attributed to them was committed by Curly-headed Doctor's little band. The charges of bad conduct against any of the Modocs off the reservation finally

MODOC SQUAWS

settled down to these: that they scared women and children by boisterous conduct when they came to the houses of the settlers; that they killed cattle; and that they used and carried off hay belonging to certain settlers. Major Elmer Otis investigated these charges in the spring of 1872. It was testified by some settlers that Jack and his band claimed their old home on the theory that they were not bound by the treaty, and demanded compensation from those who settled on these lands; that they were insolent and threatening; that they were guilty of thefts and of stealing cattle. On the other hand, one settler testified that he had never paid anything for settling on their lands, and did not believe that any one was asked to pay; that the Indians were no more insolent to whites than whites are to whites; that from inspection of the trails made by marauders, he believed that the Klamaths were the parties who were guilty of killing the cattle. Another settler testified that he had lived near the tribe for ten years, and did not consider that there was any danger to settlers from them; that the parties whose hay was taken had agreed to pay the Indians for cutting hay on lands claimed by them and had failed to do so. It may be mentioned, in this connection, that the general charge was made, all through the Modoc troubles, that the Indians were influenced by "low whites," who advised them to resist removal to the reservation. This position is hardly tenable. On his trial, when there was every inducement to state anything that would excuse him, Captain Jack solemnly denied that he had ever been advised to resist by any white man. He denied always that he or his tribe had been guilty of wrong-doing, and said that if any thefts had been committed, the Klamaths or Curly-headed Doctor's men were the guilty parties. Certain it is that all these Modocs lived off the reservation, without causing any serious trouble until the winter of 1872. They roamed over a large extent of country at will. On the 4th of July they usually turned up at Yreka, in California, where their friends and advisers, Judge Roseborough and Judge Steele, resided; and on the national birthday in 1871, when that town was destroyed by fire, the Modocs did good service at the engine and elsewhere, in aiding to fight the flames.

No complaints were made of their conduct anywhere, except those mentioned, which were by some of the settlers near their usual homes.

During all this time an effort was being made by the local military and Indian authorities to have a small reservation set off for these people, where they might live without the continual annoyance of the Klamaths. It was their desire to have their lands in severalty and become citizens, though it was questionable whether all of them were sufficiently advanced in the white man's ways for that. They had, as all Indians had, a true friend in Gen. E. R. S. Canby, commanding the Department of the Columbia. He had served continuously in the army since 1839; had won notice in the Seminole and Mexican wars; had stood firmly for the Union in New Mexico, at the outbreak of the civil war, when his senior officers went over to the South; had led the forces that drove the Texan invaders from the mountains; had commanded at the capture of Mobile; and had compelled the surrender of the rebel forces in the Southwest. During his long service he had many dealings with Indians, and had treated them with uniform fairness and honesty. One tribe had named him "the Indian's Friend." He said, on February 7, 1872, "I am not surprised at the unwillingness of the Modocs to return to any point on the reservation where they would be exposed to the hostilities and annoyances they have heretofore experienced (and without any adequate protection) from the Klamaths; but they have expressed a desire to be established upon Lost River, where they would be free from this trouble, and the superintendent informed me last summer that he would endeavor to secure such a location for them." The land they wanted was about three miles long by one mile wide, bordering on Lost River. There were less than two thousand acres of it, and it was not occupied by settlers. In addition to the reasons mentioned, they wanted their reservation on Lost River because that stream and Tulé Lake abounded in fish, a staple food of theirs. "There are black, silver-sided, and speckled trout, of which first two species specimens are taken weighing twenty-five pounds; buffalo fish, from five to twelve pounds; and very large, fine suck-

MAJOR-GENERAL E. R. S. CANBY.

ers—such only in name and appearance, for they are not bonier than common fishes. In spawning time the fish school up from the lake in extraordinary numbers, so that the Indians have only to put a slight obstruction in the river, when they can literally shovel them out."

Superintendent Meacham desired and urged that a separate reservation be established for them, but in the spring of 1872 he was relieved by F. B. Odeneal, who appointed two agents to hold a council with the Modocs and report. He accepted all complaints against them as true, and enlarged them, without seeing the tribe himself; he reported that the leaders of the Modocs off the reservation were "desperadoes," and foes to civilization. "As well," says this eloquent and judicious man, "might we expect our own youth to grow up in the practice of Christian virtues under the tutorship of the 'road-agents' of Montana, or the guerillas of Mexico, as to think of instilling any good into the minds of the Modocs while under the exclusive control, as they have been, of their present, leaders." He advised that the leaders be arrested and the others compelled to go on the Klamath reservation. This advice was taken by the Indian Bureau, although General Canby had reported, but a few weeks before, that the previous Commission had "authorized the Modocs to remain where they were until the superintendent could see them. This has been understood as a settlement of the question until some permanent arrangement could be made for them; and unless they have violated some subsequent agreement, I do not think that the immediate application of force as asked for would be either expedient or just. They should at least be notified that a new location has been selected for them, and provision made for their wants."

Troops had already been placed in the vicinity of the Modocs, on account of the complaints before mentioned, and to them was assigned the task of bringing the Indians to the reservation. The instructions from General Canby to the officer commanding the District of the Lakes, were: "If the military force is to be used, it will only be in aid of the Indian Department and after peaceable means have been exhausted, but you should be prepared for the possibility that the attempt to remove them may result in hostilities, and be able to act promptly in that event for the protection of the frontier." It was thought necessary, however, by the commanding officer, to surprise their camp, which was on Lost River—at that point a deep stream three hundred feet wide. Jack's Indians were located on one side and the Doctor's on the other. In the night of November 28th, Captain Jackson with forty men and ten citizens quietly made their way to the camp. On the 30th the captain reported concerning the outcome of this strategic movement. "I have the honor to report that I jumped the camp of Captain Jack's Modoc Indians yesterday morning soon after daylight, completely surprising them. I demanded their surrender and disarming, and asked for a parley with Captain Jack. Captain Jack, Scar-faced Charley, Black Jim, and some others, would neither lay down their arms nor surrender, and some of them commenced making hostile demonstrations against us, and finally opened fire. I immediately poured volley after volley among the hostile Indians, took their camp, killed eight or nine warriors, and drove the rest into the hills. During the engagement I had one man killed and seven wounded, three of the last severely and perhaps dangerously. The band that I attacked was on the south side of the river; another small band on the north side was attacked by a party of ten or twelve citizens, and their surrender demanded; but when the firing commenced in Captain Jack's camp, these Indians opened on the citizens and drove them to the refuge of Crawley's ranch. One citizen was killed during the fight, and two others coming up the road, unconscious of any trouble, were shot; one (Mr. Nuss) mortally wounded, and the other (Joe Pennig) badly. My force was too weak to pursue and capture the Indians that made off, owing to the necessity of taking immediate care of my wounded, and protecting the few citizens who had collected at Crawley's ranch. . . . From the best information I can get, Captain Jack, Scar-faced Charley, and Black Jim are killed or mortally wounded." Neither one of them was killed, but the Curly-headed Doctor's band was made furious. The leadership of this band was shared, to a certain extent, by Hooker Jim (Hooka, Jooka, Hocker, Hawkey), who was probably the worst man of the lot. There was no control over them by any one. They acknowledged Jack to be chief of the tribe, as they had always done, but they did what they chose, without regard to his orders. They at once began attacking the scattered settlers, and within forty-eight hours had killed twelve men. No women or children were killed by either Indians or soldiers, except one Indian child, reported as accidentally shot. With the killing of these settlers Captain Jack and his band proper had no connection. Judge-Advocate Curtis said, at the trial, "I do not accuse Captain Jack of any participation in those murders. I acquit him of them entirely. I know almost to a demonstration that he was ignorant of their occurrence until after they had taken place. I have investigated that matter somewhat since I have been here, and I do not believe he was concerned in them or knew of them in advance."

It was at once realized that the surprise was a mistake. Lieutenant-colonel Wheaton, commanding the district, placed the blame on Superintendent Odeneal and his agents. There is no room for doubt that the fighting qualities of the Modocs were underestimated by the military as well as by the agents of the Indian Bureau. Captain Jack's band moved at once to the Lava Beds, on the south side of Tulé Lake, where they were soon joined by Hooker Jim's party, who had added six more to their list of victims. This now celebrated stronghold of theirs covers about fifty square miles of country in Northern California, partly in Siskiyou County and partly in Modoc County. It is what is known in scientific parlance, as also locally in the West, as a pedregal (pay-dray-gahl'), a name adopted from the Spanish, meaning a stony place. It is impossible to give any adequate idea of the place by words. The rock is volcanic, and appears to have been broken in fragments again and again by explosions, as the lava was cooling; after each explosion the fragments dropped back into the gradually solidifying lava, to be again thrown up and again fall, until the whole became cool, and the explosive element lost its force. If you will go to the end of a slag dump at a blast-furnace, where the refuse has been tumbled from the slag pots, chilled outside and molten within, bursting, shooting in the air, hissing, crackling, rolling, and flowing, there to cool and solidify—if looking at such a ragged surface you can imagine with what ease an ant could make its way over it, you will have an idea of the progress of a man across the Lava Beds—only you must remember that an ant has three times as many legs as a man, and that its feet have the power of suction, by which it is enabled to walk as easily on a window-pane or a ceiling as on a floor. There are rocks, from the sharp-edged pebble that cuts through a cowhide boot, to the bowlder as large as a church. They are in heaps, of all sizes and shapes. This is the surface; but it is cut in every direction by innumerable chasms and crevices, some of them a hundred feet deep, with occasionally a wholly subterranean passage, through which a man can pass from one point to another. Such is this mighty pedregal, and in the northern end of it, near Tulé Lake, the Modocs had established their camp, in what were called the Modoc Caves.

Against the Modocs, in this Gibraltar, troops were soon preparing to move. In the middle of January they were on

A VIEW OF THE CAVES.

the ground, anxious for the attack. There were four hundred of them, two hundred and twenty-five regulars, all well-armed and equipped, with a battery of howitzers. They were confident and determined. Said their commander: "If the Modocs will only try to make good their boast to whip a thousand soldiers, all will be satisfied." Over in the chaotic heap of lava were fifty Modoc warriors, and about one hundred and seventy-five women and children. They were armed with muzzle-loading rifles and revolvers. On the morning of the 17th, the advance into the pedregal was begun by three hundred of the troops, including twenty Indian scouts, the remainder being employed in guarding the stores and as a reserve. The advance was well planned, but the nature of the country had not been realized. It is impossible to realize it without going over the ground. The movements contemplated could not be made. The junction of detachments was prevented by deep chasms. The troops could move only at a snail's pace. Constantly before them were the Modocs, picking their shots and firing carefully. They were not exposed to a return fire, for they were behind lava bowlders, shooting through crevices. The troops had no targets but puffs of smoke. After hours of painful creeping they would gain the place of the smoke, but nothing would be found. A hundred yards away would be another puff, spitting out its leaden missiles. All day the troops heroically advanced under these difficulties, protected to some extent by the dense fog that rested over the lake and the Lava Beds until two o'clock, now lifting a little and now settling again—an almost constant phenomenon of the place. At evening the soldiers were withdrawn. They brought out their wounded, twenty-eight in number, but ten dead were left behind, after strenuous attempts to bring them away. Officers and men now understood that they had a serious task before them, and Colonel Wheaton reported: "In the opinion of any experienced officer of regulars or volunteers, one thousand men would be required to dislodge them from their almost impregnable position, and it must be done deliberately, with a free use of mortar batteries." He asked for three hundred more men and four howitzers.

On receipt of reports of this attack, the authorities at Washington decided to "give the peace men a chance." Pity it had not been done three months earlier. The Modocs were now confident and well supplied with ammunition. They obtained powder and lead from cartridges found on the field.

VIEW OF CAMP AND LAKE.

They captured also some breech-loading guns. They swore afterwards that they obtained caps from the Klamaths. They had been made suspicious by the surprise of their camp in November. They had been kept in a continual state of distrust by the people in their neighborhood. In December the band of Hot Creek Indians, who had no connection whatever with the troubles, had started for the Klamath reservation, under care of authorized agents. At Link River, Oregon, they were met by an Indian agent, who informed them that the citizens were collected beyond, to mob them. On hearing this the Indians became frightened and scattered into the mountains. It was with the utmost difficulty that a portion were gathered and placed on the reservation. The remainder fled to the Lava Beds and joined Jack's Indians. The Modocs testified that whites told them they would be executed, and that one, Nate Beswick, informed them that the commissioners wanted to get them out to kill them. They swore (those who were tried and others) that the Klamaths encouraged them to fight, and furnished them with ammunition. General Gillem says he learned, on what he considered good authority, that Sam Blair, a man of the neighborhood, sent word to them, "That he had an order in his pocket from the governor of Oregon to hang the nine Indians engaged in killing the citizens as soon as they came in." Notoriously, almost all the Pacific slope was clamoring for their extermination, and Governor Grover, of Oregon, on February 10th, in a pathetic open letter to the commissioners, protested against any settlement of the matter on terms which did not include the surrender for trial of the men who massacred white settlers "on the 29th and 30th of November last," although they "had not been attacked by the soldiery or otherwise molested." The reader will remember that Captain Jackson's surprise was at daybreak on the 29th.

On January 30th instructions were given for the suspension of hostilities, and a commission was ordered. It was made up of A. B. Meacham, Jesse Applegate, his nephew Oliver Applegate, agent at Yainax, and Samuel Chase. They were all men whom the Modocs distrusted and disliked except Meacham. Nothing could be done under the circumstances. The Modocs were afraid to meet where they would be in the power of the whites, and the commissioners declined to meet where they would be in the power of the Modocs. So they dawdled along until the 1st of March, by which time General Canby had arrived, and the authorities at Washington had been made to understand that the Commission would be useless until its personnel was altered. It was decided to change it, and Judge Roseborough, of Yreka, Rev. E. Thomas, of Petaluma, and

THE REV. DR. THOMAS.

L. S. Dyer, of the Klamath Agency, were substituted for the Applegates and Chase. The Commission, as it now stood, was unexceptionable from the peace people's stand-point—also from the stand-point of unbiased people; the Indian-haters did not like it—"too much milk-and-water and all that." Five weeks were consumed in completing these changes, and during this time a change was going on among the Modocs

THE TRAGEDY OF THE LAVA BEDS. 561

also. This statement will be disapproved both by those who have decided that all the Modocs were always good, and by those who have ordained that all the Modocs were always bad; nevertheless it is true. There were in the Modoc camp eight men known as "the murderers," which meant that they were the men who killed the settlers, after the surprise by Captain Jackson. These men knew that they were considered guilty of murder by the white people, and that all the people who lived about them were in favor of trying, convicting, and hanging them. They knew also that if they made peace, and had a reservation set off for them on Lost River, it was very questionable whether the United States could protect them. The offences had been committed within the State of Oregon; Lost River was within the State of Oregon; and the people and authorities of Oregon, while always very ready to claim monetary recompense from the General Government for injuries by its "wards," were ever jealous of any interference with its jurisdiction over those wards. These things were explained to the Indians by the Commission, or members of it, from time to time. The explanation was necessary in order to try to induce them to move elsewhere. It was proposed to them that they should be temporarily located on Angell's Island, in the Pacific, and subsequently placed on a reservation in Arizona or Indian Territory. They agreed to this at first, but there still remained the trouble that they must surrender to the soldiers, to begin with. They were afraid to do this. They knew that the soldiers, both regulars and volunteers, "had bad hearts towards them," on account of the deaths of their comrades. Consequently "the murderers" objected to surrender and urged war, and they were gradually bringing the other Indians over to their views.

It was a situation where two parties were desirous of peace, on a basis of amnesty for the past and harmony for the future, but neither dared trust the other. The Indian-hater may say that the idea that they were afraid to trust our commissioners and officers is preposterous, but it is not. Just around the lake, in constant view when the fog lifted, was Bloody Point, where Ben Wright invited them to make a treaty, and murdered thirty-eight of them, in 1852. Just there, on the edge of the Lava Beds, were sons and nephews, neighbors and friends of men who took part in that "lesson to the Modocs." In command of a part of those volunteers was General John Ross, who led the Jacksonville volunteers that operated with Ben Wright. It is idle to talk of the Modocs having no reason to fear bad faith, especially in consideration of the fact that a part of them were afterwards murdered while they were prisoners. On March 6th Captain Jack sent a message to the commissioners then present by his sister Mary. He said, "I am very sad. I want peace quick, or else let the soldiers come and make haste and fight. . . . I am nearly well; but I am afraid of the soldiers on the road. There are so many soldiers around. There are soldiers on Lost River, on Clear Lake, and Bernard's soldiers. Wouldn't they be afraid if they were in the same situation? . . . I wish to live like the whites. Let everything be wiped out, washed out, and let there be no more blood. I have got a bad heart about those murderers. I have got but a few men and I don't see how I can give them up. Will they give up their people who murdered my people while they were asleep? I never asked for the people who murdered my people. I only talked that way. I can see how I could give up my horse to be hanged; but I can't see how I could give up my men to be hanged. I could give up my horse to be hanged, and wouldn't cry about it; but if I gave up my men I would have to cry about it. I want them all to have good hearts now. I have thrown away everything. There must be no more bad talk. I will not. I have spoken forever. I want soldiers all to go home. I have given up now and want no more fuss. I have said yes, and thrown away my country. I want soldiers to go away so I will not be afraid."

Of course the soldiers could not be sent away. It would have been inconsistent with the position the government had taken—inconsistent with the usages of every civilized nation —to withdraw its forces pending a treaty, while the submitting force remained as it was. Besides, there was the fear that the Indians intended treachery. It was impossible that the Commission should overcome these obstacles, but it hoped on. If the Modocs had felt that they were whipped—if they had realized the hopelessness of their struggle—they might have submitted to the chance of life or death that they saw in a surrender; but they did not. They had more and better arms and more ammunition than before. Their confidence in the strength of their position was unbounded. The Klamaths were promising to assist them. It was reported that the Indians of Washington, Oregon, and Idaho were on the verge of declaring war. It was evident, however, that the Modocs were not united; that there was a war party and a peace party. Jack and part of his followers wanted peace; the murderers wanted war, and Schonchin John, Scar-faced Charley, and others leaned towards them. The commissioners were satisfied that Jack was under duress; that he was in fear of the others. Others thought that he was trying to gain time; but he had no object to gain by that. Certain it was that he acted like a man in great trouble: he was sad and gloomy; much of the time he was weeping. Finally the Modocs offered a new solution; they would take the Lava Beds for a reservation. This could not be accepted. To the whites it meant establishing a den for wild beasts, from which they could issue for rapine and plunder; to the Indians it meant a home in a castle where no sheriff's posse could arrest them for killing the people in November. The commissioners were satisfied that no permanent settlement of the trouble could be made if the Indians remained in that part of the country, and so matters drifted along until the second week of April.

Captain Jack sat on a rock in the Lava Beds. His heart was bowed down. He had talked with the commissioners and was no nearer a solution of his troubles. He had been informed that the soldiers could not be sent away. He had been told that his people could not remain in the Lava Beds. He could find no answer to the arguments of the murderers, for from his stand they were not much to be blamed. They had not killed the settlers till the soldiers had surprised his camp. They had not killed women and children. They had fought the soldiers like brave men. If he surrendered they would probably be hanged, and that was a dreadful death; it killed both the body and the soul. The rope closed up a man's throat so that his spirit could not come out, and take up its journey to the happy hunting-grounds. It must die in his body. He could not feel satisfied that the soldiers would not shoot all the Modocs when they came out, as they had done twenty-one years before. The murderers came around him. They saw that the time for argument was past, and the time for appeal to passion had come. They taunted him. Hooker Jim said, "You are like an old squaw; you have never done any fighting yet; we have done the fighting and you are our chief. You are not fit to be a chief." Then came George, another of the murderers, and said, "What do you want with a gun? You don't shoot anything with it. You don't go any place to do anything. You are sitting around on the rocks." After a while Scar-faced Charley came up: He was a Rogue River Indian, of the Tipsie Tyee's (Bearded Chief) band, who had joined the Modocs many years before, after the separation of his tribe. He had been with Captain Jack's band, and was the oldest of his warriors. He said, "I am going with Hooker Jim. I can fight with them. You are nothing but an old squaw." Jack winced a little when they called him a squaw. They brought a dress and a squaw's bonnet and put them on him. They mocked and jeered their squaw chief. He had sat there through the morning, bearing it all. Now the fog had parted and risen, and the sun was shining on them. He rose and threw the humiliating garments from him. With blazing eyes he turned on his tormentors and hissed: "I will show you that I am no squaw. You say you want war. We will have war, and Krent-poos will not be the one who asks for peace." He had fought his temptation and it had proved too strong for him. The perplexity pushing on one side and the eight devils tugging on the other had started him in the evil path. The dormant savage in him waked with renewed strength. His good angel fled from him, as Vivian from old Merlin, who lay in the dark spell "of woven paces and of waving hands," shrieking back, "Oh, fool!" From that hour on his heart was bad.

Arrangements were being made with the commissioners for another meeting. Judge Steele, of Yreka, an old resident, in whom the Indians had the utmost confidence, who had been the arbiter of their petty troubles for many years, acted as one messenger to them. Riddle, the interpreter, and Toby, his squaw wife, acted also on behalf of the Commission. At Steele's last visit to the cave the Indians became angry, and his life was saved only by Captain Jack and Scar-faced Charley standing guard over him during the night. He told the commissioners that the Modocs meant treachery and refused to go to their camp again. As Toby left the cave, on the occasion of her last visit, a Modoc named William-they called him "Whim"—followed her and warned her to keep away, and to keep the commissioners away; that the Indians were going to kill them. The commissioners were in a quandary. There had been acts that appeared evidences of treachery before, but they had come to nothing. They had consulted the Commissioner of Indian Affairs then, and he had replied, on March 5th, "I do not think the Modocs mean treachery. The mission should not be a failure." An agreed meeting had not been attended by the Commission on April 8th because the lookout had discovered twenty armed Modocs in ambush near the place of conference. On the 10th, Bogus Charley came from the Modocs, proposing that General Canby and the commissioners, unarmed, should meet an equal party of Modocs, unarmed, at the council tent, about three-quarters of a mile from General Gillem's camp, and on the day after they would all come in and surrender. The Commission discussed this plan. They all felt that the meeting would probably be dangerous. Mr. Thomas said they ought to go; that it was a duty which they could not conscientiously evade. General Canby thought that the importance of the object justified some risk. He believed that the Indians would not kill them, though he considered them capable of it, because it was not to their interest. Meacham and Dyer insisted that the meeting ought not be held; that it was going to certain death.

Riddle told them that the Indians meant to kill them possibly not that day, but probably then; that if they went they must free him from all responsibility. Meacham then proposed that they should go armed, and add John Fairchild, a frontiersman of the neighborhood, to the party, but Dr. Thomas protested that this would be a breach of faith. Meacham then proposed that in case there appeared indubitable evidences of treachery, they should agree to anything that the Indians might ask, until they could make their escape. Dr. Thomas replied, "I will be a party to no deception under any circumstances; this matter is in the hands of God." General Canby said, "I have dealt with Indians for thirty years, and

GENERAL ALVIN GILLEM.

I have never deceived an Indian. I will not consent to it—to any promise that cannot be fulfilled." Riddle insisted that the commissioners accompany him to General Gillem's tent, and there, again, he repeated his warnings, and called Gillem to witness that he washed his hands of the whole matter. He added that if they were determined to go, he would go with them rather than be called a coward. Gillem thought

THE TRAGEDY OF THE LAVA BEDS. 567

the Indians would not dare to commit the anticipated treachery. Canby and Thomas said they would go. Meacham and Dyer said they would go also rather than subject themselves to a charge of cowardice, or have the Commission fail for want of action on their part. Before starting, Meacham and Dyer gave John Fairchild what valuables they had about them, and indicated their last wishes, as men preparing for death. Each of them also put in his pocket a small derringer pistol. Some have said that Canby and Thomas were foolhardy to do as they did. To those who are incapable of understanding lofty motives it most ever appear so. They went to their fate drawn by a destiny as irresistible as that which led Krentpoos to his, but of an opposite nature. They knew that the trouble had been caused by the wrong-doing of white men, and their consciences would not permit them to throw their personal safety in the balance on the question of going. They felt bound to leave no stone unturned in their attempt to right this wrong peacefully.

The place of meeting was at what was called the peace tent, or council tent. It was in a little open space at the foot of a high bluff, in the edge of the pedregal. The approach was sufficiently level and clear to permit of riding a horse into it, and a tent had been placed there for the use of the Commission. Thither the little party of peace-makers started at eleven o'clock. General Canby and Dr. Thomas, with Boston Charley, who came to the camp that morning, walked ahead; Meacham, Dyer, and Toby rode; Riddle and Bogus Charley, who had been in the camp over night, came last, on foot. At the tent they found six Modocs: Captain Jack, Schonchin John, Ellen's Man, Black Jim, Hooker Jim, and Shack-nasty Jim. It was at once noticed that, they were armed with revolvers, but as they had been armed at, previous councils, no remark was made concerning this. Twenty or thirty feet from the tent a small fire of sage brush had been made, and around it was a row of stones, in a half-circle. On these the party seated themselves, excepting Dr. Thomas, who reclined on the ground. They talked together about the proposition for this meeting and the surrender on the morrow. Captain Jack made a speech, the substance of which was that he did not want anything from the President, but wanted the soldiers taken away. As he concluded, Hooker Jim stepped back and fastened Meacham's horse, which had been left loose. He took Meacham's overcoat from the pommel of the saddle and put it on, remarking, "I am Meacham." This was understood as a bid for an objection on which a quarrel might be based, but Meacham merely said, "Take my hat, too." Jim replied, in Modoc, "I will, presently." General Canby, apparently understanding the meaning of this by-play, arose and began to speak. He told them how he had dealt with other Indians, and had been named by them "the Indian's Friend;" how he had met those Indians afterwards and been thanked by them for his just treatment of them; how he hoped that in some future time the Modocs would thank him for getting them happy homes. He said he could not send away the soldiers-that the President had sent them there-but that whatever the commissioners promised should be done, and the citizens should not interfere. Dr. Thomas rose to his knees, rested his hand on Meacham's shoulder, and, with uncovered head, said "I believe the Great Spirit put it in the heart of the President to send us here to make peace. I have known General Canby fourteen years, Mr. Meacham eighteen years, and Mr. Dyer four years. I know all their hearts are good, and I know my own heart. We want no more war. I believe that God sees us, what we do; that he wishes us all to be at peace; that no more blood should be shed."

Jack said that he did not want to leave that country; that he did not know any other country. If he could not have a reservation on Lost River, he would take one on Willow Creek and Cottonwood Creek. Meacham tapped him on the shoulder, and said, "Jack, let us talk like men, and not like children. You are a man that has common-sense; isn't there any other place that will do you except Willow Creek and Cottonwood?" Schonchin interrupted, and told him to hush; that he could talk a straight talk; to let him talk. As he began, Jack stepped back to the horses. Schonchin said, "Give us Hot Creek for a home, and take away your soldiers." The commissioners tried to explain that they would

THE TRAGEDY OF THE LAVA BEDS. 569

have to see first whether they could get lands there, but Schonchin cried, very excitedly, "Take away the soldiers and give us Hot Creek, or stop talking." Just then two Indians, Barncho and Slolox, jumped up from some rocks fifty yards away, and came running forward, each carrying three guns. At the same time Steamboat Frank and another Indian appeared from another direction. The commissioners turned, and one said, "What does this mean, Captain Jack?" As he did so Jack stepped forward, cocking his revolver; said "At-we'" (all ready); and levelled his revolver at General Canby, within three feet of his face. The cap snapped at the first attempt, but quick as thought it was cocked again. At the second the ball struck General Canby under the eye, and he fell back.

At the word each of the Indians sprang at his appointed victim. Dr. Thomas was shot in the left breast by Boston Charley. He rose and ran, followed by Boston Charley and Bogus Charley. At about seventy yards he fell, killed by a rifle shot from Bogus. Schonchin John fired at Meacham, at a distance of three or four feet, and missed him. Meacham ran back, drawing his pistol. Schonchin and Black Jim followed him, firing, and Meacham fired back once. He had gone about fifty yards when a ball struck him in the head and he became unconscious. General Canby also sprang to his feet and fled after the first wound: the ball had ranged down and come out at the back of the neck. He ran about as far as Dr. Thomas, when Ellen's Man shot him with a rifle, and Captain Jack killed him by a stab in the neck. Dyer ran, pursued by Hooker Jim, who fired as he ran. At about two hundred yards, Dyer faced on his pursuer and pointed his derringer at him, whereupon Jim ran back and Dyer escaped. Riddle was followed by Shack-nasty Jim and Barncho, who were joined by Ellen's Man after Canby fell. They were all firing at him, but he escaped with the touch of a rifle-ball on his ear. Toby was struck across the back with a rifle by Slolox, who was trying to get possession of her horse, but was saved from further violence by Captain Jack, who ordered that she should not be injured. By this time the wild excitement of the assassination was over. The Indians quickly stripped all the clothing from the bodies and started to move away. Boston Charley ran back and began to scalp Meacham, but Toby cried out, "Soldiers! soldiers!" and they all fled. The soldiers were not yet in sight. She used this stratagem in order to prevent the mutilation.

The soldiers were coming, however, at a double-quick; the camp had received the alarm before the assassination began. Around on the east side of the lake, where Major Mason's command was posted, two Indians had appeared, under a flag of truce, at a little after one o'clock. Lieutenant Sherwood and Lieutenant Doyle went out two or three hundred yards to meet them. The Indians said they wanted to talk to the "Little Tyee" (Major Mason), but were informed that no one there could talk to them. Scar-faced Charley and another Indian, who were concealed in the rocks, then opened fire, inflicting wounds in Lieutenant Sherwood's arm and thigh, from which he died three days later. This treachery was signalled to General Gillem's camp. A message was being prepared to send to Canby when the firing was heard, and the signal officer reported that the commissioners were being murdered. The soldiers sprang to their arms at the sound of the shots, and advanced towards the council tent on a run. In a few minutes Dyer appeared, almost exhausted, reporting that all the others were killed. A little farther on Riddle reached the lines. The soldiers hurried on to the scene of the tragedy. About seventy yards from the tent were found the bodies of Canby and Dr. Thomas, stripped of everything. The former had two bullet wounds through his head and a cut in the neck; the latter had several wounds in his body. A little farther on was Meacham, also stripped. He had one bullet wound under his right eye, one in the side of the head, one through his right arm, a grazing shot on the temple, a finger shot from his left hand, one ear cut, and a long knife-wound on his head, where Boston had begun to scalp him. It was not expected that he would live, but, after four bullets had been extracted from his head, he grew better and rapidly recovered. The soldiers advanced a short distance beyond the council tent, and then withdrew, bearing the remains of the victims in sadness to the camp.

THE TRAGEDY OF THE LAVA BEDS. 571

There has never been an occurrence in any of our Indian wars that excited such wide-spread indignation as this act of treachery. The high esteem in which both General Canby and Dr. Thomas were held, their disinterested efforts in behalf of these Indians, and the atrocity of the assassination stirred public feeling to its depths. The Modocs were the objects of universal execration, and their outlandish names quickly became household words. For a time there was but one sentiment, and that was that the tribe should be exterminated. The soldiers had the same feeling, but extermination was not so easily accomplished. The entire force moved forward on the 14th, in the face of a stubborn resistance by the Indians, to positions from which the mortar batteries could reach the caves. The stronghold was shelled during the 15th and 16th. On the morning of the 17th the troops advanced again and took possession of the cave, all of the Indians having moved away, except a small rear-guard, which was driven out by a dashing charge. The famous retreat was found to be a long crevice, extending for more than a mile in a north and south direction, connected at various points with deep sink-holes. All along it were fragments of bursted shells, and here and there the body of an Indian. The body of one man was literally torn to pieces. It was learned afterwards that the man had picked up a shell and was trying to bite off the fuse when it exploded. Another man was killed by the same explosion. Altogether there were eleven bodies found, three of them men, as the product of the three days' work. There were no wounded reported. No quarter was given. The loss to the troops, from the morning of the 14th, was six men killed and fourteen wounded. In addition to this the Indians had cut off Eugene Hovey, a young citizen, killed him, and captured four horses. The Indians took a new position about four miles south of their old place, but kept closely hidden for several days.

Prior to this time the troops had been reinforced by a party of sixty Warm Springs Indians, under Donald McKay, their interpreter. They proved invaluable assistants, the only objection to them being that they absolutely refused to do anything on Sundays. Supposed discoveries of the new hiding-place of the Modocs were made on several occasions, but they were not found until the morning of the 23d. Early on the 26th, a party under command of Captain Thomas of the 4th Artillery was sent on a reconnoissance to a sand-hill in the centre of the Lava Beds, to ascertain the practicability of taking the pack-train with the mortar battery to that point. The command consisted of six officers, sixty-four men, and thirteen of the Indian scouts, under McKay. They marched in column of twos, with a company deployed across the front, and flankers on either side. It was soon apparent that many of the men were inspired with a dread of the foe, which had been dealing death among them from its hidden fastnesses. The skirmishers kept lagging until the column was upon them, and the flankers continually edged in from the sides, notwithstanding the orders of the officers. The base of the sand-hill was reached by noon, without sight of the enemy, and the party stopped for luncheon. They were in comparatively low ground. On all sides of them but the front, which was occupied by the sand-hill, were rough lava ridges, from four to six hundred yards distant. Two men were sent to reconnoitre the ridge to the east of the sand-hill. When about half-way to it, two shots were fired at them from the rocks to which they were going, and immediately fire was opened from the lava ridges all about them. A large portion of the men became panic-stricken. They rushed to and fro, crying, "We are completely surrounded," and paid no attention to commands. A number sought hid-

DONALD McKAY, LEADER OF THE SCOUTS.

ing-places, and sneaked away as soon as the engagement of the Indians with the others gave them opportunity. The rest, with the officers, at first pushed up the sand-hill.

Lieutenant Wright was ordered to advance with one company and occupy the ridge to the west. Lieutenant Cranston, with five men, volunteered to take the ridge to the north. All of this party were killed, the position of their bodies indicating that they had died while bravely trying to accomplish the task they had undertaken. The main body, now reduced to less than thirty men, soon started to follow Lieutenant Wright, but Wright's command had gone to pieces, and no trace of them could be found. The others reached a little hollow about fifty yards from the ridge, supposing it to be occupied by Lieutenant Wright's men, but on calling for them received a volley of rifle-shots for an answer. By death and desertion they had been cut down to only twenty, and these saw that they were lost. Captain Thomas said, "We are surrounded. Let us die like brave men." They sheltered themselves as best they could behind rocks and sage bushes, but they were helpless. There were twenty-one Indians here. They separated and, by paths known only to them, gained positions on two sides—fourteen on one side and seven on the other—from which they maintained a deadly cross-fire, they being in perfect safety. About the time the firing began, the Warm Springs Indians, who had been scouting, came up and tried to join the troops. They were mistaken for Modocs and fired upon. They used every device to show who they were, but in vain. They captured an escaping bugler and made him sound the whole list of bugle calls, but the soldiers did not understand. Being under two fires the scouts could do nothing but keep concealed. All of them escaped unhurt. In the mean time Major Green, with all available forces, was hastening in the direction of the firing. They reached the place in time to save but few of the party. Captain Thomas (son of Gen. Lorenzo Thomas), Lieutenant Howe (son-in-law of General Brady), Lieutenant Wright (son of Gen. George Wright), and Lieutenant Cranston were dead. Lieutenant Harris was mortally wounded. Dr. Semig, who had performed his duties everywhere, regardless of flying bullets, received a wound in the leg which necessitated amputation below the knee. Eighteen enlisted men were killed and seventeen wounded, several mortally. The troops held the ground through the night, but the Modocs crept through the lines to scalp and rifle the dead. In the morning the Indians retired and the troops withdrew to the lake. All the wounded and the greater part of the dead were brought in. Over twenty of the soldiers of Captain Thomas's command straggled into camp, reporting that they had been "cut off." Gen. Jeff. C. Davis, who arrived a few days later to take General Canby's place, denounced them as "cowardly beef-eaters."

When Davis took command of the troops, he found them so dispirited over this series of failures and losses, which left always the same desperate task before them, that he considered it injudicious to move actively at once. There was much raillery at the time at the army's want of success; but the outside world had no idea of the situation, or of the high order of courage in the common soldiers that it called for. There have been many thousands of men who dared to march up to the cannon's mouth, but what if such marching be required to be done by inches, when there is no opportunity for harming the cannoneer, and with the certain knowledge that when the cannon was reached it would be whisked away to another safe position, there again to belch out its iron death? The Modocs added not a little to the apprehensive feeling by keeping perfectly quiet. They gave no intimation as to what part of that wilderness of stone they occupied. They might be hidden in its nearest edge; they might be resting peacefully in the centre. No one knew. On May 6th two friendly squaws were sent into the pedregal. They returned after two days, almost exhausted, and reported that the Modocs had moved towards the southeast. On the evening of the 8th some Warm Springs Indians were sent out. They confirmed the report of the squaws, and also reported that fifteen or twenty Modocs had attacked and captured a supply-train of four wagons, attended by an escort equal in number to the attacking party, on the east side of Tulé Lake. The casualties to the escort were three men wounded. Two squadrons of cavalry, with the Indian scouts, were at once sent in that direction. They discovered some signs of Indians near a small, dry lake, and pitched their camp there for the night. At daybreak the next morning (the 10th) the Indians attacked them. The troops were surprised, but the men seized their

GENERAL JEFFERSON C. DAVIS.

guns and returned the fire so gallantly that the Indians began to retreat. They were followed for three miles, fighting all the way, till they reached the Lava Beds. The troops followed them in at a distance, and at the same time detachments were thrown in on the other sides, the plan being now adopted of making permanent camps in the pedregal. By this means the Indians were kept continually on the watch, which, owing to their small number, was a great hardship to them.

There was a more serious trouble than this in the Modoc camp. Over at the dry lake there had occurred a quarrel between Hooker Jim and Jack, in which the murderers sided with Jim. The bad feeling then created grew with the hardships of the fighting, and these warriors began to think that Jack was tyrannical. The quarrel became so bitter that the band separated about the 15th. Thirteen warriors, with sixty-two women and children, composed the murderers' party; thirty warriors, with fifty-two women and children, followed Jack. Both parties left the Lava Beds, thereby throwing away their greatest protection as completely as did Roderick Dhu when he cast down his targe and bared his breast to Fitz-James's blade. The trail of the murderers' party was soon discovered. Hasbrouck's cavalry followed it, and overtook them after a hard march of fifty miles. For seven miles or more a sharp running fight was kept up, and then the Indians scattered for safety. The cavalry horses were so exhausted that further pursuit was abandoned for that night. Some Indians captured in this chase said the band desired to surrender. Messengers were sent to them in the morning. They asked for terms, but none were given, except safe conduct to General Davis's quarters. On May 22d they all came in and laid down their arms. Hooker Jim volunteered to go to Jack's camp and secure his surrender; he wanted eight men to go with him for protection, but only three were allowed. He was assured, through a mistake of the interpreter, it is said, that they would have immunity from punishment. Under this arrangement Hooker Jim, Bogus Charley, Shack-nasty Jim, and Steamboat Frank were furnished with horses and Springfield rifles, and started on their search for Jack's band, which, it was believed, had either gone south towards Pitt River, or east towards Goose Lake. The latter supposition proved correct. The four scouts found them, on the 28th, on Willow Creek, one of the head-waters of Lost River, east of Wright's Lake. The scouts had a stormy interview with Jack, in which he denounced them as cowards and squaws, who had induced him to go into this war and deserted him in the hour of peril. He said that he would never surrender; that he would die with his gun in his hand.

The scouts returned to the troops, who were moving in the same direction. At two o'clock the next day the command surprised Jack's band in the cañon of Willow Creek, near the crossing of the old emigrant road. Boston Charley came out and held up his hands in token of surrender. He was permitted to come into the lines. Seven women were captured also, including Jack's sister Mary, commonly known as "Queen Mary," or "Princess Mary." The rest escaped by running down the cañon, which is about forty feet deep and impossible of access to horses. On the next morning the troops followed their trail over hill and valley, through cañons and across beds of sharp lava rocks, to a bluff bordering on Langell's Valley. As they approached the bluff four shots were fired from it, and immediately after two warriors came bounding down the rocks, crying, "We surrender; don't shoot!" Five warriors came in. With these Dr. Cabanisse, who was well acquainted with the Modocs, went into the rocks to make arrangements for the surrender of the rest. He remained with them overnight. In the morning twelve warriors, including Schonchin and Scar-faced Charley, surrendered. Jack, with three warriors, fled in the night. There were nine others who scattered in different directions.

On June 1st, an hour or so before noon, a Warm Springs scout, with Colonel Perry's squadron of the First Cavalry, struck a fresh trail three miles above the mouth of Willow Creek. The squadron followed it, and in a short time found and surrounded the Modocs, who occupied a small pedregal. A warrior bearing a white flag appeared from among the rocks. He said that Jack desired to surrender. The scouts went in to meet him. He came out cautiously, glared about him for a few moments, and then, with the hopeless, desperate air of a man

"Who had thrown, and had missed
His last stake,"

he came forward and extended his hands to the scouts. His only remark was, "My legs have given out." He was taken to the camp at Applegate's ranch, near Clear Lake. The news of the capture had been carried before them, and was received with enthusiasm and rejoicing. Jack was the centre of attraction. Dressed in old, dilapidated clothes, and wrapped in a faded army blanket, it was still the universal sentiment that he looked every inch a chief. He stood apart, silent as a statue. The Indians said he was insane.

There surrendered with Jack two warriors, fifteen squaws, and seven children; the remainder of the band were captured during the two days following, excepting Long Jim and his father, who were caught on the 11th. The Modoc war was ended. In it the whites had lost in killed eight officers, thirty-nine enlisted men, sixteen citizens, and two Warm Springs scouts; in wounded sixty-seven. This was the loss to the army proper. To it should be added eighteen killed and about as many wounded, for the settlers who were attacked in November. The loss of the Modocs from the massacre of the commissioners to the close of the war was five warriors. Three were killed during the advance on the cave—two by the explosion of a shell, and one by a rifle-ball; one was killed at the dry lake, and one during the attack on Thomas, of the 26th. Their other killed were all women and children. The cost of the war was over half a million of dollars. The quartermaster-general reported the cost to his department at $355,000. We paid Oregon and California $76,000 for the services of their militia. Then there were the claims for destroyed property and other contingent expenses. The reservation that the Modocs asked for was of less than 2000 acres. If they had been settled in severalty the cost, including the value of the land, would have been about $10,000. An agency might perhaps have come as high as $20,000. Beyond dispute, the Modoc war would have been prevented at a cost of not to exceed one-twentieth of the outlay that occurred. It is, in fact, usually cheaper to be fair and honest with Indians, just as in other affairs in this world.

Governor Grover was on hand, demanding that the Modocs should be turned over to the civil authorities for trial. General Davis was not in favor of "the law's delay," and decided to hang eight or ten of them without any formality of

THE TRAGEDY OF THE LAVA BEDS.

CAPTAIN JACK AND HIS COMPANIONS.

judge or jury. While the scaffolds were being prepared, a telegram came from Washington, directing their trial by a Military Commission. The Commission sat from July 5th to July 9th, at Fort Klamath, Oregon. The prisoners arraigned were Captain Jack, Schonchin John (Schonchis), Black Jim,

Boston Charley, Barncho, *alias* One-eyed Jim, and Slolox, *alias* Lolocksalt, *alias* Cok. Ellen's Man was dead. The charges were murder and assault to kill, in violation of the rules of war. The prosecution made a clear case by the testimony of Riddle, Toby, Meacham, Dyer, Shack-nasty Jim, Hooker Jim Bogus Charley, Steamboat Frank, William, Lieutenant Anderson, and Surgeon McEldery; the defence introduced Scarfaced Charley, Dave, and One-eyed Mose, who testified that the Klamaths furnished them, gun-caps and were guilty of other acts of treachery. This may have been introduced in mitigation of their offence, or from an ignorant belief that they could shift the guilt to others. There is another possibility, which is very strong. Jack may have intended his defence solely for futurity. He may have been actuated by the same desire of a justification by posterity that moved Robert Emmet to the words, "Let not my epitaph be written till other times and other men can do me justice." He did not deny his guilt; he admitted that he had done wrong. He did not hope for a realization of his motives by his judges. He told them as much. The members of the Commission were strangers to him; they did not know his past surroundings or the events that had driven him on. He saw around him the men he had attempted to assassinate, the whites he had fought, and his enemies the Klamaths, who had urged him on. In the midst of them he saw the men who had brought him to ruin and betrayed him, sitting as his accusers. What room had he to hope for mercy there? He addressed the Commission. He tried to tell how he had been adopting the customs of the whites; how he had treated them generously; how he had dealt so fairly with all men that no one called him mean except the Klamaths. He said, "I have always lived like a white man, and wanted to live so. I have always tried to live peaceably and never asked any man for anything. I have always lived on what I could kill and shoot with my gun and catch in my trap. Riddle knows that I have always lived like a man, and have never gone begging; that what I have got I have always got with my own hands, honestly. I should have taken his advice. He has always given me good advice, and told me to live like a white man; and I have always tried to do it, and did do it, until this war started. I hardly know how to talk here. I don't know how white people talk in such a place as this; but I will do the best I can." The Judge-Advocate said, in a kindly way, "Talk exactly as if you were at home, in a council." Jack went on to tell how he and his people had become fearful of treachery on account of Captain Jackson's surprise, on account of the treatment of the Hot Creek Indians, on account of the threatening word sent to him by white men, on account of the misrepresentations of the squaw messengers. He told how his warriors refused to obey him; how they attacked the settlers without his knowledge; how they taunted him; and, as he came to the point where he gave way under the awful pressure that was brought upon him, he broke down. His throat choked up; he could speak no further. At his request the Commission adjourned to the next day, with permission to him to continue then. On the next day he resumed his address, but the flood of tender feelings that had overwhelmed him on the preceding day had given way to the stoical desperation which characterizes his race when the shadow of death is over them. In a few curt sentences he pointed out the guilt of the four informers, and sat down.

The Judge-Advocate submitted the instructions and detailed report of Captain Jackson, showing that he had acted in accordance with his instructions when he surprised the camp on Lost River. He acquitted Jack of any complicity in the attack on the settlers immediately following this occurrence, and submitted the case without argument. There could be but one result. The prisoners were found guilty on both charges and sentenced to be hanged. A strong influence was exerted with President Grant for a commutation of the sentence. The National Association to Promote Universal Peace, the American Indian Aid Association, and many individuals, petitioned in their behalf. One good Quaker brother offered, if the President would commute their sentence to imprisonment on some ocean island, to go there and devote his life to their enlightenment and salvation. For the information of the President, the Judge-Advocate, H. P. Curtis, reported that Barncho and Slolox were common soldiers, who appeared to have acted under the orders of their chief; that they were ignorant and devoid of perception—in short, little above the level of the brute; that they did not seem to understand the nature of their trial or appreciate their danger; and that Slolox, from choice, sat on the floor during the trial, much of the time asleep. Under this statement the sentences of Barncho and Slolox were commuted to imprisonment for life on the Island of Alcatraz, in the harbor of San Francisco. The others were executed at Fort Klamath on October 3, 1873, in accordance with the sentence. They were all hanged from one long scaffold. They mounted it firmly, and with no tremor stood through the preliminary proceedings, though Jack showed the signs of internal torment in his face. He had asked for delay that morning, but on being assured that it could not be granted—that he must die—he said, "I am ready to go to the Great Father." The orders for execution and the reprieve for Barncho and Slolox, which had arrived the night before, were read from the scaffold. The chaplain prayed fervently and the signal was given. As the drop fell, an involuntary cry of horror went up from the throats of over five hundred Klamaths, who had assembled to witness the execution. From the stockade, where the Modoc captives stood, in full view of the scene, rose shrieks and wails of anguish. It was over. The white man's justice was satisfied.

The decision of the President was just. It seems wrong that these men should be hanged for the very offence for which Ben Wright and his men were fêted and rewarded, but the wrong done was in failing to punish the white assassins. If criminals were to be pardoned because equally guilty men have escaped, there would be an end to all punishment. They knew they were committing a crime. Few criminals have a keener sense of their offending than did Captain Jack. He would not have debated so long before taking the fatal step if he had not known its evil nature. It was right that he should be hanged—and yet we killed him much as you would kill the mad dog that bites the hand extended to caress him, and we had helped to make him mad. Was it strange that the son of Dr. Thomas said, "The wickedness of white men caused my father's death?" The remainder of the tribe, excepting those who were murdered while prisoners, were sent east. Most of them were located at the Quapaw Agency, where, under chief Bogus Charley, they have become models of industry and good-behavior. Several of the worst men were sent to Fort Marion, at St. Augustine, Florida, and put under charge of Captain Pratt, of training-school fame. Under his labors they were converted to Christianity, and if testimony can be believed they underwent an actual change of heart. In 1879 Steamboat Frank, the unhanged murderer of 1873, was installed as pastor in the Modoc church on the Quapaw reservation. It is well that by penance and good works they should expiate their wrong-doing, but great must be the grace that has come upon them if the face of Krent-poos does not haunt them. Unfortunate man! Drawn by forces whose power we can scarcely imagine, he fell—fell hopelessly. Who shall reproach his memory? It was a divine wisdom that taught us all to pray, "Lead us not into temptation," for if the right temptation come, in open strength, or hidden under deceptive covering, who shall withstand it?

CHAPTER XVIII.

THE LITTLE BIG HORN.

THE Sioux war of 1876 was more like the wars between civilized nations, in its inception, than any conflict that ever occurred between the whites and the Indians. There were the same violations of compacts on both sides, the same diplomatic skirmishing, and the same deliberate preparation for wholesale killing, that the civilized world has decided to be proper when two nations have reached so belligerent a feeling that peace is no longer satisfactory to either. On paper, our relations with the Sioux remained as they were established in 1868, when we abandoned the Montana road. There was then set off to the western tribes, as a reservation, all of Dakota Territory west of the Missouri River and south of parallel 46—practically, the southwest quarter of the territory. This reservation, by the treaty, "is set apart for the absolute and undisturbed use and occupation of the Indians herein named, and for such other friendly tribes or individual Indians as from time to time they may be willing, with the consent of the United States, to admit amongst them; and the United States now solemnly agrees that no persons except those herein designated and authorized so to do, and except such officers, agents, and employés of the government as may be authorized to enter upon Indian reservations in discharge of duties enjoined by law, shall ever be permitted to pass over, settle upon, or reside in the territory described in this article, or in such territory as may be added to this reservation for the use of said Indians; and henceforth they will and do hereby relinquish all claims or right in and to any portion of the United States or Territories, except such as is embraced in the limits aforesaid, and except as hereinafter provided." The subsequent provision referred to is Article 16, as follows:

"The United States hereby agrees and stipulates that the country north of the North Platte River and east of the summits of the Big Horn Mountains shall be held and considered to be unceded Indian territory, and also stipulates and agrees that no white person or persons shall be permitted to settle upon or occupy any portion of the same; or without the consent of the Indians, first had and obtained, to pass through the same." The land covered by this article is "the Powder River country," and the article closes with the agreement that the Montana road, and all the posts along it, shall be abandoned.

During these eight years material changes had been taking place in other respects which altered the relations of the two races. The completion of the Pacific Railway, and the wonderful advance of minor lines into the plains, had carried an enormous population into the West. Kansas, Iowa, Nebraska, Colorado, Wyoming, Montana, and Eastern Dakota were filling up rapidly, and assuming the appearance of long-settled countries. The whites were strong in their numbers and their facilities for transportation. They had grown used to the Indian as the loafer and drunkard, and had no great fear of him in any character. Among the whites were many miners who looked with longing eyes on the Black Hills (a literal translation of the Sioux name, Pah-sap-pa), which lay wholly within the reservation. This tract of mountain country was almost unknown. It was partially surrounded by the Bad Lands, which formed a barrier that the emigrant shunned. The Indians went into the Hills but little. They considered it a "medicine" country, inhabited by their supernaturals, and not to be rashly invaded, though they occasionally hunted in its borders, or cut lodge-poles in its pine woods. Lieutenant Warren (afterwards a Confederate general) attempted to go into it in 1857, but when in the neighborhood of Inyan Kara, a peak on the western side, he was met by a delegation of Sioux chiefs and warned back. They said it was sacred ground. It was commonly believed that there was gold in the Black Hills, even before gold was discovered in California. In 1847, Parkman recounted how his trapper friend, Reynal, had stood on one of those mountains and said: "Many a time, when I

THE BAD LANDS.

was with the Indians, I have been hunting for gold all through the Black Hills. There's plenty of it here; you may be certain of that. I have dreamed about it fifty times, and I never dreamed yet but what it came out true. Look over yonder at those black rocks piled up against that other big rock. Don't it look as if there might be something there? It won't do for a white man to be rummaging too much about these mountains; the Indians say they are full of bad spirits; and I believe myself that it's no good luck to be hunting about here after gold. Well, for all that, I would like to have one of those fellows up here, from down below, to go about with his witch-hazel rod, and I'll guarantee that it would not be long before he would light on a gold mine."

No one knew whether there was gold in the Hills or not, but there grew up that strong faith in its existence which miners always have in regard to a country difficult of access. Man ever hopes for much from the unknown. Imagination furnishes the only statistics by which it may be judged, and imagination is liberal. The first recorded discovery of gold in the Black Hills was made by Toussaint Kensler, a half-breed who had worked in the placers of Alder Gulch, Montana. He had been under arrest for murder, but escaped, and for a long time was not seen in the haunts of men. He then reappeared at the agencies on the Missouri, with several goose-quills full of gold dust, and a fossil skull which he said he had found in the Bad Lands, when returning from these diggings that he had discovered. He was rearrested, convicted, and hung for the murder, but he left a map which shows a full acquaintance with the country he claimed to have examined. He said he found the gold on what is now called Amphibious Creek, a tributary of the South Fork of the Cheyenne, about ten miles above its mouth. The Indians sometimes brought in pieces of rock, bearing gold, and trappers occasionally reported discoveries of the metal. It is quite probable that Wetmore, the man who started the story of the "Lost Cabin," that great *ignis fatuus* of the miners, obtained the gold, which he brought home, from the Black Hills.

The interest in the country grew so strong that influence was brought to bear on the government, and an exploring expedition was ordered. It consisted of over twelve hundred men, with four Gatling guns and a large supply-train, accompanied by sixty Indian scouts, all under command of General George A. Custer. The movement was called a military reconnoissance, and said to be a military necessity; but the expedition certainly devoted more time to investigating the mineral and agricultural resources of the region than to anything else. It was accompanied by a number of miners and prospectors, who carefully examined the country along the lines of march and exploration. Custer mentions one instance in which they excavated to a depth of eight feet in their exploitations. They demonstrated the existence of gold beyond all reasonable questioning, but owing to some controversy that arose afterwards, the government sent another party to the Hills, in the following year, for the express purpose of investigating the gold indications. If this fact does not lift the thin disguise of military necessity from the first expedition, one could hardly imagine what would. The Custer expedition did not return until September, and the reports from it were so golden-hued that the excitement grew feverish. Parties were organized to go into the Hills, treaty or no treaty, and some of them did go. The Indians complained, and threatened to attack them if they were not removed. The military authorities denied for a time that any one had gone in, but on December 24 it was conceded that one party of twenty-one had evaded their watchful eyes. A company of cavalry was sent after them, but returned, after almost perishing from cold, without finding them. They remained in the Hills all winter and greeted many others in the spring.

There was no little dissatisfaction among the Indians over this invasion, and war was seriously contemplated. The far-sighted Red Cloud sent men to ascertain the probable number of buffalo, and their report showed that no reliance could be put on this food supply for any great time. The slaughter of buffalo in the past six or eight years had been prodigious. Careful investigators have estimated it at a million a year. It may have been less than that, but it was enormous. The buffalo had disappeared from the eastern side of the mountains altogether. The plains of Kansas, Colorado, Nebraska, and Dakota, which had once been alive with them, no longer shook beneath their migrations. The valleys of the Arkansas, Platte, Cheyenne, and their tributaries were deserted. The buffalo range was limited to the Powder River country. Red Cloud took in the situation. He decided for peace. In January, 1875, he and Spotted Tail expressed a desire to visit Washington and make arrangements for selling the Black Hills. To this request the government acceded. In the spring, miners began to flock into the Hills. The Interior Department called on the military to put them out. The troops made several trips for this purpose, brought out the gold-hunters, and turned them over to the civil authorities for trial. The civil authorities turned them loose, and they went back. Each time they went back their numbers were greatly increased. During the summer Professor Jenney made his exploration of the Hills, to settle the question of the existence of gold. He had no difficulty in learning that there was gold, from the miners who were there extracting it. The Hills contained probably a thousand miners in the fall of 1875. Custer City had been laid out, and people were coming in, with but little show of resistance.

It has often been claimed that the Black Hills question had nothing to do with the Sioux war of 1876, but the claim is partisan and untrue. In June, 1875, a commission was appointed by the President to secure from the Indians the right of mining in the Black Hills. They met with all the Teton tribes, the Northern Cheyennes and Arapahoes, and representatives of the Yanktons and Yanktonnais, September 17, 1875, at the plain north of Crow Butte, eight miles east of Red Cloud agency, on White River. They found the Indians in two parties, as to the sale. The larger party favored sale, but demanded sums ranging from thirty to fifty millions in payment. The smaller party, nearly all young men, opposed selling, on any terms. Their dissension became so bitter that a fight would probably have ensued but for the efforts of Young Man Afraid of his Horses, the leader of the "soldiers," or police force. The form in which the Indians who were willing to sell put their demand was, "Subsistence for seven generations ahead, or so long as we live." Their argument, as repeated by all the chiefs who spoke, was substantially as made by the Cheyenne chief, Little Wolf. He said: "You are here to buy the gold regions in those Black Hills. There has been a great deal stolen from those Hills already. . . . If the Great Father gets this country from us, it is a rich country and we want something to pay us for it. We want to be made rich too. There is gold and silver and a great many kinds of mineral in that country. The Great Father gets that for the whites. They will live on it and become rich. We want him to make us rich also." They refused absolutely to sell the Powder River country, and it was dropped from consideration on the first day. They dwelt much on the value of Pah-sap-pa. It was their "house of gold." It was "worth more than all the wild beasts and all the tame beasts in the possession of the white people." Said Crow Feather: "Even if our Great Father should give a hundred different kinds of live-stock to each Indian house every year, it seems that would not pay for the Black Hills. I was not born and raised on this soil for fun. No, indeed. ... I hope the Great Father will look and see how many millions of dollars have been stolen out of the Black Hills, and when he finds it out, I want the Great Father to pay us that." They offered to allow one road, and only one, which they designated as "the thieves' road." This, on inquiry, was found to be Custer's trail, over which several parties of miners had gone into the Hills. Little Bear claimed that white men had been in the Hills for four years, and Lone Horn said seven. The commission offered to lease the country at $400,000 per year, so long as the whites should use it, or to give them $6,000,000 in fifteen annual instalments for their title, which propositions the assembled Sioux received with derisive laughter. The commission was obliged to return unsuccessful. It reported: "We do not believe their temper or spirit can or will be changed until they are made to feel the power as well as the magnanimity of the government." It recommended that the government set its own price, and force the Sioux to accept it. In justice to the commission, it should be remembered that the same chiefs, who demanded $50,000,00 in the morning, would be begging for a shirt in the evening, and that it was believed that white men had urged them to ask this large sum. However, irrespective of all other questions, it is evident that the Sioux valued the Hills highly, part of them because they desired the country itself, and part of them on account of what they hoped to obtain for it. There appears no reason for supposing that either party would be contented to see it taken by the miners without payment to them, or for a much smaller payment than they considered it worth.

At this time the Sioux nation could hardly be said to have the same divisions that were formerly recognized. The Teton Sioux had become divided into four main bodies after the treaty of 1868, and had mixed largely with the Yanktonnais and Sissetons. Their agencies had all been on the Missouri until 1874, and then, on stated grounds of the contaminating effects of the settlements, Red Cloud and Spotted Tail agencies were removed to the southeast of the Black Hills. With the usual care that marks the transaction of Indian business, both agencies were located in Nebraska, off the reservation. At Red Cloud agency there were supposed to be 9100 Ogallallas and 3700 Cheyennes and Arapahoes. There was no such number of genuine Ogallallas. The tribe had been reinforced by other Sioux, attracted by Red Cloud's fame. At Spotted Tail (Whetstone) agency there were reported 8400 Brulés and 1200 Minneconjous. At Cheyenne River agency, on the Missouri, there were 7600 Two Kettles, Sans Arcs, Minneconjous, and Blackfeet Sioux. At Standing Rock agency, on the Missouri, were 7300, of whom 4200 were Yanktonnais, and the remainder Oncpapas and Blackfeet Sioux. At Fort Peck agency (Milk River), Montana, were 6000 Indians, sometimes called Tetons, but not, in fact, for 2000 of them were Assinaboines, and the remainder Yanktonnais and Sissetons, except about 400 who were Tetons proper. These were all the Tetons except the roaming tribes, which were estimated at 3000, as follows: Black Tigers, 150; Long Sioux, 200; Shooters, 900; Tatkannais, 700; Oncpapas, 450; White Eagles, 200; Yellow Livers, 350. These Indians lived in the Powder River country, and roamed extensively, all of which they had the right to do, under the treaty of 1868. The most celebrated chiefs of these bands were Crazy Horse and Sitting Bull. Crazy Horse was an Ogallalla, although the Indians with him, in the spring of 1876, were chiefly Northern Cheyennes and Minneconjous, numbering not more than five or six hundred. Sitting Bull's band was still smaller, consisting of only thirty or forty lodges in times of peace, but in war times increasing rapidly.

Sitting Bull (Ta-tan-kah-yo-tan-kah) was a born fighter. He is said to be a half-breed Oncpapa, though he signed the treaty of 1868 as an Ogallalla. At this time he was somewhat broken by disease, but he was still of fine physique. His hair was brown, his complexion light, his face badly scarred by smallpox. There was probably no other Sioux who could make so proud a showing of individual prowess as he. About the year 1870 a Yanktonnais Indian brought to Fort Buford an old roster of the 31st Infantry, which had, on the blank sides of the leaves, a series of portraitures of the doings of a mighty warrior. They were quite skilfully executed, in brown and black inks, with coloring added for the horses and clothing. The totem in the corner of each pictograph, a buffalo bull on its haunches, connected with the hero by a line, revealed the fact that it was a history of Sitting Bull, who, with a following of sixty or seventy warriors, had been depredating in the neighborhood for several years. The Yanktonnais finally admitted that he had stolen it from Sitting Bull, and sold it for a dollar and a half's worth of supplies. The first twenty-three pictures

SITTING BULL'S FIRST ADVENTURE.

showed his slaughter of enemies of all descriptions, men, women, and children, Indians, teamsters, mail-men, frontiersmen, railroad hands, soldiers. He was as impartial as death itself. The next twelve show his exploits as a collector of horses, a pursuit in which he displayed good taste and an insatiable craving for horse-flesh. He may fairly be considered one of the ablest horse-thieves the country ever produced. The last two pictures show him as leader of the Strong Hearts, a Sioux fraternity for war purposes—Knights of the Terres Mauvaises, as it were—storming two Crow villages.

SITTING BULL STORMS A CROW ENCAMPMENT AND TAKES THIRTY SCALPS.

In one of these fights thirty scalps were taken. These picture records are usually accurate. Ordinarily they are made on buffalo robes, and kept by the hero for display among his own people, who are acquainted with the facts of which he boasts. In this case the pictorial history was confirmed by knowledge that the whites already had of this doughty warrior.

While, therefore, Sitting Bull was not a chief of any particular prominence during times of peace, he had a record as a fighter, and a reputation as a skilful commander, that made him a loadstone to the discontented Sioux of the agencies. Even the agency Sioux who were not discontented were not averse to the society of their roaming brethren. Every summer they would slip away in small parties for a few months' sport with the bad Indians. Sometimes they would massacre a few Crows, or Blackfeet, or Arickarees. Sometimes they would practice shooting at the miners of Montana. Sometimes they would gather some cattle and horses from the settlers in Wyoming. These statements are not flights of fancy. The official records for seven months, from July 1, 1875, to the spring of 1876, show seventeen attacks on the whites in

Yellowstone Valley alone, nine men killed, ten wounded, and a large amount of property stolen. These depredations caused general complaints from whites and friendly Indians. The Crows, especially, who were trying to adopt civilization, suffered severely from these attacks. We were under obligations to protect them, and all other tribes that had accepted reservations in good faith, but we neglected to do so for many years. It was an established custom of the early days for the whites to stand neutral when two or more Indian tribes were at war among themselves. Each tribe would object to any interference except as an ally to it, and interference could therefore result only in making one or all the tribes hostile. It was clearly politic for the whites to stand back and permit them to enjoy themselves; so the mountain tribes and plains tribes kept up a perpetual warfare, as they had done from traditional times.

As the country became more settled these wars became more annoying. If a band were disappointed in its search for Indian enemies, it was liable to take some lonely settler as a substitute. Many such affairs occurred, one of the most

SITTING BULL SCALPS A TEAMSTER.

SITTING BULL STEALS A DROVE OF HORSES.

celebrated being the Rawlin's Springs massacre of June 28, 1873. On that occasion a party of Arapahoes went on the war-path against the Crows, but hearing that *les Corbeaux* were on the alert, they turned to try the Utes. Near Rawlin's Springs they crossed the Pacific Railroad, and chanced to meet a lone teamster driving four mules. They attacked him, but he fired on them and escaped. A party at once started after the Indians, who, on being overtaken, claimed to be friendly Utes. They would have gone unharmed, on that theory, had they not happened to have some stolen horses which were recognized by the whites. These were demanded, and during the controversy that ensued the Arapahoes undertook to run, firing back with their pistols as they went. The whites opened fire, killed four of them, and returned in triumph with eight captured horses. As we placed the more tractable tribes on reservations and endeavored to lead them into civilized ways, our duty of protection became stronger. The reservation Indian who honestly desired to work had to go to the field with his rifle in one hand and his hoe in the other. They complained bitterly. The Crows said: "We might just as well go out and kill white men as to try to be good Indians, for we get neither protection nor reward for being good." The depredations of the roaming Sioux were infractions of the treaty, justifying hostilities on our part. The only bad-looking feature of our sudden resolve to make them behave was that it came so quickly on the heels of the failure of the commission to purchase the Black Hills and the Powder River country. This feature is the more striking because the reservation Sioux refused to consider the sale of the latter, on the ground that the roaming bands would not consent to it. It was also pretty well established that the roaming bands were not guilty of all the depredations, and that Indians from the reservations were doing their share of these misdeeds, yet Sitting Bull's band got credit for nearly every wrong committed, a false reputation to which, however, they had little objection.

It was determined that the roaming tribes, or, as they were often called, "the hostiles," should be forced to go on the reservations. This determination was the immediate result of a report on their behavior by Inspector Watkins, on November 9, 1875. On December 6 of the same year, after consideration of this report by the Interior Department, orders were sent to all the Sioux agencies to notify "Sitting Bull's band and all other wild and lawless bands" that "unless they shall remove within the bounds of their reservation (and remain there) before the 31st of January next, they shall be deemed hostile, and treated accordingly by the military force." This notice was given, and the roaming bands refused to comply with it. They were then turned over to the military, and for this they were ready. Sitting Bull coolly sent word to General Terry to come on. "You need not bring any guides," he said; "you can find me easily. I will not run away." It was the original intention to strike the Indians before the spring opened, while their ponies were in bad condition and the weather prevented them from travelling, but movements from General Terry's department were made impracticable by the cold. General Crook prepared an expedition from Fort Fetterman, from which point, it was supposed, the troops could operate at any time.

The expedition was composed of ten troops of cavalry and two of infantry (700 men), with a large train, it being necessary to carry all forage for the horses and pack animals. The command marched down Tongue River almost to the Yellowstone. A trail was discovered, and Colonel Reynolds, with nine troops of cavalry, pushed forward over it, on the night of March 16. In the morning they discovered the camp of Crazy Horse, near the mouth of Little Powder River. The situation of the village, beneath the precipitous bluffs of the river, made it impossible to charge at once. The horses had to be conducted to the valley through almost impassable gorges, a work which required two hours, and even then Captain Moore's battalion of dismounted men, which had been assigned a position on the eastern side, had not been led to the designated point by the commander. Only two officers and five men advanced to where they had been ordered. At nine o'clock Captain Egan charged the camp, with one company, while Captain Noyes, with another, drove off the herd. Both movements were successfully executed, though Egan was put on the defensive before the supporting column came up. On its arrival the Indians fled to the rocks, and the soldiers began destroying the camp. One hundred and ten lodges, with numerous buffalo robes and property of all kinds, were burned. The troops lost four killed and six wounded; the Indian loss was trifling. Immediately after destroying the village, the troops retired rapidly to Lodge Pole Creek, twenty miles away, where they expected to meet Crook, but he had not arrived. The soldiers had now been thirty-six hours in the saddle, or fighting, and were much exhausted. Supperless and blanketless, they rested as well as they could during the intensely cold night. No guard was stationed with the captured herd, in consequence of which nearly all of them escaped and were retaken by the Indians. The cold grew so intense as to make further operations impossible. The thermometer repeatedly fell to thirty degrees below zero, and on several occasions went below registry. The command returned to Fort Fetterman, and the troops were distributed to their posts.

This movement and its results have been subjected to spicy criticism, beginning with some sharp talk by the Indian Department. In his report General Crook said that the village was a "perfect magazine of ammunition, war material, and general supplies. . . . Every evidence was found to prove these Indians in copartnership with those at the Red Cloud and Spotted Tail agencies, and that the proceeds of their raids upon the settlements had been taken to those agencies and supplies brought out in return." This raised the wrath of the Indian Bureau. Agent Howard, of Spotted Tail agency, reported at once: "No proceeds of raids upon settlements have been brought here; no supplies taken north in return. No arms have been sold by the agency trader to Indians for more than two years, and but little ammunition; and, for two months, none of either. . . . I respectfully suggest that General Crook be requested to produce some of the abundant evidence which he found." Agent Hastings, of Red Cloud agency, was more savage. He said: "I learn from one of the half-breed scouts, who was with Crook's expedition against the hostile camp, that it was a complete failure, with the exception of the killing of an old squaw and two children, and the destruction of about forty lodges, with a loss to the troops of four killed and six wounded. Seven hundred Indian ponies were captured, but were recaptured on the following day, with the exception of about seventy head. A dozen or more officers have been placed in arrest for cowardice, and the command have returned to the railroad. Five pounds of powder, twenty of lead, and six boxes of percussion caps comprised all the ammunition that was found in the abandoned camp." The truth probably lies between these extremes. While some of the statements of the latter extract are exact, its tone is so venomous as to destroy confidence in others. On the other hand, General Crook's statement savors more of opinion than of demonstration. It is difficult to conceive of any evidence that could possibly be in the Indian camp which would prove that the proceeds of raids on the settlements had been taken to the agencies and traded for goods. If such were the fact, the evidence would be at the agencies, not at the camp.

The plan adopted for the campaign was an advance in three columns, as soon as the weather permitted. General Crook was to march north from Fort Fetterman, with fifteen troops of cavalry and four companies of infantry, 1300

OLD FORT RENO—CROOK'S SUPPLY CAMP.

men; Colonel Gibbon was to come east from Fort Ellis, Montana, with four troops of cavalry and six companies of infantry, 400 men; General Custer was to move west from Fort A. Lincoln, with the 7th Cavalry, six companies of infantry, and three Gatling guns, 1000 men, besides the train men. This plan was followed, except that General Terry commanded the last force, Custer having been deposed by order of General Grant. The trouble between them was occasioned by Custer's testimony before the celebrated Heister Clymer committee, in the Belknap investigation. Clymer learned that Custer had reported his suspicions of certain transactions to the War Department, and that orders had been given that the transactions referred to be not interfered with. He at once summoned Custer, by telegraph. This was in the middle of March, and Custer was preparing to start his column early in April. He protested, and asked to be examined by deposition, but without effect. Mr. Clymer was gunning for big game, and did not propose to feel around in the dark by means of interrogatories. Custer had to go on to Washington. The main point elicited from him was that certain government contractors had turned over to him a large amount of grain, in sacks which bore the Indian Department's mark. He suspected that the sacks had been stolen from the Indian Department through a conspiracy between the Indian ring and the contractors, and reported the matter through his superior, General Terry, in accordance with military etiquette, at the same time refusing to receive the grain. He received peremptory orders to take the grain, which orders, he naturally believed, came down from the Secretary of War. This belief, however, was erroneous, as Custer learned of General Terry, on his return. Terry had given the orders himself, under certain instructions intended for the protection of the government. Custer at once telegraphed this fact to Clymer, and asked that the telegram be made part of his testimony, but the evil had already been done.

Grant was furious. He considered the attack on Belknap as an attack on himself and his administration, as well as an unjustifiable assault on his personal friend. The same quality of persistence that made Grant successful as a general, got him into trouble as an executive. He stuck to his friends in rough weather just as when the sky was smiling. He always fought it out on the line he had begun with—an excellent policy if the line be correct, but very bad otherwise. The verdict of history will probably be that Grant was an honest man who fell an easy prey to tricksters. The partisan effort to defend his administration, and the partisan effort to involve Grant personally in its corruption, will both fail under the test of time. Whether, in fact, Belknap was guilty in the Fort Sill tradership affair, or whether the folly of his wife occasioned his ruin, is not very material. It is beyond doubt that he was saved from impeachment solely by the legal theory of the defence, that a man out of office cannot be impeached, for of the twenty-five Senators who voted "not guilty," twenty-three explained their votes as being wholly on the ground of lack of jurisdiction. Whether guilty or not, there is clearly no reason why any one who knew any material facts should not be called as a witness, or why any witness should be reproached for telling what he believed.

Custer was in disgrace at court. In court opinion the probability of his antipathy to the administration was heightened by the fact that he was a Democrat in politics. He had joined that party soon after the war, on account of a feeling that the Southern States were treated unjustly. He now felt that he was misunderstood, but Grant refused to see him or hear any explanation. Three times Custer called at the White House and failed to obtain an audience. During the last call, as he waited in the anteroom, General Ingalls notified the President that Custer desired to speak to him, but Grant said he did not wish to see him. Custer then sent in a note stating that he desired the interview solely to correct certain unjust impressions which he believed were held concerning him. Grant still declined to see him. Custer started for his post. At Chicago he was overtaken by a despatch, through General Sheridan, ordering that he should stop and await further orders, while the expedition went on without him. A telegraphic correspondence ensued, which disclosed the fact that the instigator of the order was Grant, and that

Custer's offence as a witness was the cause of his hostility. The first concession obtained was that Custer might go on to his post, and remain there on duty. This did not satisfy the warrior. He appealed personally to Grant by telegram, saying: "I appeal to you as a soldier to spare me the humiliation of seeing my regiment march to meet the enemy and I not to share its dangers." This message General Terry kindly endorsed: "I do not know the reasons upon which the orders already given rest; but if those reasons do not forbid it, Lieutenant-colonel Custer's services would be very valuable with his command." This brought Grant around one step more, and Custer was permitted to go with his regiment, under Terry.

Unfortunately for Custer, the press got hold of the matter, and it became the subject of partisan dispute. The worst thing that can befall a man is to become a political martyr for the benefit of an opposition. His temporary friends cannot assist him, and usually care nothing for him, except as a viaduct for attack, while to the other and powerful side he becomes an object of execration. The Democratic papers attacked Grant for his treatment of Custer, and the Republican papers, as in duty bound, abused Custer, in defence of Grant. Between his policy friends and his unreasonable enemies poor Custer was well-nigh ruined.

The expeditions finally started. Crook met the enemy first. He moved to the hostile country, and, on June 8, established a large supply camp on Goose Creek. This he left under a strong guard, and marched on the 16th in search of the enemy, with nearly one thousand men. He had mounted his infantry on the train mules, and supplied each man with four days' rations. The Indians were believed to be on the Rosebud, about sixty miles away. Crook advanced for forty miles and went into camp. His Crow scouts refused to make a night march, having secured some buffalo during the day, and being determined to feast before they fought. The next morning an advance of seven miles was made, after which the troops camped at the mouth of a deep and rocky cañon with steep, timbered sides. The scouts were out ahead. Suddenly the reports of guns were heard, and soon the scouts came racing over the hills, chased by a large force of Sioux. The soldiers were quickly formed in line of battle, and the right centre was advanced to the summit of the bluffs, the position of the camp being untenable except these were held. In this general position the fight was carried on from eight in the morning until two in the afternoon. At the latter hour the left wing was ordered to retire, or connect with the main body. This movement was effected with considerable loss, the Sioux at once occupying the deserted position, and pouring a heavy fire into the retiring troops. Their advance was checked by a charge of the infantry and Indian allies from the left centre. Orders were then given for an advance, the purpose being to strike the Indian village, which was supposed to be about six miles ahead, but this was abandoned on account of the shortness of the supply of ammunition, and the discovery that the advance would have to be made through a cañon where the troops would be at the mercy of the enemy. After a brief pursuit of the Indians, who were now withdrawing, General Crook went into camp on the field. The loss to the troops was nine killed and twenty-one wounded. Eleven dead Indians were found on the field. The surprise of the village being now impossible, the wounded needing care, and the enemy being in much greater force than had been expected, Crook determined to fall back on his supply camp, which he did without further molestation.

Communication had not yet been established with the other two columns, and this withdrawal took Crook out of the range of practicable communication. Terry and Gibbon had communicated on June 1. On the 7th Terry established his supply camp at the mouth of Powder River. From this point Major Reno made a scout up Powder River to the mouth of the Little Powder, about one hundred and fifty miles, thence across to the Rosebud, and down it to its mouth. He could find nothing of Crook and nothing of the Indians, but on the Rosebud he found a heavy Indian trail, about nine days' old, which he followed for a short distance. In the mean time the main command had proceeded up the south bank of the Yellowstone to a point opposite Gibbon's camp,

ROSEBUD RIVER.

the steamer *Far West* moving up the river at the same time. A conference was held, and it was determined to make a grand surround, it being now reasonably certain that the Indians were between the Rosebud and the Big Horn, probably on the Little Big Horn. Gibbon was to cross the Yellowstone near the mouth of the Big Horn, march to the mouth of the Little Big Horn, by June 26, and then up the last-named stream. Meanwhile Custer was to march up the Rosebud with the 7th Cavalry, to the trail discovered by Reno. Beyond that point Custer had virtually *carte blanche*, by his written orders, but it was understood that if the trail were found to lead to the Little Big Horn he would pass it and continue southward long enough to allow Gibbon, who had all the infantry, to reach the mouth of the Little Big Horn. This he could not do before the 26th. This understanding is substantially set forth in Custer's orders, as the views of General Terry, with the desire that Custer should "conform to them" unless he should "see sufficient reason for departing from them." It was evidently the object of the movement to get the Indians between the two forces, but it is equally evident that either command was supposed to be large enough to safely engage all the hostiles. The object of division of forces was to prevent the escape of the Indians, to surround the hostiles, and bring the campaign to a close at one blow. No one, as yet, had any suspicion of the number of Indians they were to meet.

Custer moved up the Rosebud on the afternoon of the 22d twelve miles, and encamped. On the next day he advanced thirty-three miles, striking the lodge-pole trail that Reno had found. On the 24th he followed this trail for twenty-eight miles, still up the Rosebud, and went into camp. The scouts were kept ahead. At half-past nine a council was called, and Custer announced his intention of crossing the divide to the Little Big Horn that night, in order to avoid detection by the hostiles. At eleven o'clock the regiment moved on up one of the small feeders of the Rosebud, towards the Little Big Horn. The divide between these two streams is only about twenty miles across at this point, but by the course followed, up the tributary of the Rosebud, and down a tributary of the Little Big Horn, it was thirty-three miles from Custer's camp, on the evening of the 24th, to the Indian village. At two o'clock in the morning, after making ten miles, the column again halted until five o'clock in the morning, the scouts reporting that the divide could not be crossed until daylight. Coffee was made, and the troops moved on. At eight o'clock the first Indians were seen. It was then evident that no surprise could be made, but it was determined to attack the village, at any rate. The regiment was divided into four commands. Custer took five companies; Major Reno had three; Captain Benteen had three; and Captain McDougal, with one, was placed in charge of the pack train. Benteen was ordered to ride with his detachment to some bluffs on the left front, and to report if he could see anything of the village from there. He reached these bluffs, but could see nothing, and went on to some others beyond, making an offing of some ten miles. The rest of the command kept on down the creek until half-past twelve. Custer then sent word to Reno that the village was only two miles ahead and the Indians were running away. Reno says his orders were "to move forward at as rapid a gait as prudent, and to charge afterwards, and that the whole outfit would support me." He rode at a fast trot for two miles, crossed the river at a ford, halted ten minutes to gather his battalion, and moved on down the valley with his men in line of battle. The small number of Indians who appeared fled before him for two miles and a half, making scarcely any resistance.

"I soon saw," says Reno, "that I was being drawn into some trap, as they certainly would fight harder, and especially as we were nearing their village, which was still standing; besides, I could not see Custer, or any other support, and at the same time the very earth seemed to grow Indians, and they were running towards me in swarms, and from all directions. I saw I must defend myself, and give up the attack mounted. This I did, taking possession of a point of woods, and which furnished, near its edge, a shelter for the horses; dismounted, and fought them on foot, making headway through the wood. I soon found myself in the near vicinity of the village, saw that I was fighting odds of at least five to one, and that my only hope was to get out of the wood, where I would soon have been surrounded, and gain some high ground. I accomplished this by mounting and charging the Indians between me and the bluffs, on the opposite side of the river. . . . I succeeded in reaching the top of the bluff, with a loss of three officers and twenty-nine enlisted men killed, and seven men wounded." Benteen had struck the trail of the main body, just in advance of the train, and come on at a trot. He met a messenger with orders to McDougal to bring on the train as rapidly as possible. A mile farther on he met another messenger with the order: "Benteen, come on; big village; be quick; bring packs. P. S. Bring packs." Says Benteen: "A mile or a mile and a half farther on, I came in sight of the valley and Little Big Horn. About twelve or fifteen dismounted men were fighting on the plain with Indians, charging and recharging them. This body (the Indians) numbered about nine hundred at this time. Colonel Reno's mounted party were retiring across the river to the bluffs. I did not recognize till later what party this was, but was clear that they had been beaten. I then marched my command in line to their succor. On reaching the bluff I reported to Colonel Reno, and first learned that the command had been separated, and that Custer was not in that part of the field, and no one of Reno's command was able to inform me of the whereabouts of General Custer."

The two united commands, numbering three hundred and eighty men, now moved down the river, keeping on the bluffs. Firing had been heard in that direction, and the inference was that Custer was engaged. On reaching the summit of the highest bluff nothing could be seen of him, and no more firing was heard. Reno stopped until the pack train came up, meanwhile sending Captain Weir, with one company, to open communication, but he quickly sent back word that he could make no progress; that the Indians were surrounding him. A heavy fire from his force showed that his enemies were not imaginary. It now seemed certain that Custer had been driven back and had retired down the river. Weir was called back, and the whole force moved to Reno's first position after retreating across the river, which was the most available point for defence yet found. Here they were rejoined by scout Herndon and thirteen men, who had become separated from the command in the timber. The place was a small depression, surrounded by the crests of the hills that formed it. The animals were scarcely placed in the depression, and the men stationed on the crests, when the Indians attacked them in strong force They maintained an incessant fire from six till nine o'clock in the evening, during which the troops lost eighteen killed and forty-six wounded.

All through that night the soldiers worked at their intrenchments, making rifle-pits and barricading with dead animals. Below them, in the valley, the Sioux were holding a scalp-dance over those already fallen, and the wild sound came plainly on the night air to the little band, who knew that their scalps would be in demand on the morrow. Day broke at half-past two, and the attack was renewed at once, by a part of the enemy. The remainder came in crowds, riding up the valley from the scene of their orgies of the night, until all the élite of Sioux chivalry had taken their places about the tiny fortress. For seven hours they maintained a continuous fire of rifles, themselves out of reach of the carbines of the cavalrymen. At half-past nine they made a desperate charge, advancing close enough to use their bows and arrows, but were driven back by a counter-charge from the lines, led by Captain Benteen. They then charged on the other side, but were repulsed by a like counter-charge under Major Reno. It was now ten o'clock, and the men, especially the wounded, were suffering for water. Volunteers were called for, and a party was soon scrambling down to the river, under cover of the fire of their comrades. They secured enough to moisten the lips of all, but they left half a dozen brave men on their road. The Indians then began moving to the valley, presumably either to get something to eat or more ammunition, and the soldiers hastened to get a good supply of water before they should return. They did not come back. At two o'clock they fired the grass in the valley, and under cover of the heavy smoke began preparations for their final departure. About sunset they emerged from the clouds of smoke and filed away in the direction of the Big Horn Mountains. Reno moved his position that night, so as to secure a full supply of water, but the Indians had gone to stay. The only arrival during the night was Lieutenant De Rudio, who had become separated from the command in the timber, where he had been hiding ever since. In the morning Terry and Gibbon came up. They had seen nothing of Custer.

Until this time no one had felt any serious apprehension for Custer's command. Reno and Benteen supposed he had fallen back, down the river, and united with Terry. Terry and Gibbon had received word by the Crow scouts that Custer had been defeated, but did not believe it. Captain Benteen was sent out with a company of cavalry to make a search. He struck the broad trail that Custer had left, and in that trail was read the record of their progress to death, as plainly as though it were written in words. From the point where Reno crossed the river, Custer had marched rapidly down the north bank, keeping back of the crests of the bluffs, for a little more than three miles. Then his trail swung around to the river, but did not cross it. It turned back on itself and still bore down the river. The fighting began at this turning-point, as was shown by the bodies of men and horses first appearing there. Custer had probably intended to strike the lower end of the village, but, not knowing its extent, had attempted to cross the river near the middle of the village. He had been ambushed and driven back. He had been pressed so closely that there was no opportunity for a stand. Three quarters of a mile back from the river Captain Calhoun's company had been thrown across the line of retreat as a rear-guard. They died at their posts. Stretched across the trail in irregular line, with Calhoun and Lieutenant Crittenden in place at the rear, were the bodies of all the company—dead, where they had been stationed, in the attempt to save the remainder of the command. Under cover of this check, the rest of the force had fallen back a mile farther and gained a better position; but the remorseless Sioux were on their heels. The force was now disposed in something like military order. The centre, on a small ridge, was held by Yates's company. On the left was Keogh's company, with its right flank resting on the ridge. On the right was Smith's company. Captain Tom Custer's company was probably in the right centre.

The brunt of the attack came first on Keogh's company, which went down, as Calhoun's had, in line. There was no chance to aid them. The Indians were pressing on every side. It has been learned from Sitting Bull that at this point the Indians captured most of the horses, by circling the hill to the right (of the Indians) and driving them away from the rear. The superior forces of the Indians, and the shrewdness and daring of their fighting, can be judged from this movement. They knew where the horses were and that they wanted only these to make their prey secure. The plains Indians have not the nerve to ride to certain death, but they charge as gallantly as any cavalrymen that ever rode, when they are confident of success. They had trampled down Keogh's men like ripened grain, as they dashed to the rear to secure the horses. The attack now came on the left centre—from the front, rear, and left flank. The fire poured in on the little ridge must have been terrific. Custer fell there, with nearly all his officers. Around his body were those of Captain Yates, Colonel Cook, and Lieutenant Riley. Close by were Boston Custer, the general's brother, Autie Reed, his nephew, and Kellogg, the *Herald* correspondent, all civilians who had accompanied the expedition. Around these were the bodies of Yates's company. Just beyond was the corpse of Tom Custer, the general's brother, with part of his men; and a little farther on lay Captain Smith. The positions of the bodies showed that the remnants of Custer's and Smith's companies, their officers all dead, and themselves surrounded on three sides by the foe, had fallen back through a ravine to the river, leaving twenty-three dead along the line of retreat. Near the river they stopped. They had all the surviving uncaptured horses with them. It is probable either that the sight of the village, extending yet below them, showed them there was no chance for escape, or that they were here met by some new force. Here, at least, they died.

The only man of the entire command that escaped was "Curly," a Crow scout. When Custer was surrounded on the

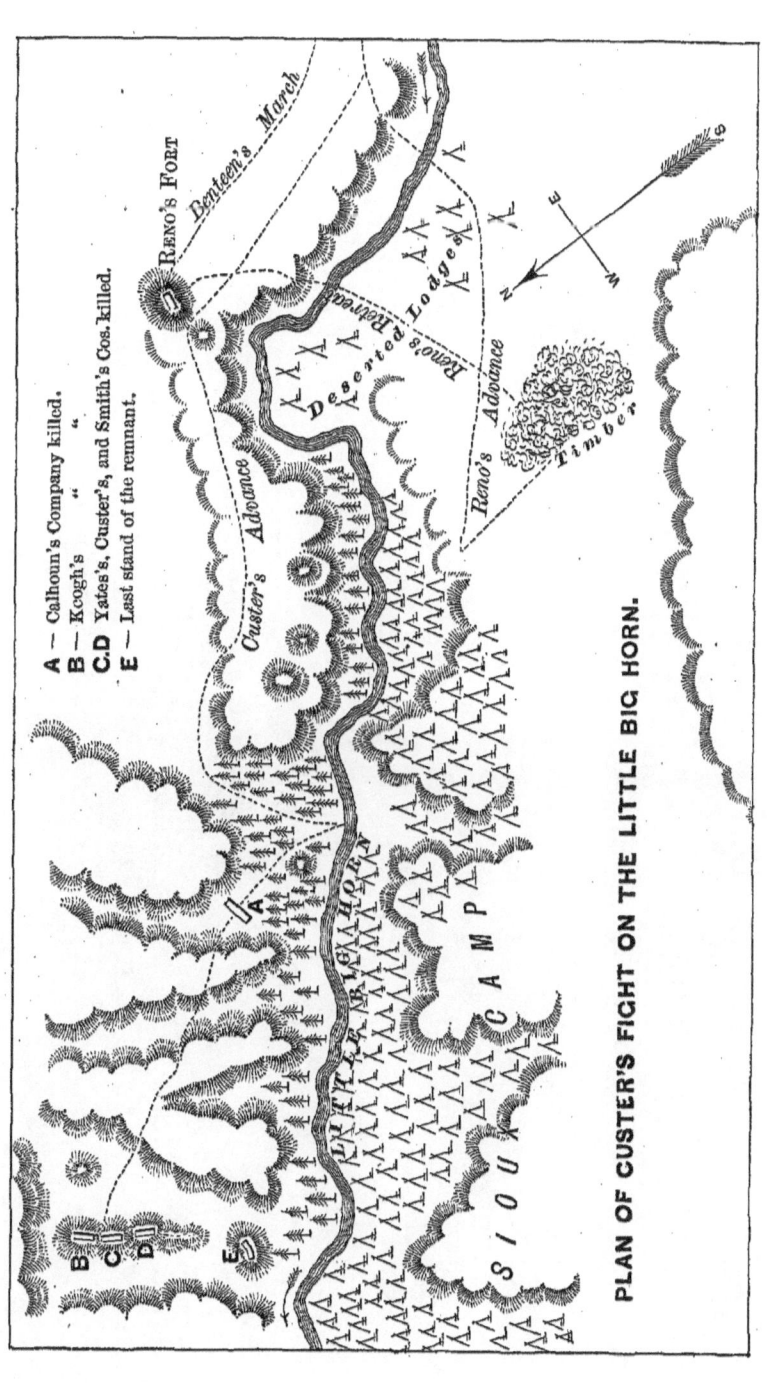

THE LITTLE BIG HORN. 615

hill, he slipped down a ravine, let down his hair in Sioux fashion, changed his paint, secured a Sioux blanket, and succeeded in getting among the enemy during a charge. He mounted the horse of a fallen warrior and made his escape during the confusion of the battle. He says he did not leave Custer until the fight on the hill was almost ended. He saw Custer sink to a sitting posture, from a shot in his side, and then fall back, struck by a second bullet. It has been reported as having been claimed by some of the hostiles who fled into British America, that Custer was the last to fall; and that he died, sabre in hand, shot by Rain in the Face. The story is hardly credible. Custer was not the last to fall, beyond question. The evidence that has been obtained all goes to show that he was not even the last officer who fell on the ridge, but that Lieutenant-colonel Cook survived the others. Curly says that as he rode away, when nearly a mile distant, he looked back and saw a dozen or more soldiers, in a ravine, fighting the Sioux, who hemmed them in on all sides. This was after Custer's death, as the position of the bodies and the trail itself proved. The opinion most prevalent among Dakota people, to whom the talk of the Indians drifts, sooner or later, is that no one knows certainly who killed Custer—that he died by some bullet that could never be identified among the hundreds that were flying.

Of course it is possible that Rain in the Face shot him; but the real basis of this story was the imprisonment of this Indian, and his probable desire for revenge. In 1873 Custer had been sent with an expedition to protect a surveying-party of the Northern Pacific Railroad Company, from the Missouri to Montana. They crossed the country which had been guaranteed the Sioux, by the treaty of 1868, and which was consequently occupied by "hostiles." On this expedition the troops were attacked by the Sioux, and, at the time of the attack, two non-combatants were killed while separated from the command. They were Dr. Honzinger, the veterinary surgeon, and Mr. Baliran, the sutler of the 7th Cavalry. They were elderly men, of scientific tastes, and were searching for fossils, in which the bad lands abound. Their slayer was unknown; but, eighteen months later, while Custer was in winter quarters at Fort Abraham Lincoln, he was discovered at Standing Rock agency. The Sioux were there drawing rations, and, as usual, held dances in which they recounted their prowess. In one of these Rain in the Face, a young brave, described how he had killed these two men, and displayed articles that had belonged to them. Unfortunately for him, Reynolds, the scout —Lonesome Charley Reynolds, he was called; a brave man with a pathetic history, who fell in Reno's first skirmish on the Little Big Horn—was looking on, and understood the story. He notified Custer, who sent a company to arrest the man. They brought him out, after many threats and much begging by the Indians, and took him to Fort Lincoln. His arrest caused much anxiety to the Sioux, who expected him to be hung. He was a great brave, and so were his five brothers; one of them, Iron Horn, being a chief of prominence. He had especially distinguished himself in the sun dance—the Sioux test of endurance—by remaining suspended for four hours and refusing to be cut down, although the judges decided that he had passed the test.* He confessed his guilt to Custer, and was retained in the guard-house. In the spring of 1875 some white hay-thieves, confined in the same place, made their escape by cutting through the side of the building, and Rain in the Face slipped out after them. When next heard from he was with Sitting Bull, and sent in word to his tribe that he was awaiting an opportunity for vengeance.

It is to be regretted that Major Reno and General Terry should have felt it necessary to reflect on the course of Custer in attacking the Indians before the other troops were within supporting distance, and equally so that Custer's friends should have returned the attack by accusations of disobedience and cowardice against Reno and Benteen. There was no occasion for either. The affair is pardonable on one account, and one

---

* The tortures of the sun dance are about the same as those of the Mandans, described and illustrated by Catlin. The suspension test is made by hanging the candidate on cords passed under various muscles or sinews, until the flesh gives way under the strain and he falls to the ground. Sometimes weights are attached to the limbs to hasten the desired result. Rain in the Face was hung by cords passed under the muscles at the base of the shoulder-blades.

only; and all of its minor happenings fall under the same excuse. No one with Custer's command, or with Terry or Gibbon or Crook, had any thought that there was so large a force of hostiles; and none of them had any reason to suspect its real strength. The roaming Indians were reported by the Indian Department to number 3000, which meant a fighting force of 600 possibly 800. The information from other sources did not indicate any excess over this figure. On March 22, General Crook, reporting the attack on Crazy Horse's village, said: "Crazy Horse had with him the Northern Cheyennes and Minneconjous, probably in all one half the Indians off the reservation." This camp consisted of 110 lodges, or less than 600 people. From this statement it would appear that the military expected a hostile force of not to exceed 1200, or a fighting force of about 250. Agent Howard, of Spotted Tail agency, replying to Crook's report, said, on April 1: "Very few, if any, of these Indians have been north this season, and I have heard of none who were in copartnership with those of the North." Agent Hastings, of Red Cloud agency, in a similar communication, on April 3, said: "The agency Indians appear to take but little interest in what has transpired north; but the disastrous result may have a tendency to awaken the old feeling of superiority. I have experienced no difficulty whatever in taking the census, but have been somewhat delayed on account of the weather." There was in these reports no cause to anticipate that the hostiles would be materially reinforced from these agencies. General Sherman, whose position put him in possession of all the information that could be had, referring to Custer's departure on June 22, said: "Up to this moment there was nothing official or private to justify an officer to expect that any detachment could encounter more than 500, or, at the maximum, 800 hostile warriors." There was nothing, after that moment, from which Custer or any of his officers had any reason to change that estimate, until they were fairly within the clutches of the enemy.

This was a wide miscalculation. The Indians from all the Sioux agencies began slipping away to the hostiles as soon as spring gave signs of approach, and when Custer struck them, there were together, as nearly as can be judged, about one half of all the Sioux in Dakota. As soon as the fight on the Little Big Horn had shown what the real state of affairs was, the military authorities insisted on taking control of the agencies, and, on July 22, the Secretary of the Interior acceded to the demand. The soldiers at once took possession of the agencies, and made a careful census of the Indians remaining on the reservations. At Red Cloud, instead of 12,873 Indians, there were 4760. At Spotted Tail, instead of 9610, there were found to be 2315. At Cheyenne River, instead of 7586, there were found 2280. At Standing Rock, instead of 7322, there were found 2305. In other words, there were 25,800 less Indians at these four agencies than belonged there, according to the reports of the Indian Bureau. These, with the 3000 roaming Indians, who were always off the reservations, make 28,800, to which there could safely be added a considerable number as representatives from other agencies, notably from Fort Peck. It is certain that a large portion of the Indians, off the reservations when the censuses were taken by the military, had left after reports of the Little Big Horn fight reached them and stimulated them to a desire for war, but, deducting one half for this, we may still count at least 3000 warriors for that engagement. Reno says, of the horde that surrounded his intrenchment on the 26th: "I think we were fighting all the Sioux nation, and also all the desperadoes, renegades, half-breeds, and squaw-men between the Missouri and Arkansas, east of the Rocky Mountains, and they must have numbered at least 2500 warriors." This is more probably an underestimate than an overestimate. The hostiles had assembled at this point, Crazy Horse, Sitting Bull, and all the rest. The Indians say so, and the scouting that had been done previously had shown that all the hostiles were in that neighborhood. The two main bodies joined about the 23d, as was shown by a heavy trail into the valley, about five days old, discovered by Captain Ball, on the 28th. The village extended three miles down the river, and in addition to the lodges there were a large number of brush shelters, such as are commonly called wick-i-ups in the West. Officers who estimated from the size of the village thought there were at least 3000 warriors.

MASSACRE MONUMENT.

The belief has been held by some military men that the Indians were not expecting an attack when the soldiers struck them, but this theory is not supported by the facts. The inference from all the evidence is irresistible that Custer advanced into a remarkably complete and well-planned ambuscade. The Indians had ample notice of his approach. He did not advance on them rapidly. At five o'clock in the morning, when he re-began his march, he was twenty-three miles from the village. At half-past twelve, when Reno was ordered to charge, they were still four miles from it. In seven hours and a half they had advanced nineteen miles. They first saw Indians at eight o'clock, and at their rate of marching they were then about fifteen miles from the village, with the Indians still nearer. If we suppose these first Indians seen to have been the first Indians who saw the troops, it is evident that they could have notified the village with ease by ten o'clock. No one at all acquainted with Indian methods will believe that the troops mere out of sight of Indian scouts at any time after eight o'clock. There are two facts going to show that they desired the troops to suppose that the village had not been alarmed. They did not make any signal-fires for communication, as they usually do. These would have informed the soldiers that their presence was known to all the Indians in the vicinity. Secondly, Trumpeter Martin (the last white man who saw Custer alive), who brought back the message to Benteen, says he left the general at the summit of the bluff overlooking the village, and that, as he turned, "General Custer raised his hat and gave a yell, saying they were asleep in their teepees and surprised, and to charge." It is known that only a part of the village was visible from any point on the bluff that the soldiers reached before the fight, but the part Custer saw was quiet. It must have been kept quiet intentionally, for the warriors were at that time waiting for Custer below, and under such circumstances there would naturally have been an appearance of activity in the village, whatever its size might have been. Custer drew the correct conclusion on his theory of the number of Indians there. If there had been only from five to eight hundred warriors, and they had been notified of the coming of the troops, the squaws would have been taking down the lodges and packing at that time. The only inference that could be drawn was that they were surprised, and Custer acted on it, as they probably desired that he should.

The Indians were in at least two bodies before the fight began, one at the upper end of the village, and one at the ford where Custer attempted to cross. When Reno retired across the valley from the timber he was pursued by all the Indians there, who followed him until he reached the top of the bluff. His heaviest loss occurred while ascending the bluff. From the summit he heard firing, down the river, where Custer had gone. Custer was on the retreat from the time he was attacked, as is shown by the trail. Consequently, an overwhelming force of Indians was fighting each party at the same time. The number of Indians fighting Reno was estimated by Benteen at 900, and by Reno to be at least that number. So far as is known, the remainder, numbering probably 2000, were fighting Custer. The record of time given by Reno also shows that they were fighting simultaneously. Custer ordered Reno forward at half-past twelve. His own command followed Reno's to a point near the ford, and then moved rapidly three miles down the river, in all five miles. He must have been engaged by two o'clock, and probably was fighting from half-past one. It was half-past two when Reno reached the top of the bluff and was joined by Benteen. It is not probable that Custer's fight lasted long after that time. There has been published an account of this massacre, purporting to come from a trapper named Ridgely, who was a prisoner in the Sioux camp and escaped during the jubilee on the night of the 25th, in which it is stated that the fight with Custer lasted only fifty-five minutes. This story contains numerous errors, and is therefore unworthy of belief except as corroborated. In this particular it is corroborated by Reno and Benteen, who say the firing bad ceased when they advanced on the bluffs, and Captain Weir was sent beyond to learn Custer's whereabouts. This movement was made shortly after Reno and Benteen united, and before the pack train had come up. Another fact which shows conclusively that Custer's fight was short, was the small number of Indians killed. The estimates of their killed, in the entire affair, by the officers engaged, were from forty to one hundred. The Indians conceded a loss of thirty-five. Most of these were killed by Reno's command in the fight on the 26th.

With these points in mind, it is easy to see the plan of the Indians. They knew that a force of about six hundred men was approaching. They saw Benteen's detachment leave the others and ride to the left. They arranged their forces, part at the end of the village nearest the soldiers, and part at the first accessible ford below the approach to the upper end of the village If the soldiers reunited they might possibly charge through at either place, but if they did they would be surrounded on all sides. If they came in two detachments there would be enough warriors at both points to overwhelm them. At the upper end a few Indians remained among some scattered teepees, above the main village. As the soldiers advanced these were to retreat, and draw their pursuers into the midst of the main body at this point. They failed in this, because Reno became suspicious of their action, and, seeing nothing of Custer, who, he understood, was to follow him, halted before reaching their ambuscade. They then advanced on him, passing constantly to his rear, to surround him, whereupon he cut through them to the bluffs. At the other end

MAJOR-GENERAL GEORGE A. CUSTER.

Sitting Bull had his main force at the ford, with a strong band advanced six hundred yards on the right bank, and concealed in the timber. Sitting Bull so states, and his statement is verified by the fact that Custer, instead of falling back by the road over which he advanced, retired farther down the stream. This he would not probably have done from choice, for it took him away from Reno and Benteen, and placed him in very bad ground, much cut up by ravines. He was struck in the rear by this band, turned down the river, and hurried on by a force vastly outnumbering him, until completely swept away.

It has been quite commonly believed that Custer recklessly charged his command into a force that outnumbered him from five to ten times over, and that his recklessness was more or less due to his trouble with General Grant. That this last made him more anxious for action is probably true. One can readily see how the soldier, who has unwittingly been drawn into the muddy pool of politics, would wish for an open field and the enemy before him. The people understood that, and they looked on the attack as some of "Custer's dash," but they did not blame him, for it was that same "dash" that carried him into their hearts long before. There was another consideration, too, that might well have palsied the tongue of criticism—the terrible loss to the Custer family. The general, his two brothers, his brother-in-law, Captain Calhoun, and his nephew, were certainly sacrifices enough to have expiated any common mistake. But this estimate, though it may be intended to be a kindly one, is unjust to Custer's memory. In fact, there has been injustice done to all the officers engaged in the battle, and it has arisen chiefly from the efforts of themselves or their friends to evade the supposed fault in the affair. There was not fairly any fault in it. It is evident that Custer attacked a force which he believed, and had every reason to believe, was about equal to his own. In that belief he concluded logically that the Indians were surprised when he saw their quiet camp. With that belief his division of his force into detachments, to strike on two sides, was a most excellent plan. He had not overmarched his command. His advance was only sixty-one miles, from five o'clock on the morning of the 24th, to the time of the fight, or about thirty-two hours. It is plain enough that Terry's plan was to get the Indians between Custer and Gibbon, but this was not from any supposition that either command was not large enough to handle the Indians singly. It was for the purpose of preventing their escape. Terry had no more knowledge of the number of the Indians than Ouster had, and neither Terry nor Custer can justly be blamed for relying on what information they had.

On the other hand, Reno and Benteen are equally justifiable. Reno saw that he was being drawn into a trap, and fell back in time to save the greater part of his command. It was most fortunate that he did so as quickly as he did. Army officers, in blaming one another for failures, almost invariably weaken their common defence, and this case is no exception. Custer's biographer, Captain Whittaker, in assailing Reno for falling back, labors to prove that the number of all the Indians at the village, including squaws and children, was about 4500. If this were correct, the maximum number of warriors that could fairly be counted would be 1500. The number assailing Reno, by the estimates of both Reno and Benteen, was about 900. The result of Whittaker's argument, therefore, would be that Custer was driven back by a party smaller than that assailing Reno, and Custer had two companies more than Reno. Benteen's course is also attacked by Captain Whittaker, but in this his premises are incorrect. His argument is based on the time consumed in Benteen's movements, and his time and distances are fixed by the time when Benteen watered his horses, which he assumes to have occurred when crossing the river. The horses were watered at a morass, some distance back on the main trail. The unjustness of the estimate of our officers has been increased by an underestimate of the Indian leaders. That they were men of ability to handle their forces is certain. That was a matter of notoriety all through the campaign of 1876. No more complete evidence of their skill could be given than the fact that neither of the three armies searching for them secured any knowledge of their numbers or position in advance. Crook had no idea of their strength until they fought him and turned him back on the 20th of June. Custer did not suspect it until they swarmed about him on the 25th. Terry and Gibbon did not believe it possible for Custer to have been defeated, when the Crow scouts brought them word of it. It is a task requiring much tact and skill for a commander to conceal 15,000 people from the scouts of armies which are on all sides of him.

The struggle with the Sioux was protracted. The hostiles

of the Little Big Horn separated into two bands, Sitting Bull's Indians remaining in the west, and Crazy Horse's moving towards the east. The war spirit was awakened throughout the Sioux nation, and warriors were constantly leaving the reservations. Colonel Merritt intercepted and drove back a party of 900 Cheyennes, that had started from Red Cloud, but many others gained the hostile camps. In a short time small parties were raiding in all directions. Reinforcements and supplies for the troops were hurried forward, but autumn had arrived before they were ready for active operations. On September 29, Captain Mills, of Crook's command, with 150 men, surprised the camp of American Horse (Wa-se-chun-Ta-shun-kah, *i.e.,* Washington Tashunkah) at Slim Buttes, Dakota. American Horse was mortally wounded, four of his men killed, and a dozen captured. The Indians lost their lodges, supplies, arms, ammunition, and 175 ponies. A number of articles belonging to the 7th Cavalry were found in this camp. In October, after a desperate and fruitless attack on a large supply train, escorted by Colonel Otis, Sitting Bull

SITTING BULL. (FROM A PORTRAIT BY D. F. BARRY, BISMARCK, DAKOTA.)

met Colonel Miles with propositions for peace. Miles, who had been put in command of the active troops in Dakota, told him that he could have peace if he would go on a reservation, or camp near the troops, where he would be in subjection to the government. Sitting Bull said he would come in and trade for ammunition, but wanted no rations or annuities, and desired to live free, as an Indian. The council dissolved with the assurance to the Indians that non-acceptance of the government's terms would be considered an act of hostility. Both parties took positions for action, and a battle ensued, in which the Indians were routed, and chased for over forty miles. On the 27th more than 400 lodges surrendered. Sitting Bull, with his band proper, escaped to the North, and was afterwards joined by several others. One band of 119 lodges, under Iron Dog (Shon-ka-Ma-za) gained the Yanktonnais reservation and dissolved. Just previous to this time the Indians on the reservations were disarmed and dismounted. The same policy was pursued towards all the hostiles that came in subsequently. Red Cloud, who had remained at his agency, was deposed for his hostile bearing, and Spotted Tail was put in charge of all the Indians at both agencies.

Late in the fall a new expedition was fitted out by General Crook. The cavalry with this force (ten troops), under Colonel Mackenzie, surprised the camp of Dull Knife, a Cheyenne chief, at daybreak, on November 25. The Indians escaped with heavy loss, but their village of 173 lodges was destroyed, and 500 ponies were captured. Owing to cold weather, operations were thereafter suspended in this department, but were maintained in the Department of Dakota. On December 7 Lieutenant Baldwin, with 100 men, attacked Sitting Bull's camp of 190 lodges, and drove him across the Missouri into the bad lands. On the 18th Baldwin surprised their camp and captured all its contents, together with 60 horses. The Indians escaped across the Yellowstone in a state of destitution. Hearing of the reverses of Sitting Bull, Crazy Horse sent him word to join his camp, as he had plenty of men and supplies; but General Miles learned of this from spies, and kept a force between the two bands which prevented their union. On Dec. 29, Miles started with 436 men and two cannons against Crazy Horse, who had his winter camp on the Tongue River. The Indians abandoned their village on his approach, and were driven up the river from January 1 to January 7. On the evening of the 7th, the advance captured a young warrior and seven Cheyenne women and children, who were relatives of one of the Cheyenne head men. The Indians made a desperate attempt to recover them that evening, and on the following morning 600 warriors engaged Miles. This fight occurred on a spur of the Wolf Mountains. The ground was covered with snow and ice, and a blinding snow-storm came on during the action. The Indians were driven back over three rugged bluffs, which horses could not cross, and which men could surmount only with great difficulty. They then fled, having lost heavily, and went through the Wolf Mountains in the direction of the Big Horn range.

Communication was opened with them through the captives. On February 1 Miles sent word to them that they must surrender unconditionally or he would attack them again. In March, after consultation, they concluded to submit, and left nine men as hostages for their surrender, either to Miles or at the agencies. 300, under Two Moons, Hump, and other chiefs, surrendered to Miles on April 22. Over 2000, under Crazy Horse, surrendered at Red Cloud and Spotted Tail agencies in May. Sitting Bull fled into British America with his little band, and was there joined by Iron Dog, Gall, and other chiefs. Crazy Horse remained on the reservation near Camp Robinson, until September. It was then learned that he was trying to bring about another war. He was arrested, but tried to escape, while on his way to the guard-house, by running amuck through the crowd, striking with his knife at all who opposed him. He received a fatal wound, and died on September 7. The only band remaining at large was Lame Deer's. They were Minneconjous, with some renegades, who broke off from Crazy Horse's band when he determined to surrender, numbering in all 51 lodges. Colonel Miles surprised and routed them, on the morning of May 7, on the Rosebud, near the mouth of Muddy Creek. They lost 14 killed, including Lame Deer, all their supplies, and 450 ponies. The remaining Indians scattered, and Miles was soon after called away to stop the Nez Percés, who were retreating through Montana. On September 26, 1876, the "hostile" feeling having become somewhat subdued, the Sioux concluded the agreement by which they surrendered the Black Hills and the Powder River country to the government, and accepted in lieu thereof a substantial ration for each member of the tribe until they should become self-supporting.

Sitting Bull's party was visited in British America by a commission, with the object of inducing them to return and surrender. They returned a defiant refusal to the emissaries of the government which "had made fifty-two treaties with the Sioux and kept none of them," declaring their intention to become subjects of her majesty. The new situation did not long suit them. The British government gave them protection merely, with no assistance, and this on the understanding that they would not be allowed to depredate across the line. One by one they concluded to come back to the flesh-pots of the republic. They kept coming in small parties and surrendering to the troops until, on July 20, 1881, Sitting Bull, with his little band, reduced to 45 men, 67 women, and 73 children, surrendered at Fort Buford. Two days later all the captive hostiles, numbering 2829, were turned over to the agent at Standing Rock. There has been no trouble of any importance with the Sioux since 1877, and they are reported to be making remarkable progress in civilization.

CHAPTER XIX.
JOSEPH'S NEZ PERCÉS.

THE meanest, most contemptible, least justifiable thing that the United States was ever guilty of was its treatment of the Lower Nez Percés. It will not be necessary to tell the reader of the preceding pages that the conduct of the Nez Percés had been of uniform friendship and kindness towards the Americans. Their call for missionaries, their support of the settlers against the overbearing Hudson's Bay Company, their offer of protection to the Lapwai Mission when Whitman had fallen a victim to the Cayuses, their protection and escort of Governor Stevens's party in 1855, their stand for peace when the other tribes were for war in 1855 and 1856, their rescue of Steptoe's party in 1858, their assistance to our troops against hostile Indians, have all been recorded. They also rejected proposals for hostilities from the Mormons, both before and during the civil war. It may also be remembered that their friendship was of older date than the matters treated of in the foregoing chapters; that they gave Lewis and Clarke a reception which brought joy to the hearts of those weary explorers; that they furnished them food and refused pay for it; that they cared for the horses and other property while the expedition made its way down the river, and returned them safely in the spring. It is true that there was some difference of opinion among these Indians in regard to adopting the white man's religions and customs, but not one whit as to remaining his friends. Cur history ran its cycle of a hundred years with the record of but one American's blood being shed by a Nez Percé—a case of manslaughter, about the year 1862. Seventy years of friendly intercourse—seventy years in which the Indians patiently endured what they justly considered hardships, for their friendship to the white man-seventy years of self-sacrifice, of forbearance, of sacred faith on their part-before the folly or weakness or dishonesty, whichever it may have been, of our governmental agents roused them to madness, and the worms we so knavishly trod upon turned to sting us.

The Nez Percés, while one in feeling, were composed of

YOUNG JOSEPH.

several independent, confederated tribes. The most common method of dividing them, used by the whites, was into the Upper and Lower Nez Percés, a distinction referring to their lands, as the names imply. The chief of the Wal-lam-mute-kint (Wal-lam-wat-kin) band, which was usually called the Lower Nez Percés, was Joseph, the chief who came to meet the Oregon volunteers after the Whitman massacre, and said to them, "When I left my home I took the Book in my hand and brought it with me; it is my light. I heard the Americans were coming to kill me. Still I held my Book before me and came on." There was never any head chief who claimed full control over all the bands, and none in whom we recognized such power, except those who had been appointed through our agency. The first one was appointed by Elijah White, their first agent, a man who meant well enough; but who was probably mistaken in his idea that he had discovered the Northwest passage around all Indian troubles. He appointed Ellis head chief in 1842; but Ellis had no control over the tribe, and after his death, in 1847, there was no head chief until 1855. The authority of Lawyer as head chief was formally recognized in the treaty made by Governor Stevens in 1855, but it was never understood by the Indians that this gave him any authority to dispose of their lands. As a matter-of-fact he was arbitrarily appointed by Governor Stevens for the purposes of the treaty, and was never acknowledged by half of the Indians. Among the Indians, the Lower Nez Percés were conceded to own the country south and east of the Blue Mountains, and west of the Snake River, as far south as the Powder River, a tributary of the Snake. It is true that the other bands had the privilege of hunting and fishing there, just as the Lower Nez Percés had the privilege of roaming over or camping in the upper country, but the right of control—their highest idea of a fee-simple—of both sections was never disputed to be in the bands respectively. The Lower Nez Percés moved to the upper country when Whitman and Spalding came, in order to receive "the Book" from their hands, but there was no change in the ownership of the lands; and afterwards, when jealousies arose between Joseph and Big Thunder, a chief of the Upper Nez Percés, Joseph was unceremoniously ordered to return to the land where he belonged, and he did so.

Joseph and his people seemed to love that country of theirs. It was not the most attractive region in the world to the white man, but it suited them. On one side of it the Snake surges and foams over its rocky bed. On the other the Blue Mountains rise majestically, and along their eastern base the Grande Ronde River sweeps through its great arc to the Snake. Between them is a rugged country impossible of cultivation. Through it, towards the east, runs the Imnaha (Immaha), down a narrow, rugged vale; through it towards the northwest flows the Wallowa (Wall-low-how, Way-lee-way—the Winding Waters), with a valley larger and better than that of the other stream. The valley of the Wallowa was the very best of the land claimed by the Lower Nez Percés, and it was not much to be desired. Captain Whipple reported of it, on August 28, 1875, "The valley is only fit for stock-raising, as a business, and not desirable for that in consequence of the long winters; but the Indian horses would live through where the white man's cattle would perish." It was even so worthless that Americans did not desire it. Says Captain Whipple, "The average American is not, as a rule, slow to take advantage of eligible openings to secure land 'claims' which may probably become valuable, but none of them seem anxious to locate them in Wallowa Valley. . . . The population is less than it was a year ago. Since the valley was restored to settlement, three families have disposed of their improvements for a trifle, and moved away; nor do I believe any others have come in. Not a man has taken a claim in the valley since that time. One of the most enterprising, reliable, and best citizens in the settlement, has told me, within the past week, that he thought the people of the valley were disappointed to learn it was not to be taken for an Indian reservation; that he regretted it for one; that he should sell out at first opportunity, and settle in a more promising locality. This shows how the white people who reside here regard this valley. On the other hand, the Indians love it."

A strange man was old Joseph, a sturdy, strong-built man, with a will of iron and a foresight that never failed him but once—when he welcomed the Americans to his country. He had some strange notions too, one of which was that "no man owned any part of the earth, and a man could not sell what he did not own." He was an aboriginal Henry George in his idea that ownership in land should be limited to occupancy, and, if we may judge by the converts that gentleman is making, he was not without reason. Joseph continued friendly to the whites, but he grew suspicious of their trading abilities, and bade his people be careful how they made bargains; the land he would look after himself. Surely the white man would not get it away from him. He was very careful, indeed. He would not join in the treaty with Governor Stevens until his own land was reserved out of the cession. To be candid, he and his tribe claimed that he did not sign the treaty at all, though his name is affixed, but they evidently mean that he never signed a treaty ceding his land, which is true. After the ratification of the treaty, in 1859, the other Indians received presents from the government and annuity goods; they had tools and bright clothing and guns, but Joseph and his people took none. He said to them, "These presents are the price of the land which is sold. If we take the pay, the white man will say he has bought our land also." So, for all those years after the treaty the Lower Nez Percés refused to receive any of the annuity goods, contented to know that the land of the Winding Waters was their own. Foolish Indians! to think that they could escape our clutches in that way.

In 1863 the whites had so encroached on the lands of the Nez Percés, and whiskey was doing so much damage, that another treaty was considered necessary. Calvin H. Hale, Charles Hutchins, and S. D. Howe negotiated it. The Upper Nez Percés accepted their present reservation of Lapwai, in Western Idaho. The Lower Nez Percés refused to join in the treaty. They had seen nothing to make them believe that their own course was not the best. The other tribes had been getting very few of the fine things that Governor Stevens had promised them, and what they did get was in gewgaws that they did not want; for the Nez Percés always asked for substantial and useful goods. It must be confessed that the Lower Nez Percés twitted them a little, too, which was annoying, though natural. Agent Hutchins said of this in 1863, "The old men of the tribe look with sorrow on the fact that they cannot rebut these flings by pointing to real evidences of the good faith of the white man's chief." But Joseph's band did not save their land by refusing to join.

The Upper Nez Percés sold all their land except the reservation, and that took away all the land of the Lower Nez Percés. Do you not understand it? It is the simplest thing in the world. Governor Grover discovered the way—the same Governor Grover that tried so hard to prevent the Republican party from stealing the government in 1876, by stealing the vote of Oregon himself—who was sent to the Senate for his distinguished services. This is the process. In 1855 Joseph joined with other chiefs in the treaty by which they sold a certain amount of land; hence the land that they did not sell belonged to all of the tribe in common. By joining in that treaty, Joseph acknowledged the tribal organization; hence the tribe had authority to bind him afterwards. A majority of all the chiefs, counting all the bands together, joined in the treaty of 1863, and sold all their land except, the Lapwai reservation; hence they sold Joseph's land. You may be inclined to call that thieving; it is also idiocy.

There is no pretence that the Upper Nez Percés intended to sell the land of the Lower Nez Percés, or claimed any power to do so, or that the commissioners understood that they were purchasing it. It does not appear that any one anticipated such a result at the time, for this construction was not adopted for years afterwards. Old Joseph went to his grave in 1871, in blissful ignorance of the fact that his land was not his land. Captain Whipple says, "Uniformly and with vehemence, to his last hour, he asserted to his children and friends that he had never surrendered claim to this (Wallowa) valley, but that he left it to them as their inheritance, with the injunction never to barter it away." His son says, "I saw he was dying. I took his hand in mine. He said, 'My son, my body is returning to my mother earth, and my spirit is going very soon to see the Great Spirit Chief. When I am gone, think of your country. You are the chief of these people. They look to you to guide them. Always remember that your father never sold his country. You must stop your ears whenever you are asked to sign a treaty selling your home. A few years more, and white men will be all around you. They have their eyes on this land. My son, never forget my dying words. This country holds your father's body.

Never sell the bones of your father and your mother.' I pressed my father's hand, and told him I would protect his grave with my life. My father smiled and passed away to the spirit land. I buried him in that beautiful valley of

OLLACUT.*

Winding Waters. I love that land more than all the rest of the world. A man who would not love his father's grave is worse than a wild animal."

This son was worthy his father's legacy. His name was In-mut-too-yah-lat-lat— the Thunder-Travelling-Over-the

---

* This cut was originally published as a portrait of Joseph, Ollacut having been mistaken for his brother by the artist.

Mountains. To the Americans he was known as Young Joseph, and to the world, since 1877, he is Chief Joseph the Nez Percé. He was six feet in height, well-formed, of serious and noble countenance. He was grave and thoughtful, as becomes a ruler. He was shrewd and cautious, as becomes one who transacts business for a nation. He was exact and resolute, as becomes one who must preserve peace between two factions prone to misunderstanding and jealousy. Nearest and dearest to him, after the death of his father, was his brother Ol-la-cut, a little younger than himself, tall, handsome, and gay. Both of these youths were students in Mrs. Spalding's school in the happy olden time. Probably the good seed which was sown then ripened into good deeds afterwards; possibly it accounts for their honorable conduct when war came. If so, it were well worthy of record in some Ely volume. The white men grew more numerous in the West. They came into the Nez Percé country to search for gold, and many of them remained there. They did not treat the Indians well, but the young chieftain ruled his people so wisely that no warfare occurred. Says Joseph, "They stole a great many horses from us, and we could not get them back because we were Indians. The white men told lies for each other. They drove off a great many of our cattle. Some white men branded our young cattle so they could claim them. We had no friend who would plead our cause before the law councils." Still there were no hostilities. In 1871 an Indian was killed by a white man. The Indians took no revenge, but insisted that the whites should leave their country. Troops were sent into the country for the protection of both parties. In March, 1875, a white man named Larry Ott killed a Nez Percé in a quarrel, and the grand-jury returned no bill against him. In August, 1875, one Benedict shot at some drunken Indians who came to his house at night demanding admittance, and killed one and wounded another. This man was accused of selling liquor to the Indians. In the spring, also, one Harry Mason whipped two Indians; the council of arbitration chosen in this matter—three white men—decided against the Indians. In June, 1876, a settler named Finley killed a brother of Joseph. None of these offences were punished, and for none did the Indians take revenge, still urging only that the whites should leave their lands.

The question of title had drifted along until 1873, when the Interior Department took steps to set the Wallowa off as reserved land for the Lower Nez Percés. The improvements of the eighty-seven squatters who were to be bought out were appraised at $67,860. For eighteen months the matter rested in that way, all parties satisfied, but in the spring of 1875 Congress refused to confirm the purchase and reservation. Why it did so is beyond imagination, except it may have been from the influence of Governor Grover, who had put his fine-spun theory before the Government in the summer of 1873. As we have seen, the disappointment was almost as great to the settlers as to the Indians. Some of my readers may not understand the theory of settling for the purpose of being bought out. If a man discover where a reservation is to be located, he cannot do better financially than to locate upon it. Appraisers for government purchases are usually liberal. The Indians were cast down in spirit. When Joseph learned of the decision, Captain Whipple says "he looked disappointed, and after a short silence he said he hoped I could tell something of a possible doubt of their being obliged to relinquish this valley to the settlers. I told him the case was decided against the Indians by higher authority than that of any army officer. This declaration did not make the countenances of the Indians more cheerful. They all realize that after they go to Lapwai reservation, or one similar, they will be obliged to give up their horses, which constitute their main wealth, and that as a community they will cease to exist."

The outlook for the Lower Nez Percés was gloomy, but there was yet one ray of hope. There were still a few people in Oregon who remembered the good services of the Nez Percés in the past, and did not wish to see them robbed. Rev. A. L. Lindsley, celebrated for his mission work in the Northwest and in Alaska, with others, asked that a commission be appointed to investigate the matter and make some equitable settlement with the Indians. Gen. O. O. Howard, commanding the District of the Columbia, endorsed the proposition, and suggested that he be made a member of the Commission. A commission was appointed, and General Howard was made a member. They came to Lapwai to talk with Joseph and the other "non-treaties" that had never been able to understand Governor Grover's logic. There was White Bird's band, which occupied the country adjacent to the Salmon River. There was a band that roamed over the rugged country between the Salmon and the Snake, under the old chief and "medicine-man" Too-hul-hul-sute. There was a small band on Ashotin Creek, north of Joseph's country, and above this were several small bands under the authority of the young chief Hush-hush-cute (Hus-es-cruyt, Hus-ses-kutte—the Bald Head). There was also the band of Looking Glass, on whose land the Lapwai reservation had been located, and who retained their home in common with the "treaties" who had been put with them. These bands were sufficiently confederated in interest, and sufficiently sensible of Joseph's ability, to make him the common leader of the "non-treaty" party. The Commission talked with them in November, 1876, in the mission church at Lapwai, but Joseph nonplussed the commissioners. They say, "An alertness and dexterity in intellectual fencing was exhibited by him that was quite remarkable." It was remarkable. They were unable to answer his arguments. He said "that the Creative Power, when he made the earth, made no marks, no lines of division or separation on it, and that it should be allowed to remain as then made. The earth was his mother. He was made of the earth and grew up on its bosom. The earth, as his mother

GENERAL O. O. HOWARD.

and nurse, was sacred to his affections, too sacred to be valued by or sold for silver and gold. He could not consent to sever his affections from the land that bore him. He was content to live upon such fruits as the Creative Power placed within and upon it, and unwilling to barter these and his free habits away for the new modes of life proposed by us. Moreover, the earth carried chieftainship (which the interpreter explained to mean law, authority, or control), and therefore to part with the earth would be to part with himself or with his self-control. He asked nothing of the President. He was able to take care of himself. He did not desire Wallowa Valley as a reservation, for that would subject him and his band to the will of and dependence on another, and to laws not of their own making. He was disposed to live peaceably. He and his band had suffered wrong rather than do wrong. One of their number was wickedly slain by a white man during the last summer, but he would not avenge his death. But unavenged by him, the voice of that brother's blood, sanctifying the ground, would call the dust of their fathers back to life, to people the land in protest of this great wrong."

The commissioners knew that Joseph's statements were true. His brother had been killed, as stated, in a quarrel about some stock, by a man named Finley, and the Indians had refused even to appear as witnesses against the murderer in court. Joseph said, "When I learned that they had killed one of my people I was heart-sick. When I saw all the settlers take the murderer's part, though they spoke of bringing him to trial, I told them that the law did not favor murder. I could see they were all in favor of the murderer, so I told them to leave the country. As to the murderer I have made up my mind. I have come to the conclusion to let him escape and enjoy health and not take his life for the one he took. I am speaking as though I spoke to the man himself. I do not want anything in payment for the deed he committed. I pronounce the sentence that he shall live." The causes for removal given by the Commission were not brought into prominence in the council. They were not of a nature that would admit of consistent urging. The first was of a religions character. A part of the Nez Percés had become

Catholics; a part adhered to "Mr. Spalding's religion;" and a part had become believers in a form of spiritualism which had recently been introduced in Eastern Oregon by Smo-hallie, a chief who dwelt with a little band of followers across the Columbia from Wallula, the village on the site of old Fort Walla-Walla. He was a small and deformed sorcerer, but the abnormally large head that surmounted his humped shoulders had evolved the mystic faith of the "Drummer-dreamers," which threatened to stop the progress of good, old-fashioned, orthodox conversion. They were a queer lot. Their young men saw visions and their old men dreamed dreams. They taught that land ought not be divided up, or forced by cultivation to yield more than its natural fruits; that schools and churches were innovations of the devil; and that a savior would be raised up in the East who would bring their dead to life, expel the white man from the country, and restore the Indians to their own. This last was probably a relic of the story of the second coming of Christ, which Brigham Young had left in their country twenty years before. These theories seem odd, but the Indians defended them in a way that was hard to answer. Said General Shanks to Joseph, "Do you want schools and school-houses on the Wallowa reservation?" "No," said Joseph, "we do not want schools or school-houses on the Wallowa reservation." "Why do you not want schools?" "They will teach us to have churches." "Why do you not want churches?" "They will teach us to quarrel about God, as the Catholics and Protestants do on the Nez Percé reservation, and at other places. We do not want to learn that. We may quarrel with men, sometimes, about things on this earth, but we never quarrel about God. We do not want to learn that." These tenets apparently stood in the way of an adoption of our customs, but there is certainly nothing about them that is either criminal or improper, notwithstanding they so impressed Father Wilbur in that way that he recommended that the Indians be "brought within the Christianizing influences of the reservation," even if force were necessary to accomplish the removal. Apropos of this, are not the Indians entitled to a share in the temporal comforts of spiritualism, considering the immense amount of service their disembodied spirits have to perform as "controls" in the white man's séances? Our spiritualistic brethren have not had any tribe assigned to them for missionary labor—in fact they do not appear to be ardent missionaries—and, in consequence, the red man has been obliged to get along without any rappings, or materializations, or dark cabinets.

Another objection was that they went every year to the "buffalo illahie"—the Powder River country—to procure their winter's supply of meat. They did not disturb any one in going or coming, but it made the "treaty" Indians jealous and restless to be thus reminded that they had sold their birthright for a mess of pottage. Their unhappiness was increased by the fact that they did not always get the pottage. A fellow named Langford had taken and held possession for months of the old mission claim of six hundred and forty acres, on which the agency buildings were situated, and shut down the mills, forcing the treaty Indians to sell their grain at a sacrifice and buy flour. One Finney claimed and occupied six hundred and forty acres of the reservation; one Colwell claimed and occupied seventy-five acres; one Randall claimed fifty acres, and had a permit to place a stage station on the land. The deeds which had been promised the Indians for their twenty-acre lots had never been issued to them. There was due them $4665 for services and for horses furnished the Oregon volunteers in 1856, which it had been definitely agreed should be paid in the treaty of 1863. It was only thirteen years since that treaty had been executed, and the governmental agents had not had time to attend to these minor details. It is quite possible that these things made the "treaties" jealous of the "non-treaties" also. In connection with the objection to the "non-treaties" going to hunt buffalo, it is interesting to remember that the Sioux and their allies were doing the same thing, and that we had kindly guaranteed them the right to do so, because they were strong, and fought back, and made our occupation of the buffalo illahie so uncomfortable that we were glad to abandon the Montana road and leave them as they were.

Now why did these Nez Percés object to going on the

Lapwai reservation? The first reason was that they preferred their own country, and, in connection with this feeling, they knew that the money, goods, and the rest that were so glibly promised them in the councils, in payment for their country, would not be forthcoming. They had the experience of their "treaty" brethren constantly before them in proof of that. The second reason was that they desired personal liberty to go from one place to another. They knew that going on a reservation meant staying there, except on permission of the authorities, and also a practical dissolution of their tribal organization. After the wrong was consummated, when Joseph had been permitted to go to Washington and talk to our wise men, he said, "I have asked some of the great white chiefs where they get their authority to say to the Indian that he shall stay in one place, while he sees white men going where they please. They cannot tell me." The third reason was that their chief wealth was in herds of horses, from the increase of which they had a plentiful support, with but little labor, and these they would have to give up if they went on the reservation. Why? Because, on the reservation, twenty acres of land, and no more, were allotted to each head of a family, out of which he was to make his living. Stock-raising on twenty acres is necessarily a limited business. The care of these herds, the visits of the Indians to the settlements to trade, and their annual buffalo hunts, are what constituted the "nomadic habits" that the Commission objected to.

The "judicious men" came to a conclusion at last. They revamped that false and fallacious theory of Governor Grover's, that Old Joseph's joining in the treaty of 1855 "implied a surrender of any specific rights to any particular portion of the whole reserve." They adopted his monstrous proposition that from the treaty of 1863 a contract should be implied which neither of the contracting parties contemplated and neither had a right to make. The thing is too absurd for serious argument. Joseph disposed of it, though he did not put his case so strongly as he might, in this manner: "Suppose a white man should come to me and say, 'Joseph, I like your horses, and I want to buy them.' I say to him, 'No, my horses suit me; I will not sell them.' Then he goes to my

LAPWAI.

neighbor, and says to him, 'Joseph has some good horses. I want to buy them but he refuses to sell.' My neighbor answers, 'Pay me the money and I will sell you Joseph's horses.' The white man returns to me and says, 'Joseph, I have bought your horses and you must let me have them.' If we sold our lands to the Government, this is the way they were bought." In short, the Commission recommended that if the Lower Nez Percés did not peaceably take up their residence on the Lapwai reservation within a limited time, that they should "be placed by force upon the reservation, and, in satisfaction of any possible rights of occupancy which they may have, the same aid and allotments of land granted to the treaty Nez Percés should be extended to them on the reservation." The same commission recommends that the Umatilla reservation —the peaceful home of the Cayuses, Umatillas, and Walla-Wallas for twenty years past—be vacated, because it "would be eagerly purchased," was "of the best quality of land," and was "occupied by a mere handful of Indians who are incapable of developing its rich treasures." By all means, put all Indians on lands that have no rich treasures to develop. Then nothing will be lost. To be sure, there are a few millions of acres, with undeveloped treasures, that can be had for the pre-emption, but they are not quite so convenient.

But, it will be said, surely the commissioners did not understand the real state of affairs. Go softly. General Howard had been looking over the matter ever since he was put in command of the Department of the Columbia. Papers containing full statements of the historic services of the Nez Percés, of the rights of the "non-treaties," and of the influences actuating them, had passed through his hands and received his endorsement and approval. In his report of September 1, 1875, he had said, "I think it a great mistake to take from Joseph and his band of Nez Percé Indians that [the Wallowa] valley. The white people really do not want it. They wished to be bought out. I think gradually this valley will be abandoned by the white people, and possibly Congress can be induced to let these really peaceable Indians have this poor valley for their own." Lieut.-Col. H. Clay Wood was another member of the Commission who was fully posted. On August 1, 1876, he reported at length on "The Status of Young Joseph and his Band of Nez Percé Indians," and gave his opinion that the government had so far failed to comply with its agreements in the treaty of 1855, that none of the Nez Percés were bound by it. Let us also record, to his honor, that he made a minority report, as commissioner, recommending that although Joseph's band would have to be moved eventually, yet that "until Joseph commits some overt act of hostility, force should not be used to put him upon any reservation." The other commissioners were D. H. Jerome, William Stickney, and A. C. Barstow. What previous knowledge they had of the matter I cannot say; but there was leaven enough for the whole lump in the two military members.

The Commission made its report, and the Department of the Interior, acting on its recommendations, ordered the non-treaties to be placed on the Lapwai reservation. By virtue of his office, General Howard was the agent to enforce this order. He met the non-treaties in May, and found, as he must have anticipated, that they were unwilling to go to the reservation. He held three councils with them—the last on May 7th. Too-hul-hul-sute, the *too-at* ("Drummer-dreamer" priest) and chief, was their spokesman. He talked boldly, and as word came back to word he said, "The Indians may do what they like, but I am not going on the reservation." Howard threatened him with arrest. "Do you want to scare me with reference to my body?" asked the old man. He was arrested and led out of the council. The Indians murmured. Should they kill Howard and the rest? They were well-armed and self-confident. Joseph bade them not. The position of the government was now plain to the Indians. They must go to the reservation or fight. They decided to go. Would you have done so, reader? Would you have swallowed the injustice, and meekly agreed to go, without striking one blow at least for liberty and right? I remind you that the Nez Percés had never fought the white man, and Joseph was not the man to begin. He says, "I said in my heart that rather than have war I would give up my country. I would give up my father's grave. I would give up everything rather than have the blood of white men upon the hands of my people." The Indians were given thirty days from May 14th, in which to gather their cattle and move; Hush-hush-cute's band had thirty-five. They say it was not time enough, but that was of no consequence. We must have firmness in dealing with Indians, even if we have nothing else.

The Indians went to make their preparations. They looked on their old home, and their love for it doubled under the realization that they must leave it. Too-hul-hul-sute's spirit burned because of his imprisonment for the offence of telling his determination in the council. There was a warrior whose father had been killed by a white man, five years before, who brooded over the unavenged wrong. There were the two warriors who had been whipped by Harry Mason. There were the kinsmen of the murdered men. They assembled at Rocky Cañon. Several hundred of their horses and cattle were missing. They held councils. A desire to resist removal sprang up and spread rapidly. They determined, over Joseph's counsel, to fight the soldiers when they came. It was the desire of a part that the settlers should not be molested, in the hope that they would remain neutral, but the others overruled them; they said it was the settlers that had brought all the trouble. They bought arms and ammunition where they could. They practised military movements, in which they were already quite proficient. General Shanks says, that "Joseph's party was thoroughly disciplined; that they rode at full gallop along the mountain side in a steady formation by fours; formed twos, at a given signal, with perfect precision, to cross a narrow bridge; then galloped into line, reined in to a sudden halt, and dismounted with as much system as regulars." June 13th arrived; the thirty days were up; the soldiers had not arrived. Over on Salmon River three Indians killed an old hermit ranchman named Devine. The taste of blood whetted their appetites. On the morning of the 14th they killed three more, and in the afternoon another. They mounted the horses of their victims, and hurried to Camas Prairie, where the main body of Indians was encamped. They rode through the camp displaying the spoils of their bloodshed, and calling on others to join them.

Joseph and Ollacut were not in the camp; they had placed their teepees away from the others on account of Joseph's wife, who was sick. White Bird, the next in rank and influence, gave way. He rode through the camp, crying, "All must join now. There is blood. You will be punished if you delay." Seventeen warriors joined the three, and they hastened back to the Salmon River. Eight more fell victims to them, including Harry Mason, who had whipped the two Indians. On the night of the 14th another party attacked the people of the Cottonwood house—a ranch on the road between Mount Idaho and Fort Lapwai—who were trying to escape to Mount Idaho. Two men and a boy were killed and the others badly wounded, two men subsequently dying of their injuries. It is said that two women were outraged. Joseph denies it, by implication. It may have been done without his knowledge. He was not there. He protested against hostilities until they had gone so far that war was inevitable; then he took command, and the Indians moved to White Bird Cañon, where they prepared to fight soldiers.

They had not long to wait. Colonel Perry was hurrying down from Fort Lapwai with ninety men. He reached Grangeville, four miles from Mount Idaho, on the evening of the 16th, was joined by ten citizens, and marched on through the night to White Bird Cañon, sixteen miles away. He reached the head of the cañon at daybreak, and began his descent of the broad trail, to surprise the Indians and prevent their escape across the Salmon. Down in the cañon Joseph watched his approach through a field-glass. Some of the Indians became nervous, and suggested that it would be better to move across the Salmon, where the soldiers could not reach them. Joseph said, "We will fight them here." A party of mounted warriors were put in ambush behind a hill on the south side of the cañon. The rest, under Joseph, were crouched on the ground, squarely across the trail, hidden behind rocks and in hollows. On came the soldiers until well within range, when every bush and rock poured out its fire. At the same time the party of mounted warriors appeared on the left. The foremost ranks deployed to engage the force in front, and the rear wheeled to meet the flank movement. Men were falling; the Indians were moving up on the hills, making towards the rear; some one cried to fall back to the next ridge. The next ridge was gained, with the enemy on their heels. There was no time to stop. The attempts of the officers to rally the men were only momentarily successful. The Indians were pressing along the sides of the cañon to gain the head and cut off retreat. Part of the command reached the ascent and hurried out. The remainder, under Lieutenant Theller, were cut off. They saw the bar across the way, and wheeled into a ravine to the left. The Indians were upon them in a moment, thinning them out with their murderous fire, through which only a few stragglers made their way unscathed to the summit. Across the rugged country the Indians pursued the flying troops for twelve miles; but the soldiers were out of that dreadful cañon now and had regained their wits. The officers obtained control, and the retreat of the sixty-five who escaped from the cañon was conducted in order. Four miles from Mount Idaho Joseph withdrew his men. He had fought and won his first battle.

The military reputation of the Nez Percés was altered. It would require more men to whip them. Reinforcements were started from all neighboring points. Skirmishing and minor engagements continued. A detachment was sent to arrest Looking Glass, who had not yet joined the hostiles, and bring him in. His camp was destroyed and seven hundred and twenty-five ponies captured, but the Indians all escaped and went to Joseph. Lieutenant Rains, with ten men and a scout named Foster, was sent on a reconnoissance. The party was surrounded and every man killed. A company of volunteers, under Captain Randall, was attacked on the Mount Idaho road; two were killed and two wounded. The remainder would have been killed if relief had not arrived. On July 11th General Howard and his assembled troops were in sight of the enemy, who had crossed the country to the Lapwai reservation, and taken position on the Clearwater to give him battle. Howard had four hundred fighting men besides his teamsters and train men. He had a howitzer and two Gatling guns. Joseph had about three hundred warriors, with the squaws for assistants. The soldiers advanced in line of battle, leaving the supply trains unguarded. Joseph saw this and sent thirty warriors to attack them. The glass of an officer caught this movement just in the nick of time. A messenger was sent back to hurry them into the lines, and a company of cavalry galloped to their protection. The Indians gained the smaller train first, killed two packers, and disabled their animals, but the fire of the cavalry drove them off. The large train gained the lines uninjured. All that afternoon the battle raged, with its charges and counter-charges, its feinting and fighting. All night both parties strengthened their breastworks and kept up a desultory fire. In the morning the battle was renewed and kept up, with no perceptible advantage to either side until the middle of the afternoon. Then a fresh company of cavalry appeared to reinforce Howard. The artillery moved back to meet them, and, having made a junction, they struck the enemy's line on the left and charged down it. The Indians fought stubbornly for a few minutes, gave way, and fled. The victorious troops pressed after them so hotly that the artillery covered their camp, beyond the Clearwater, before their lodges could be struck. The Indians, however, made their escape with their herds, and sufficient supplies for their purposes, and, before the troops could cross, a large body of warriors was seen on the right front, apparently returning for an attack. While preparations were being made to meet this force, the remainder of the Indians continued their flight; and when the preparations of the soldiers were complete, the returning warriors, having accomplished their purpose by this feint, were found to have disappeared. In the morning the troops continued the pursuit of the retreating Indians, who were still in sight from the heights, only to fall into an ambuscade by the Nez Percés rear-guard and be thrown into confusion. Night found the Indians safely encamped, in an almost impregnable position, at the entrance to the Lolo trail. Joseph had fought his second battle, against heavy odds, and though beaten had brought off his forces most creditably.

What was to be done? There was another trail which formed a junction with the Lolo, fifteen miles back of Joseph's position; send a detachment, by a masked movement, to that point, to cut off his retreat and strike him from the rear. General Joseph was not so easily trapped. The detachment was hardly under way, on its pretended march to Lapwai, before Joseph's camp was broken, and the Indians were falling back beyond the dangerous point. It was at first intended to follow him closely, but that plan was abandoned. A small force, which was started up the trail, ran into the rear-guard rather disastrously, and then that ubiquitous rear-guard dropped back on the settlements and carried off a lot of horses. The settlers were sure that as soon as the soldiers were started on the trail the Nez Percés would be back, by some other route, devastating the settlements. What a wonderful trail that was for a highway! It begins on Lolo Creek, a tributary of the Clearwater, crosses the Bitter Root Mountains, and comes to the lowland again by the Lou-Lou fork of the Bitter Root River on the east. Any mountain trail, especially any Indian trail, is bad enough, with its sharp rocks, its fallen timber, its slippery pitches, and its roaring torrents; but this one seems to have been made for its sterling impassable qualities. Says General Sherman, "This is universally admitted, by all who have travelled it—from Lewis and Clarke to Captain Winters—as one of the worst *trails* for man and beast on this continent." The Nez Percés came safely across it. In the valley of the Lou-Lou they were confronted by a hastily prepared fort, held by Captain Rawn with a few regulars and some volunteers. Looking Glass talked to them. "We will not fight the settlers if they do not fight us. We are going by you to the buffalo country. Will you let us go in peace?" Rawn refused to let them pass, but the volunteers rebelled. The Nez Percés had always been "good Indians" on the Bitter Root. The settlers had no grounds for complaint in their conduct, as they had passed annually to and from the buffalo country. They decided that, in the expressive frontier phrase, "they had not lost any Indians," and consequently were not hunting for any. The Nez Percés might go by, and God speed them out of the country. The Indians not only passed in peace, but they stopped at the villages of Stevensville and Corvallis and traded with these pacific whites. They also left a spy at Corvallis, who stopped until Howard had come up and passed on, and then sped away on his cayuse to General Joseph with full particulars.

Meantime a potent ally of the white man had been at work. The telegraph had ticked its message of alarm all through the country to the east, and the troops at the various posts were on the alert. General Gibbon, with one hundred and ninety cavalrymen, had hastened from Helena across to Fort Missoula, on the Bitter Root, but arrived too late to intercept the Indians. They had gone on to the south, up the Bitter Root valley, past Ross's hole, and into the valley of the Big Hole River. Gibbon followed on their trail. He came close up to them on August 8th, while they were all unsuspecting. He waited through the night, and in the stillness of "the hour before the dawn" he swept through their camp in a furious charge, completely surprising them. Surely now the Nez Percés were whipped. Not a bit of it. They rallied and retook their camp. They drove the soldiers back to a wooded point where, behind rude barricades and in hastily dug trenches, they defended themselves through the following day. At eleven o'clock that night, having captured Gibbon's howitzer, they withdrew, leaving Gibbon wounded, and his command so crippled that it could not pursue. Joseph had fought and won his third battle. Howard joined Gibbon here, and in the presence of officers and men, his Bannock scouts scalped and mutilated the bodies of the Nez Percé dead. There were many dead, men, women, and children, but worst of all Looking Glass, their ablest diplomat, lay stark upon that field. The Nez Percés neither took scalps nor mutilated during this war. They were neither civilized nor the allies of civilization. They were only defrauded Indians. A few days later they captured an Indian scout attached to Howard's command, and said to him, "Your men kill our women and children; your men are worse than the Indians." "No, no," said the scout, "my chief is kind. I saw him and his officers bury the women and children with their own hands. They don't want to hurt the women and children." Then his captors released him unharmed.

PLAIN OF THE GEYSERS.

Sunday, August 19th, Joseph had crossed the continental divide again into Idaho, and camped on the great Camas prairie which lies west of the National Park, on the Yellowstone. He had captured two hundred and fifty good horses, replenished his supplies and put his forces in excellent condition. Howard's forces were one day's march behind him. They camped on the prairie also. A detachment had been sent ahead, under Lieutenant Bacon, to hold Tacher's Pass, the most accessible roadway across the divide into the park. The sentinels and pickets were properly posted and the weary soldiers slept peacefully. In the faint starlight swarthy forms crept through the long grass. Hobbles were cut and bells were removed from bell-mares. Off to the east a troop of horsemen came in sight, riding back over the trail of the Nez Percés. They rode in column of fours, regularly and without haste. "It must be Bacon's men coming back," said the pickets. They came within hailing distance and were challenged. Their answer betrayed them. The picket opened fire. Then arose a wild yell that startled the soldiers from their sleep, and a confused discharge of small-arms, after which all the horses and mules that were not fastened were seen scampering away with a crowd of Indians after them, yelling like demons. Fortunately enough horses and mules were left to mount three companies of cavalry. They hurried out into the night after the Indians, came up with part of them, and recovered half a hundred of the lost animals. Before morning the Indians were back after these, and stampeded a part of them. Then they went on with their retreat, leaving the soldiers with one dead and six wounded men to care for; also to wait till more horses and supplies could be obtained from Virginia City. We must credit General Joseph with a successful surprise.

On went the Nez Percés through Tacher's Pass, where Bacon had missed them, and into the park; on through the pleasant open country of the western portion to the region of the hot springs, the geysers, and the sulphur lands. Here they met Cowan's party, consisting of Mr. Cowan, his wife, sister-in-law, brother-in-law, and two others. Three of the men were left for dead; one and the two ladies were carried away. Horrible fate!—carried into Indian captivity. General Howard says they were "afterwards rescued." Joseph says, "On the way we captured one white man and two white women. We released them at the end of three days. They were treated kindly. The women were not insulted.

THE STINKING WATER.

Can the white soldiers tell me of one time when Indian women were taken prisoners and held three days, and then released without being insulted? Were the Nez Percé women who fell into the hands of General Howard's soldiers treated with as much respect? I deny that a Nez

Percé was ever guilty of such a crime." On went the Indians, down by Yellowstone Lake, over the Yellowstone River, burning Baronett's Bridge behind them, and then, after a feint in the direction of the Stinking Water, they slipped through a narrow cañon to Clark's Fork, and down it to the Yellowstone again. By this movement Joseph avoided Colonel Sturgis, who had been warned, and come over from the Powder River country with six companies of cavalry (three hundred and fifty men) and some friendly Crows. Deceived by Joseph's movement, and by the messages he had received, Sturgis hastened to block up the trail down the Stinking Water. He discovered his mistake quickly, however, and took up the chase at once. On September 13th he overtook the Nez Percés on the alkaline, sage-brush plains across the Yellowstone. The rear-guard of the Indians engaged

GENERAL S. D. STURGIS.

the troops, while the remainder turned into the narrow valley of Cañon Creek; but a detachment under Captain Benteen circled around the fight and pressed the retreating herds so closely that over four hundred ponies had to be abandoned. The Indians then reunited at the mouth of the cañon, posting themselves wherever there was a chance for shelter. There was but one way of reaching them, and that was direct pursuit. All day the Indians dropped back, fighting for every foot of ground, and at dark the exhausted soldiers withdrew to camp at the mouth of the cañon. In the morning Sturgis was reinforced by a large party of Crow Indians, who pressed the Nez Percés so vigorously that five hundred more of the ponies were abandoned. March as they would, the soldiers could not lessen the distance between themselves and the Nez Percés, who retired up the Mussel Shell River, and then, circling back of the Judith Mountains, struck the Missouri at Cow Island on the 23d. Joseph had fought his fourth battle, had held in check a greatly superior force, and brought off his people in comparative safety.

Cow Island is the limit of low-water navigation on the Upper Missouri, one hundred and twenty-three miles below Fort Benton, which is the high-water limit. The boats that run up to it are little steamers that have, in addition to ordinary steamboat machinery, long wooden arms, which are thrust out and worked by steam windlasses, to push the boat off from sand-bars and snags. Their navigation is much like that of those big water-beetles, which swim where there is water enough, and crawl where there is not. The landing is close by the mouth of Cow Creek. There was no settlement at the place; only a landing, with a little intrenchment near by, held by twelve soldiers and four citizens. The Nez Percés attacked it, but drew off at night, after wounding two of the garrison and burning all the freight at the landing. Major Ilges came down from Fort Benton with a small force, and followed them for a day or two, but wisely abandoned the pursuit after a skirmish with them. The Indians moved on leisurely to the north. They were now coming into a beautiful country, a "very Eden" it has been called, lying about the Bear Paw and Little Rocky Mountains. It is a country of romance also, the reputed locality of the celebrated "Lost Cabin of Montana," that miners have been crazy over for the last decade. They established their camp in a crescent curve of Snake Creek, a tributary of Milk River, thirty-five miles south of the British line. They had rid themselves of every force that had attacked them, but the telegraph and the messengers of the whites had done their work again. From Fort Keogh, away over on the Yellowstone, Col. Nelson A. Miles was coming with nine companies of mounted men, a company and a half of infantry, a company of white and Indian scouts, a breech-loading Hotchkiss gun, and a 12-pounder Napoleon. They reached Oarroll, on the Missouri, below Cow Island, and learned of the events at the latter place. On the evening of the 25th three hundred and seventy-five men began their march from Carroll to cut off the retreating Nez Percés. Joseph did not know of this new and powerful enemy. He was resting quietly only one day's march from his bravely-earned safety. If he had only known—but he had no telegraph wires.

On the morning of the 30th the camp of the Indians was attacked by the soldiers. The Nez Percés knew of their coming only long enough to gain the ravines which led into the creek valley along the bluffs. Their herd, to the number of eight hundred, was cut off by one battalion of cavalry, while two more, with the scouts, charged the camp. These barely reached the village before they recoiled under the fearful fire of the Indians, with one-fifth of their force killed and wounded. For four days and nights the forces remained facing each other. The whites controlled the situation. They were unwilling to attempt the capture of the camp by storm, for that would involve a heavy loss of life, but they had the Indians surrounded and were damaging them with shells. The Indians could not escape through the lines without abandoning their wounded and helpless. Says Joseph, "We could have escaped from Bear Paw Mountain if we had left our wounded, old women, and children behind. We were unwilling to do this. We had never heard of a wounded Indian recovering while in the hands of white men." How deftly does this spiritualistic heathen strike us, and how keenly do his blows cut! There was only one power on earth from which they could hope for aid. Over the British line was Sitting Bull, who had been fighting Miles all summer. Perhaps this chief, who had said, "There is not one white man who loves an Indian, and not a true Indian but hates a white man," actuated by enmity to the whites, would come to the rescue. So they sent messengers, improved their defences, and held their ground, occasionally parleying with Colonel Miles; but Sitting Bull did not come, and on the morning of October 5th they surrendered—those who were left. Ollacut had fallen here at Snake Creek, and so had the old Dreamer-drummer, Too-hul-hul-sute, with twenty-seven others. White Bird had fled in the night with a band which, it was afterwards learned, numbered one hundred and five. They reached British America. Joseph, be it understood, surrendered on honorable terms. Colonel Miles says, "I acted on what I supposed was the original design of the government to place these Indians on their own reservation, and so informed them, and also sent assurances to the war parties that were out, and those who had escaped, that they would be taken to Tongue River, and retained for a time, and sent across the mountains as soon as the weather permitted in the spring." The Indians understood also that they were to retain what stock they still had. General Howard had come up and was present at the surrender. The negotiations were conducted through his Nez Percé scouts. He issued directions to Colonel Miles to send the Indians to his department in the spring, unless he received "instructions from higher authority." "Thus," says General Sherman, "has terminated one of the most extraordinary Indian wars of which there is any record. The Indians throughout displayed a courage and skill that elicited universal praise; they abstained from scalping, let captive women go free, did not commit indiscriminate murder of peaceful families, which is usual, and fought with almost scientific skill, using advance and rear guards, skirmish lines and field fortifications."

Of course the Nez Percés were sent back to the Lapwai reservation, as Colonel Miles had agreed. Well, no. They were sent to Fort Lincoln; then to Fort Leavenworth, where they remained for a few weeks; and then to the Quapaw Agency in Indian Territory. Says Commissioner Hayt, in his report of November 1, 1877, "Upon the capture of Joseph and his Indians, the first question that arises is, 'What shall be done with them?' Humanity prompts us to send them back and place them on the Nez Percé reservation, as Joseph and his followers have shown themselves to be brave men and skilful soldiers, who, with one exception, have observed the rules of civilized warfare, and have not mutilated their dead enemies. There is, however, an insuperable difficulty in the way, owing to the fact that at the beginning of the outbreak of the Nez Percé war, twenty-one whites in the immediate vicinity of Joseph's home were murdered in cold blood

JOSEPH'S LAST BATTLE.

by the Indians, and six white women were outraged. Because of these crimes, there would be no peace nor safety for Joseph and his Indians on their old reservation, or in its vicinity, as the friends and relatives of the victims would wage an unrelenting war upon the offenders. But for these foul crimes these Indians would be sent back to the reservation in Idaho. Now, however, they will have to be sent to the Indian Territory; and this will be no hardship to them, as the difference in the temperature between that latitude and their old home is inconsiderable." How complacently does this gentleman sit in his easy-chair in Washington, and thrum the heartstrings of this outraged people. "Humanity," indeed! What did honesty and common decency prompt? Was it nothing that these warriors laid down their arms on Colonel Miles's promise, in General Howard's presence, that they should be returned to Idaho? Cannot a commander in the field plight the faith of this nation and have his word respected? "Foul crimes!" What men were "murdered in cold blood?" and what "six white women were outraged?" There seems to be a feeling here that an Indian should never shoot any one but a soldier. Had the soldiers done them any injury? Had any one injured them directly except these settlers who located on their lands and "wished to be bought out?" Had Harry Mason and Finley and the rest done them no wrong? But suppose there were here twenty-seven cold-blooded crimes, how many times over did the whites exceed that number in this trouble? What of the four Indians murdered before they lifted a hand? What of the stock-stealing? What of the scalping and mutilation, on three different occasions, by Bannock and white scouts? What of the treatment of captured women? What of our cold-blooded steal of their country? What of our cold-blooded violation of Colonel Miles's agreement? What of the one thousand or more of horses that they had when they surrendered, which were to be returned to them, and of which Joseph says only, "Somebody has got our horses?" What of the cold-blooded refusal of the authorities to return the Indians to Idaho, when Joseph told them he would never have surrendered if Colonel Miles had not promised this—when he begged them to keep that promise? We have too much "humanity;" it might be profitable to experiment with honesty and good faith for a time.

But passing the coloring of the commissioner's statement, what truth was there in his two reasons for locating the Nez Percés in Indian Territory; namely, that there would be no hardship from the change of climate, and the existence of a thirst for revenge in Idaho? To avoid question as to the truth of Joseph's sad story, we will take up only official statements. In his report of November 1, 1878, Commissioner Hayt says, "The number of prisoners reported by the War Department, December 4th last, was as follows: 79 men, 178 women, and 174 children, making a total of 431. A few scattered members of the band were subsequently taken by the military and also sent to Fort Leavenworth. . . . The number reported to have been turned over to the inspector and agent was 410, three of whom—children—died on the route. Inspector McNeil reported that the camping-place selected by the commandant for these Indians, and where he found them, was in the Missouri River bottom, about two miles above the fort, 'between a lagoon and the river, the worst possible place that could have been selected; and the sanitary condition of the Indians proved it.' The physician in charge said that 'one-half could be said to be sick, and all were affected by the poisonous malaria of the camp.' After the arrival of Joseph and his band in the Indian Territory, the bad effect of their location at Fort Leavenworth manifested itself in the prostration by sickness at one time of 260 out of the 410, and within a few months they have lost by death more than one-quarter of the entire number. A little care in the selection of a wholesome location near Fort Leavenworth would have saved very much sickness and many lives." In addition to the facts mentioned, the agent, H. W. Jones, reported that they had been without medicine, and concluded thus: "I am now glad to be able to say that their sickness is abating, and I believe the worst is over. They now number 86 men, 168 women, and 137 children." Was this all due to the malaria from the Missouri bottom-lands? Let us see.

In June, 1879, the Nez Percés were removed to a new

reservation, just west of the Ponca agency (strange that these two shamefully mistreated tribes should be thrown together), on the Salt Fork of the Arkansas River. The philosophic Agent Whiteman reported of them on August 31, 1879: "The location, I think, is a healthy one, and the Indians are as healthy as could be expected. There is this fact about the Nez Percés, which, perhaps, is hardly ever considered, viz., that most of the young, able-bodied men and women were engaged in their late war with the government, and many of them were killed and wounded, and a large proportion of the Nez Percés brought to the Indian Territory were old people and children, which accounts in a great measure for the many deaths which have occurred among them. I have also observed both among the Nez Percés and Poncas, who came from northern climates, that lung diseases are very prevalent. I think that seven Indians out of every ten have their lungs diseased so badly that they could not live in any climate; and while I do not desire to depreciate the fearful ravages made by malaria on Northern Indians in the Indian Territory, yet I give it as my opinion, which I believe will be borne out by statistics, that more Indians die from pulmonary diseases in the Northwest than die from the effects of malaria in the Indian Territory . . . . The Nez Percés number at this time three hundred and seventy." It is to be regretted that Mr. Whiteman did not explain why, under his theory, the Indians of the Northwest were not extinct many years ago. On August 31, 1880, Agent Whiting reported: "The old Ponca saw-mill was removed to the Nez Percé reservation in July last, and we are now sawing out lumber for the purpose of erecting houses for the Indians, and I hope to have them all comfortably housed before cold weather." The statistical tables for the same year show nine births and twenty-one deaths for the year, but give the total remaining on the reservation at only three hundred and forty-four.

On September 6, 1881, Agent Jordan reported: "The Nez Percés located at Oakland comprise three hundred and twenty-eight souls, and I am sorry to be compelled to report that there has been a large amount of sickness and many deaths among them during the last year. This arises from the fact that they have not become acclimated, and are to a great extent compelled to live in teepees, the cloth of which has become so rotten from long wear and the effects of the weather as to be no longer capable of keeping out the rain, by which they were soaked during the last spring. The tribe, unless something is done for them, will soon become extinct. . . . They are greatly in need of a church in which to hold services, and for want of one are compelled to meet under an arbor covered with branches and leaves. They keep the Sabbath-day holy, abstaining from all kinds of work, and the service at the arbor is attended by every member of the tribe, whether a communicant or not. . . . Poor as they are, they have contributed forty-five dollars with which to buy the lumber, etc., necessary to build a house for their pastor. . . . Love of country and home, as in all brave people, is very largely developed in this tribe, and they long for the mountains, the valleys, the streams, and the clear springs of water of their old home. They are cleanly to a fault, and most of them have adopted the dress, and as far as possible the habits, of the white man. They keep their stock in good order, and are a hard-working, painstaking people. I hope by the time winter comes on to have them all in comfortable houses." This is enough to show the justice of Mr. Hayt's statement that a removal to Indian Territory would be "no hardship" to them. It is probably enough for all present purposes. Picture to yourself these wretched people, sick, destitute, with no decent shelter, longing for the clear waters and balmy breezes of their stolen home. God help the victims of our "humanity." In all seriousness, it would have been far more humane to have put them in some penitentiary, where they could at least have had medical attention, and shelter from the rain and snow.

Comment on Mr. Hayt's climate proposition is needless. How about the revengeful whites? It does not appear that the government took any active steps to find what the sentiment of their former white neighbors was. Mr. Hayt's theory was evidently put on paper before investigation, for it is dated less than a month after the surrender. There was subsequently much difference of opinion, in a speculative way, as to what the feeling was. In 1883 Rev. A. L. Lindsley set about ascertaining it definitely. He prepared a series of questions, which he submitted to prominent residents of the Wallowa and Salmon River country, and from their answers drew the following conclusions: "There appears to be no active ill-will cherished towards these Indians, nor any opposition to the return of the exiles. There was a general agreement, in Judge Leland's opinion, who thought the aggrieved whites will take revenge. This will excite the Indians to retaliation; and that again will probably occasion another outbreak, or at least create public disturbances. There is only one way of prevention: to surrender to the authorities of Nez Percé County the survivors of the thirty-two Indians who were indicted for outrage and murder committed before the war began. It is known that a number of these are still living; some of them are with White Bird, who is in Canada, and some with Joseph. The Attorney-general of the United States answered a former demand for them by advising a suspension of all action in the case, with which the Idaho court complied. It is a suspension only; the return of these indicted men free will not escape the notice of the court. Even if it should, there are men who would excite a popular demand for justice. There is great reason to fear, however, that there are men in Kamiah Prairie and Mount Idaho who would not wait for the court to take action if these indicted Indians return free. A frequent remark used to be heard that certain Indians would be 'shot on sight.' Agent Monteith and others have no doubt that some men would carry out their threats. One of them is well known—'he don't think he'd hunt 'em up to kill 'em; he thinks it mean to shoot even an Indian in the dark; but it wouldn't be safe for any of them to come where he is.' I must restrain my pen and assume much. The sum is this: that the peace can be preserved in the return of these Indians by the surrender of the indicted ones to the Idaho authorities—or sending them off to join White Bird in Canada. What the full effect of the alternative would be it would be difficult to estimate."

I submit that there is here no desire for revenge which

would justify the nation in breaking its faith with these Indians. I submit that an American who is sufficiently civilized to admit that it is "mean to shoot even an Indian in the dark," is humane enough not to have harassed the wretched remnant of these victims when he had been informed of their sufferings in exile. But supposing it were otherwise, what force was there in this plea? Is the nation to be prevented from being just because a score of men threaten to be lawless? Where was our army? There was no trouble in finding soldiers when it was anticipated that the Indians would rebel under the outrage put upon them. There had been no trouble in finding soldiers to station in the South when it was claimed that negroes were deprived of the right of suffrage. There had been no trouble in finding soldiers when strikers interfered with the property of capitalists. Is it unlawful to protect Indians, or was the government afraid of these desperate people of the West? If the latter, would it not have been well to have appointed a committee of "judicious men" to beg them not to become murderers? There remains another matter for consideration back of this. supposing that the blood-thirsty people of Idaho could have been satisfied only by leaving the Nez Percés in Indian Territory, and that it were necessary to satisfy them, why were these Indians left in such destitution? (The alternative of surrendering the indicted Indians is not considered, because the government could not honorably have adopted it.) Why were not their ponies returned to them? What became of the lumber that was sawed for them in 1880? How did it happen that they must deepen their poverty by purchasing lumber for their pastor's house in 1881, while they sat under the drippings of their rotten teepees? Why were they not paid for their share of the Nez Percés lands, if the government must persist in holding them bound by the treaty of 1863? They had certainly received none of the purchase-money before they were sent to Indian Territory.

It was not possible that Mr. Hayt's flimsy reasons for keeping them in exile should long be regarded by any one but himself, although the lack of information concerning their case was not supplied in the Indian Bureau for years. In

1882 Commissioner Price said of Joseph's band: "Not in the least excusing or attempting to palliate the crimes alleged to have been committed by them, it is but fair to say that their warfare was conducted with a noticeable absence of savage barbarity on their part, and that they persistently claim that when they surrendered to General Miles it was with the express stipulation that they should be sent back to Idaho. Whether this alleged stipulation be true or not [General Miles had said officially that it was], it is a fact that their unfortunate location near Fort Leavenworth, when in charge of the military, and the influences of the climate where they are now located in the Indian Territory, have caused much sickness among them; their ranks have been sadly depleted, and it is claimed that if they are much longer compelled to remain in their present situation, the entire band will become virtually extinct. It is now about five years since the surrender, and a sufficient time has probably elapsed to justify the belief that no concerted effort will be taken to avenge wrongs alleged to have been perpetrated by these people so many years ago. The band now numbers only about three hundred and twenty-two souls, and the reservation in Idaho is ample to accommodate them comfortably, in addition to those who are already there, who are substantially self-supporting and who have enough to spare a portion for their less fortunate brethren, and, as I understand, are willing to give them such aid. The deep-rooted love for the 'old home' which is so conspicuous among them, and their longing desire to leave the warm, debilitating climate of the Indian Territory for the

GENERAL N. A. MILES.

more healthy and invigorating air of the Idaho mountains, can never be eradicated, and any longer delay, with a hope of a final contentment on their part with their present situation, is, in my judgment, futile and unnecessary. In view of all the facts, I am constrained to believe that the remnant of this tribe should be returned to Idaho, if possible, early next spring, and I respectfully suggest that this matter be submitted to Congress at its next session, with a recommendation that an appropriation be made sufficient to meet the necessary expenses of a removal thither."

No immediate action was taken on this recommendation, but in the succeeding year the work of undoing this great wrong was begun. When the agency school broke up for vacation in May, 1883, the teacher, James Reuben, started for Idaho with twenty-nine of the exiles, mostly widows and orphans. James Reuben, by-the-way, was a Nez Percé, who had been educated and converted through the labors of Miss McBeth, a lady who went among the Nez Percés many years ago, and has devoted her life and her fortune to their advancement. Success has attended her devotion, and her preachers and teachers have done excellent work among other bands. It was, indeed, chiefly to the efforts of native missionaries, whom she had prepared for the work and sent out, that the rapid growth of Christianity among Joseph's band in the Indian Territory was due. The remainder of the band was still left there to suffer and mourn. On August 15, 1884, Agent Scott reported: "They are extremely anxious to return to their own country. They regard themselves as exiles. The climate does not seem to agree with them; many of them have died; and there is a tinge of melancholy in their bearing and conversation that is truly pathetic. I think they should be sent back, as it seems clear they will never take root and prosper in this locality." Whether this report moved the government, or whether the pleadings of their friends in Oregon at last induced the authorities to abandon the cruel injustice of the past eight years, I do not know; but last spring the remnant of the band, now numbering only two hundred and sixty-eight, were sent back to their mountain homes. Joseph and a few others were placed at Colville

Agency, in Washington Territory, and the remainder were put with their brethren on Lapwai reservation. The return of the exiles was a great occasion at Lapwai. The Indians collected from every part of the reservation to greet them. Addresses of welcome were made by Silas Whitman and James Lawyer, native preachers, and then, says a witness of the scene, "an earnest response was made by 'Tom Hill,' on behalf of the returned wanderers. His heart was too full for him to command his words, but as it was, he made a most impressive speech, delivered with matchless oratory. He touched on their long confinement in a dreary land, a land of many sorrows; spoke feelingly of their constant longings for their mountain home, which they had given up all hopes of ever seeing again; humbly acknowledged the goodness and mercy of God in permitting some of them to stand once more on the banks of the Lapwai in the presence of so many old-time friends; referred gratefully to the interposition of the Church and the law in their behalf, and closed with the announcement that their only desire now is to be henceforth law-abiding people and believers in the God of heaven. At the close of the speech hand-shaking began, which lasted for over an hour. Headed by your correspondent (Rev. G. L. Deffenbaugh), the long procession of our people filed past, and took the hand of every man, woman, and child. Friend met with friend, fathers and mothers with their long-lost sons and daughters. It was very touching to watch the play of features as the mind went through the process of identifying the face of a relative or friend, and then, after the decision was made, to hear the glad expressions, 'Is this you?' mentioning the name; 'Is it you, father?' or 'Is that you, brother?' Only one who had a heart of stone could have stood by and not entered with spirit into the joys of the occasion. But to one standing near the end of the line a different scene presented itself. Some having taken the hands of all present, and missing the faces of those they had hoped to see, gave vent to their sorrow in uncontrollable weeping. Certainly, the most cruel-hearted Indian-hater could not have stood by unaffected." And Joseph could not share in even this small recompense for past suffering. It was feared that local prejudice would make it dangerous for him to come. Joseph—ah no! he had been guilty of fighting like a man for justice and for the right. He was a criminal—in Idaho.

Who is to be blamed for all this wickedness and wrong? Incidentally, various persons who have been mentioned, but the greatest responsibility is apparently with the Commission of 1876, sent out to arrange for an equitable settlement with these Indians, who, with the exception of Lieutenant-colonel Wood, reported that the Indians ought to be sent to the reservation, by force, if necessary. Their names are Gen. O. O. Howard, D. H. Jerome, William Stickney, and A. C. Barstow. It has been mentioned that in 1875 General Howard took the position that the Lower Nez Percés ought to have the Wallowa country. Why he changed his mind in 1876 does not appear. Joseph says that when Howard came back he said, "I will not let white men laugh at me the next time I come." Whether Joseph means that he used these words, or merely thus indicates his own guess at the general's motives, the chances are that he struck the correct theory. In the spring of 1879, when there appeared in the *North American Review* Joseph's statement of his case—the most magnificent piece of Indian eloquence that was ever known, with the exception of the much disputed speech of Logan—General Howard rushed into print with a reply. Therein he promised a book on the subject, which appeared in 1881. If the existence of the publications be not sufficient evidence of his sensitiveness to public opinion, the inquiring reader will find ample confession of it in the pages of both productions. I do not find that his part in the work of the Commission is brought prominently forward in either. If there is any mention of the fact that he was a member of the Commission, in his book I have failed to discover it. I do find his objection to the public holding responsible an "army officer who is subject to the requisition of the Indian Department," and his statement that "the Indian management did not belong to my department." I do find him giving a summary of Governor Grover's letter, the ideas of which the Commission adopted, and then adding these words, "So much for our ideas of justice. First, we acknowledge and confirm by treaty to Indians a sort of title to vast regions. Afterwards we continue, in a strictly legal manner, to do away with both the substance and the shadow of title. Wiser heads than Joseph's have been puzzled by this manner of balancing the scales." Who would read these words and imagine that their author had sat as a judge in this case, and recommended the injustice over which he sighs.

I do not presume to criticise General Howard's conduct of the campaign. It is quite probable that he did the best he could—possibly as well as any one would have done. He had for an enemy the hardest fighting Indians on the continent, led by the ablest uneducated chief that the world ever saw. I do criticise him for his part in the Commission, where he could probably have induced a recommendation of fair and honorable treatment of these Indians, instead of the mistreatment that was recommended. I do criticise him for writing in 1879, those cruel words: "Let them settle down, and keep quiet, in the Indian Territory, as the Modocs have done, and they will thrive as they do." I do criticise him for evading the real issue in his attempted defence. I do criticise him for trying to make a defence. I would that he had been noble enough to say, "I was mistaken." I would that he had said to the government and the people, "When I recommended the removal of these Indians, I thought they would go without fighting. I thought that they would have real advantages on the reservation which would compensate them for their loss of freedom. I did not imagine that they would be roused to madness by the wrong we were doing. I did not think that the plighted faith of Colonel Miles and myself would be broken. I did not dream that the Indians would be taken to swampy bottom-lands and shelterless plains to die of unknown diseases. I was wrong, and I wish to have my wrong righted, as far as possible, by having them sent back to their mountain homes." If he had said this, the wrong would probably have been righted long ago.

The great majority of the American people desire that the Indians should be treated fairly and honorably—not because they are Indians, but because they are men, and we desire that all men should be so treated. It can but be humiliating that our second century should begin with such a wrong against that race, which, it must be confessed, has suffered at our hands, despite the wishes of the people. Yet there is nothing to relieve its monstrosity. It was not committed by rude and lawless men of the border, but by men selected from the nation for their supposed fitness for the work. It was not done when public sentiment might have been supposed to sustain harsh and unjust measures, but in the day of "advanced ideas" and under the lauded "humanitarian Indian policy" of our government. How tarnished are the tinsel vauntings of the admirers of that policy, in the light of this case! Taking it all in all, from the first time an Indian was kidnaped on the New England coast, and sold into slavery, down to the present day, Conestoga, Sand Creek, Bloody Point, and all, the treatment of the Nez Percés is the worst crime that the white man has perpetrated upon the red man. Heedless of this beam in our own eye, we have groaned over the wrongs of the Bulgarian Christians, waxed indignant at the harrying of the Russian Jews, and raged about England's treatment of the Irish. Look to your hands! They are red with innocent blood and dark with the stains of plunder. We may seek to justify ourselves by shallow casuistry, but if the time shall ever come when a just God shall judge between us and the Lower Nez Percés, what answer can we make?

CHAPTER XX.
WHITE RIVER AGENCY.

"THE Utes must go!" How that cry resounded through Colorado in 1879 and 1880. "The Utes must go!" Everybody said so. If any one had been rash enough to dispute the proposition he would have been denounced as an enemy to public peace and prosperity. The newspapers kept the words standing for head-lines. People talked it, met together and resolved it, and finally accomplished it. It was a sentiment that arose several years before and gained strength steadily. Its original basis was that their reservation was rich in minerals and included the best agricultural and grazing lands in the state; that the Utes did not and would not develop these resources; and that the whites desired to develop them. At first this feeling was not so strong, because the whites were not numerous; and there were hundreds of acres of arable land that had not been taken up, and thousands of acres of mineral land that had not been prospected. But Colorado and all the adjoining territory were destined to a mighty revolution. It originated in the obscure mining-camp of Slabtown, or Oro City, in California Gulch, on the head-waters of the Arkansas River. The place first attracted attention in the time of the Pike's Peak excitement, when hardy gold-hunters were searching all through the ranges nearest the plains for deposits of the yellow metal. California, Stray Horse, and Iowa gulches were discovered; the towns of Oro, Malta, and Granite were established; and a population estimated at 10,000 occupied the region. In the course of four years they took out about $13,000,000 of gold; but after that the placers decreased in value, and were gradually abandoned until, in 1874, they were practically deserted. Work was prosecuted on them at intervals, however, and ranches which had been established along the Arkansas and its tributaries were still occupied.

During the placer mining in California Gulch, the miners had been much annoyed by a peculiar heavy substance, resembling clay, that clogged their rockers and interfered with their work. In 1878 it was ascertained that this stuff was carbonate of lead, and that it carried enough silver to make it valuable. It was already known that there were large deposits of it above the town. Then ensued the most remarkable mining excitement ever known in America. Times were hard in the East. The country was still suffering from the financial disorders of 1873 and 1875. Railroads afforded speedy and cheap transportation almost to the mines. Why not try the West? In August, 1877, the camp of Slabtown was composed of a score of shanties. In June, 1878, it had a population of 400. In October, 1878, the city of Leadville had 6000 inhabitants; in April, 1879, it had 12,000, with additions coming at the rate of from 300 to 500 per day. But this represented only a fraction of the people coming West. The rival railroad lines across the plains had placed before the public everywhere their most alluring prospectuses of the country bordering on their lines, and beyond their termini, inducing thousands, who had been originally awakened to the desirability of Western fields of labor by the Leadville discoveries, to go to other points. It was as well that they did, for Leadville was already overloaded, and the neighboring country for miles was staked out in mining claims, that were worth less, actually, than the cost of surveying them, though their market value was for a time quite respectable. The same thing occurred in many other places. There were hundreds of acres that looked like overgrown prairie-dog towns, so covered were they with the dumps of sanguine prospectors, who had about as much knowledge of mining as they had of the precession of the equinoxes. "Got any indications?" some new arrival would ask. "Nothin' very good, but you've got to dig for it if you find it. That's the way George Fryer struck it." Then the inquiring tenderfoot would seek the most convenient unclaimed spot, adjust the red flannel rag around his neck, worn to prevent pneumo-

THE SNOW RANGE.

nia, and begin digging. He had the same answer stored away for any one who asked him the reason of his faith.

The immigration increased until the summer of 1880, before it began its gradual return to a natural basis. Every train over the Union Pacific, Kansas Pacific, and Atchison, Topeka, & Santa Fé roads was uncomfortably overloaded. It appears, from the best data that are obtainable, that by railroad and wagon there came into Colorado on some days as many as five thousand people, and very seldom less than one thousand. Many of these returned, after a short stay, but the major part remained, or pressed on into the wilder country beyond. The influx of humanity was like a rising river. It filled the eastern valleys, crept up the mountain ranges, and poured into the valleys beyond. Onward, ever onward, it moved, gaining strength continually, until it was beating against the barrier of the reservation lines. Then the sentiment that "the Utes must go" gained strength rapidly. It was told in mysterious whispers that the reservation was a very treasure-house; the Elk Mountains were full of silver; there were placers on all the rivers. It was known that there were large deposits of coal and iron, and gold generally goes with iron. The impossibility of verifying the stories made them ten times greater, and increased credence in an equal ratio. What was the use of having the Utes there? There was plenty of land elsewhere, not rich in mineral, that would do just as well for them. Blank blank the Utes, any way. They were a miserable, lousy lot of savages, and a detriment to the country. Still, the sentiment did not obtain universally until the outbreak of 1879; then the whole state was put in a furor. The Utes were strong in numbers, well-armed, well supplied with horses, and were warriors of no mean repute. They could cross either the Saguache or the Snow range, and strike the eastern settlements by a dozen different routes. The northern and southern settlements were at their mercy. Information was meagre and contradictory. There were hundreds of wild rumors. The only way to be safe was to be prepared for anything. Accordingly, men abandoned their work and organized for defence, at dozens of points, where there was, in fact, no danger at all. After the trouble was all over, it was learned that two or three hundred Indians, who had no intention of fighting except on their own lands, had thrown into confusion a hundred thousand people; but the scare had settled the matter. There were few who knew who the Utes were, or cared what they were. It made no difference what were their rights or what had been their wrongs. They were an injury to the interests of the entire state. If the United States did not remove them the people of Colorado would. The Utes must go!

There is no doubt that the Utes had been treated badly; there is no doubt that at least nine tenths of the charges made against them were unfounded. On the other hand, it is clear that their mistreatment had little, if anything, to do with the outbreak. The country of the Utes was not affected by any of the transcontinental thoroughfares. It lay south of the Sonth Pass routes, and north of the road through the Spanish settlements. To the settlements on their borders they had been of so little trouble that no treaty with them was considered necessary until 1863. In the early days of the West some bands of them engaged in marauding, jointly with their allies, the Navahos and Apaches. On Christmas Day, 1854, a hundred Utes and Jicarillas, under Tierra Blanco, destroyed the settlement on the Arkansas, above the mouth of the Huerfano, killing fifteen men, capturing two women and some children, and running off all the stock of the settlement. Colonel Fauntleroy marched against these Indians from Fort Massachusetts, which had been established as a threat, for the preservation of peace, in the San Luis valley. His force consisted of two companies of regulars, two companies of volunteers, and Kit Carson's scouts. They surprised the Utes on the night of April 28, 1855, on the Arkansas, near Chalk Creek, about twenty miles above Poncha Pass.* The Indians had been holding a

---

* This pass leads from San Luis Park to the South Arkansas valley. The name was originally *Puncha* or *Punché*, the Ute word for a small plant, that they use for kil-li-kin-nick, which grows abundantly in the pass. When the post-office was established at Poncha Springs, in 1879, some backwoods philologists thought the word was the Mexican *Poncho*, a blanket cloak; and the Post-office Department, with an admirable spirit of compromise, named it Poncha, which does not mean anything.

scalp-dance all night, and were struck at daybreak. Forty were killed, many wounded, six children were made prisoners, and all their property was captured. This blow had a very salutary effect on them. There were afterwards some petty depredations by the southern tribes, occasional disturbances with the Colorado miners, and some rather serious troubles on the Utah side, arising from Mormon influence, but never anything in the way of a general war. It has been claimed that as many as forty men were killed by them from 1860 to 1879; but many of these were people who were found dead, or had disappeared, and their taking off was blamed to the Utes in the absence of any other known cause. It should be remembered, also, that the plains Indians often entered this country, on war expeditions, and were at times mistaken for Utes. The Arapahoes engaged in the Rawlin's Springs massacre claimed to be Utes, and were supposed to be until after that affair was over. On the whole, the Utes may be called friendly, and were so regarded; but they were not admirers of civilization, and, with the exception of a few of the New Mexican bands, never showed much disposition to adopt "the white man's road." They preferred to live by the chase.

In 1863 the Tabequache Utes made a treaty accepting, as a reservation, a part of the lands they had always held in Western Colorado. There was some dissatisfaction, because payments were not made to them as they should have been; but it was smoothed over, and peaceful relations were maintained. In a few years it was thought best to put all the eastern Utes together. A treaty to effect this purpose was made with the principal bands on March 2, 1868, by Kit Carson, N. G. Taylor, and Governor Hunt; and the western part of Colorado, included between longitude 107°, a line fifteen miles north of latitude 40°, and the southern and western boundaries of the territory, was set apart to be theirs forever. There were seven principal bands. The Yampas (Bear Rivers) and Grand Rivers were located in the northern part of the reservation, with their agency on White River. The Tabequaches and Uncompahgrés were in the central part, with their agency at Los Pinos. The Wee-mi-nu-ches, Mu-a-ches, and Ca-po-tes, who were Southern Colorado and New Mexican Indians, were located in the southern part of the reservation. They had their agency at Los Pinos, with the Tabequaches and Uncompahgrés, until the San Juan cession, in 1873, and then a separate agency was established for them in their own country. A number of these southern Indians, principally Muaches (Maquaches), had land under cultivation on the Rio La Plata and other tributaries of the Rio San Juan, of which they retained possession for several years, but were then forcibly dispossessed by settlers who claimed that the Indians had no rights off the reservation. The annuities promised in this treaty were not paid until after unreasonable delay. The lines established were claimed by the Indians to be fraudulent. They said the lines were explained to them as being on the tops of the mountains, *i.e.*, the continental divide, but the line as surveyed cut off the beautiful valleys of the Gunnison, Tomichi, and other streams. It took away also Middle Park and North Park, which they said they did not sell. Worst of all, the whites continually invaded the reservation. It had been the great desire of the Utes to have a country that was absolutely their own, and accordingly the following strong promise was put in the treaty: "The United States now solemnly agrees that no persons, except those herein authorized so to do, and except such officers, agents, and employés of the government as may be authorized to enter upon Indian reservations in discharge of duties enjoined by law, shall ever be permitted to pass over, settle upon, or reside in the territory described in this article." The Indians considered this treaty as giving them the fee-simple of these lands. The first proceeding of part of the bands was to move off the reservation, which they said they intended to keep for a hunting-ground. They abandoned this plan, after remonstrance by their agents, and located on their reservation, with the privilege of hunting outside of it.

Looking back through the years, it seems questionable whether the men who negotiated this treaty, or the senators who ratified it, had any expectation that these agreements would be kept, so repeatedly had similar ones been broken. The Utes had scarcely received their first payments before the mines of the San Juan country were discovered, and great crowds of people went to them, notwithstanding they were wholly within the Ute reservation. The Indians complained, and soldiers were ordered to remove the intruders. Before the enforcement of the orders began, the President was "informed that their chief, Ouray (Uré, Uray—The Arrow), had expressed a willingness to negotiate for the sale of a portion of the reservation," and the orders were countermanded. Who vouchsafed this information does not appear from the published records. A commission was at once sent to the Utes (in 1872), and they utterly refused to sell. The miners remained undisturbed, and in the following year Felix Brunot was sent to talk to the Indians. He persuaded them that he came from pure friendship for them, and induced them to make a cession of the San Juan and San Miguel countries, a block of land sixty-five miles wide by ninety-five miles deep. This left them a strip fifteen miles wide along the southern line of the state, and one twenty miles wide along the western line up to ten miles north of parallel 38, above which the reservation stood as formerly. This cession was made on the express understanding that it was not to include any farming lands, but only the mines on the mountains. Most of the farming lands on the reservation were in the southern part. The Tabequaches and Uncompahgrés had only a limited amount of arable land—a strip on the San Miguel, the Uncompahgré Park, and a small tract on the Uncompahgré River. No one, white or Indian, thought

OURAY.

at that time that the lands on the Gunnison and the Grand, in the western part of the reservation, which are now farmed so profitably, were worth anything for agriculture.

The Utes said they thought the north line of the proposed cession would cut off part of the Uncompahgré Park. To meet this objection it was agreed that, if it did, an offset would be made to exclude it from the cession. This understanding was inserted in the treaty in these words: *"Provided,* that if any part of the Uncompahgré Park shall be found to extend south of the north line of said described country, the same is not intended to be included therein, and is hereby reserved and retained as a portion of the Ute reservation." This agreement was ratified by Act of Congress, April 29, 1874, "treaties" with Indians being at that time prohibited by law. The former agreement as to the exclusion of white persons from the reservation was reaffirmed, but the Indians agreed to allow one road, across the southern part of the reservation, to the ceded lands. The Utes made this cession with much hesitancy, and chiefly in the hope that it would avoid any further trouble from miners, but they still feared that the miners would want more. Said Ouray to Brunot: "The lines in regard to the mines do not amount to anything; it is changing them all the time—taking a little now and a little again–that makes trouble. You said you do not know anything in regard to these lines [those established under the treaty of 1868], and it may be the same in regard to lines you make. There are many men talk about it to us; they say they are going to have the lines as they want, whether the Utes like it or not. It is common talk; everybody tells it to the Utes. The miners care very little about the government. It is a long way off in the States, and they say the man who comes to make the treaty will go off to the States, and it will all be as they want it." True old Arrow! He went straight to the mark.

This treaty was not complied with by us in three important particulars, not to mention minor ones. In the first place, the Utes were to receive $25,000 annually forever, in compensation for the cession, but Congress provided for this by placing bonds to their credit, the interest on which was to meet these payments, and the first instalment did not fall due for one year. Consequently the first, or cash payment, was not provided for. After several years of protestation and bickering this was made good, but by this time there had been twice that amount withheld from the annual payments under "the discretion of the President." The amount thereafter continuously due the Utes, under this agreement, fluctuated from $65,000 to $90,000. At the time of the outbreak it was $65,000. In the second place, the south line of the cession was run so as to cut off a large amount of farming and grazing lands. Sapavanari, a young Uncompahgré chief, went with the surveying-party, to protect them from interference, "until he saw with his own eyes" that the line was cutting off some 15,000 acres of farm lands, including some of the Ute farms. Then he left them, fearing that he would be compromised with his tribe, and his tribe compromised with the government, if he did not protest against the line. The Indians said that as the agreement was explained to them they were to have ten miles more on the south side, and twenty miles more on the west side, than was given them. In the third place, the north line of the cession was run through the centre of Uncompahgré Park, and no offset was made to cover the part cut off. This fact was pointed out to the surveyor, J. W. Miller, and he promised to correct it, but, instead of doing so, went on to Washington, had his survey approved, got his money, and dropped out of the controversy. The Indians were greatly disappointed, and begged to have justice done them in this matter. After much correspondence the authorities concluded to humor them by complying with the treaty, and on August 17, 1876, President Grant issued an order withdrawing from the public domain four miles square of the cession, including the part of the Park that had been cut off, and adding it to the Ute reservation.

By this time a number of settlers had located in this part of the Park, which was the only convenient farming land in the neighborhood of Ouray, the principal mining-town of the San Juan country. They declined to remove except at the point of the bayonet. Some of their attorneys advised them that the President had no right to add to a reservation after it had been established by Congress, and one, C. H. McIntyre, prepared and forwarded to the Interior Department a brief maintaining this proposition. It seems to have escaped Mr. McIntyre's notice that this had nothing to do with the question. The reservation as established by Congress included all of the Uncompahgré Park. The trouble was that an executive officer had wilfully failed to comply with the provisions

HENRY M. TELLER.

made by Congress, and this the Executive Department not only had the right, but was in duty bound to rectify. Under Mr. McIntyre's profound logic, a United States deputy surveyor had abrogated an Act of Congress. Troops were ordered to remove the intruders in the spring of 1877, but H. M. Teller, of counsel for the settlers, since Secretary of the Interior, of Backbone Land-grant fame, wrote a touching letter to Secretary Schurz, detailing the hardships that this would cause to these people, who "went on the land in good faith," and Mr. Schurz weakly allowed them six months of grace, in which to harvest their crops and move. None of them agreed to move—their attorney, even, did not promise it—in order to obtain this kind concession of the rights of a third party, and none of them did move. In the spring of 1878 another order was made for their dispossession, but by this time the Park was full of defiant settlers. They refused to move, and said that if the soldiers put them off before the commission, which had been sent to treat for the four miles square, had been heard from, they would kill Indians and precipitate an Indian war. This threat so terrified the Ute agent, J. B. Abbott, that he withdrew the troops.

The commission arrived in August, 1878, headed by General Hatch. Their mission was to purchase the four miles square and also the southern strip, below the San Juan cession. At first the Indians refused to talk to them. They had not yet received the first payment for the San Juan cession. They said they would not talk of selling land to people who would not pay for what they had already bought. Finally, on promise that this should be made right, they went into council. There was no difficulty about the southern strip. The southern Utes had already proposed to take another reservation, "provided the government would pay them the previous indebtedness," and this the commission did, to the amount of $15,534, letting the remainder stand. In this transaction the southern Utes gave up over 1,800,000 acres of land and took a reservation of something over 700,000 acres, with the understanding that they should have compensation for the excess of 1,100,000 acres. This was left out of the treaty by the commissioners, but shows in the minutes of the council, as the Indians claimed. (During the past summer, by the way, they have been reported as reduced to starvation and becoming desperate.) The four miles square was more troublesome. The Utes wanted all of the Park because it was their best, almost their only, winter range for their stock—they had about six thousand horses, besides cattle and sheep. In addition to this, it contained a hot spring which was valuable to them for medicinal purposes. It was urged by the commission that the President wanted to give the miners some land, on which to raise vegetables. Said Ouray: "I can't see that the President wants it; the settlers want it." It was urged that the settlers and their backers were making strong claims to the government. Said Ouray: "If the government wants to take it and break the treaty, all right." It was urged that the land was not of importance, but that it was very desirable to end all difficulty. Said Ouray: "I don't think that would end it. They would want more." The value of $10,000, the price offered, was dwelt upon. Said Sapavanari: "We don't want to sell it; don't want money." The commissioners said they were talking for the good of the Indians, not the white men. Said Ouray: "If you were talking for the Indians, you would put the settlers out." The commission abandoned the task, in despair, but a delegation of Utes was brought on to Washington in the following winter, and the purchase was accomplished. The Utes wanted one thing distinctly understood, and they had it put on record; it was that they consented to this sale, not because they desired it, but because the government did. They wanted the $10,000 paid in cash, but were informed that they would have to wait until it was appropriated by Congress. They got it several years later.

While all these things are true, and while they are very dirty spots on our enlightened Indian policy, it is not true, as some have inferred, that they caused the Ute outbreak. They were all settled several months before it occurred. The Indians simply agreed to submit to these wrongs, and as disturbing forces they were removed. Moreover, the Indians who made the outbreak were not materially affected by these wrongs. Soon after the establishment of the reservation the Indians divided themselves into three groups, with independent governments, corresponding to the three agencies. The smaller tribes, principally Pah-Utes, who were afterwards placed on the reservation, joined one or the other of these groups. Ouray was treated as head chief of all the Utes, by the whites, but he did not, in fact, have general authority. The Southern Utes did not recognize him at all. Their head chief was Ignacio, a Muache, who was aided by several sub-chiefs, including Ka-ni-a-che (The One Who was Taken Down), An-ka-tosh (the Red), and others. Ignacio would have nothing to do with Ouray. This was chiefly owing to the fact that, by the Brunot agreement, Ouray was to receive $1000 annually for his services, an arrangement at the time unknown to the other Indians. The Los Pinos and White River Utes did not even claim any interest in the southern and western strips of land. When the commission of 1878 desired to purchase these lands, they said they would agree to whatever Ignacio said; that they had no claim to the lower country. The Tabequaches, Uncompahgrés, and others of the Los Pinos agency recognized Ouray's authority fully. Among their minor chiefs were Sha-va-no (Chavanaugh, Shawana —Blue Flower), Guero (Wa-ro—Light hair), and Captain Billy, of the Tabequaches, and Un-com-mute (Un-kum-good, Uncom, Uncah, Unqua), and Sapavana-ri,* of the Uncompah-grés. The White River Utes recognized Ouray's authority to

CAPTAIN BILLY.

---

* There is some confusion about this name. In official reports it is often mistaken for the Spanish Saponiere (Xaboniere—a soap-maker), Saponavero (which may be translated "genuine soap"), or Saponaria (soapwort). The agent at Ouray writes me, on August 13, 1885: "I have made inquiry and learn that 'Sappovanaro' means anything white, and I am free to confess there are many of the Utes who seem to know more about it than 'Old Sap' himself. One says 'something white, all same pony or paper,' and another explained by pointing to a white toad-stool. The interpreter says it means a water-cloud or water-spout. Sappovanaro says the name was given him by Kit Carson, and was taken from the Mexican Indians." In his correspondence Mr. Carson spelled the name Sa-pa-wa-ne-ri.

a very limited extent; in ordinary affairs not at all. They were in two factions; one led by Douglas, and the other by Jack. Among the lesser chiefs were Colorado (Red), commonly called Colorow, Piah (The Black-tailed Deer), Sa-rap (The Rainbow), Sah-patch (White Hot), and Johnson. These Indians had no real interest in the San Juan cession, the south-line dispute, or the four miles square. The first concerned both of the other groups; the second affected only the Southern Utes; and the last was the affair of the Los Pinos Indians. The White Rivers took very little interest in these matters. They received no part of the money for the San Juan cession, and claimed no interest in it. The lands ceded did not belong to them. They said the other bands were fools for selling their land, and that it was good enough for them if they were cheated. The Uintah Utes were not on this reservation. Their chief was called Tabby (Taw-vi), and they were located on a reservation in Utah.

The trouble with the White River Indians arose from disagreements with their agent, N. C. Meeker. He was best known as the leader of the colony that settled the town of Greeley, Colorado, under the patronage of Horace Greeley, and was, for a long time, a correspondent of the *New York Tribune,* over the initials N. C. M. His reputation for honesty was excellent, but he prided himself on his practical qualities, and greatly overestimated his ability to civilize savages. He said, in a letter to Senator Teller, on December 23, 1878: "When I get round to it in a year or so, if I stay as long, I shall propose to cut every Indian down to bare starvation point if he will not work. The 'getting around to it' means to have plenty of tilled ground, plenty of work to do, and to have labor organized so that whoever will shall be able to earn his bread." A friend characterized him thus: "A man of the Puritan stamp, an enthusiast in whatever work he undertook, he had given his whole soul to the work of civilizing the Utes. It is a waste of words to say that he was honorable and upright in all his dealings with them, for his life has been public and his character beyond reproach." Admitting this to be true, the fact still remains that he did not understand the Indian character, and could not manage them.

He took charge of the agency in May, 1878, and began operations by moving the agency to Powell's Valley, on White River, fifteen miles below the old agency. The Indians opposed this because they used this valley for a winter camp, it affording the best pasturage for their horses. Meeker studied the situation, and adopted the plan of playing one of the factions against the other. He first took up the Douglas faction, which was recognized as "the government," although Jack's party was the larger. The feeling had become such that whatever one faction favored the other would oppose. The next difficulty, after moving the agency, to which the Indians yielded a reluctant assent, on being assured that the commissioner would be "a heap mad" if they did not, was to get their consent to the appropriation of $3000 of their money, for an irrigating ditch. This was never obtained directly, but was taken for granted, because a part of the Indians were employed in the work, on the theory that by taking part in the work they consented to the appropriation, "as much so as, when a man marries a woman, they consent." The Indians who assisted in the work, for which they received in all $303, were twenty-five men of the Douglas faction. Jack's party not only refused to work, but also objected to the others working, on the grounds that it was the white men's business to do all the work, and that the Indians at Los Pinos did not work. After being threatened with report to the commissioner, he withdrew this objection, and all his party, with a number of the others, went on a hunting excursion off the reservation, as had been their custom every summer.

To understand what Meeker was contending against, it must be borne in mind that the Utes had not yet emerged from "the hunter state." They subsisted on game to the extent of fully fifty per cent., and derived most of their money from the products of the chase, particularly buckskin. Deer were yet very numerous in the mountains of Colorado, and the greater part of them made their way beyond the divide in the summer. Their habit is to spend the winter months in the foot-hills, bordering on the plains, but in the spring to run back into the mountains, ranging as far as the beginning of the desert lands in Western Colorado. Elks were quite abundant, and a small herd of buffalo remained in Middle Park. The Indians roved where they chose, but their best hunting-grounds lay between the reservation and the divide, in Middle Park, in North Park, and in the country west of it. This country, they claimed, belonged to them under the treaty of 1868, being west of the Continental Divide. North Park is east of it, but is drained to the north by the North Platte. They also hunted buffalo on the plains east of Denver, where these animals were quite numerous until 1875. Their last visit to the plains was in 1878. They prided themselves on being "peaceable," but their visits were regarded by settlers with much the same dread that Eastern people have of a camp of gypsies or a colony of tramps. Undoubtedly they committed some trespasses and frightened some timid people in 1879, but the reports that were made concerning them were so wildly exaggerated as to deserve the name of falsehoods. The principal charge that was urged against them was that they were setting out fires by which the forests were destroyed and the improvements of settlers put in jeopardy. It was explained by some that this was a custom of theirs, the object of which was to drive the game so that it could be more easily killed. The charge and explanation were untrue and absurd. The Utes never had such a custom. The existence of millions of acres of virgin forests ought to have been sufficient proof of it. No people preserve game more carefully than Indians, and none know better than they that continuous fires would drive it away. Their hunting was like the white man's; the chief object was to induce a deer to stand still long enough to be shot. There were great and destructive forest fires that summer, but the Indians were responsible for very few of them. Major Thornburgh, commanding at Fort Fred Steele, Wyoming, investigated this charge thoroughly, by writing to reliable settlers, and by sending out men to look for evidence of it, but the reports, without exception, were that the Indians had killed no cattle, offered no violence to settlers, and set no fires. One man went over their trail and satisfied himself that no fires originated from their camps. They did set fire to the grass at several places in Middle Park, "to make good grass next year," but they claimed that Middle Park belonged to them, and repeatedly ordered settlers and others to leave it. They ordered the miners out in 1869, the first year after the treaty.

The truth is that nearly all the fires were occasioned by the carelessness of white men, and particularly from the carelessness of men in the "tie camps," *i.e.*, men who were cutting ties for the Denver, Rio Grande, and South Park railways, which were then being pushed through the mountains. It was notorious that most of these fires occurred in localities where there were no Indians. Many a prospector,

SOUTHERN UTES.

who never saw a Ute, saw hundreds of acres of pine consumed. I resided in a district that was nearly all burned over in 1879, and there was not an Indian in it, though it was within fifty miles of the reservation. Old settlers said there had not been a mountain fire in the region for seventeen years before. They also said the year was unusually dry, and that fires travelled and caught easily. It is true, however, that, owing to the reports, the whites generally believed that the Indians were firing the forests at other places, to drive out the miners. It is true also that the Indians killed large quantities of game, as was complained, but so did every one. A man who failed to shoot at a deer because it was against the law would have been laughed at. Venison retailed, in season, at four and five cents the pound, while beef was fifteen to twenty. There was not a mountain stream in which dynamite was not exploded to kill trout, if there were any trout in it. So with the forests. The United States law against cutting timber on public lands was no more regarded than if it had not been on the statute-books. The forests of stumps are there to-day to prove the statement. The people of Middle Park sent a memorial to General Pope, in 1877, representing that the Indians were slaughtering the game, "when a white man is not allowed to kill a pound more than he can use to sustain life;" but if the people of Middle Park were any more virtuous or law-abiding, in this respect or any other, than the rest of the people in Colorado, no one ever discovered it. It was not many months later that half the county officials of Grand County (Middle Park) conspired to murder the county commissioners, and did murder them. It is notorious that two of the signers of that memorial have committed suicide on account of their participation in that crime, and that Grand County to-day is a slumbering volcano of hate, remorse, distrust, and revenge, as a result of that awful tragedy enacted on the shore of Grand Lake. Let it be distinctly understood that there were reputable, law-abiding people in Middle Park, and elsewhere in Colorado—plenty of them—but to all such representations of uniformly proper whites and uniformly villainous Indians, coming from any frontier settlement, I say: "In the name of the Prophet—Bosh!"

While the Utes behaved comparatively well in their summer excursions, it cannot be questioned that these trips were a serious impediment to their civilization. Of course they would not settle down to farming while they could live by hunting. That would have been unnatural. But, worse than that, there were no restrictions to trade with them, off the reservation. There were four stores on Bear River, and many at other points, where they could obtain guns, ammunition, whiskey, or anything else that they were able to pay for. They were also thrown in contact with the worst class of whites, and there were some very bad white people for them to come in contact with. Aside from the ordinary riff-raff, there were a number of cattle-men about the reservation with more property than character. Two of these, who were the subjects of repeated complaints by the agent, were the Morgan brothers. They had large herds of cattle near the reservation, and were accused of permitting them to mix with the herd belonging to the White River agency, for the purpose of claiming the unbranded increase (mavoricks) of the agency herd. They were also charged with taking branded cattle and burning their brand, a double box (••), over the "I D" of the Indian Department. They were not the only ones. When the outbreak came, and the agency herd was scattered and uncared for, about twelve hundred of them disappeared. It was supposed at the time that the Indians had taken them. It was afterwards learned that they were stolen by white men, rebranded, and sold to the government for beef. I had the honor to be acquainted with Wes Travis, one of the men engaged in this robbery—since succumbed to the combined powers of bad whiskey and death—and have heard him tell, with great gusto, how he and a companion, after finishing the cattle job, killed an Indian that they met when coming out of the reservation. They cut him open, removed his intestines, filled him with stones, sewed him up, and dumped him into a deep hole in Grand River. Morgan's partner, W. B. Hugus, and John Gordon, *alias* Samuel Lemon, were brought to trial for this affair, in Denver, but they had the good fortune to be acquitted. The Morgans escaped from the country.

The complaints made against the Utes, in the summer of 1879, flew on wings of the wind, growing as they went. The only palpable foundation for them was the alleged destruction of some property by two Utes called Bennett and Chinaman. It had been agreed by the Utes that they would deliver up accused persons for trial, and they had complied with this agreement usually, but on this occasion Douglas refused to surrender these men to the officer who came for them, and informed him that he could not make the arrest on the reservation. The treaty also contained this clause: *"Provided,* That if any chief of either of the confederated bands

JACK.

make war against the people of the United States, or in any manner violate this treaty in any essential part, said chief shall forfeit his position as chief, and all rights to any of the benefits of this treaty: *But, provided further,* Any Indian of these confederated bands who shall remain at peace, and abide by the terms of this treaty in all its essentials, shall be entitled to its benefits and provisions, notwithstanding his particular chief and band may have forfeited their rights thereto." Meeker, although he had no personal knowledge of what was occurring off the reservation, joined in these complaints. On March 17 he reported that part of the Utes were going north "probably to supply ammunition to the hostiles," *i.e.,* certain Sioux who were said to be on the war-path, and asked that the military send the Indians back to the reservation. Jack was several times confronted with reports of wrong-doing, and the statement that his party wanted to go to war. Being conscience clear, he, with three others, went to Denver to see Governor Pitkin. He complained of this treatment and asked for Meeker's removal; but being there confronted by Meeker's letters, complaining of some things of which he had no knowledge, and of others that he could meet only by denial, he became disheartened and went back to the agency. In this interview he backed up his claim of Meeker's evil deeds by the statement that Meeker wanted their children to go to school and learn to work, neither of which the Utes wanted. Meeker had also promised him a wagon, and failed to give it to him, which satisfied him that Meeker could not be trusted. At the agency he got no satisfaction, and became impressed with the idea that Meeker was responsible for everything that was said about the Utes in the newspapers, a theory which the other Indians soon adopted. A more oppressive burden could not be placed on any man's shoulders than such a responsibility. The Colorado press was sensational, to say the least, and the contents of the papers were frequently communicated to the Indians by their white acquaintances.

In the mean time a new trouble had arisen. Powell's Valley had been subdivided by Meeker with a view to its permanent settlement by the Indians. One street crossed it lengthwise, and another at right angles to the first. The agency was located at the crossing, but the cross-street was as yet on paper only. Several small plots had been marked off for Indians who desired to work. The first one provided for was Johnson, a chief with "three cows and two wives," who showed a commendable disposition to civilize. A log-house was built for him, near the agency buildings, and for several months he was the "brag Indian" of the place. Horses were broken for him, and fed from the agency supplies to keep them in condition for work; but, finally, Meeker discovered that Johnson was using these horses to race with the other Indians, whose ponies were picking a precarious living where they could find it. Johnson stock fell rapidly thereafter. Instead of cultivating the land set off for him, Johnson used it to pasture his ponies, of which he had about a hundred and fifty. Early in

September Meeker undertook to plough up a large amount of land near the agency, including that set off to Johnson and two or three others. These Indians objected, and could neither be talked out of their objections nor induced to take other locations. They got their guns, and ordered the ploughing stopped. The ploughing went on. In a few minutes a gun was fired in a clump of bushes near by, and a bullet whizzed unpleasantly near the ploughman's ears. Meeker then stopped the work and appealed to Douglas; but Douglas said the men who claimed land wanted it, and that Meeker should plough in some other place. Having exhausted his influence in that quarter, Meeker thought he would try the other faction. He sent for Jack, who came at once with his retainers. A council was held, and the conclusion reached that Jack and his men cared nothing about it, but that Meeker might plough a strip one hundred feet wide and half a mile long. He told them that this would do no good; that he wanted at least fifty acres, besides meadow land. He understood that they consented to this, but on the following morning the work was stopped again. Jack was sent for once more and another council was held. They finally decided that Meeker might have the land if he would give Johnson a stove, move his corral, dig a well, and help build a house, to which the agent consented. He said, however, "that it was the wish of all the Indians that ploughing might be stopped, and that no more ploughing at all shall be done; but that the conclusion which they reached was based upon the danger they ran in opposing the government of the United States."

This influence wore off and the bad feeling of the Indians grew. Two days later (September 10) Johnson assaulted Meeker in his own house, drove him out, and beat him badly. Meeker would probably have been killed but for the interference of the employés. He sent at once for military aid, and telegraphed the commissioner: "Ploughing stops. Life of self, family, and employés not safe; want protection immediately. Have asked Governor Pitkin to confer with General Pope." On the same day he wrote to W. N. Byers, of Denver, in regard to Johnson's attack, and added: "I think they will submit to nothing but force. How many are rebellions I do not know; but if only a few are, and the rest laugh at their outrages, as they do, and think nothing of it, all are complicated. I didn't come here to be kicked and hustled out of my own house by savages, and if government cannot protect me, let somebody else try it. You know the Indians and understand the situation. Please see Governor Pitkin," etc. From that time to the outbreak, work at the agency was at a stand still. The feeling of the Indians, with very few exceptions, was that they would do no work; that the ploughing must stop; that Meeker was their enemy; that the soldiers were coming to have the land ploughed, to arrest Johnson, Chinaman, Bennett, and others, and, probably, to make everybody work; that the soldiers ought not to come. Meeker's feeling may be inferred from his telegram to the commissioner, of September 17: "There is no particular change, either for worse or better. No ploughing is done, nor will until it can be done in safety. It remains to be seen whether the business and industries of this agency are to be conducted under the direction of the Indians or of yourself."

In response to Meeker's application for protection, Major T. T. Thornburgh marched from Fort Fred Steele with a hundred men—three companies of cavalry and one of infantry. This post is in Wyoming, at the Union Pacific Railroad's crossing of the Platte. The road, which was the only ordinary approach to the agency, runs to the southwest, crossing the Sierra. Madre at Bridger's Pass; thence south, bearing east, to the crossing of Bear River, at the mouth of Elk Head Creek. From this point its general course is southwest, striking the reservation at Milk Creek. On the 26th, Thornburgh was met at Bear River by a party of five Utes, including Jack and Colorow. They wanted to know why he was coming. He explained that the agent had sent for him; that the Indians had been acting badly. They denied everything, and asked that the soldiers should not come on the reservation. They proposed that he should leave the soldiers and go to the agency, with four or five companions, to investigate the truth of the charges. Major Thornburgh informed them that his orders were to go on, but that he would find a good place to camp, closer to the agency, and leave his men there while he went on. After conversation, by which he thought they were brought into a pacific state of mind, they went away. They returned to the agency and asked Meeker to stop the soldiers, but he said it was none of his business. Finally he yielded to their importunities, and, on the 27th, sent a letter to Thornburgh advising him that it would be the better course to come on alone. To this Thornburgh replied on the 28th that he would discontinue his march on the 29th, and come on with five men. On the 29th, in the morning, the command reached Milk Creek and entered the reservation. The road, after Milk Creek is passed half a mile, enters a cañon, the sides and top of which are covered with oak brush. It is called Red Cañon. An Indian trail runs along the adjoining ridge, or "hog-back," and joins the road near the creek. The Indians were in ambush along the tops of the cañon. Just as the troops were beginning to enter it, shortly before noon, the advance guard, under Lieutenant Cherry, discovered some Indians moving over a hill, half a mile in advance, and separated to reconnoitre. After flanking the cañon about two hundred yards, the ambuscade was discovered and at once reported. Cherry was ordered to make a reconnoissance on the right, and, if possible, communicate with the Indians, on the supposition that hostilities might be averted by a parley. At the same time Jack started from the Ute position to talk with the soldiers; but when Cherry's command galloped off to the

COLOROW.

right a body of Indians went out to oppose the movement, and both parties deployed. An Indian fired, and the fighting began on both sides.

Captain Payne's company was at once thrown out on the left and Captain Lawson's on the right, in skirmish line. The wagon train, which was crossing a small plateau, between one and two hundred yards from the stream, was ordered to park. The Indians pressed the troops hotly. They were in strong force. Major Thornburgh saw that they were massing to cut off his retreat, and ordered his men to fall back on the wagon train. The movement was executed in excellent order, but in the midst of it the commander was shot and instantly killed. Captain Payne took command, being next in seniority. He set the entire force at work fortifying. Wounded horses were killed for temporary shelter for sharpshooters. Boxes, bundles of bedding, sacks of corn and flour, and everything available were piled up for cover, while pick and shovel were plied to make the protection more substantial. The men worked desperately—the groans of the dying, the agonized cries of the wounded, and the incessant cracking of the Indians' rifles serving only as incentives to greater activity. To add to the peril of the situation, the Indians fired the grass and sage brush, and the wind was hurrying the roaring flames upon the little band. They worked on with feverish haste. The fire reached them, and stretched out its forked tongues to lick them up. There was no water within reach. They dropped their tools, and smothered the flames with blankets, blouses, and sacks. Some of the wagons took fire; but, under cover of the stifling smoke, these were extinguished also. The greatest danger was now past. By burning the brush the Indians had deprived themselves of cover for close approach, and were compelled to do their firing from the surrounding bluffs, at a distance of from four to six hundred yards. They commanded the situation, but could inflict no material damage. So long as the soldiers remained in their trenches they were safe from the bullets that were poured in on them.

The news of the attack was carried to the agency, twenty-five miles below, by an Indian messenger who arrived at about one o'clock. The Indians did not breathe a word about it to the whites. They had held another council with Meeker, on the arrival of the messenger from Thornburgh, in regard to the advance of the soldiers, just as though nothing had occurred. Meeker prepared a note to Thornburgh, as follows: "I expect to leave in the morning with Douglas and Serrick to meet you; things are peaceable, and Douglas flies the United States flag. If you have trouble in getting through the cañon to-day, let me know in what force. We have been on guard three nights, and shall be to-night, not because we know there is danger, but because there may be. I like your last programme; it is based on true military principles." This message was dated September 29, 1 P. M. He little dreamed that Thornburgh was then lying cold and stark at the month of the cañon. The "last, programme" referred to was Major Thornburgh's letter of the 28th, in which he informed Meeker that he would bring his troops "within striking distance" of the agency on the 29th. He said: "I have carefully considered whether or not it would be advisable to have my command at a point as distant as that desired by the Indians who were in my camp last night, and have reached the conclusion that, under my orders, which require me to march this command to your agency, I am not at liberty to leave it at a point where it would not be available in case of trouble." Meeker received this message at noon on the 29th. Previous to that hour, it seems certain that he was deceived in regard to Thornburgh's intentions. On the day of the attack, the 29th, he telegraphed Washington: "Major Thornburgh, 4th Infantry, leaves his command fifty miles distant, and comes to-day with five men. Indians propose to fight if troops advance. A talk will be had to-morrow. Captain Dodge, 9th Cavalry, is at Steamboat Springs, with orders to break up Indian stores and keep Indians on reservation. Sales of ammunition and guns brisk for ten days past. Store nearest sent back 16,000 rounds and 13 guns. When Captain Dodge commences to enforce law, no living here without troops. Have sent for him to confer."

Meeker knew that Red Cañon, to which he refers in the one o'clock message, was less than twenty-five miles from the agency, and within the reservation. If he knew that Thornburgh was within a day's march of it, he was trying to deceive the Indians. If he had not received Thornburgh's message of the 28th, before writing his telegram to Washington, of the 29th—which is most likely—he probably misunderstood Thornburgh's intentions, but communicated his understanding to the Indians. The Indians were misinformed by him in either event, and undoubtedly thought they were misinformed intentionally, for they were fully posted concerning Thornburgh's movements, by their scouts, and believed that Meeker was hostile to them. With this belief they decided to meet treachery with treachery. It is not within the range of credibility that the attack and massacre were planned before the 26th. If they had been, Ouray would have known it sooner. There was no evidence of it at the agency. According to Meeker's statement, guards were first posted on the night of the 26th. It was the opinion of Mrs. Meeker, Josie Meeker, and the employés that the plot was arranged on the 28th, when the soldiers had passed the fifty-mile limit. There was a war-dance that night, in Douglas's camp, which continued till daybreak the next morning. The action of the Indians on Monday was marked by deep cunning; their behavior at the council deceived Meeker completely. He despatched his note to Thornburgh by Wilmer Eskridge, a man employed at the agency as a sawyer. He was accompanied by two Indians—

ANTELOPE.

Antelope (Wah-sitz) and Ebenezer. After going two miles the Indians murdered Eskridge, and hastened back to the agency. In the mean time the other Indians had managed to get into the store-room and secure all the agency guns, without attracting attention.

The people at the agency were wholly unsuspecting. Mrs. Meeker and Josie were washing dishes in their house. Mrs. Price was washing clothes outside. Shaduck Price, post-farmer, and Frank Dresser, laborer, were in a wagon, throwing dirt on the roof of the new building. Arthur Thompson, laborer, was on the roof, spreading the dirt. Meeker and William H. Post, storekeeper and carpenter, were in the larger storehouse. The other employés were scattered about the place, engaged in their various duties. As Ebenezer and Antelope returned, about twenty Indians, armed with guns, started up from the river. They met Donglas, who was walking towards his teepee, and all came on to the buildings together. They began firing as soon as they reached the new building—Ebenezer, Antelope, and others having by that time secured positions for attacking the other men. At the first volley Price was killed and Thompson fell from the building. Frank Dresser was wounded in the leg, but managed to run to Meeker's house through a rain of bullets. Mrs. Price picked up her little boy and ran to her room. Dresser followed her. She gave him Price's gun, which lay on the bed. As he came out, the windows of the dining-room were broken in. He fired through the window and mortally wounded Johnson's brother. The Indians then left them and began plundering the stores. The inmates of the house went into Josie's room and hid under the bed, but as soon as their wits cleared they saw that this position afforded no safety. They then ran into the milk-house, a small adobe building close at hand. Here they remained all the afternoon undisturbed, Frank Dresser, the three women, and the children. They had the entrance barricaded, however, so that they could not see what was being done outside. For half an hour the firing was kept up quite steadily; then there were intervals of quiet, broken by volleys. It is probable that some of this firing was from the explosion of cartridges in the burning buildings, and the rest was drawn by some of the employés who had secured weapons and were fighting for their lives.

Mrs. Price tells their story thus: "We were in the milk-house until nearly sundown. They set Meeker's house on fire first. The house sat east and west, with wings built on the south and north sides. The south wing was Josie's bedroom, and on the north was my bedroom. In the east part of the house was a room used as a dining-room and kitchen, and on the north of that the milk-house. They set Josie's room on fire first, and we stayed until we began strangling in the milk-house, and had to go out. We ran into Meeker's house. I do not think it is ten feet to the corner of my bedroom. We opened both doors and thought of secreting ourselves under the bed of Mr. Meeker. I said: 'No, that will not do.' We looked out to the north. The blinds were open. They were busy taking out goods; they were taking the blankets, shirts, and everything else they could. I said: 'Let's try and escape to the north, in the sage brush; it will not do to stay here; they will be here in a minute.' Frank said, 'Let's go while they are so busy,' and we went. I ran outside of the fence; Josie, Mrs. Meeker, and Frank opened the gate and went into the field, and I crossed over through the wire-fence. They then saw us; we had not got more than ten or fifteen steps from the corner of the fence north before they saw us and fired. They came running, on foot and ponies, and fired at all of us, and hit Mrs. Meeker. The bullets whizzed by my head and hit beside me. They shot at Frank Dresser, and, as he would take a step, the dust would fly. The last I saw of him he was about a quarter of a mile from the agency, in the field, still running. The Indians took us, and said we had to go with them. As I was going, I said I had read so much about their treatment of captives, that I was afraid they would want to burn me. They said: 'No kill white squaw; heap like them.' I said, 'You are going to burn me,' and they said, 'No burn white squaw.' Then they took me on through the brush to the river."

Mrs. Price's captor was Ahu-u-tu-pu-wit, a small, ill-favored Uncompahgré. Josie Meeker says of her capture: "One called to me and said, 'Come to me; no shoot you.' I said, Going to shoot?' He said, 'No.' I said, 'Better not.' He said, 'Come to me.' And then they took me down to the camp." This was Persune, a Yampa warrior. Douglas tried to take his captive from him, but Persune pushed him away. They had an angry dispute, after which Douglas went away and took Mrs. Meeker, whom no one else had claimed. The Indians moved that night about twelve miles to the south, and camped on Pi-ce-ance Creek, on the Great Hogback of the Roan or Book plateau. They had all been drinking. They were laden with plunder and flushed with success. That night the three women were "taken for squaws" by their respective captors, and were so held during their captivity. Mrs. Price was also outraged by Johnson.

The news of these affairs came to the settlements slowly. There were weary days of suspense, in which no trustworthy tidings could be had, and no assurance as to the extent of the war. Ouray was on a hunting expedition with his band. A messenger brought him word of the outbreak, and he returned at once to Los Pinos to report to the agent. A letter to the White River chiefs was prepared and signed by Ouray, directing them to stop fighting. This was carried by Joseph Brady, miller at Los Pinos, accompanied by Sapavanari. On receipt of Ouray's message the Utes agreed to obey his directions. Brady also communicated with the soldiers, who were now under command of Colonel Merritt. The remnant of the original command had held their fortification alone, without further loss, until the morning of the 2d, when Dodge's company of colored soldiers arrived. These had marched from Grand River on September 27, on orders to report at White River agency. On the 1st of October they found a paper, on a sage bush by the road, with the words: "Hurry up. The troops have been defeated at the agency.—E. E. C." A few miles farther they reached the village of Hayden, which was deserted, but while here a party of citizens came up, and the facts of the situation were learned. The command moved on down Bear River and went into camp as usual, to deceive the Indian spies, if any should be watching. At half-past eight they packed up again. The train was sent to the supply camp on Fortification Creek, and the remainder of the force, forty in number, took an Indian trail for Milk Creek. They reached the intrenchment at daybreak, without molestation, and did gallant service there. Merritt arrived with

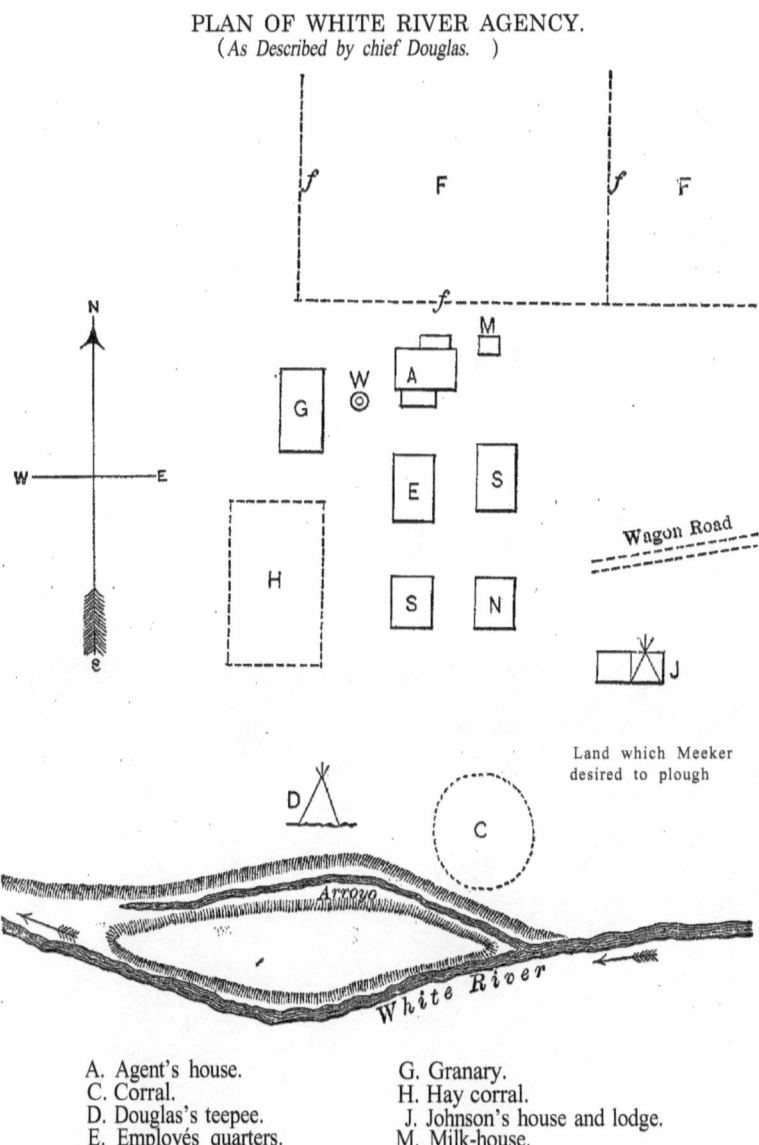

PLAN OF WHITE RIVER AGENCY.
(*As Described by chief Douglas.*)

Land which Meeker desired to plough

A. Agent's house.
C. Corral.
D. Douglas's teepee.
E. Employés quarters.
FF. Ploughed fields.
SS. Stores.
G. Granary.
H. Hay corral.
J. Johnson's house and lodge.
M. Milk-house.
N. New building.
W. Well.
fff. Fences of enclosed fields.

reinforcements on the morning of the 5th. He found the besieged men in good trim. No more killed had been added to the thirteen who fell on the first day, though several had been struck. The wounded numbered forty-three, nearly all of the wounds being slight. The Indians were preparing to fight Merritt when Brady arrived with Ouray's order. No fighting was done afterwards, except that Lieutenant Weir and Captain of Scouts Humme were killed, and the scouting party of Lieutenant Hall, from which they had detached themselves, was attacked. The Indians claimed that this resulted from Humme's shooting at some Indians that he met, and this is the only evidence extant on the subject. On the 9th word was received at Los Pinos that the White Rivers would fight no more, and that the Southern Utes would not join in any hostilities.

On the 11th Merritt advanced to White River agency. All along the road were ghastly evidences of savage fury. In a gulch, six miles from the agency, lay the body of Carl Goldstein, a contractor who was taking supplies to Meeker. A hundred yards away was Julius Moore, one of his teamsters, with two bullet-holes in his breast, and his body hacked and mutilated. A little farther down the cañon the soldiers came to the old coal-mine, in which was found the body of Henry Dresser, engineer at the agency. He lay on his back, with his head pillowed on his folded coat. By his side was a Winchester rifle containing eight cartridges. In one of his pockets was Meeker's message to Thornburgh, with which Eskridge had started. It is evident that Dresser had escaped from the agency wounded. He found Eskridge's body, and, remembering that he bore a message, had taken the letter from his pocket to carry it forward. He had become weak, and crawled into the cave to rest, but his life was spent. The Indians had not found him. Two miles from White River Eskridge was found, naked, with a bullet-hole through his head. The agency was a scene of overwhelming desolation. All the buildings but one were burned down. No sign of life was near, and the absence of life was emphasized by the haphazard scattering of articles of all kinds over the ground, indicating a season of riotous pillaging before the burning. Lying here and there were the bodies of the victims. Father Meeker lay naked, on his back, one hundred yards from the ashes of his house. A bullet had pierced his brain, and the left side of his head was mashed in with a club. A barrel stave was driven into his mouth. Around his neck was a chain, by which he had probably been dragged from the storehouse. These indignities to him meant that their hatred was directed chiefly towards him. Frank Dresser's corpse lay over in the field, with a bullet through the heart. George Eaton, one of the laborers, lay naked, shot through the left breast. From some strange fancy, the Indians had placed a bundle of paper bags in his arms, after stripping him. The wolves had been eating him. These bodies, with those of Thompson, Price, and the others, were all picked up and buried.

DOUGLAS.

The first object to which the government directed its attention, after the outbreak was checked by Ouray, was the recovery of the captive women. This was undertaken by General Charles Adams, special agent of the Indian Department, who, with an escort of fifteen Utes, started from Los Pinos for the hostile camp, on October 21, to secure their release. A stormy council was held on his arrival. Part of the Indians wanted to give up the captives and make peace. The rest wished to kill Adam's and go on with the war. It was understood that the Uintahs, Shoshonees, and others promised assistance, but this was largely a result of Mormon misrepresentations. There were a few members of other tribes who would have aided the hostiles, but the majority favored preserving the peace. The Mormons unquestionably tried to help on the war. There were two of their emissaries in the hostile camp while Adams was there, The friendly Utes always said that the Mormons promised aid, and the hostiles would neither admit nor deny it. There was found, behind the breastworks of the Indians who besieged the force on Milk Creek, the body of an unknown white man, in the attitude of firing, just as he had been killed. He did not belong in that locality. The chances are about ten to one that he had a Mormon brand on his soul. Opposing these influences were Ouray's authority, the apprehension of being worsted by the soldiers, and the influence of a little knot of friendly Indians. Prominent among these were two squaws, Susan and Jane. Susan was a wife of Johnson and a sister of Ouray. She felt under obligations to the whites. Years before, when Governor Evans presided over the affairs of Colorado Territory, she had been captured by the Arapahoes. They were making preparations to burn her, when she was rescued by soldiers and taken to Fort Collins. Anxious to get to her people, she slipped away from the fort and narrowly escaped recapture by the Arapahoes, who were looking for her. She was saved by a ranchman, who hid her under some cabbages in his wagon when he saw the Arapahoes coming. She was taken to Central City, furnished with a horse, and returned in safety to her people. She not only treated the captives kindly, but also went boldly into the council, an almost unheard-of thing among the Utes, and insisted on their release. Jane was the wife of Pah-vitz. She had been cured of a serious illness by Mrs. Meeker, and had been treated kindly by her and her daughter. She manifested her gratitude by numerous acts of friendship.

There was another influence that affected the Indians. It was their rage over some pictures that they claimed to have found on the body of some dead person, but this was directed more particularly towards Meeker. The story is somewhat incoherent, and possibly was not correctly understood. It was to the effect that they had found, on this body, pictures of

Meeker, Mrs. Meeker, Josie, and Mrs. Price, each showing a wound in some mortal part, and each covered with blood. Meeker's showed a wound in the head, Josie's in the breast, and the others similarly. These, the Indians said, had been sent to make bad feeling against them. Whenever the subject was introduced they became furious. Some thought there was nothing in it, but Miss Meeker and Brady were both of the opinion that there was, because the story was repeated so often, by different Indians, and always the same. Captain Payne offered two possible explanations. One was that in his trunk, which was captured by the Indians, there was a picture of an Indian that had been given him a short time before by one of the scouts. When Thornburgh's body was recovered this picture was lying on his breast, held by a small stone. The Indian was not known to Payne, but was said by the Utes to be one of the Uncompahgrés. This occurrence, however, has so little identity with the story that it may be left out of consideration as an explanation. The second was that a teamster found on a bush a sheet of paper bearing rough drafts of the bodies of three or four men, with holes through them, that might have been meant for representations of bullet-wounds. Under the figures were wavy lines like writing. This was brought to Payne on the night of the attack at Milk Creek. The only objections to this are that the pictures were recognized by the Indians as those of the persons mentioned, and that this picture did not fall into the hands of the Indians. On the other hand, it may have been in the possession of the Indians before it was found, and the identity of the figures may have been indicated by some of the signs used in their system of pictography. It is possible that the body referred to may have been that of Eskridge, and he may have had in his pockets photographs, which had been defaced, as photographs sometimes are, by pencil or ink marks.

But to resume: the tribe at length decided that the captives should be given up, and there remained no objection except from Persune, who had become madly infatuated with Miss Meeker. He implored her to remain with him; promised that she should never do any work; that all his possessions should be hers, and similar rash vows. He wept like a

MAJOR T. T. THORNBURGH.

child, but his prayers and tears were of no avail. The other Indians regarded all this as a good joke on Persune, and afterwards, when the news of her death, while a Treasury clerk in Washington, came to them on Uintah Valley reservation, they nudged one another slyly, winked significantly, and said that Persune ought to put on his mourning paint for his wife. General Adams, with the captives, reached Merritt's camp on the night of the 23d, and conveyed them thence to Los Pinos. The captives then claimed that they had not been subjected to indignity, and General Adams stated afterwards that this was his reason for urging the withdrawal of the troops. They did not make a full statement of their treatment to any of the officials until their depositions were taken at Greeley, on November 4, and then very reluctantly, and under promise that the newspapers should not have information of it. The public did not learn the facts for several weeks.

The story of the remainder of the Ute trouble is mainly the record of the tedious sessions of two commissions. The government demanded the surrender of the parties guilty of the massacre and the attack on Thornburgh, but could get no legal evidence of their identity. The white survivors could not testify to the killing of any white man by any Indian. The Indians denied everything, except what favored them. They had learned the white man's maxim: "No man can be compelled to criminate himself," and had evidently added to it the words, "or any of his friends." Not a man could be found who knew any one that had been implicated. The chiefs who undoubtedly led in the attacks swore that they were not present, or, if present, were trying to preserve the peace. Finally, General Hatch demanded the surrender of the parties against whom there was the greatest show of evidence; *viz.:* Douglas, Johnson, Antelope, Ebenezer, Persune, Ahu-u-tu-pu-wit, Johnny (Douglas's son-in-law), Sah-witz (Sawa-wick, Sow-er-wick, Serwick, Serrick), Crepah, Tim Johnson, Thomas (an Uintah), and Pah-vitz. The proceedings were also delayed by the death of Ouray, on August 24, 1880, and of Ka-ni-a-che, who was struck by lightning two days after the death of Ouray. In one sense the death of Ouray furthered the final adjustment of the difficulty. He did not wish to move, though he finally consented to it, and he did not wish to leave his tribe. He had repeatedly said: "Ouray will never leave the great mountains." He and his tribe had the clear right to remain and retain the reservation, under the treaty. They had not only not been hostile, but also had prevented a general war. If Ouray had desired war—if he had even refused to interfere with the White Rivers—the frontier settlements would have been damaged incalculably. Inspector Pollock well wrote from the San Juan: "Saltpetre would not save this country but for the counsel of Ouray." No commissioner with a sentiment of decency or honesty could advise forcing him or his people to give up the reservation, and yet the rabble forgot his services, and could no longer see a distinction between good and bad Indians. Their skins are all of the same color, are they not? They are when the white man wants their property, at any rate.

The work of the commission was further complicated, and perhaps hastened, by the invasion of the reservation by armed bands of prospectors, and gangs of railroad graders. In the fall of 1880 war was almost precipitated by the murder of Young Johnson, a son of Shavano, by a drunken teamster, and the lynching of the teamster by the Indians. An adjustment was at length arranged, on the basis that none of the Indians should be punished, but that they should all move to new reservations. Strict justice would have required that the guilty Indians should be punished and the peaceable ones allowed to retain the reservation, but this would not have been satisfactory to either party. The Indians did not wish to be punished, and the whites wished to get the reservation. Under the circumstances, the solution arrived at was perhaps the best that could have been made. The Southern Utes were given land in severalty on the Animas, Florida, and other streams in Southern Colorado. The White Rivers were sent to the Uintah agency. The Los Pinos Indians were put on a new reservation on Green River, east of and adjoining the Uintah agency. It was stated by the Indians, accepted by the commission, and adopted by the government, that the guilty parties had fled beyond the jurisdiction of the United States. Of course this was a fiction. Those parties are all on the reservations in Utah; at least, they were eighteen months ago. But there was no special object to be gained by their surrender. There was not evidence to convict them, and the tribe was willing to purchase immunity by the surrender of the reservation. It is rare that any tribunal has an opportunity to settle a question so satisfactorily to all parties concerned, and, being so settled, it is to be hoped that our differences with the Utes are henceforth, forever, *res judicata*.

CHAPTER XXI.

CRUELTY, PITY, AND JUSTICE.

ON July 20, 1867, was passed "an act to establish peace with certain hostile Indian tribes," providing for the creation of a board of peace commissioners. As members of this board, there were named in the act N. G. Taylor, J. B. Henderson, J. B. Sanborn, and S. F. Tappan, to whom the President was empowered to add four army officers. He named Generals Sherman, Harney, Terry, and Augur. The discussion connected with the emancipation and citizenship of the negroes had educated the people to a just appreciation of the natural rights of all men, and an awakening public conscience pointed to the Indian as a victim of past injustice. The "peace policy of General Grant," as it was commonly called, received the approval of a great majority of Americans. The labors of the peace commissioners were considered so valuable, and the advantages to be gained by authorizing a committee of citizens to aid in the conduct of Indian affairs were so evident, that by an act of April 10, 1869, a permanent Board of Indian Commissioners was organized. It was composed of ten civilians, who received no compensation for their services, but had their expenses paid, and were to assist in procuring and maintaining peace with the Indians, for which purposes an appropriation of two million dollars was made. Unfortunately for the Indian, the feeling in his favor wandered off into the channel of abstract compliment. From a demon he was raised to the position of a temporal deity by the extremists who were now given an opportunity to aid him. The gentlemen who wrote the reports of the commissioners revelled in riotous imaginations and discarded facts, as a part of the old and offensive *régime* which was henceforth to be abandoned. Take, for instance, this picture of the Indian's character from one of the reports: "His only compromise is to have his rights, real or fancied, fully conceded. To force he yields nothing. In battle he never surrenders, and is the more excusable, therefore, that he never accepts capitulation at the hands of others. In war he does not ask or accept mercy. He is then the more consistent that he does not grant mercy." This statement is astounding, in the face of the fact that for over three centuries the Indian had been yielding to force, surrendering, accepting mercy, and compromising his rights, if be ever had any. It is hardly possible that the commissioners ever read carefully the balderdash that has been printed over their names. Certainly the four military members of the peace commission did not realize to what they were assenting; it has been quoted to them at times when it must have been very embarrassing, from a logical stand-point, as, for example, in the case of Wendell Phillips's open letter to General Sherman during the Modoc war. These officers knew, as any sane man does, that the Indian is not an angel. He is merely an uncivilized man who has some good qualities and some bad ones, like other mortals. What he needs is honesty and justice, more than admiration or maudlin sympathy, and what success the peace policy has had has been in the line of the extension to the red man of that justice and reasonable aid to which Americans generally believe he is entitled.

The earlier years of commission work were devoted to the plains Indians and to those in the more settled parts of the country. During this time the extermination policy was pursued in Arizona. In June, 1869, Major-general Thomas relieved General Halleck, in command of the Military Division of the Pacific, and General Ord succeeded to the command of the Department of California. General Ord was an enthusiastic exterminator, so far as the Apaches were concerned. He writes, in September, 1869: "I encouraged the troops to capture and root out the Apache by every means, and to hunt them as they would wild animals. This they have done with unrelenting vigor. Since my last report over two hundred have been killed, generally by parties who have trailed them for days and weeks into the mountain recesses, over snows, among gorges and precipices, lying in wait for them by day, and following them by night. Many villages have been burned, large quantities of arms and supplies of ammunition, clothing, and provisions have been destroyed, a large number of horses and mules have been captured, and two men, twenty-eight women, and thirty-four children taken

HAUNTS OF THE APACHES.

prisoners; and though we have lost quite a number of soldiers, I think the Apaches have discovered that they are getting the worst of it." A more profitable result was obtained in Western Arizona, where the less nomadic bands of the Apaches were located. These Indians were more closely surrounded by white neighbors and nearer to the locations of the troops; besides which they were of a more peaceable character than the other tribes. There were several bands that were quite agricultural in their pursuits, notably that of

Miguel, who kept back in the mountain valleys and took little or no part in any of the wars. Miguel's village, with a white flag flying over each lodge, was found in the heart of the White Mountains by Captain Barry, whose forces were on an exterminating expedition, but these Indians showed so much sincerity in their professions of peace that even the Mexican scouts said they could not fire on them. For these Apaches the White Mountain reservation was first established, and to it others gathered as they learned that they could surrender and remain at peace in their own country.

Although extermination was not being satisfactorily accomplished in Arizona, the legitimate object of war was being obtained. The Apaches were gradually being brought to a realization that peace was a better mode of life than war. They were learning that their enemies could invade their homes, destroy their property, and keep them in constant apprehension of death. Some of them were ready to live peaceably at places where they could be protected, but for this result, which ought to have been the primary object of the war, there had been no adequate preparation. Indians who desired to surrender could go to the White Mountains, but Indians living elsewhere, who desired to make peace and settle in their old homes, had no one who could talk to them with authority. In February, 1871, a party of Indian women came to Camp Grant, near the junction of the San Pedro and Arivapa rivers, in search of a captive boy. They were treated kindly, and through them communication was had with Es-kim-en-zin, the chief of their band. They were Arivapa or Pinal Apaches, about one hundred and fifty in number. The chief said that they wished to make peace. Lieut. Royal E. Whitman, commanding the post, told them to go to the White Mountains. They were not willing to do this; some of their number had been there and found the locality unhealthy; the Indians there were people with whom they had never mixed. More than this, their home was on the Arivapa. They said, "Our fathers and their fathers before them have lived in these mountains, and have raised corn in this valley." Lieutenant Whitman told them that he had no authority to make a treaty or to promise them a permanent home at that place, but that they might surrender to him, and he would feed and protect them as prisoners until the authorities could be heard from. To this they agreed. They came in about March 1st, and were immediately followed by other small tribes, bringing the number, by March 5th, to about three hundred. Whitman expressed a full account of the matter to Division head-quarters, and six weeks later received an answer. The answer was that his communication had not been endorsed in accordance with official etiquette, and it was returned therewith. There was no comment on the contents. The fate of three hundred people was of less importance than the manner of addressing a report.

EFFECT OF EXTERMINATION POLICY ON ARIZONA SETTLER.

Lieutenant Whitman had located the Arivapas half a mile from the post, and counted them every other day. Their number gradually increased till it reached five hundred and ten. They were very destitute and almost naked, but it was found that they were willing to work to obtain clothing, so they were set to gathering hay. They cut it with their knives and brought it in on their backs, but by this slow method they furnished the post with one hundred and fifty tons in less than two months, besides gathering large quantities of mescal for their own use. As the weather grew warmer they were allowed to move four or five miles farther up the Arivapa, to some land that they wished to cultivate, and here they were counted and rationed every third day. About April 1st Captain Stanwood arrived and took command of the post, with instructions to hold and feed any Indians he might find there as prisoners of war. He examined the status of the Arivapas and left them as they were. On April 24th he started to the south, on a scout, leaving Lieutenant Whitman in charge of the post, with fifty infantry. The Indians were well-behaved, and the system of counting made it impossible for them to go any great distance from their camp. The ranchmen in the neighborhood were on friendly terms with them, and had made some contracts for their services in the coming harvest.

On April 28th a large party of Americans, Mexicans, and Papago Indians left Tucson, with the avowed determination of killing these Arivapas. Captain Penn, commanding at Fort Lowell, sent word of this movement to Lieutenant Whitman by a messenger, who arrived on the morning of April 30th. Whitman at once sent two men to the Indians to tell them to come in, but in an hour the messengers returned and informed him that it was too late. The camp was strewn with the mutilated bodies of women and children, and their lodges were burning. The post-surgeon, Doctor Briesly, with twelve men, was at once despatched to the place with a wagon, to bring in any wounded that might be found. Doctor Briesly said, "On my arrival I found that I should have but little use for wagon or medicine; the work had been too thoroughly done. The camp had been fired, and the dead bodies of some twenty-one women and children were lying scattered over the ground; those who had been wounded in the first instance had their brains beaten out with stones. Two of the best-looking of the squaws were lying in such a position, and from the appearance of the genital organs and of their wounds, there can be no doubt that they were first ravished and then shot dead. Nearly all of the dead were mutilated. One infant of some ten months was shot-twice, and one leg hacked nearly off. While going over the ground, we came upon a squaw who was unhurt, but were unable to get her to come in and talk, she not feeling very sure of our good intentions."

The next morning Lieutenant Whitman went out with a party to bury the dead. He says, "I thought the act of caring for their dead would be an evidence to them of our sympathy at least, and the conjecture proved correct, for while at the work many of them came to the spot and indulged in their expressions of grief, too wild and terrible to be described. That evening they began to come in from all directions, singly and in small parties, so changed in forty-eight hours as to be hardly recognizable, during which time they had neither eaten nor slept. Many of the men, whose families had all been killed, when I spoke to them and expressed sympathy for them, were obliged to turn away, unable to speak, and too proud to show their grief. The women whose children had been killed or stolen were convulsed with grief, and looked to me appealingly, as though I was their last hope on earth. Children who, two days before, had been full of fun and frolic kept at a distance, expressing wondering horror. I did what I could; I fed them, and talked to them, and listened patiently to their accounts. I sent horses into the mountains to bring in two badly-wounded women, one shot through the left lung, and one with an arm shattered. These were attended to, and are doing well, and will recover. Their camp was surrounded and attacked at daybreak. So sudden and unexpected was it, that no one was awake to give the alarm, and I found quite a number of women shot while asleep beside their bundles of hay which they had collected to bring in on that morning. The wounded who were unable to get away had their brains beaten out with clubs or stones, while some were shot full of arrows after having been mortally wounded by gunshot. The bodies were all stripped. Of the whole number buried, one was an old man and one was a well-grown boy—all the rest women and children. Of the whole number killed and missing—about one hundred and twenty-five—only eight were men. It has been said that the men were not there—they were all there. On the 28th we counted one hundred and twenty-eight men, a small number being absent for mescal, all of whom have since been in. . . . About their captives they say, 'Get them back for us; our little boys will grow up slaves, and our girls, as soon as they are large enough, will be diseased prostitutes, to get money for whoever owns them. Our women work hard and are good women, and they and our children have no diseases. Our dead you cannot bring to life, but those that are living we gave to you, and we look to you, who can write and talk and have soldiers, to get them back.' I will assure you it is no easy task to convince them of my zeal when they see so little being done. I have pledged my word to them that I never would rest easily, day or night, until they should have justice, and just now I would as soon leave the army as to be ordered away from them, or to be obliged to order them away from here. But you will know the difficulties in the way. You know that parties who would engage in murder like this, could and would (and have already) make statements and multiply affidavits without end in their justification. I know you will use your influence on the right side. I believe with them, this may be made either a means of making good citizens of them and their children, or drive them out to a hopeless war of extermination. They ask to be allowed to live here in their old homes, where nature supplies nearly all their wants; they ask for a fair and impartial trial of their faith, and they ask that all their captive children living may be returned to them. Is their demand unreasonable?"

Unhappily for the good repute of Arizona, the press, and apparently the people, justified or apologized for this monstrous crime. The frontier press does not always represent the feeling of a majority of the community in these matters. It is sensational on all subjects, and it is down on Indians on all occasions, on the supposition that this course is popular. It is popular in time of war. Misrepresentation may then be carried as far as in politics, or farther, for then there is but one side to be heard. But there is no community so depraved as to favor assassination in time of peace, and this was downright assassination. Whatever provocation there existed was in the offence of other people. The massacre cannot even be justified on the theory that it was an application of lynch law, for lynching is resorted to for the purpose of just punishment, irregularly of course, but still for the exclusive purpose of punishment. The accompaniments of this deed showed that no such motives actuated these murderers. The camp was plundered, women were ravished, and the children carried away were sold for the profit of their captors. Lust and plunder are not motives consistent with the savage justice that sometimes makes lynching almost excusable. It seems unjust to charge this wrong against the American people, for most of the perpetrators were Mexicans and Indians, and there were Americans near by who would have given protection to the victims if it had been in their power. It ought to rank as a crime committed by criminals.

The offence of the people of Arizona was in defending it, and the method of defence was worse than the abstract wrong of defending a wicked and shameful action. The papers of Arizona attacked Whitman, charging him with being a debauchee and a consorter with Indian women. Even if these charges had been true, they did not make the massacre any less wrong; and they did not weaken Whitman's statements, for these were confirmed in every particular by other men. But the charges were not true, if we may believe the solemn statements of the officers, men, contractors, and employés of the post. Men of all classes, who voluntarily stated that they had come to Camp Grant prejudiced against the Apaches, swore that these Indians were peaceable and well-behaved, and that the charges against Lieutenant Whitman were false. One hundred of the participants in this affair, Americans, Mexicans, and Papagos, were indicted and brought to trial that year, in the December term of the United States District Court. The jury remained out for twenty minutes and returned a verdict of "not guilty." It is such verdicts as this that are bringing the jury system into disrepute. Nevertheless, the prosecution had some effect. It is a great step towards civilization even to have men indicted for murder. It tends to repress the light-hearted assassin. There is only one consideration that affords any shadow of excuse for Camp Grant: the Apaches made war similarly. With them it was the highest science of war to lull an enemy's suspicions and then murder him. Under similar circumstances hostile Apaches would probably have committed the Camp Grant massacre and gloried in it. This consideration is more than offset by the inexpediency of the act. This horrible warfare had to be ended in some way, and the military had the task to perform. There were but two ways of doing it; one was to exterminate the Indians; the other was to require both sides to observe the laws of civilization until confidence was restored. Years of warfare had shown the first to be impracticable. It was suicidal to place any obstacle in the way of attaining the second. As a matter of expediency, carrying away the children was worse than the murders, for this was a continuing wrong. Of the twenty-nine children taken, two escaped and five were recovered from Arizonians. The remainder were sold into slavery in Sonora.

An unfortunate misunderstanding occurred, soon after the massacre, that resulted in another attack on these Arivapas, and apparently gave them reason to believe that there were no white men who could be trusted. The grief-stricken remnant of the tribe gathered again in the valley, under promise of protection, and assurance that the soldiers had no part in the bloody work. Among them was Eskimenzin, the chief who first came to the post. In the massacre he lost two wives five children, and about fifty of his tribe. He came back during the burial and assisted in this mournful task, although nearly crazed with grief over his loss. As the Indians slowly returned, they camped in small parties, fearing to get together lest another attack should be made. On one of these parties, consisting of Eskimenzin and the remnant of his family, a party of soldiers suddenly came while returning from the White Mountains, about a month after the massacre, and by mistake, in the confusion of the moment, fired upon them. No one was killed, but Eskimenzin lost all confidence in the protectorate. He fled to the mountains with his remaining people, and killed a white man as he went.

The Camp Grant massacre naturally raised a whirlwind of indignation in the East among those who advocated peace, and even conservative people who had not been inclined to Indian-worship recoiled at this atrocity. In July, President

Grant gave Mr. Vincent Colyer plenary powers to go into Arizona and adjust the Indian troubles there as appeared proper to him. His advent as a representative of the government was heralded by the Arizona press with the same fiery defiance that used to characterize the Mormon papers when the government proposed to take a hand in Utah affairs. Still the government was not observed to tremble, and Mr. Colyer's policy was enforced. The Arizona papers simply weakened their cause by their absurd threatenings. Mr. Colyer was notoriously ultra in his peace theories, and evidently did not understand the situation in Arizona and New Mexico, but he was quite as correct as his assailants. There were in reality a large number of Indians there who were sufficiently humbled by war to be ready for reservation life, under control of the Indian Department. There were also many who had not been humbled, who had never been conquered, and who considered themselves the superiors of white men in all respects except numbers and equipments. It was as erroneous to suppose that the latter class would live peaceably on reservations, as it was barbarous to continue war against the well-disposed. No warlike Indian ever submitted to reservation restrictions until he had been whipped. He cannot be a savage ruler and an humble pupil at the same time. He cannot feel that fighting is the only work that a man ought to do, and yet take kindly to ploughing. His spirit must be broken in some way, or his nature changed, before he will submit to it. The right or wrong of breaking his spirit is another question; the fact remains that he must be born again into civilization, if he ever attains civilization.

It is but just to say that Mr. Colyer did not have full opportunity to talk with either the Indians or the people. The Indians were afraid to come in, being apprehensive of treachery, and Colyer did not care to interview the white population on account of the violent tone of the press. His changes of the location of the Indians were rather extensive, and none of them produced good results. The more peaceful portion of the Mimbreños had been living at and about Cañada Alamosa (Cottonwood Valley), and for these he selected a reservation in the Tularosa valley, to which the hostile Mimbreños with their allied Chiricahuas were also expected to come. None of the Indians wanted to go there, and many refused to go. Cochise, the Chiricahua chief, who had surrendered in September, 1871, with a band of about two hundred, went back to his old haunts in the spring of 1872, when the removal occurred. More than six hundred others followed their example. Less than half of the sixteen hundred Apaches gathered at Cañada Alamosa consented to go to Tularosa valley, and these were wretched and discontented. The water there was bad, the climate was cold, and the Indians were frightened by superstitions. They had warning legends of the destruction of the ancient races who once inhabited the ruins there, and they viewed the sickness which prevailed among them with great alarm. By fall their discontent was so great that the reservation was recommended to be abandoned, and the Indians placed on a reservation at Ojo Caliente, near their old home, which was done in 1874. Mr. Colyer established a reservation for the Pinaleños and Gileños at the mouth of the San Pedro River. It contained about one hundred square miles, extending west from the San Pedro and south from the Gila. These Apaches remained there for about a year, and then, on account of sickness, the proximity of settlers, and the inadequate supply of water, were established on a reservation on the Gila, south of and adjoining the original White Mountain reservation, and known as the San Carlos division. The Indians who had assembled in the White Mountains were gathered about Camp Apache (known at various times as Camp Ord, Camp Mogollon, and Camp Thomas), in the northern part of the present reservation, and these were left as they were. The Chiricahua reservation, in Southeastern Arizona, extending from the Mexican line to the Peloncillo Mountains, and including the Chiricahua range, was established in the following year by General Howard, as special agent. A very satisfactory reservation was set off for the Yampais, or Apache Mohaves, about Camp Verde, by Mr. Colyer; no other changes were made by him, except in the treatment of the hostiles.

As to these, his plans came in conflict with those which had been adopted by General Crook; who had taken command of the Department of Arizona on June 4, 1871. General Crook was the beau-ideal Indian-fighter of the frontiersmen at that time, and continued to be until his recent fair treatment of the Apaches has made him objectionable to the more rabid exterminationists—not that his treatment was not formerly fair; there has been no change in his expressed opinions concerning the Indians, though his opinion of their white neighbors in Arizona appears to have lowered somewhat. He was not an exterminator. His policy was to subdue the Indians and then treat them honestly. He said in September, 1871, "I think that the Apache is painted in darker colors than he deserves, and that his villainies arise more from a misconception of facts than from his being worse than other Indians. Living in a country the natural products of which will not support him, he has either to cultivate the soil or steal, and as our vacillating policy satisfies him we are afraid of him, he chooses the latter, also as requiring less labor and being more congenial to his natural instincts. I am satisfied that a sharp, active campaign against him would not only make him one of the best Indians in the country, but it would also save millions of dollars to the Treasury, and the lives of many innocent whites and Indians." General Crook had begun preparations for an active campaign against all hostiles when Colyer arrived, but Colyer's powers were made superior to his, and Colyer desired to try coaxing. Later on, Crook was given power to proceed

GENERAL GEORGE CROOK.

against all who failed to respond to Colyer's appeals, but finding that the prosecution of his plans would interfere with the negotiations of the peace agents, he undertook no active hostilities, and contented himself with pursuing and punishing, as far as possible, parties who made raids on the settlements. Mr. Colyer's plans for the procurement of peace were given a fair trial for over a year, and they failed. The hostiles did not come in, and they did not remain quiet. From September 1, 1871, to September 4, 1872, they made fifty-four separate attacks on the whites in Arizona, with recorded results as follows: soldiers killed, 3; citizens killed, 41; citizens wounded, 16; government horses and cattle stolen, 68; same stolen from citizens, 489. The actual depredations were slightly in excess of this statement. It may be remarked, parenthetically, that this damage and fourteen months' delay in obtaining peace, were caused by the Camp Grant massacre; but for that affair Mr. Colyer would not have been sent to Arizona, and General Crook would have conquered the hostiles in 1871. In view of the results mentioned, General Crook announced in September, 1872, his intention of proceeding to "punish the incorrigibly hostile."

For the first time in the history of that part of the country, the fair and sensible manner of dealing with the Apaches was adopted. Its results have proven this, and have shown General Crook to be the right man in the right place. It must be remembered that he had left to him a legacy of the hatred of three centuries between the peoples whom he had to pacify; that a large portion of the white population were as barbarous in their modes of warfare as the Apaches themselves; that Arizona was still a refuge for the criminal and lawless men of other states and territories; that war and pillage had been bred into the Apaches, until they were the most savage and intractable Indians in the country; that large bands of their nation still infested Northern Mexico, and had almost impregnable strongholds there; that Mexico pursued war in the old way, and still paid bounty for Apache scalps, no matter where procured; that slavery still existed in Mexico, and it was next to impossible to recover Indians once carried across the line. During the winter a vigorous campaign was prosecuted against the Tontos, Coyotéros, Yampais, and Hualapais, and by the summer of 1873 they were subdued. Del-Shay's band of Tontos were captured in the Sierra Ancha by Captain Randall, on April 22d, with that notorious chief himself, who had played fast and loose with Mr. Colyer, and earned a reputation for unblushing treachery by his dealings with others. Jemaspie's band of Hualapais surrendered to Captain McGregor, in the Santa Maria Mountains, on June 12th. Lieutenant Babcock handsomely whipped the Tontos under Natatotel and Naqui-naquis, on June 16th, and forced their surrender. Soon afterwards Captain Burns captured two hundred Yampais, the last organized band in Northern Arizona, and peace was practically established.

The Hualapais, or Apache Yumas, numbering about eight hundred, were gathered at Beale's Springs, whence the Indian Department moved them, much against their wills, to the Colorado River reservation. When the removal was first proposed to them, they fled to the mountains and said they would resist to the death, but, through fear of the soldiers, they came back and were removed. The Indians at this reservation were unfriendly to them, and the climate was unendurable to these people of the mountains. In four months nearly all of them were afflicted with an epidemic eruptive disease; many of their children were nearly blind from a disease of the eyes, brought on by the heat and dust; and half of their horses had starved to death. The troops stationed there suffered almost as much as the Indians. After a year's residence there the Hualapais left the place in a body and went back to their old homes, but without committing any depredations. They lived there on friendly terms with the whites for a time, and were then removed to San Carlos, through the intercession of General Crook. The Yampais, or Apache Mohaves, and part of the Tontos, numbering nearly two thousand, were located on a reservation about Camp Verde. The Pinaleños, with a few stragglers from other tribes, in all about twelve hundred, were sent to San Carlos, where they still remain. There were about sixteen hundred Apaches, known as the White Mountain Apaches, grouped about Camp Apache. It was estimated that about one thousand renegades, one-third of whom were warriors, still remained at large in various parts of the Territory, but there were not probably more than one-third to one-half of that number. Against these an unceasing war was waged.

The Indians placed on the reservations were kept under rigid surveillance. Each warrior was furnished with a metal check marked with his number and the name of his tribe. The officers in charge kept record of them and their families by these numbers, and as a full description of each man was recorded, and rations were issued on these checks, it was impossible for them to leave the reservation undetected. The remarkable success of General Crook in conquering these tribes so quickly was obtained by fighting Apaches with Apaches. The friendly White Mountain Indians and Hualapais were used against the others. They acted in the best of faith, rendering services that were invaluable. They knew the country as well as the hostiles, and could interpret all their signals, besides being adepts in the ruses of Apache warfare. After being brought on the reservation they were still used as police, with such gratifying results that the Indian police system has since been extended to all reservations. The Apaches were informed that their welfare would rest mainly with themselves; that white people punished their own offenders, and they must do the same. This was especially beneficial in the case of the Apaches, because they are thoroughly democratic in their tribal government. They have no hereditary chiefs; each warrior has a large amount of independence, and the rivalry between various aspirants for power usually affords any wrong-doer a certain amount of backing. The only way in which the guilty could be certainly singled out was by making the Indians the agents of the law. There were, of course, many who awaited only an opportunity to resume their old life, and the machinations of these could be detected and repressed by the Indians alone. In the spring of 1873, certain of these conspired to kill all the whites at San Carlos and make their escape. On May 27th the attempt was made prematurely, resulting in a failure. Chan-Deisi, a malcontent chief, tried to spear Agent Larrabee, but was prevented by Yomas, another Indian. He then shot and killed Lieutenant Almy. The bands of Cochinay and Chuntz, to which he belonged, at once fled to the mountains, and for over a year they were hunted by the troops and the reservation Apaches. Many of the Indians became worn out, and begged to return to the reservation, but they were met with the reply that they could come only when they brought Cochinay, Chuntz, and Chan-Deisi, dead or alive. One by one they joined the troops in hunting down their fugitive kindred. Cochinay was killed on May 26, 1874; Chan-Deisi was killed on June 12th; and Chuntz on July 25th. Del-Shay, the Tonto chief, tried to play treachery at the Verde reservation, to which he had been permitted to remove, by murdering all of the whites there. He had them surrounded, and would have killed them but for the prompt resistance of the police and other Indians. He was brought to bay and killed by his own people on July 27th. The punishment of these chiefs is conclusive evidence that a new era had dawned upon the Apaches.

The Apaches under General Crook's supervision were also giving other evidences of reformation. They were farming extensively and building houses for themselves. At Verde they made an excellent irrigating canal at no expense to the government. The White Mountain Indians, in 1874, raised 300,000 pounds of corn and 5000 pounds of beans, besides delivering 750 tons of hay to the post and making five miles of irrigating ditches. Everywhere they were quiet, except the few renegades, who were hunted diligently. For the first time in its history Arizona was at peace. The Indians were all on reservations that suited them, except the Hualapais, and they had seen the hopelessness of war. The whites also were satisfied, except that class who prey upon their fellow-men, and search out the helpless because they are the more easy and profitable victims. Governor Safford said, in his message of January 6, 1875, "At no period in the history of Arizona have our Indian affairs been in so satisfactory condition. Comparative peace now reigns throughout the Territory, with almost a certainty that no general Indian war will ever occur again. General Crook, in the subjugation of the Apaches, has sustained his former well-earned military reputation, and deserves the lasting gratitude of our people." Let it be remembered that this result was effected neither by the extermination policy nor by the so-called peace policy. It was the work of a man who said, "Vengeance is just as much to be deprecated as a silly sentimentalism." His policy was simple justice to red and white alike. Bear this in mind, as we proceed, and consider how fully its abandonment answers the question, Why did not this state of affairs continue?

The little cloud, like a man's hand, was already in the sky. In his report of August 31, 1874, General Crook said, "There are now on the Verde reservation about fifteen hundred Indians; they have been among the worst in Arizona; but if the government keeps its promise to them that it shall be their home for all time, there will be no difficulty in keeping them at peace, and engaged in peaceful pursuits. I sincerely hope that the interests that are now at work to deprive these Indians of this reservation will be defeated; but if they succeed, the responsibility of turning these fifteen hundred Apaches loose upon the settlers of Arizona should rest where it belongs." Although this was said of the Verde reservation only, it may be applied to the other Arizona reservations. The Indians were all at peace on reservations that suited them, and the responsibility of driving them to desperation by taking them from their native homes and placing them among enemies, in unhealthy and unpleasant localities, must rest where it belongs. We must turn our eyes to the Indian Bureau—our humanitarian, sympathetic, religious, peace and civilization Indian Bureau. It has been charged time and again that the Indian Department has been controlled by a corrupt ring, which manages to keep its hold on men of every profession and every party who are appointed to represent the government in this branch of its interests. It has been charged that they have had such a control over Congress that they can turn it whither they will, and break down any man who tries to stand up for honesty and justice. Considering the professions that various Indian Commissioners have made, it is but too evident that the control of that department has been in the hands either of men who "stole the livery of Heaven to serve the devil in," or of arrant fools who have been played upon like shepherds' pipes by the land-grabbers, who have secured the spoils. For present purposes it is immaterial which is the correct alternative.

In 1874 the reservations of Arizona passed from the control of the War Department to that of the Indian Bureau, and the latter inaugurated what it was pleased to call "the policy of concentration." In other words, it began taking away from various tribes the lands on which they were peacefully settled, and which had been promised them for their future homes. The interests that were at work to get the Verde reservation did get it, notwithstanding General Crook's hopes, and he was forced into the humiliating position of seeing the Indians taken away from the lands that had been promised them through him. He told the agent sent to remove them that he would give him all the assistance in his power except force; he would not use his soldiers to compel a removal. The Indians did not wish to go, but they went peaceably. They were informed that the President ordered their removal, and they had learned that what the President said must be obeyed. They gave up their houses, their irrigating ditches, and their fields, and went, because they dared not refuse. General Crook did not remain to see the undoing of his work. He was relieved, on March 22, 1875, by Colonel Kautz, and sent to the Department of the Platte, where the Sioux were beginning to be troublesome. Colonel Kautz held the same opinions as to the propriety of keeping faith with Indians that General Crook did, and managed to preserve peace for some months longer. To the statement of the Commissioner of Indian Affairs: "I believe now no one in the territory questions the wisdom of the removal of the Verde Indians," Colonel Kautz bluntly replied: "So far as my observation goes, I have seen no one who endorses it, except those connected with the Indian Department."

The next outrage committed by the Indian Bureau was the removal of the White Mountain Indians—that is, those who had been about Camp Apache, in the northern part of the White Mountain reservation—to the neighborhood of San Carlos agency. The advantages claimed to be gained by this were better and more extensive farming lands, a mild climate, excellent roads, a saving of the expense of an extra agency, and "last, but not least, to the people of the territory, it would avert the trade with these Indians from New Mexico to Arizona, where it properly belongs." The disadvantages were that these were mountain Indians, who were unused to the hot, stifling climate of the Gila Valley; that the region of the new location had proven so unhealthy to the soldiers at Camp Goodwin that the post had to be removed; that the Indians would be placed in close proximity to the white settlement of Pueblo Viejo; and that the Pinal Apaches, already at San Carlos, were their enemies by feuds of many years' standing. There were other considerations that would seem serious to some persons, though these humanitarians, who were desirous of having trade go in its proper channels, did not trouble their minds about them. A large majority, if not all, the Indians were bitterly opposed to the removal, and they had been good friends to us. These were the Indians on whom Mexican scouts had not felt willing to fire; who had helped General Crook to subdue the hostile Apaches; who were living on the little farms that had long supported them; who had raised greater crops than all the other Apaches together. Every inducement to move was used with them, except actual force, and that was refused by the military authorities. They were threatened with force, however, and their agency buildings were burned down by the representatives of the peace policy. Under these kindly arguments nearly half of the Indians consented to go. Their state of mind may be imagined from the fact that, on the way, they had a fight among themselves, in which five were killed and ten wounded—"Not a great loss where so much lead was expended," said the philosophic special agent, L. E. Dudley, who effected the removal. In the fall of the same year (1875) large numbers of these Indians left San Carlos and went to the Chiricahua reservation, stating that they were unable to live at the former place on account of the hostility of the Pinals. That winter they had a falling-out with the Chiricahuas; a Southern Chiricahua chief was killed; and our White Mountain Coyoteros had to flee from that reservation to escape the indiscriminating vengeance of his tribe.

The bands of Pitone, Eskyinlaw (alias Diablo), and Pedro, a majority of all the White Mountain Indians, refused to remove to San Carlos. They said that General Howard, as agent of the Indian Department, had promised them that they might remain there so long as they were peaceable; that they had not only been peaceable, but also had fought other Indians, in aid of the Americans. They did not want to leave their farms or their native mountains, and they begged Colonel Kautz to interpose for them at Washington. He did so, and his plea was met with the answer of "(hostility of the War Department to the peace policy." Search you now the history of the whole world and find a more wanton act of tyranny than the removal of these Indians from their homes. They would have saluted a Gesler's hat without a murmur; they would have paid a tax on tea without much remonstrance; a foreign lord might have lived in their Dublin Castle without making them desperate. It is almost questionable whether Nero would have been capable of treating his friends and allies as the humane gentlemen treated these unfortunate bands, and yet men ask why the Apaches cannot be made peaceable. No war resulted in this case, because the soldiers could not be induced to compel the removal of the three obdurate bands. But it came finally. There are some Indians into whose necks it will not do to grind your heels too far.

The next victims of humanity were the Chiricahuas. There were, on the Chiricahua reservation, in Southeastern Arizona, the Northern Chiricahuas, under Tah-za, a son of old Cochise, who had died in peace on the reservation some eighteen months before, the Southern Chiricahuas, whose head chief was Juh (Hoo, Who), and a mixed band of Mogollons, Mimbres, and Coyoteros. The management of these warlike bands by the Indian Bureau had been criminally inefficient, and its faults had been pointed out repeatedly. To begin with, their reservation had been made to join the Mexican line, giving every opportunity for raiding from either side. It will be remembered that there were large bands of predatory Apaches in Northern Mexico, and that the Mexicans were still pursuing the old, treacherous system of warfare. The authorities of Sonora complained that the Chiricahuas committed depredations within their borders, which was true in a number of cases. The agency people did not keep count of their Apaches, as General Crook was doing, and there were no restrictions imposed upon them that were sufficient to keep them on their reservation. On the other hand, the Mexicans were constantly coming on the reservation to sell whiskey, or in search of scalps. On July 23, 1875, a party of Chiricahuas who were gathering acorns on the reservation, fifteen miles north of the Mexican line, were fired upon by a party of Mexican soldiers. Notwithstanding these acts of lawlessness, there were no troubles with the whites, on our side of the line, during the four years, from 1872 to 1876, that the Indians were located there. In April of the latter year two white men were killed by two Indians at Sulphur Springs, a mail station on the reservation. The killing was not justifiable, and yet the victims were not entitled to the slightest sympathy. Their death resulted from a violation of the laws of the United States. The Indians were hunting in the Dragoon Mountains, about thirty-five miles from the agency, owing to the fact that their supply of food was exhausted, and the agent had sent them out to procure some for themselves. They obtained whiskey from Mr. Rogers, the station-keeper at Sulphur Springs, who had several times been warned against selling it to them. They got drunk and had a fight among themselves, in which two men and a child were killed; a part of the band then returned to the agency, leaving a chief named Eskina (Skinya), with a dozen warriors and their families. Two of these, a sub-chief named Pi-hon-se-nay and his nephew, went to Sulphur Springs for more whiskey. Rogers sold them small quantities two or three times, and then refused to let them have more, they being drunk. They watched their opportunity, killed Rogers and an employé named Spence, stole the whiskey, ammunition, and horses at the place, and returned to camp. Eskina's entire party got drunk and decided to go on the warpath, which they did, with the result of an American killed, another wounded, and four horses stolen on the next day. A company of cavalry was sent after them, but. failed to capture them. Early in June, after committing other depredations, Eskina and his men came to Tahza's camp and tried to induce him to join them. Tahza and his people refused, and a fight ensued, in which six men were killed and three wounded. Pi-hon-se-nay was shot in the shoulder by Tahza, and Eskina was killed by Tahza's youngest brother.

In the mean time Governor Safford had been consulted by the Indian Bureau, and had recommended the removal of all the Chiricahuas, either to Ojo Caliente, in New Mexico, or to San Carlos. Removal to Ojo Caliente had been proposed to them the year before, and they had replied that they "would sooner die than live there." The department, instead of cutting off the southern part of the reservation and asking for troops to guard the Mexican line and punish the guilty Indians, decided to send the innocent ones to San Carlos, the guilty being at large. Tahza reluctantly agreed to go, but said he could not answer for the other bands. On June 7, Juh, Geronimo (Heronemo—Jerome), and Nolgee, who had sided with Eskina in the fight, agreed to go also, but on the same afternoon they fled with all their people and went into Sonora. 320 of the Chiricahuas went with Tahza to San Carlos, in June; a small band, under Gordo, had gone to Ojo Caliente just after Rogers and Spence were killed; the remainder of the 965 Indians reported to be on the reservation, which was three or four hundred more than were in fact there, went to war. By October the hostiles had stolen 170 head of stock and killed 20 persons—probably more; because a number of prospectors who were known to be in the mountains were never accounted for.

The evil did not stop there. In the spring of 1877 Mr. E. A. Hayt, the man of many removals, became Commissioner of Indian Affairs under Secretary Schurz. His policy was "a steady concentration of the smaller bands of Indians upon the larger reservations." It was found that about 250 of the Chiricahua renegades had taken refuge on the Ojo Caliente reservation, and made raids from there, assisted by some of the Hot Springs Indians; hence the Hot Springs reservation must be broken up, and the Indians removed to San Carlos. A force of 103 Indian police was sent over from San Carlos, and the available troops stationed in New Mexico were concentrated about the reservation. Geronimo and other renegades were found there and arrested. None of the Indians wished to leave Ojo Caliente, but there was no chance for resistance. Very few escaped, the principal party being some 40 warriors led by Victorio, a chief who made himself unpleasantly notorious later on. 453 of them arrived at San Carlos in May. There had been reported 2100 Indians at this place in 1875, and 1600 in 1876, but it was evident that no such number had been there. On September 2, 300 of these Hot Springs and Chiricahua Apaches escaped from San Carlos. They were pursued by the agency Indians, but only 30 women and children were brought back. The remainder made their way to New Mexico, attacked a settlement there, killed 8 persons, and ravaged, the neighboring country. Troops were hurried after them, and on September 10 a fight occurred, in which 12 of the hostiles were killed and 13 captured. On October 13, 190 of them surrendered at Fort Wingate, and 50 came in afterwards. All these were taken to Ojo Caliente to await orders for their final disposition. It was decided to take them all back to San Carlos, against which they protested, saying they were willing to go anywhere else, and a number took their chances on a break for the mountains rather than go; 80 of them got safely away. In December 67 of these came to the Mescalero reservation and asked leave to stay there, which was granted.

In February, 1878, Victorio and his band, who had been in Mexico, surrendered at Ojo Caliente, but announced their intention to resist any attempt to take them to San Carlos. In April it was decided to remove them to the Mescalero reservation, but they refused to go, and fled to the mountains. Towards the last of June they went to the Mescalero agency, of their own accord, and promised to remain there. Their wives and children, who were at San Carlos, were sent for, and there appeared to be a prospect of their final settlement, when, most inopportunely, the judge, prosecuting attorney, and other officials of Grant County appeared at the Mescalero reservation on a hunting excursion. Victorio and others of his band were under indictment in Grant County, and they took this to be a move for their arrest. They left the reservation, taking with them all the Chiricahuas who had taken refuge there, and made a most destructive raid through Southwestern New Mexico and Southeastern Arizona, until they were chased into Mexico by the soldiers a few weeks later.

Victorio's stay in Mexico was short. On September 4, 1879, he suddenly appeared near Ojo Caliente with 60 warriors; they killed the post herders, and captured all the horses of the cavalry stationed there. Major Morrow, with the 9th Cavalry, was sent after them, but was able to accomplish but little. Victorio roamed the mountains of Southern New Mexico, depredating in all directions, and spreading terror everywhere. About 200 Mescaleros were induced to join him, and he was further reinforced by at least 100 renegade Comanches and other warriors from Mexico. When dislodged in one mountain range they would fall back to another which afforded a position of equal strength, and if too hard pressed they would scatter in small bands, to unite at some well-known rendezvous. In April, 1880, Colonel Hatch, who had returned from his labors with the Colorado Utes, disarmed all the Indians remaining on the Mescalero reservation and then took up the chase of Victorio. The hostile bands were driven back through the San Mateo, the Mimbres, and the Mogollon mountains. The Arizona forces, under Colonel Carr, turned them to the south, and they were soon driven into Mexico. This outbreak occasioned an unusual loss of life to the scattered herders of New Mexico. These people, mostly Mexicans, had formerly been left unharmed by the Apaches, who secured provisions from the herds and frequently obtained arms and ammunition from the herders. The Mescaleros, Comanches, and other renegades, who had joined Victorio, abandoned his shrewd policy of maintaining friendly relations with these convenient commissaries, and killed them at every opportunity. The result, as nearly as could be ascertained, was that of 73 persons killed during the outbreak 53 were Mexicans, of whom a large percentage were herders. It was claimed that the number of persons killed was in excess of this, and it is probable that a correct list would reach 100.

The bitterness of this warfare, against such desperate odds, set the people of Arizona and New Mexico to thinking of the cause of it all. Said General Willcox, commanding the Department of Arizona: "It is believed by many that Victorio was unjustly dealt with in the first instance, by the abrupt removal of his people from Ojo Caliente, New Mexico, to San Carlos; and that such removal, if not a breach of faith, was a harsh and cruel measure, from which the people of New Mexico have reaped bitter consequences." General Pope, of the Division of the Missouri, was even more pointed in his remarks, and his opinion in this case is the more weighty as he was never an admirer of the Apaches; he had unreservedly expressed his opinion that they were "idle vagabonds, utterly worthless and hopeless," and again, that they were "a squalid, untrustworthy people, robbers and thieves by nature." He said: "This outbreak of Victorio, and the severe campaign against him, still in progress, involving the loss of many of our men, and the murder by Indians of about seventy persons, mainly Mexican herders, were due to the determined purpose of the Interior

GENERAL POPE.

Department to effect the removal of the band to the San Carlos agency in Arizona. There is already a large number of Indians collected at that agency, mainly Indians of Arizona. Victorio and his band have always bitterly objected to being placed there, one of the reasons given by him being the hostility of many of the Indians of the agency. He always asserted his willingness to live peaceably with his people at the Warm Springs (Ojo Caliente) agency, and, so far as I am informed, gave no trouble to any one while there. I do not know the reasons of the Interior Department for insisting upon the removal to San Carlos agency, but certainly they should be cogent to justify the great trouble and severe losses occasioned by the attempts to coerce the removal. The present is the fourth time within five years that Victorio's band has broken out. Three times they have been brought in and turned over by the military to the Indian Bureau authorities. Both Victorio and his band are resolved to die rather than go to the San Carlos agency, and there is no doubt it will be necessary to kill or capture the whole tribe before present military operations can be closed successfully. The capture is not very probable, but the killing (cruel as it will be) can, I suppose, be done in time. I am trying to separate the Mescaleros from Victorio, and yet hope to do so, but there is not the slightest prospect that Victorio or his band will ever surrender under any circumstances. He and others of his band are understood to be indicted for murder in the courts in New Mexico, and they are well aware of it, and prefer being shot in battle to being hung. It is proper to represent this state of facts, that the work still before the troops in New Mexico may be clearly understood, and prosecuted to the end if the authorities in Washington so desire and direct. Although I entertain strong convictions on the merits of the controversy which has resulted in this Indian war, I do not consider it my duty to express them in this report, but I think it would be well for the Secretary of the Interior to ascertain what were the engagements entered into and the promises made by the agents of that department from the time of General Howard's mission to this band of Apaches down to the late outbreak. It is probable that much would be developed by such investigation to extenuate, at least, the feeling, if not the conduct, of the tribe."

It will be observed that neither of these officers goes back to the original source of the trouble—the removal of the Chiricahuas. Two drunken Indians killed two whiskey smugglers, and forthwith the Indians who happened to live on the same reservation, who had no connection with the killing, were ordered to be removed from their homes; fugitives from this reservation took refuge at Ojo Caliente, and forthwith the Indians there, guilty and innocent alike, were ordered to be removed; fugitives from Ojo Caliente invaded the Mescalero reservation and induced half of that tribe to go, to war; New Mexico and Arizona reaped a harvest of five years of savage murdering and plundering—nay, more, for this war was not stopped until 1882, and the dissatisfaction caused by these removals has had its weight in every outbreak since then. In this connection it may be well to look at other parts of the country, where the success of the concentration policy was being demonstrated in 1879. In the spring the much-abused Poncas were snatched by writ of *habeas corpus* from the hands of the military, who, in accordance with the wishes of the Indian Bureau, were dragging them back to Indian Territory, from their homes in Dakota. Later in the year the Northern Cheyennes were fighting with a desperation that was bloodcurdling—fighting soldiers, with knives made of pieces of stove-pipe, and slungshots made of fragments of the stove in their prison—to escape being taken back to Indian Territory. In the Indian Territory were Joseph's Nez Percés, sickening and dying in their rotten teepees. In Arizona the Hualapais would have starved to death, or into hostility, if the War Department had not relieved them. South of these, the Papagos were relapsing into barbarism for want of proper teachers; their school-houses were stripped of windows and doors, and the grand old cathedral of San Xavier del Bac was robbed of its consecrated vessels. And yet the Commissioner of Indian Affairs was on hand, with the annual recommendation for more concentration. If concentration were beneficial, why were not some of its good effects shown on the tribes that had been concentrated at the cost of life, treasure, and broken faith? It is a perversion of the English language to call such a system a peace policy.

In January, 1880, Juh and Geronimo came voluntarily to the White Mountain reservation, with 108 Chiricahua renegades. They were induced to leave the fastnesses of the Sierra Madre, in Northern Mexico, by Lieutenant Haskell and Interpreter Jeffords, who went to their haunts and reasoned them into returning. Victorio depredated and fought Mexican troops for a few months, and in August crossed into Texas, one hundred miles below El Paso del

Norte. He was twice driven across the Rio Grande by Colonel Grierson, and then remained in Mexico, at war with the people there. He was killed by the Mexican troops some weeks later. In July, 1881, Nané, with 15 warriors, who had been with Victorio, crossed the Rio Grande and made his way into New Mexico, when he was joined by some 25 Mescaleros. He then made a rapid and bloody raid across Southern New Mexico, falling upon herders and prospectors, who had no warning of his coming, and murdering them without mercy. He was chased back into Mexico by the troops, in the latter part of August. In Arizona there were two outbreaks during the year: one, among the White Mountain Indians, was caused by the arrest of a medicine-man, named Nockay-Delklinne, who was holding dances for the purpose of bringing dead warriors to life, with the ultimate design of repeopling the country and driving out the whites. It was considered advisable to suppress him, although it did not appear that he had succeeded in reviving any of the departed—it would have been a splendid time to tell the Indians he was a humbug, and let him prove it; his arrest only made them think the whites were afraid of his powers. While removing him, the Indian scouts with the command took up his cause, and a fight ensued, in which the medicine-man and five soldiers were killed. The Indians then killed all the whites they could find, and attacked Camp Apache, to which Colonel Carr's party had retired. They killed in all ten soldiers and eight citizens. On the approach of reinforcements they fled, but, with the exception of about a dozen, who escaped and became outlaws, they were driven back to the reservation without any fighting. Five of the scouts were tried by court-martial; three were hung, and two were sent to prison on Alcatraz Island. On the night of September 30, a number of Chiricahuas, under Juh and Nachez, broke away from the reservation. The reasons given for this were that the agency authorities would not help them make an irrigating ditch, and treated them worse than the other Indians in various respects. They were driven into Mexico early in October, after a sharp fight at Cedar Springs.

In April, 1882, a number of the hostiles from Mexico made

SAN XAVIER DEL BAC.

their way quietly to the San Carlos agency, and induced all the remaining original renegade Chiricahuas, and also Loco's band of Ojo Caliente Indians, to leave the reservation and run for Mexico. They were pursued by the troops from several posts, and struck by two detachments; Lieutenant-colonel Forsythe attacked them at Horse Shoe Cañon, in New Mexico, and Major Tupper followed them into Mexico and whipped them badly in the Hatchet Mountains. They fled, leaving five dead warriors and two squaws, but carrying off others; and two days later were ambushed by Lieutenant-colonel Garcia, of the Mexican army, who inflicted severe punishment upon them. On July 6, a part of the White Mountain Indians at San Carlos, under Nan-tia-tish and Ar-shay, known as the Cibicu Indians, from their former location on Cibicu Creek, killed four of the Indian police and escaped from the reservation. They committed several robberies and killed six people within ten days. On the 17th they were overtaken and terribly punished at the "Big Dry Wash," on the old Moqúi trail, a wild, desolate cañon, two hundred feet deep, with rocky side cañons and forbidding surroundings. They left sixteen dead, including Nan-tia-tish, and lost all their property. They scattered in the night, and, under cover of a heavy hail-storm, which obliterated their trails, straggled into the reservation completely destitute, and sated with war.

Some important changes in the affairs of the Arizona Indians were made in 1882. One of the most noticeable was the treaty effected with Mexico, on July 29, by which troops of both countries were authorized to pursue fleeing savages across the line in "unpopulated or desert parts." This made the punishment of the hostiles a possibility for the first time. Before that they had only to reach the Mexican line to be safe; our troops could pursue them no farther. Another important change was the return of General Crook to the command of the department. No dereliction can fairly be charged against Colonel Kautz or General Willcox, who had commanded there since Crook left; but nature has made a difference in men, and General Crook is one whose character has made him phenomenally successful in the management of Indians. Most important of his qualifications is his habit of keeping strict faith with the Indians; they are never contented under the control of a man whom they cannot trust. Next to this is the possession of common-sense, a qualification in which some people who have held responsible positions have been sadly lacking. Consider this statement, made by him in 1879: "During the twenty-seven years of my experience with the Indian question I have never known a band of Indians to make peace with our government and then break it, or leave their reservation, without some ground of complaint; but until their complaints are examined and adjusted, they will constantly give annoyance and trouble." He does not say that the Indians are always right nor that they are always wrong; but he does not leave room for a single case of their making war from "pure deviltry." This language was not called forth, however, by the mistreatment of Indians at the hands of lawless whites, or by the dishonesty of Indian agents; it was used in regard to the attempted removal of the Northern Cheyennes to the Indian Territory. Concerning this he further says: "In the present case, the Cheyennes claimed that they had been wronged, and had become desperate as a pack of wolves. The army had orders to take them back to the Indian Territory, and had no option in the matter. It seems to me to have been, to say the least, a very unnecessary exercise of power to insist upon this particular portion of the band going back to their former reservation, while the other fragments of the same band, which surrendered to the troops on the Yellowstone, or escaped to the Red Cloud and Spotted Tail reservations, had been allowed to remain North unmolested." And who were these Cheyennes that must be hounded back to the chills, fever, and starvation that they had run away from? He says: "Among these Cheyenne Indians were some of the bravest and most efficient of the auxiliaries who had acted under General Mackenzie and myself in the campaign against the hostile Sioux in 1876 and 1877, and I still preserve a grateful remembrance of their distinguished services, which the government seems to have forgotten." Do you think that any of the concentration humanitarians will ever rank with this stern Indian-fighter in the lists of humane men?

Immediately after General Crook's return there came about a reasonable harmony between the representatives of the Indian Bureau and the War Department in Arizona, which had not existed during his absence. Just how this was effected has not been made public, but the fact was soon notorious. He then talked to the Indians, publicly and privately, until he learned the state of their feelings. He found them sullen, distrustful, and, as they confessed, on the verge of going to war. Conflicting statements had been made to them till they had lost confidence in every one; they had been told that they were to be disarmed, attacked by troops, and removed from Arizona. He explained to them that their enemies, who wanted their reservation, were trying to get them to make war.; and that they would certainly lose their reservation and everything else if they did. He showed them that their well-being must depend mainly on themselves, and secured their co-operation in reinstating all the old measures he had used so successfully ten years before, but which had since been discontinued. Every male Indian capable of bearing arms was required to wear constantly a metal tag with his number and the designation of his band. The police were reorganized, and frequent roll-calls were required. He next obtained permission for six or seven hundred of the White Mountain Indians to leave the hot valleys of the Gila and San Carlos rivers, and return to their old homes in the northern part of the reservation. To obtain this privilege he became personally responsible for their good behavior; and the Indians agreed to be self-supporting after they got their first year's crop. Both of these promises have been kept, notwithstanding that the Indians had to use sharpened sticks for planting and case-knives for harvesting implements. The lot of these Indians was so much more pleasing to many of the red men than that of the "fed savages" at the agency, that over one third of the forty-five hundred Indians there (not counting the Chiricahuas) have gathered in the northern part of the reservation, and are supporting themselves with very little assistance. To the officers explicit orders were given to give and require "justice to all—Indians as well as white men." There were to be no wrongs and no mistakes. The orders were: "There must be no division of responsibility in this matter; each officer will be held to a strict accountability that his actions have been fully authorized by law and justice, and that Indians evincing a desire to enter upon a career of peace shall have no cause of complaint through hasty or injudicious acts of the military."

Having adopted these means for the preservation of peace on and about the reservation—means which have proven completely successful, without any exception—General Crook next turned his attention to the hostiles in Mexico. They were the worst product of the bad faith and bad policy of the past six years, and the most difficult to dispose of. Their native homes could not be restored to them. There was nothing that could be offered them except fair treatment on the White Mountain reservation, and that had little attraction to savages whose tastes led them to piratical lives, and who had experienced our fair treatment. He tried to open negotiations with them, but succeeded only in learning that a raid was imminent. All that could be done was to prepare for it as well as possible, for which purpose pack-trains were put in readiness and the troops stationed at the most available points. In March the Chiricahuas began operations. A party of fifty warriors, under Geronimo, swept through Sonora to obtain stock, while Chato (Flat Nose—a mule had kicked him in the face and flattened his nose), with twenty-six men, dashed, through Arizona and New Mexico, chiefly to obtain ammunition. The latter party killed about a dozen persons in Arizona, circled through Mexico, and crossed back near the Hatchet Mountains. The atrocity committed by them that attracted the greatest attention was the murder of Judge McComas and wife, and the capture of Charley McComas, on March 28.

On the day previous to this terrible tragedy an event occurred which led to the final overthrow and capture of the renegades. It was the desertion from Chato's party of a warrior named Pe-nal-tishn, commonly called "Peaches." He made his way to San Carlos, was there arrested, and was induced by General Crook to guide the troops to the stronghold of the Chiricahuas. General Crook made hasty visits to Sonora and Chihuahua, and secured promises of co-operation there. He stationed troops along the line to watch for any future raiders, and, with 193 Apache scouts, 42 men, and 9 officers, started for the hiding-place of the Chiricahuas. It was situated in the Sierra Madre, the range that separates Sonora from Chihuahua, one of the roughest mountain countries in America, but covered with forests of pine and oak, and furnished with an abundance of good water. Here were a series of natural and almost impregnable fortresses which the Mexican troops had never been able to reach, and which Crook might not have penetrated if the Chiricahuas had not been

CROOK'S BATTLE-FIELD IN THE SIERRA MADRE.

wholly unsuspicious of his approach. As it was, his forces moved quietly into the mountains; his scouts located Chato's camp; and the party would have surrounded it but for the haste of some scouts, who fired on two Indians. The camp was at once attacked, and the Indians were defeated, with a loss of about a dozen killed and five captured. There was now no hope of securing the Indians by pursuing them, for they scattered, as usual, and the pursuing force could not scatter to follow them. The only chance of getting them was to induce them to surrender, if possible. Communication was obtained, through the captives, and they were soon satisfied that they had better surrender on the terms offered, which were substantially an agreement to overlook the past and start with a clean page on the White Mountain reservation. Almost all the renegades came in under this arrangement, among them Geronimo, Nachez (a son of Cochise), Chato, and Bonito. Juh had fallen out with the band and gone away to the South, with one man and two or three squaws, before Crook arrived.

By an agreement made between the War and Interior departments, in July, 1883, the Chiricahuas were placed under the exclusive control of General Crook; and the police authority of the entire reservation was put in his hands. By his permission the renegades selected lands for themselves on Turkey Creek, near Camp Apache, and, with the aid of the soldiers, began cultivation. In 1884, Geronimo and Chato had farms which were among the most creditable on the reservation. The prejudice of the Apache men against labor was never so strong as that of the average Indian, and on the reservation no disgrace attached to a man who worked. In 1884 more than one half of all the labor was performed by men and boys. The results of the Indian work on the reservation for that year were 3,850,000 pounds of corn, 550,000 pounds of barley, 540,000 pounds of beans, 20,000 pounds of potatoes, 50,000 pounds of wheat, 200,000 pumpkins, and 90,000 melons, besides garden stuff; and this, notwithstanding that the Apaches on the Gila lost nearly all their crops by freshets, and those in the northern part of the reservation lost about one third of theirs by late rains and early frosts. They also supplied large quantities of wood and hay, made ditches, and performed other labor. There was only one appearance of trouble during the year, and this was occasioned by Ka-e-te-na (The Looking-glass), a young chief of a Mexican tribe, who was with the renegades at the time of their surrender. At one of their dances he made a speech which was calculated to raise hostile feeling; for which offence he was arrested by Chiricahua police, convicted by an Apache jury, and sentenced to three years' imprisonment, in irons, at Alcatraz Island, in San Francisco Bay.

CRUELTY, PITY, AND JUSTICE.   753

With such a record, continued till the recent outbreak of Geronimo, that outbreak was naturally unexpected. Theories of its cause should not be hastily formed; and yet the only one thus far announced--detection in the manufacture of tiswin, and flight from fear of punishment--is not improbable. Tiswin, or p'tis wing, is a fermented drink of native manufacture, somewhat resembling beer. Its basis is usually corn, but other materials are sometimes used. It had long been a favorite drink with some of the tribes; and on the reservation, owing to the enforcement of the intercourse laws, it was the

ALCATRAZ ISLAND.

popular intoxicant. Es-kim-en-zin, the unfortunate Camp Grant chief, was a large manufacturer of it, and had grown quite wealthy from selling it to the other Indians. The results of its use were practically as deplorable as those resulting from liquors sold by the whites, in consequence of which determined efforts have been made of late years to break up the manufacture. Through the aid of the Indian police these efforts have been very successful, and but few who have made it have escaped punishment. If this were the cause of the outbreak, the escaped Indians apparently deserve severe punishment for their crimes; but in any event, General Crook is entitled to the confidence of the people that he will do what is just.

It is hardly to be supposed that there will never be any more troubles with the Apaches, for there are causes which will produce trouble, if not removed, and our government is slow of motion. There are coal mines on the southern part of the reservation, that are very valuable, on account of the scarcity of fuel in Arizona, which certain white men have been trying to secure. It has been thought possible by some that difficulty in regard to these might best be avoided by leasing them. A proposed law for that purpose was submitted to Congress in 1882, and bills to cut off the parts of the reservation containing them have since been introduced; but no action has been taken on any of them. Possibly a good solution would be to make miners of the Apaches. They are industrious and quick to learn, and could dig coal as well as plant corn. The whites would then be supplied with coal and the Indians would have the benefit of the mines, besides being initiated in a new field of industry. The Apaches are anxious to obtain the release of their people now held in Mexico, some of whom were captured within the past five years. The Mexican captives, held as hostages for the return of these, were released by General Crook in 1883; but the Apache captives are still slaves. The government cannot neglect this matter and retain the respect of civilized men. There were indications of a rupture between the military and Indian authorities in Arizona under the late administration; but the firm stand of Commissioner Atkins against disarming the Apaches indicates that he is in harmony with General Crook. It would be folly to disarm them, even if it could be accomplished. They would be left subject to the outrages of the Arizona outlaws, who prey on every one, and also at the mercy of the rabid exterminationists. In 1883 a company of "rangers" was organized, to attack the peaceable Indians at San Carlos, and marched nearly to the reservation. No time was wasted in begging these men to be law-abiding. The Indians were notified that they would be expected to defend themselves; and the rangers, on learning this, concluded that they had not lost any Indians. They marched back to Tombstone without making an attack. There has been much talk of removing the Apaches from Arizona, which, if it were attempted, would produce war; it would be a terrible war too. The Apaches cannot be driven about like cattle. On the other hand, if the policy of the past three years is followed to its proper limits—if the Apaches are treated fairly, and all disturbing causes are removed, as far as possible—there is no reason why these demons of the past should not continue to develop into a quiet, self-sustaining people.

LIST OF AUTHORITIES.

OWING to the great extent of territory covered in this book, it has been thought best to classify the authorities, in order that those who desire to investigate any subject herein discussed may be directed at once to the evidence relating to it. It is hoped that those who are interested in Indian affairs, or in local history, will thus be relieved of needless search through irrelevant documents. In furtherance of this object, many authorities consulted by the author are omitted altogether, only those being mentioned which are considered of material value. The Executive Documents referred to are documents of the House of Representatives. Up to 1861 the same documents will usually be found in the Senate Documents for the same years, as also Senate Documents referred to, prior to 1861, will usually be found in the Executive Documents. Some authorities have been used in almost every chapter; and these, to avoid repetition, will, except as to matters of unusual importance, be mentioned but once, and

IN GENERAL:

Historical and Statistical Information respecting the History, Condition, and Prospects of the Indian Tribes of the United States, etc. Henry R. Schoolcraft. In 5 vols. Philadelphia, 1851–55; also a sixth volume of same, under title Archives of Aboriginal Knowledge, etc. Philadelphia, 1860.

Reports of Generals of the Army, and accompanying documents: 1846–84.

Reports of Commissioners of Indian Affairs, and accompanying documents: 1849–84.

Reports of Pacific Railroad Surveys, Ex. Docs. 1854–55, vol. xi. (in 11 parts); same in Sen. Docs., vol. xiii.; also Supplemental Report, Ex. Docs. 1859–60, vol. xi. (in 2 parts); same in Sen. Docs. 1858–59, vol. xviii.

The Native Races of the Pacific States of North America. Hubert Howe Bancroft. In 5 vols. New York, 1875.

All Ratified Treaties, prior to 1843, are in U. S. Stats. at Large, vol. vii. For those of later date, see vol. ix. U. S. Stats. at Large, and subsequent volumes.

CHAPTER I.
INTRODUCTORY.

Report of Joint Special Committee on Condition of Indian Tribes, under Joint Resolution of March 3, 1865. Washington, 1867.

Report of Special Commission appointed to Investigate the Affairs of Red Cloud Indian Agency. Washington, 1875.

Report of Committee on Indian Affairs on Indian Frauds, House Rep., No. 98, 1872–73.

The Legal Position of the Indian. G. F. Canfield, in *Am. Law Rev.,* vol. xv., p. 21.

The Red Man and White Man in North America, etc. G. E. Ellis. Boston, 1882.

Indian Titles to Land; in Commentaries on American Law, vol. iii., pp. 379–400. James Kent.

CHAPTER II.
THE ACQUISITION OF THE MOUNTAINS.

Thirty Years' View of the American Government. Thos. Benton. New York, 1871.

Commerce of the Prairies, etc. Josiah Gregg. New York, 1844.

Oregon. W. Barrows. Boston and New York, 1884.

A History of Oregon, etc. W. H. Gray. New York, 1870.

Oregon and California in 1848. J. Quinn Thornton. New York, 1849.

The American Statesman: A Political History, etc. Andrew W. Young. New York, 1855.

Discussion of the Oregon Question; in *Congressional Globe,* First Sess. 29th Congress, pp. 44–692, and Appendix.

CHAPTER III.
THE ONE OFFENCE OF THE PUEBLOS.

The History of Mexico and its Wars, etc. John Frost, LL.D. New Orleans, 1882.

The Conquest of New Mexico and California, etc. Gen. P. St. G. Cooke. New York, 1878.

El Gringo; or, New Mexico and her People. W. W. H. Davis. New York, 1857.

Adventures in Mexico and the Rocky Mountains. Geo. F. Ruxton. New York, 1848.

Report of Colonel Price. Ex. Doc. No. 8, 1847–48, pp. 520–538.

CHAPTER IV.
MURDER OF THE MISSIONARIES.

Gray's Oregon (*supra* ch. ii.).

Barrow's Oregon (*supra* ch. ii.).

Protestantism in Oregon: Account of the Murder of Dr. Whitman, etc.

LIST OF AUTHORITIES. 759

Rev. J. B. A. Brouillet, S. J. New York, 1853. Reprinted in Ex. Doc. No. 38, 1857–58.

Portraits of North American Indians (with biographical notes). J. M. Stanley. In Smithsonian Mis. Coll., vol. ii.

The Ely Volume. T. Laurie, D.D. Boston, 1881.

Recollections and Opinions of an Old Pioneer. P. H. Burnett. New York, 1880.

Papers and Correspondence relating to Indian Affairs on the Pacific, from War and Interior Depts. Ex. Doc. No. 76, 1856–57, vol. ix.

CHAPTER V.
THE CURSE OF GOLD.

Mormon Discovery of Gold. Geo. M. Evans. In *Hunt's Merchants' Magazine,* vol. xxxi., p. 385.

Memoirs of Gen. Wm. T. Sherman, by himself. New York, 1875.

Thornton's Oregon and California (*supra* ch. ii.). Appendix.

American Adventure. *Blackwood's Magazine,* vol. lxvii., p. 34.

Discovery of the Yosemite, and the Indian War of 1851, etc. L. H. Bunnell. Chicago, 1880.

Ex. Doc. No. 76, 1856–57 (*supra* ch. iv.).

Correspondence on California Indian Affairs. Sen. Doc. No. 4, Special Sess., 1853.

Correspondence and Reports on California Agencies. Sen. Doc. No. 46, 1859–60 (vol. xi.); also Ex. Docs., 1856–57, vol. ix., pp. 136–145.

Report of Special Agent Bailey. Ex. Docs. 1858–59, vol. ii., pt. 1, pp. 649-657.

The Coast Rangers. J. Ross Browne. In *Harper's Magazine,* vol. xxiii., p. 306.

Mission Indians. Report of J. G. Ames. Ex. Docs. 1873–74, vol. iv., pt. 1, p. 397.

Mission Indians. Report of B. C. Whiting. Ex. Docs. 1871–72, vol. iii., pt. 1, p. 1107.

Mission Indians. Helen Hunt Jackson. In *Century,* vol. xxvi., pp. 1, 199, 511.

CHAPTER VI.
OATMAN FLAT.

Captivity of the Oatman Girls, etc. R. B. Stratton. New York, 1858.

Adventures in the Apache Country. J. Ross Browne. New York, 1874.

Recovery of Miss Oatman. Sen. Doc. No. 66, 1855–56, p. 67.

Personal Narrative of Explorations, etc. J. R. Bartlett. Vol. ii., p. 203. New York, 1854.

Lieutenant Sitgreave's Expedition. Sen. Docs., 1852–53, vol. x.

Notes on the Tonto Apaches. Capt. Charles Smart. In Smithsonian Report for 1867.

Ex. Doc. No. 76, 1856–57 (*supra* ch. iv.).

CHAPTER VII.

THE ROGUE RIVER, YAKIMA, AND KLICKITAT WARS.

Gray's Oregon (*supra* ch. ii.).
Ex. Doc. No. 76, 1856–57 (*supra* ch. iv.).
Military Reports. Sen. Docs. 1856–57, vol. iii., pp. 147–203.
Papers and Correspondence, with affidavits. House Mis. Doc. No. 47, 1858–59, vol. i.
Local Legislative Action. House Mis. Docs. Nos. 64, 77, and 78, 1855–56; also House Mis. Docs. Nos. 71 and 116, 1857–58.
Report of J. Ross Browne on Indian Wars of Oregon. Ex. Doc. No. 38, 1857–58, vol. ix.
Report of J. Ross Browne on Indian Reservations of the Northwest. Ex. Doc. No. 39, 1857–58, vol. ix.

CHAPTER VIII.

ASH HOLLOW AND THE CHEYENNE EXPEDITION.

Correspondence and Evidence concerning Grattan Affair. Sen. Doc. No. 91, 1855–56, vol. xiv.
Harney's Report. Ex. Docs. 1855–56, vol. i., pt. 2, p. 49.
Cooke's Report. Sen. Doc. No. 58, 1856–57, vol. viii.
Sign Language. In First Annual Report of Bureau of Ethnology. Washington, 1881.
Grammar and Dictionary of the Dakota Language. Rev. S. R. Riggs. In Smithsonian Contributions to Knowledge, vol. iv.
Cheyenne Troubles of 1856. Sen. Docs. 1856–57, vol. iii., pp. 106–112.
Sumner's Expedition. Sen. Docs. 1857–58, vol. iii., pp. 96–99.
The Oregon Trail, etc. Francis Parkman. Boston, 1866.
The Plains of the Great West and their Inhabitants. R. I. Dodge. New York, 1877.
City of the Saints, etc. R. F. Burton. New York, 1862.

CHAPTER IX.

LOS NABAJOS.

Report of 1867 on Condition of Indian Affairs (*supra* ch. i.). Appendix.
El Gringo (*supra* ch. iii.).
Historical Sketch. Sen. Docs. 1858–59, vol. i., pp. 540–543.
An Account of the Navajoes of New Mexico. Major Backus. In Schoolcraft's Hist. and Stat. Inf. (*supra*), vol. iv., p. 209.
Military Reports. Sen. Docs. 1858–59, vol. ii., pp. 278–329; also, Sen. Docs. 1859–60, vol. ii., pp. 256–354.
Lieutenant Simpson's Memoir of Washington's Expedition. Sen. Doc. No. 64, 1849–50, vol. xiv.
The Undeveloped West. J. H. Beadle. Cincinnati, 1873.

LIST OF AUTHORITIES. 761

CHAPTER X.
MOUNTAIN MEADOWS.

Correspondence and Evidence from War and Interior Departments. Sen. Doc. No. 42, 1859–60, vol. xi.
Military Reports. Sen. Docs. 1859–60, vol. ii., pp. 121–255.
Trial of Gunnison Murderers. Ex. Docs. 1855–56, vol. i., pt. 2, p. 167.
Emissaries to Indians. Ex. Doc. No. 38, 1857–58.
Emissaries to Indians. Ex. Doc. No. 76, 1856–57.
Emissaries to Indians. Sen. Docs. 1859–60, vol. ii., p. 339.
Judge Cradlebaugh's Account. *Congressional Globe,* 1862–63. Appendix, p. 119.
Mormonism Unveiled, etc. (Autobiography, trials, and confessions of John D. Lee.) W. W. Bishop. St. Louis and Cleveland, 1882.
Life in Utah. J. H. Beadle. Philadelphia, 1870.
Western Wilds and the Men who Redeem Them. J. H. Beadle. Cincinnati, 1878.

CHAPTER XI.
WAR WITH THE SPOKANES, ETC.

Lieutenant Mullan's Topographical Memoir. Ex. Doc. No. 32, 1858–59, vol. x.
Father Hoecken's Account of the Attack on Steptoe. Sen. Docs. 1858–59, vol. ii., p. 127.
Military Reports and Papers. Sen. Docs. 1858–59, vol. ii., pp. 330–415.
Indian Bureau Reports and Papers. Sen. Docs. 1858–59, vol. i., pp. 566–635.

CHAPTER XII.
DEATH TO THE APACHE.

Cooke's Conquest of New Mexico (*supra* ch. iii.).
Gregg's Commerce of the Prairies (*supra* ch. ii.).
Bartlett's Narrative (*supra* ch. vi.).
Report of 1867 on Condition of Indian Tribes (*supra* ch. i.). Appendix.
Life Among the Apaches. John C. Cremony. San Francisco, 1868.
Across America and Asia. Raphael Pumpelly. New York, 1870.
Colyer's Report. Ex. Docs. 1871–72, vol. iii., p. 454.
El Gringo (*supra* ch. iii.).

CHAPTER XIII.
SAND CREEK.

Evidence. Report on Conduct of the War, 1864–65, pt. 3.
Evidence. Report of 1867 on Condition of Indian Tribes (*supra* ch. i.). Appendix.
Evidence. Sen. Doc. No. 26, 1866–67.
Documents from Interior Department concerning Custer's Fight on the Washita. Sen. Doc. No. 13, 1868–69.

Documents from War Department concerning Custer's Fight on the Washita. Sen. Doc. No. 18, 1868–69.
My Life on the Plains. G. A. Custer. New York, 1874.
Sheridan's Troopers on the Border. De B. R. Keim. Philadelphia, 1870.
New Colorado and the Santa Fé Trail. A. A. Hayes. New York, 1880.
A Century of Dishonor. Helen Hunt Jackson. New York, 1881.
The Indian and White Man. Rev. D. W. Risher. Indianapolis, 1880.

CHAPTER XIV.
CAÑON DE CHELLY AND BOSQUE REDONDO.

Lieutenant Simpson's Memoir (*supra* ch. ix.).
Beadle's Undeveloped West. (*supra* ch. ix.).
Report of 1867 on Condition of Indian Tribes (*supra* ch. i.). Appendix.
Carson's Report. MS., War Department.
Pioneer Life and Frontier Adventure. D. C. Peters. Boston, 1881.
Report of Captain Walker. Sen. Docs. 1859–60, vol. ii., p. 316.

CHAPTER XV.
FORT PHIL KEARNEY.

Papers and Correspondence from War and Interior Departments, including Report of Special Commissioners. Sen. Doc. No. 13, 1867.
Military Reports: Report of Sec. of War, 1867, pp. 31–61.
Dodge's Plains of the Great West (*supra* ch. viii.).
Absaraka, Home of the Crows. Mrs. M. I. Carrington. Philadelphia, 1869.
Absaraka, Land of Massacre. Col. H. B. Carrington. Philadelphia, 1878.

CHAPTER XVI.
PUNISHING THE PIEGANS.

Historical Sketch. Schoolcraft's Hist. and Stat. Inf. (*supra*), vol. v., p. 179.
Early Relations to U. S. Sen. Docs. 1858–59, vol. xviii.
Papers and Evidence from War Department. Ex. Doc. No. 269, 1869–70, vol. xii.; also, Sen. Doc. No. 49, 1869–70.
Baker's Report. Ex. Doc. No. 197, 1869–70, vol. vii.
Papers and Correspondence from Interior Department. Ex. Doc. No. 185, 1869–70, vol. vii.
Congressional Globe, 1869–70, pt. 2, pp. 1575–1599.
Adventures of Captain Bonneville, etc. Washington Irving. New York, 1864.

CHAPTER XVII.
THE TRAGEDY OF THE LAVA BEDS.

Papers and Correspondence from War and Interior Departments, including Proceedings of Military Commission. Ex. Doc. No. 122, 1873–74, vol. ix.
Meacham's Report. Ex. Docs. 1873–74, vol. iv., p. 442.

LIST OF AUTHORITIES. 763

Gillem's Report. Sen. Doc. No. 1, 1877 (bound with Docs. of 1876–77).
Cost of War. Ex. Doc. No. 131, 1874–75, vol. xv.
The Modocs. Stephen Powers. In *Overland Monthly,* vol. x., p. 535.

CHAPTER XVIII.
THE LITTLE BIG HORN.

Custer's Expedition to the Black Hills. Sen. Doc. No. 32, 1874–75.
Jenney's Expedition to the Black Hills. Sen. Doc. No. 51, 1875–76.
Disturbances leading to the War. Sen. Doc. No. 52, 1875–76.
Invasions by Miners. Sen. Doc. No. 2, 1875 (bound with Docs. of 1874–75).
Report of Commission to Treat for Black Hills. Ex. Docs. 1875–76, vol. iv., pt. 1, p. 686.
Report of Commission to Treat with Sitting Bull in Canada. Ex. Docs. 1877–78, vol. viii., p. 719.
Terry's Report. Sen. Doc. No. 81, 1875–76.
Sheridan's Report. Ex. Docs. 1876–77, vol. ii., pt. 1, p. 439.
Movements of Troops. Reports of General of the Army for 1876 and 1877.
Autobiography of Sitting Bull. *Harper's Weekly,* July 29, 1876.
Record of Engagements with Hostile Indians, etc. Lt.-gen. P. H. Sheridan. Chicago, 1882.
A Popular Life of Gen. George A. Custer. F. Whittaker, New York, 1877.
Dodge's Plains of the Great West (*supra* ch. viii.). Introduction.

CHAPTER XIX.
JOSEPH'S NEZ PERCÉS.

Origin of the War. Report Sec. of War for 1875, vol. i., pp. 124–131; also, Report Sec. of Interior for 1875, vol. i., p. 762; also Report Sec. of War for 1876, vol. i., pp. 91, 92; also Report Sec. of Interior for 1876, vol. i., p. 449.
Report of Commission to Treat with Joseph. Ex. Docs. 1877–78, vol. viii., p. 607.
Report of General Howard. Report Sec. of War, 1877, vol. i., pp. 119–133.
Reports of Gibbon, Sturgis, and Miles. Report Sec. of War, 1877, vol. i., pp. 68–77.
Report of General Sherman. Report Sec. of War, 1877, vol. i., pp. 7–15.
Joseph's Statement. *North American Review,* vol. cxxviii., p. 412.
Howard's Reply. *North American Review,* vol. cxxix., p. 53.
Nez Percé Joseph, etc. Gen. O. O. Howard. Boston, 1881.
The Return of the Nez Percés. Rev. G. L. Deffenbaugh. In *The Foreign Missionary,* July, 1885, p. 71.
Lindsley's Report. In Minutes of Eighth Annual Session of the Synod of the Columbia, p. 71. Seattle, W. T., 1884.

CHAPTER XX.
WHITE RIVER AGENCY.

Historical Sketch. Major Powell. House Mis. Doc. No. 86, 1873–74.

Fight near Poncha Pass. Ex. Docs. 1855–56, vol. i., pt. 2, p. 49.

Brunot's Council. Ex. Docs. 1873–74, vol. iv., pt. 1, pp. 451–481.

Ute Affairs, 1873–79. Sen. Doc. No. 29, 1879–80, vol. i.

Papers and Correspondence from Interior Department. Sen. Doc. No. 31, 1879–80, vol. i.

Report of Special Commissioners Hatch and Adams. Ex. Doc. No. 83, 1879–80, vol. xxiv.

Evidence before Committee on Indian Affairs. House Mis. Doc. No. 38, 1879–40, vol. iv.

CHAPTER XXI.
CRUELTY, PITY, AND JUSTICE.

Colyer's Report (*supra* ch. xii.).

Howard's Report. Ex. Docs. 1873–74, vol. iii., p. 533.

Reports from Department Commanders of Arizona and New Mexico, accompanying Reports of Generals of the Army, 1872–84.

Reports from Agencies of New Mexico and Arizona, accompanying Reports of Commissioners of Indian Affairs, 1872–84.

Message of Governor Safford for 1875. Journal of Eighth Legislature of Arizona.

INDEX TO VOLUMES I & II

ABBOTT, J. B., withdraws troops from Uncompahgré Park, 687.
Absaroka, same as Crows, 479.
Adams, Gen. Charles, goes to Utes to release captives, 710; brings in captives, 713; statement as to urging withdrawal of troops, 713, 714.
Ahnahaways, who are, 379.
Ahuutupuwit, Ute warrior, captures Mrs. Price, 705; surrender of, demanded, 714.
Albert, Indian boy, witnesses Mountain Meadow massacre, 298; induced to lie about it, 319.
Alcatraz Island, Modocs sent to, 582; Apaches sent to. 744, 752.
Alcedo, Antonio de, estimate of population of California, 131.
Alder Gulch, mines of, 478.
Alexander, Colonel, ordered from Utah by Brigham Young, 288, 289.
Allakaweah, who are, 379.
Allen, Lieut. J. K., death of, 352; mentioned 354.
Allen, Agent R. A., reports starvation of Piegans, 537, 538.
Almy, Lieutenant, killed, 732.
Alvord, Major, quoted, 105.
Always Ready. *See* Giannahtah.
American Horse, Sioux chief, killed, 625.
American Indian Aid Association, intercedes for Modocs, 581.
Ames, John G., reports on Mission Indians, 149.
Amoroko, Snake chief, band of, 276.
Ankatosh, Ute chief, mentioned, 689.
Antelope, Ute warrior, aids in murder of Eskridge, 703; aids in massacre, 704; surrender of, demanded, 714.
Anthony, Major, opinion of Indians at Sand Creek, 416, 417; takes command at Fort Lyon, 418; official report of, 419; sends Cheyennes away, 420; Cheyennes defy, 421; advice to Chivington, 422.
Antonio Garra, Yuma chief, conspiracy of, 180.
Apache Cañon, Kearny at, 49, 50; fight at, 407.
Apache Mohaves, same as Yampais, 358.
Apache Pass, fight at, 380; resistance to Carleton at, 382.
Apache Yumas, same as Hualapais, 358.
Apaches, location and origin of, 82, 245; damage by, to Mexican settlements, 159; common opinions of, 356; divisions of, 357; names of, 358; troubles of, with Mexicans, 359; troubles of, with traders and trappers, 360; massacres of, 361; scalp-bounty for, 362; meet General Kearny, 365; meet Bartlett's party, 366; slavery among, 367, 368, 372, 373; troubles with Bartlett's party, 373; try to drive out miners, 374; massacre White's party, 377; Mexicans attack, 378; not protected by intercourse laws, 379; hostilities of, at beginning of rebellion, 380, 381; Californians defeat, 382; operations against, 383; at Bosque Redondo, 384; Carleton's campaign against, 385, 386; extermination theory tried on, 389, 391; effect of extermination policy, 390; troubles at Bosque Redondo, 392; failure of extermination policy, 395; extermination policy continued, 717, 718; establishment at Camp Grant, 719, 720; massacre of, at Camp Grant, 721–725; peace policy tried, 726, 727; failure of peace policy, 728, 729; Crook's policy inaugurated, 729, 730; features of Crook's policy, 731; success of same, 732; removal policy inaugurated, 733, 734; effects of removals, 735–743; hostilities in 1880-82, 743–747; Crook returns to, 747, 748; renews his policy, 749; renegades brought in, 750–752; success of Crook's policy, 753, 754; causes of trouble remaining, 754, 755.
Applegate, Jesse, appointed on Modoc commission, 559; removed, 560.
Applegate, Oliver, appointed on Modoc commission, 559; removed, 560.
Arapahoes. *See* Cheyennes and Arapahoes.
Archuleta, Col. Diego, bought up by Magoffin, 50; conspiracy of, 61.
Arivapas, Apaches, who are, 357; location of, 358; capture Inez Gonzales, 366; come to Camp Grant, 719, 720; Camp Grant massacre, 721–725; attack on, 725; reservation made for, 727; sent to San Carlos, 730.
Arizona, description of southwestern part, 151, 152; established as a territory, 157, 158; description of northeastern part, 244, 245; Apache warfare in 356; a refuge for criminals, 362; Indian slavery in, 372, 373; overrun by Apaches, 380, 381; gold discoveries in, 385; operations against Apaches in, 385, 386; put in Department of California, 391; progress of, 392, 395; press of, defends Camp Grant massacre, 724, 725; threatens Colyer, 726; Crook's policy inaugurated in, 729; success of same, 732; removal policy tried in, 733; results of removals, 734–743; changes of 1882 in, 747, 748; Crook's policy renewed, 749, 750; Apache renegades brought in, 752; Geronimo's outbreak, 753; remaining sources of Apache troubles, 754, 755.
Armijo, General, commands Mexican troops in New Mexico, 49; bought up by Magoffin, 50; retires to Mexico, 51.
Arrow, the. *See* Ouray.
Arroyo Hondo, massacre at, 66–68.
Arshay, Apache chief, revolt of, 747.
Ashburton treaty, mention of 41.
Ash Hollow, location of, 234; fight at, 235; criticism of fight at, 236; fight at, praised on frontier, 433, 434.
Assinaboines, location of, 81.
Astoria, sketch of history of, 32, 33.

Athabascans, related to Navahos, Apaches, and Umpquas, 82, 245, 246.
Atsina, same as Arapahoes, 221.
Augur, General, succeeds General Cooke, 503; member Board of Peace Commissioners, 716.
BABBITT, A. W., Secretary of Utah, killed by Indians, 239.
Babcock, Lieutenant, defeats Tontos, 730.
Backus, Major, quoted, 254, 255.
Bacon, Lieutenant, sent to cut off Nez Percés, 655
Bacon, Special Agent, reports on California reservations, 137, 138.
Baillie-Grohman, quoted, 226.
Baker, Col. E. M., sent against Piegans, 528; recovers horses from Bloods; 529; report of, 530; probable facts of fight, 531; criticism of fight, 532; Sheridan's orders to, 533; supported by army officers, 534.
Bald Head. *See* Hushhushcute.
Baldwin, Lieutenant, defeats Sitting Bull, 626.
Baliran, Sutler, killed, 615; murderer of, detected, 616.
Bannocks, who are, 275, 276.
Barncho, Modoc warrior, takes part in murder of commissioners, 569; tried, 580; convicted, 581; sentence of, commuted, 582.
Barstow, A. C., member of Nez Percés Commission, 646; responsibility of, 672.
Bartlett, J. R., releases slaves of Mimbreños, 366; hostilities to, 373; leaves Copper Mines, 374.
Bateman, William, aids John D. Lee at Mountain Meadows, 295.
"Baylor's Babes," fight of, with Colorado troops, 407.
Beale, Superintendent, estimate of Indians in California, 130, 131.
Bear, the, Sioux chief. *See* Mahto Iowa.
Bear Chief, Piegan chief, becomes hostile, 524; camp of, attacked, 528.
Bear Rivers, Utes, same as Yampas, 681.
Bear Spring, treaty at, 256; fight at, 263.
Beaubien, Narcissus, murdered by Pueblos, 65.
Beckwith, Jim, guides Colorado troops, 396; a chief of the Crows, 479.
Belknap investigation, Custer's connection with, 601, 602.
Bell, Lieutenant, defeats Jicarillas, 377.
Benedict, —, shoots at Nez Percés Indians, 636.
Bennett, Captain, recommends native police for Navahos, 472.
Bennett, Ute warrior, Douglas refuses to surrender, 696.
Bent, Charles, Governor of New Mexico, character of, 152; murdered by Pueblos, 62, 63; buried at Santa Fé, 78.
Bent, George, writes letter for Cheyenne chiefs, 411; believed to be a rebel emissary, 425.
Bent's Fort, described, 52.
Benteen, Captain, sent ahead by Custer, 608; report of, 609; besieged, 610; estimate of number of Indians, 620; not in fault, 624; cuts off Nez Percés herd, 657.
Benton, Thomas, calls attention to value of Oregon, 46; regrets discovery of gold in California, 124, 125; mention of, 241.
Beswick, Nate, representations of to Modocs, 559.
Bewley, Lorinda, captured by Cayuses, 96; given to Five Crows, 99; deposition of, 113–115.
Big Bill, Pi-ede chief, at Mountain Meadow massacre, 293.
Big Thunder, Nez Percé chief, orders Joseph away, 631.

Bingham, Lieutenant, killed by Sioux, 491.
Birtsell, Dr. C. S., testimony of, concerning Sand Creek, 416.
Blackfeet, location of, 31; who are, 509; tribal organization of, 510; reputation of, 511; cause of reputation, 512; torture of, by Flatheads, 513; generosity of, 514; location of, in 1853, 515; treat with Stevens, 516; peaceful relations of, 517, 518; location in 1869, 528; neglect of, 536; sufferings of, 537; starvation of, 538; right of, to aid, 541; helplessness of, 542; harassed by Sioux, 593. *See also* Piegans and Bloods.
Black Foot, Sioux warrior, mistreats Mrs. Ewbanks, 428.
Blackfoot Sioux, who are, 231; treaty of 1866 with, 481; on the war-path, 500; not related to Blackfoot nation, 510 (*note*); location of, in 1876, 591; at war, 618; make peace, 628.
Black Hills, held sacred by Indians, 585; gold believed to exist in, 586; gold discovered, 587; invasion of, 588; Indians refuse to sell, 589, 590; Indian title to, extinguished, 628.
Black Jim, Modoc warrior, refuses to surrender, 553; meets commissioners, 567; shoots at Meacham, 569; arraigned, 579; tried, 580; sentenced, 581; executed, 582.
Black Kettle, Cheyenne chief, commands Cheyennes at Sand Creek, 408; admits hostility, 411; considered friendly, 416; escapes from Sand Creek, 417; band of, confused with Little Raven's Arapahoes, 418–420, 430; display of flag by, 422; claims authority over Dog Soldiers, 431; surprised by Custer, 440.
Black Knife, Apache chief, meets Bartlett's party, 366.
Black Tigers, Sioux, who were, 591.
Blair, Sam, representations of, to Modocs, 559.
Blanchet, Jesuit bishop, arrives in Oregon, 93; baptizes Wailatpu murderers, 102; treatment of Miss Bewley, 113–116.
Blood atonement, Mormon doctrine of, 284, 285, 290, 298, 313.
Bloods, who are, 509; treat with Stevens, 516; hostilities by, 518; steal horses, 522; encouraged by Hudson's Bay Company, 523; location in 1869, 528; surrender stolen horses, 529. *See also* Blackfeet and Piegans.
Bloody Point, fight at, 192; massacre of Modocs at, 193.
Bloody Tanks, massacre of Apaches at, 389.
Bluewater, fight on. *See* Ash Hollow.
Blunt, General, ambushed by Cheyennes and Arapahoes, 412, 444; co-operates with Carleton, 423, 424.
Board of Indian Commissioners, importance of, 15; should call for aid for destitute tribes, 538; organization of, 716.
Bogus Charley, Modoc warrior, carries message to commissioners, 565; accompanies Riddle to council, 567; assaults Dr. Thomas. 569; betrays Captain Jack, 576; witness at trial, 580; becomes chief. 583.
Bogy, Indian commissioner, did not believe in hostile Indians, 480; ignorance of Indian affairs, 485; explanation of Fetterman massacre, 501, 502.
Bolen, Indian agent, murdered by Yakimas, 204; murderers of, remain at large, 333; murderers punished, 352.
Bonito, Apache chief, returns to reservation, 752.
Bordeaux, trader, declines to accept submission of Cheyennes and Arapahoes, 230.
Boreman, Judge, sentences John D. Lee, 319.
Bosque Redondo, Mescaleros sent to, 383, 384; troubles at, 392; selected as a reservation

by General Carleton, 452; Navahos depredate at, 453; Navahos sent to, 464; Indians quarrel at, 465; agriculture fails at, 466; description of, 467; suffering at, 468, 469; Carleton's mistake, 470; decided a failure, 471; Navahos removed from, 472.
Boston Charley, Modoc warrior, at council, 567; shoots Dr. Thomas, 569; surrenders, 577; tried, 580; convicted, 581; executed, 582.
"Bostons," Indian name for Americans, 102.
Bowpiths, Sioux, same as Sans Arcs, 231.
Bozeman, Montana, settlement of, 478.
Bozeman Route, desirability of road by, 478, 479; Indians oppose road, 482; right to road, 484, 485, 507; road abandoned, 508.
Bracito, battle at, 51.
Brady, Joseph, carries message for Ouray, 706; opinion as to the pictures, 712.
Brannan, Samuel, Mormon bishop of California, 119; reports receipts of gold, 121.
Brewer, Dr. Charles, quoted, 290, 307–309.
Briesly, Dr., testimony concerning Camp Grant massacre, 721, 722.
Brooks, Major, negro servant of, killed by a Navaho, 262; demands murderer, 262, 263; expedition of, 268.
Brouillet, Father, quoted, 93; arrives at Wailatpu, 99; objects to Indian testimony, 109; statement of, 109–113; Miss Bewley's account of, 113–115.
Brown, Capt. F.H., volunteers with Fetterman's party 491; body found, 495; probable suicide of, 496, 499.
Browne, J. Ross, quoted, 107; action of, criticised, 333; opinion of Stevens's treaties, 334.
Brulés, Sioux, designation of, in sign language, 225; who are, 231; part of, in Grattan massacre, 232; got to war, 233; defeated at Ash Hollow, 235; submission of, 236; treaty of 1866 with, 481; remain friendly, 483, 484; some hostile, 500; location in 1876, 591; at war, 618; make peace, 628.
Brunot, Felix, treats with Utes, 683; Ouray's statement to, 684.
Buchanan, President, promotes General Harney, 238; quoted, 286.
Buffalo, destruction of, 2, 3, 4; belief of Indians as to permanence of, 243; extermination of, 537, 538.
Buffalo eaters, who are, 275.
Bull Bear, Cheyenne chief, desires to treat, 408; friendliness of, 411; in council at Denver, 412; a sub-chief to Black Kettle, 431.
Bunnell, Dr., account of Yosemite war, 133, 134; quoted, 135.
Burgwin, Captain, killed at Pueblo de Taos, 77.
Burke, Col. Martin, furnishes goods to Francisco, 181; letter to Olive Oatman, 183; reports her recovery, 184.
Burns, Captain, captures Yampais, 730.
Burnt Thighs. See Brulés.
Byers, W. N., Meeker's letter to, 698, 699.

CABALLO EN PELO, Yuma chief, massacres Gallatin party, 362.
Cabanisse, Dr., negotiates with Modocs, 577.
Cache Valley Indians, who are, 277.
Cadété. See Giannahtah.
Cajuenches, same as Cuchans, 358.
Calhoun, Captain, killed at Little Big Horn, 611; a brother-in-law of General Custer, 623.
Calhoun, Governor, treats with Navahos, 257, 258; releases slaves, 368; treats with Jicarillas, 377.
California, conquered, 47; discovery of gold in 118–125; early settlers of, 125–127; Indians of, 127–129; first Indian troubles of, 129, 133–135; native population of, 130–133; reservations of, 135–137; Indian ring in, 137, 138; barbarous treatment of Indians of, 138–142; Mission Indians of, 142–150; Indians in northern part of, 190, 191; sends troops against Modocs, 192; Indian titles in, 194; Mormons incite Indians of, 281; Mormons recalled from. 286; criminals from, in Arizona 362; slavery in, 371; volunteers from, in New Mexico, 382, 383; Southern sympathy in, 404; pay to militia of, in Modoc war, 578.
Calispels. See Pend d'Oreilles.
Campbell, Captain, quoted, 293.
Camp Grant, establishment of Apaches at, 719. 720; massacre at, 721–723; attempted defence of, 724; evil effects of, 725, 726, 729.
Camp Yuma, location of, 158; Lorenzo Oatman, at, 179.
Canby, Gen. E. R. S., drives back Texans, 382, 407; relieved by Carleton, 383; fight at Valverde, 404; campaign against Navahos, 451; sketch of, 550; recommends separate reservation for Modocs, 552; made a member of Modoc commission, 560; opinion as to last council, 565; refuses to deceive Modocs, 566; goes to council, 567; speech at council, 568; killed, 569; body recovered, 570; indignation at murder of, 571.
Cannon, George Q., denies guilt of Mormons at Mountain Meadows, 314.
Cannon, Lieutenant, testimony of, concerning Sand Creek, 434.
Cañon Alsada described, 455, 456; entered by Colonel Miles, 458.
Cañoncito Bonito described, 258.
Cañon Creek, fight at, 657.
Cañon de Chelly reached by troops, 256; partially explored, 257, explored, 265; expedition against Navahos in, 454; extent of, 455; description of, 456; cliff-houses in, 457; explorations of, 458; Carson marches to, 461; operations at, 462; misstatement concerning, 463; results of operations at, 464, 465.
Cañon del Trigo, location of, 456; entered by Lieutenant Simpson, 458.
Capotes, Utes, who are, 277; included in Southern Utes, 681.
Captain Billy, Tabequache chief, mentioned, 689.
Captain Jack, Modoc chief, troubles of, at Klamath reservation, 545; leaves reservation, 546; conduct of, 549; attacked by Captain Jackson, 552; takes no part in murder of settlers, 553; goes to Lava Beds, 554; joined by Hot Creek Indians, 559; message of, to commissioners, 562; desires peace, 563; decides for war, 564; saves Judge Steele's life, 565; meets commissioners, 567; speech at council. 568; kills General Canby, 569; leaves Lava Beds, 576; captured. 577; Indians call him insane, 578; arraigned, 579; tried, 580, 581; executed, 582.
Carasco, General, attack of, on Apaches, 359
Carey, Captain, accompanies Carson at Cañon de Chelly, 461; sent through the cañon, 462
Carleton, General, quoted, 125; erects monument at Mountain Meadows, 309; advances to New Mexico, 382; operations against Mescaleros, 383; sends Mescaleros to Bosque Redondo, 384; protects Arizona miners, 385; result of operations in Arizona, 386; infatuated with Bosque reservation project, 392; instructs Carson not to make peace, 423; decides to remove Navahos to Bosque Redondo, 452; operations against Navahos,

453, 454; quoted, 458; mistake of, in number of Navahos, 465; objects to interference of Steck, 467, 468; comforts the Navahos, 469; persists in Bosque Redondo project, 470.
Carr, Colonel, attacked by Apaches, 744.
Carrington, Col. H. B., sent to Powder River country, 483; locates Fort Phil Kearney, 486; constructs fort, 487; neglects scouting, 489; asks for reinforcements, 490; orders of, disobeyed, 499; removed, 500; misrepresented, 501; exonerated, 502; faults of, 503, 504.
Carson, Kit, saves Fremont's party, 191; guides dragoons against Jicarillas, 377; accepts surrender of Mescaleros, 383; commands at Fort Canby, 454; expedition of, to Cañon de Chelly, 461; immediate results of expedition, 462; misstatement concerning, 463; ulterior results of expedition, 464; sent against Comanches, 465; treats with Utes, 681.
Casas Grandas, what are, 54–57; no tradition of occupancy by Navahos, 245.
Cascades, the, described, 211; massacre at, 212.
Casino, Klickitat chief, splendor of, 201, 202, 371.
Catlin, George, meets Nez Percés messengers, 36, 37.
Cayuses, location of, 86; derivation of name, 86 (note); religious dissensions of, 90–93; massacre by, at Wailatpu, 93–100; punishment of, 101; treaty with, 217; treaty ratified, 355; removal of, abandoned, 645.
Chan-Deisi, Apache chief, attacks Agent Larrabee, 731; killed, 732.
Chandler, Special Agent, statement concerning Sioux treaty of 1876, 483.
Chapitone, Navaho chief, makes treaty, 257; murdered, 258.
Chase, Samuel, appointed on Modoc commission, 559; removed, 560.
Chato, Apache chief, raid of, 750; returns to reservation, 752.
Chavannugh. See Shavano.
Cheis. See Cochise.
Chemakane Mission, location of, 87; abandonment of, 341.
Chemehueves, location of, 157; present state of, 187.
Cherokees, in Confederate army, 424.
Cherry, Lieutenant, at Milk Creek, 700.
Chesterfield House, whiskey sold to Indians at, 515.
Cheyennes and Arapahoes, fraudulent estimates of, 16; location of, 81; treaty of 1851 with, 220; early history of, 221, 222; separations of, 222; language of, 223; designations of, in sign language, 225; government and police of, 227; first troubles with, 229, 230; hostilities of 1856, 238, 239; Sumner's expedition against, 239, 240; become peaceable, 240; treatment of, by Colorado settlers, 241, 242, 429; treaty with, 423; attack on, at Sand Creek, 396–401; sketch of hostilities, 408; effect of hostilities on whites, 409, 410; admit hostilities, 411–416; proofs of hostilities, 416, 417; not promised protection, 417–422; instructions to punish, 423; sympathy with rebels, 424, 425; treachery of, 426; brutality of, 427–430; report of Congressional committee,430–433; misrepresentations of Sand Creek affair, 433–437; treaty of 1865 with, 437; go to war, 438; supplies issued to, 439; defeated by Custer, 440; defended by Wynkoop, 443; Chivington's opinion of, 444, 445; aid Sioux against Crows, 479; aid in Fetterman massacre, 500; location of northern band in 1876, 591; at Rawlin's Springs massacre, 595; removal of northern band, 743; Crook's opinion of the removal, 748.
Chickasaws, in Confederate army, 424.
Chief Joseph. See Joseph, Young.
Chihuahua, policy of, to Apaches, 359; offers scalp-bounty, 360; results of scalp-bounty, 361–363; joins United States in fighting Apaches, 385, 386; slaves from, sold in New Mexico, 447.
Chimoneth, Cascade chief, hanged, 212.
Chinaman, Ute warrior, Douglas refuses to surrender, 696.
Chinooks, location of, 82; sacrifice of slaves by, 372.
Chiricahuas, Apaches, who are, 357; treachery to, 380; go to war, 381; fight Carleton, 382; operations against, 385, 386, 391; failure of extermination policy with, 395; refuse to be removed, 727; Coyoteros take refuge with, 735; removal of, attempted, 736, 738; cause of attempt, 737; war results, 738; effects of attempt, 742, 743; come to White Mountain reservation, 743; leave reservation, 747; raids of, 750, 751; brought in by General Crook, 752; Geronimo's outbreak, 753.
Chivington, Col. J. M., attack on Cheyennes at Sand Creek, 396–401; statement of number killed, 401; early life of, 402; enters army, 403; fight at Apache Cañon, 407; not fairly tried, 417; did not promise Cheyennes protection, 420; justification of, 422; instructions to, 423; considers Indians allies of the South, 425; report of Congressional committee on, 430–433; misrepresentation of Sand Creek, 433–437; attacked in treaty, 437; moves to Ohio, 443; address of, in Denver, 444, 445; returns to Colorado, 445.
Choate, Senator, opposes Oregon land donation bill, 42.
Choctaws, in Confederate army, 424.
Chowchillas, conquered, 131.
Chuntz, Apache chief, killed, 732.
Cibicu Indians, outbreak of, 747.
Claiborne, Capt. Thomas, report of, on Bosque Redondo, 466, 467.
Clarke, Gen. N. S., objects to Mormon influence, 332; opposes Stevens's treaties, 332; Indian messages to, 335; sends messengers to Indians, 341.
Clarke, Gen. William, Indian Superintendent at St. Louis, 36. See also Lewis and Clarke.
Clarke, M., murder of, 524, 527.
Clay, Henry, defeated by Polk, 47.
Clearwater, fight on, 649, 650.
Cliff-houses described, 58; in Cañon de Chelly, 457.
Clymer, Heister, involves Custer in Belknap investigation, 601.
Cochees. See Chiricahuas.
Cochinay, Apache chief, killed, 732.
Cochise, Apache chief, who was, 357; relation to Mangas Colorado, 374; escape of, 380; resists Carleton, 382; leaves Cañada Alamosa, 727; death of, 736.
Cocopahs, description of, 155; attacked by Mohaves, 177.
Cœur d'Alêne Mission described, 348; treaty at, 351.
Cœur d'Alênes, location of, 81; friendly before 1858, 324; menace Steptoe's command, 325; attack it, 326; fight with, 328; admissions of wrong, 330; causes of discontent, 331–336; defiance of, 342; Colonel

Wright marches against, 343; defeated at Four Lakes, 344; sue for peace, 348; country of, 348, 351; make treaty, 351.
Cok. *See* Slolox.
Colley, Major, Cheyenne chiefs' letter to, 411.
Collins, Superintendent, treats with Navahos, 451.
Colorado, early settlement of, 219, 220; discovery of gold in, 240–242; treatment of Indians by settlers, 241, 242; Indian slavery in, 371, 372; volunteers from, in New Mexico, 382, 404–407; at Sand Creek, 403; Indian troubles during the Rebellion, 408–411; Cheyenne and Arapahoe hostilities in, 411–416; loyal feeling in, 424, 425; cause of bitterness of people to Indians, 426–430; reunion of old settlers, 443–445; stands by Sand Creek, 445; desire in, for removal of Utes, 676–680; early Ute troubles in, 680, 681; San Juan excitement, 682–684; invasion of Uncompahgré Park, 665–687; conduct of Utes, 692, 693; conduct of whites, 694, 695; Utes removed from, 714, 715.
Colorado River Indians, who are, 187.
Colorow, White River chief, mentioned, 690; meets Thornburgh, 699.
Colville mines discovered, 204; trouble near, 324.
Colwell,—, settles on Lapwai reservation, 641.
Colyer, Vincent, misrepresents Lieutenant Pease and General Sully, 531, 532; sent to Arizona, 726; establishes Apaches, 727; failure of plans of, 729.
Comanches, location of, 81; in Confederate army, 424.
Concentration. *See* Removal and Concentration.
Condé, General, forwards released slaves to Mexico, 367.
Congiato, Father. Joset's letter to, 329; goes to Indians as mediator, 341.
Connelly, Governor, treats with Navahos, 451; calls out militia, 452.
Cook, Colonel, killed at Little Big Horn, 612; probably survived others, 615.
Cooke, Gen. P. St. G., accompanies Magoffin, 49; commands Mormon battalion, 51; at Ash Hollow, 234, 235; quoted, 236; Carrington asks reinforcements from, 486; blamed for Fetterman massacre, 502; relieved, 503; fault of, 504.
"Cooper's Indian" not purely mythical, 24.
Copper Mine Apaches, same as Mimbreños, 357.
Coupes-Gorges, same as Pumas, 357.
Cowan's party attacked by Nez Percés, 655.
Cow Island, fight at, 658.
Cox, Ross, quoted, 512, 513.
Coyoteros, Apaches, threaten the Oatmans, 160; who are, 357; location of, 358; permitted to leave Bosque Redondo, 470; settled at White Mountain reservation, 719; assist troops, 731; removal of, to San Carlos, 734; effects of removal, 735, 736; return to White Mountain reservation, 749; good conduct of, 752.
Cardlebaugh, Judge John. gives date of Mountain Meadow massacre, 299; investigates massacre, 312; Hamlin's story to, 319.
Cramer, Lieutenant, testimony of, concerning Sand Creek, 434.
Cranston, Lieutenant, killed in Lava Beds, 573.
Crazy Horse, Ogallalla Chief, who was, 591; fight with Reynolds, 597; controversy concerning fight, 598; fight with Crook, 604; number of Indians supposed to be with, 617; at Little Big Horn, 618; leaves Sitting Bull, 625; invites Sitting Bull to join him, 626; killed, 627.
Cremony, Colonel, statement as to Apache burials, 356, 357; Apache slaves take refuge with, 366; services of, 384.
Crittenden, Lieutenant, killed at Little Big Horn, 611.
Crook, General, opposed to Ponca removal, 21; expedition against Sioux, 596, 598; second expedition, 601; fight with Sioux, 603, 604; mistake as to number of Sioux hostiles, 617, 618; further operations against Sioux, 625, 626; opinion of Apaches, 728; inaugurates his policy, 729, 730; features of policy, 731; success of policy, 732, 733; goes to Department of the Platte, 734; returns to Arizona, 747; opinion of Cheyenne removal. 748; restores harmony in Arizona, 749; brings in renegades, 750–752; success of policy, 752; Geronimo's outbreak, 753; difficulties to be encountered, 754, 755.
Crow Creek agency, fare of Indians at, 17.
Crow Dog, Sioux chief, trial of, for murder, 10.
Crow Feather, Sioux chief, opinion of Black Hills; .589, 590.
Crows, location of, 81; designation of, in sign language, 225; description of, 479; harass Gros Ventres of the North. 510; harassed by Sioux, 593, 594; complaints of, 595, 596.
Crucifixion by Indians, case of, 178.
Cuchans. *See* Pumas.
Cuchillo Negro. *See* Black Knife.
Cullen, Special Commissioner, attempts to enforce law at Fort Benton, 522.
Cummings, Governor, reception of, in Utah, 315.
Curly, Crow scout, escape of, at Little Big Horn, 612; statement of, 615.
Curly-headed Doctor, Modoc chief, band of, 546: accused of lawlessness, 549: depredations by, 553.
Curtis, General, sends troops against Cheyennes, 412; instructions to Chivington, 422, 423; opinion of hostiles, 424; statement as to effect of flight at Sand Creek, 433, 434.
Curtis, Judge - Advocate, exculpates Captain Jack, 553; conducts trial of Modocs, 581; reports on Barncho and Slolox, 581, 582.
Custer, Boston, killed at Little Big Horn, 612, 623.
Custer, Capt. T., killed at Little Big Horn, 612, 623.
Custer, General, estimate of Indian population, 1; campaign of 1867, 438; surprises Black Kettle's camp, 440; writes up Cheyenne affairs, 443: expedition to Black Hills, 587, 588; testifies in Belknap investigation, 601; Grant's treatment of, 602; marches against Sioux, 603; starts to Little Big Horn, 607; fight on Little Big Horn, 608–615; arrest of Rain-in-the-Face, 616; mistake as to force of Sioux, 617, 618; drawn into a trap, 619–622; not in fault, 623, 624.
Cut-arms, same as Cheyennes, 225.

DAKOTAS. *See* Sioux.
Dame. Colonel, orders Mountain Meadow massacre, 295; retains standing in Mormon Church, 315.
Davidson, Lieutenant, defeated by Jicarillas, 377.
Davis. Gen. J. C., takes command against Modocs, 574; decides to execute Modocs, 578, 579.
Davis, Inspector-general, holds council with Apaches, 390, 391.
Davis, Superintendent, reports on condition of Navahos, 471.

770   INDEX.

Deaf mutes, communicate with Indians by signs, 223.
Deffenbaugh, Rev. G. L., quoted, 671.
Delano, Secretary, definition of peace policy, 19.
Delgadito, Apache chief, treachery of, 373, 374.
Delgado, Felipe, reports on condition of Navahos, 470.
Del Shay, Tonto chief, captured, 730; killed, 732.
Democratic party, favors annexation of Texas, 29; favors occupation of Oregon, 42; diversity of sentiment in, 43.
Denver, treatment of Indians by people of, 242.
De Rudio, Lieutenant, escapes at Little Big Horn, 611.
De Smet, Father, fears conversion of Indians to Protestantism, 90.
De Trobriand, General, quoted, 524; report of Baker's fight, 531, 534; opinion of Piegan hostility, 535.
Des Chutes, location of, 86; defeated by Captain Lee, 100; Stevens's treaty with, 217; treaty ratified, 355.
Devine, —, killed by Nez Percés, 647.
Diablo. See Eskyinlaw.
Diggers. See Pah-Utes and California Indians.
Dignes de pitié. See Tookarikas.
Disease, effect of, on Indian population, 5, 6; among Cayuses, 102; among Navahos, 253; among Nez Percés in Indian Territory, 664–666, 669, 670; among Hualapais, 730.
Doane, Lieutenant, destroys Piegan camp, 529.
Doctors. See Medicine-men.
Dodge, Captain, Meeker sends for, 702; relieves Payne's command, 706.
Dodge, General, quoted, 228, 243.
Dog Cañon, fight at, 383.
Dog-eaters, same as Cheyennes, 225.
Dog Soldiers, what are, 227; duties of, 228; powers of, 229; refuse to let their leader treat, 408; not an independent band, 431; do not accept treaty of 1865, 437; hostilities by, 438.
Doña Ana, massacre of Mescaleros at, 378.
Doniphan, Colonel, expedition to Chihuahua, 50, 51; expedition against Navahos, 256.
Doolittle, Senator, bias in Chivigton investigation, 431; investigates Indian affairs of New Mexico, 470.
Douglas, Stephen A., views on extension of United States boundaries, 47.
Douglas, White River chief, leader of a faction, 690; Meeker makes friend of, 691; refuses to surrender offenders, 696; opposes Meeker, 698; proposes to accompany Meeker, 702; war-dance at camp of, 703; takes part in massacre, 704; takes Mrs. Meeker, 706; surrender of, demanded, 714.
Dresser, Frank, escapes from Utes, 704; separates from women, 705; body found, 710.
Dresser, Henry, body of, found, 709.
Drew, Lieutenant, visited by scalp-hunters, 362; quoted, 365.
Dudley, L. E., removes White Mountain Apaches, 735.
Dull Knife, Cheyenne chief, camp of, destroyed, 626.
Dundy, Judge, opinion of Ponca removal, 21.
Dunn, Lieut, Clark, fight with Cheyennes, 411; Indian account of fight, 415.
Dyer, L. S., appointed on Modoc commission, 560; opposes last council, 565; goes to council, 567; pursued by Hooker Jim, 569; escapes, 660; witness at trial, 580.

EATON, GEORGE, killed by Utes, 710.

Ebenezer, Ute warrior, aids in murder of Eskridge, 703; aids in massacre, 704; surrender of, demanded, 714.
Edmonton House, illicit traffic at, 523.
Ellen's Man, Modoc warrior, at council, 567; shoots Dr. Thomas, 569; killed, 580.
Ellis, Nez Percé chief, made head-chief, 631.
Embudo, fight near, 70, 73.
Eskimenzin, Arivapa chief, comes to Camp Grant, 719; conduct of band of, 720; attack on, 721–724; second attack on, 725; manufactures tiswin, 753.
Eskina, Chiricahua chief, revolt of, 737; killed, 738.
Eskridge, Wilmer, murdered, 703; body found, 709.
Eskyinlaw, Apache chief, refuses to remove, 736.
Evans, George M., claim to discovery of gold in California, 118–121.
Evans, Governor, goes to treat with Cheyennes, 408; calls for troops, 409, 410; talk with Cheyenne and Arapahoe chiefs, 412–416; did not promise Cheyennes protection, 420; 432; did not wish to treat, 422.
Ewbanks, Mrs. Lucinda, captured by Cheyennes, 412; deposition of, 427–429; daughter and nephew die of injuries, 429.
Ewell, Captain, defeats Mescaleros, 378.
Ewtaws, See Utes.
Exkinoya, defined, 510.
Extermination policy, not possible of accomplishment, 7; failure of, in Oregon, 205–207, 217; tried in Arizona, 386, 389; effects of, 391, 392; failure of, 395; continued in Arizona, 717, 718; result of, 719; at Camp Grant, 721–724; evils of, 725, 729; not believed in by General Crook, 728, 733.

FAIRCHILD, JOHN, Meacham desires to accompany commission, 565; receives valuables of Meacham and Dyer, 567.
Fall River Indians, same as Arapahoes, 221.
Fancher's train, described, 289; treatment of, by Mormons, 290; reaches Mountain Meadows, 291; attacked, 292; defence of, 293, 294; entrapped, 295, 296; massacred, 297–299; value of property of, 300; Brigham Young's account of, 302; innocence of, 306, 307, 317; survivors of, 309, 310; heirs of, should be compensated, 311.
Faraones, same as Navahos, 358.
Fauntleroy, Colonel, fight near Poncha Pass, 680, 681.
"Fed Savages" described, 16, 17.
Fernandez de Taos. See Taos.
   490; commands troops at Fort Phil Kearney massacre, 491; crosses Lodge Trail Ridge, 492; body found, 495; probable suicide of, 496, 499; disobeyed orders, 499.
Fetterman massacre. See Fort Phil Kearney.
Fillmore, President, quoted, 194.
Finley, —, kills Nez Percé Indian, 636; Indians refuse to prosecute, 639.
Finney, —, settles on Lapwai reservation, 641.
Fire arrows, use of, in signalling, 226.
Fitzpatrick, Agent, quoted, 219.
Five Crows, Cayuse chief, how named by whites, 99; ravishes Miss Bewley, 113–115.
Flatheads, location of, 83; custom of flattening head discontinued, 83 (*note*); Stevens's treaty with, 217, 516; treaty ratified, 355; treachery by, 512; torture Blackfeet, 513.
Forney, Dr., gives date of Mountain Meadow massacre, 299; instructed to investigate massacre, 305; first report of, 306; makes

INDEX. 771

new discoveries, 306, 307; returns survivors, 309; Albert's story to, 319.
Forsythe, Lieutenant-colonel, defeats Apaches, 747.
Fort Benton, relations of Indians at, 514; hostilities at, 518; lawlessness at, 522–524.
Fort Bridger, burned by Mormons, 286.
Fort Buchanan, trouble with Chiricahuas near, 380.
Fort Buford, attack on, 504; Sitting Bull's autobiography brought to, 591; Sitting Bull surrenders at, 628.
Fort Canby, operations from, 453, 454; Carson's expedition from, 461; Navahos surrender at, 464; abandoned, 465.
Fort C. F. Smith, located, 487; abandoned and burned, 508.
Fort Craig, action near, 404; operation from, 453.
Fort Defiance established, 258; described, 259; soldier killed at, 261; negro boy Jim killed at, 262, 271; preparations for war at, 263–265; operations from, 265–272, 453.
Fort Fauntleroy, massacre of Navahos at, 448.
Fort Fillmore, taken by rebels, 404.
Fort Klamath, Modocs tried at, 579–581; executed at, 582.
Fort Laramie, treaty with Sioux at, 507.
Fort Larned, treachery of Indians at, 421, 422.
Fort Phil Kearney, location of, 486; orthography of name, 486 (*note*); description of, 487; country surrounding, 488; depredations near, 489, 490; massacre near, 491–500; misrepresentations concerning massacre, 501, 502; responsibility for massacre, 503, 504; action near, 504, 505; abandoned and burned, 508.
Fort Reno, horses driven off from, 486; General Wessels commands at, 500.
Fort Thorne, massacre of Mescaleros at, 379.
Fort Union, location of, 404; Colorado troops supplied at, 405.
Fort Vancouver, described, 87.
Fort Walla-Walla, described, 87; plundered, 206; fight near, 207; new fort built, 324.
Fort Wingate, Apaches surrender at, 739.
Fort Wise, treaty at, 242; treaty repudiated by Indians, 408, 416.
Fort Yuma, location of, 158; Grinnell at, 180; Olive Oatman arrives at, 184.
Foster, Vice-President, investigates Indian affairs in New Mexico, 470.
Foul Hand, Tookarika chief, mentioned, 276.
Four Lakes, battle at, 344.
Francisco, Yuma Indian, goes to release Olive Oatman, 181; speech to the Mohaves, 182; brings Olive to Fort Yuma, 183; is made a chief, 184; killed, 187.
Fremont, John C., crosses San Juan mountains, 41; aids in conquering California, 47; attacked by Klamaths, 191; trouble with Cheyennes and Arapahoes, 229; description of Salt Lake Basin, 275.
Fresno reservation, established, 137; abandoned; 138.
Fur trade, effect of, on settlement of Rocky Mountains, 31–34.

GADSDEN Purchase, what was, 48; caused by Southern influence, 51.
Gall, Sioux chief, flees to British America, 627.
Gallantin, John, villainy of, 362.
Gallatin, Albert, favors separate government for Pacific slope, 47.
Gallaudet, Professor, wonderful use of facial expression by, 223.
Gambler's Gourd. *See* Washikie.
Ganado Blanco, Navaho chief, leaves Bosque Redondo, 470.

Garcia, Lieutenant-colonel, defeats Apaches, 747.
Garland, General, subdues Jicarillas, 377, 378; protects Mescaleros, 379.
Garnett, Major, campaign against Yakimas, 352, 354.
Garrotéros, probably same as Coyotéros, 358.
Garry, Spokane chief, opinion of Stevens's treaties, 335; sketch of, 338, 341; message to General Clarke, 342; interview with Colonel Wright, 347; treats with Colonel Wright, 351, 352.
Gaston, Lieutenant, killed at Ingossomen Creek, 327; buried at Fort Walla-Walla, 353.
Gay, Lieutenant, ambushed by Mormons and Indians, 313.
Gazzous, Louis, murdered by Sioux, 486.
George, Modoc warrior, taunts Captain Jack, 564.
Geronimo, Apache chief, refuses to be removed, 738; comes to White Mountain reservation, 743; raid of, 750; surrenders, 752; last outbreak of, 753.
Gerry, Elbridge, sent to bring in Cheyennes and Arapahoes, 408.
Giannahtah, Mescalero chief, submission of, 383, 384; quoted, 467.
Gibbon, General, leads detachment against Sioux, 601; communicates with Terry, 604; directions to, 607; reaches scene of Custer massacre, 611; fight with Nez Percés, 652.
Gibbs, George, quoted, 331.
Gibson, Captain, murder of, 233.
Gileños, Apaches, who are, 357; hostilities by, 381; reservation for, 727.
Gillem, General, quoted, 559; warned by Riddle, 566; does not believe Modocs will attempt treachery, 567.
Gilpin, Lieutenant-colonel and Governor, winters among Cheyennes and Arapahoes, 230; expedition against Navahos, 256; recruits troops in Colorado, 404.
Gold, discovered in California, 118–125; effect of, on Indians, 125; discovered in Colorado, 240–242, 675; discovered in Arizona, 385; discovered in Idaho and Montana, 477, 478; believed to exist in Black Hills, 585, 586; discovered in Black Hills, 587–589; search for in Nez Percés country, 636; believed to exist in Elk Mountains, 679.
Goldstein, Carl, killed by Utes, 709.
Good Hearts, same as Arapahoes, 221.
Gordo, Apache chief, leaves Chiricahua reservation, 738.
Gosi-Utes, who are, 277.
Grand Coquin, Bannock chief, mentioned, 276.
Grand Lake, assassination of commissioners at, 694.
Grand Rivers, Utes, who are, 277; included in White Rivers, 681.
Grant, General, orders investigation of Fetterman massacre, 500; influence on, to pardon Modocs, 581; commutes sentence of Barncho and Slolox, 582; cause of feeling towards Custer, 601; refuses to see Custer, 602; permits Custer to accompany his regiment, 603; effect on Custer's action, 623; withdraws Uncompahgré Park from public domain, 685; peace policy of 716.
Grattan massacre, occasion of, 232; result of, 233.
Gray, W. H., emigrates to Oregon, 37; custodian of funds for Whitman monument, 117 (*note*).
Great American Desert, extent of, 34.
Great Basin described, 81, 275. *See also* Utah.
Greenhow, Robert, estimate of the West, 44, 45.
Gregg, General, gives name Apache Yumas to Hualapais, 358.

Gregory, John, discovery of gold by, in Colorado, 241.
Grierson, Colonel, drives Victorio into Mexico, 744.
Grinnell, —, search for Oatman girls, 180; sends out Francisco, 181; announces return of Olive Oatman, 183.
Gros Ventres of the North, who are, 510; troubles with Blackfeet, 514; location of, in 1853, 515; treat with Stevens, 516; remain peaceful, 517, 518; troubles with Piegans, 521; separated from Blackfoot nation, 522.
Gros Ventres of the South, same as Arapahoes, 221.
Grover, Governor, demands surrender of Modocs, 559, 578; claims Nez Percés have no title to Wallowa valley, 634; puts his theory before Congress, 637.
Grummond, Lieutenant, accompanies Fetterman party, 491; body found, 496.
Guadalupe Hidalgo, treaty of, 47; Mission Indians citizens under, 148; effect of, on Apaches, 365.
Guero, Tabequache chief, mentioned, 689.
Guerrier, Edmond, writes letter for Cheyenne chiefs, 411.
Gunnison, Lieutenant, murder of, 278, 279.

HAIGHT, Mormon bishop, orders Mountain Meadow massacre, 295; elected senator, 315.
Hairy Man. See Poemacheeah.
Hale, C. H., makes treaty with Nez Percés, 633.
Halleck, General, opinion of Apaches, 391.
Haller, Major, campaign against Yakimas, 204.
Hamlin, Jacob, Fancher's train passes house of, 291; survivors of massacre taken to house of, 299; reports to Brigham Young, 300; gives information to Dr. Forney, 306; testimony of, 318; deceit of, 319.
Hamockhaves. See Mohaves.
Hancock, General, expedition of, in 1867, 438; representations of Major Wynkoop concerning, 443; attempt to blame, for attack on Piegans, 533.
Hardie, General, quoted, 524; investigates Piegan troubles, 527; instructions to, 533; opinion of Piegan hostility, 535.
Hardscrabble, Colorado, in 1847, 219, 220.
Hare, Bishop, opinion of Indian laws, 10.
Harney, General, marches against Sioux, 234; defeats them at Ash Hollow, 235; establishes first Indian police, 236; criticism of, 236; summoned before court-martial, 237; promoted and sent to Oregon, 238; Mormon poetry on, 287; action of, admired on frontier, 433; member Board Peace Commissioners, 716.
Harris, E. R., aids in releasing Indian slaves, 371.
Hasbrouck's cavalry, capture Modocs, 576.
Haskell, Lieutenant, induces return of Apache renegades, 743.
Hastings, Agent, report on Sioux in 1876, 598, 619.
Hatch, Capt. John P., expedition against Navahos, 265, 266.
Hatch, General, treats with Utes, 687, 688; demands surrender of hostiles, 714; operations against Apaches, 740.
Hatch, Ira, takes part in Mountain Meadow massacre, 298, 299.
Hawalcoes. See Hualapais.
Hawonietah, Minneconjou chief, death of, 24.
Hayt, E. A., favors removals, 23; treatment of Nez Percés, 660, 663; misstatements of, exposed, 664–668; enforces removal policy in Arizona, 738.

Hazen, General, inspects Fort Phil Kearney, 487.
Head, Agent, quoted, 371, 372.
Heintzelman, Colonel, sends force to rescue Oatman girls, 179; chastises Yumas, 180.
Helena, Montana, settlement of, 478.
Henderson, J. B., member Board Peace Commissioners, 716.
Herrara, Sergeant, fight at Cañon de Chelly, 461.
Hickland, Hudson's Bay factor, encourages horse-stealing, 523.
Hickman, Bill, cut off from Mormon Church, 316.
Hickorias. See Jicarillas.
Higbee, Major, commands at Mountain Meadow massacre, 295; gives signal for massacre, 297; robs bodies, 299.
High Back Bone, Minneconjou chief, commands at Fetterman massacre, 499.
Higher law of Mormons, 274, 295, 320.
Hines, Surgeon, sent to look for Fetterman party, 492.
Hitchcock, General, quoted, 194, 195.
Hodt, Captain, testimony of, 448.
Hoecken, Father, Joset's letter to, 329.
Hogans, what are, 245; superstitions concerning, 246, 249.
Hokandika. See Cache Valley Indians.
Homily, love of native home, 23.
Honzinger, Dr., killed, 615; murderer detected, 616.
Hooker Jim, Modoc warrior, who was, 553; joins Captain Jack, 554; opposes peace, 561, 563; taunts Captain Jack, 564; in council, 567; action at council, 568; pursues Dyer, 569; betrays Captain Jack, 576; witness at trial, 580.
Hooper, William H., denies guilt of Mormons, 314; buys plundered property, 315.
Hosta, Pueblo chief, accompanies Colonel Washington, 257.
Hot Creek Indians, who were, 546; scattered by settlers, 559.
Hottentot Venus, case of, 14.
Hovey, Eugene, killed by Modocs, 571.
Howard, Agent, report on Sioux in 1876, 598, 617.
Howard, Gen. O. O., commissioner to treat with Joseph, 638; recommends removal, 642, 643; first opinion of case, 645; ordered to effect removal, 646; marches against Nez Percés, 649; fight on the Clearwater, 650; pursues Nez Percés, 651, 652; horses of, run off, 655; quoted, 656; present at surrender, 660; responsibility of, 672, 673; establishes Chiricahua reservation, 727.
Howe, Lieutenant, killed in Lava Beds, 573.
Howe, S. D., makes treaty with Nez Percés, 633.
Howland, Lieutenant, expedition against Navahos, 268.
Hualapais, belong to Yuma nation, 156; go to war, 391; attempted removal to Colorado River, 730; assist troops, 731; starvation of, 743.
Hudson's Bay Company, possession of Astoria by, 33; attempts to prevent emigration to Oregon, 38; post at Wallula, 87; receives Whitman kindly, 87; action and motives of, 88, 89; ransoms American prisoners, 100; responsibility for Wailatpu massacre, 102, 108; claim against United States, 116; incite Yakimas, 202; distrust of, in Oregon, 328, 329; action in Spokane war, 333; encourages slavery, 370, 371; sells whiskey to Indians, 515; buys stole horses, 522; encourages horse-stealing, 523.

INDEX.

Hugus, W. B., tried for cattle-stealing, 695.
Humboldt Bay, massacre at, 141, 143.
Humme, captain of scouts, killed, 709.
Hungate family murdered by Indians, 412, 413.
Hunt, Governor, treats with Utes, 681.
Hunter state, what is, 1, 2.
Hurt, Agent, flees from Utah, 285, 286.
Huslihushcute, Nez Percés chief, at treaty council, 638; given time to remove cattle, 647.
Hutchins, Charles, treats with Nez Percés, 633.

IDAHO, settlement and organization of, 477; feeling against Nez Percés in, 667; 668, 672.
Ignacio, Muache chief, made head-chief of southern Utes, 688; does not recognize Ouray's authority, 689.
Ilges, Major, pursues Nez Percés, 658.
Indian Bureau, should have control of Indians, 18; responsible for Apache troubles, 733, 742, 743.
Indian Commissioners. See Board of Indian Commissioners.
Indian lands purchased by all the colonies, 8; none in Mexican cession, 8, 133, 148, 379; legal status of, 8; right of appropriation, 484, 485; taken without compensation, 541.
Indian police, first established by General Harney, 236; established among Navahos, 472.
Indians, number of, in the United States, 1; legal status of, 8–14; laws governing, 9–11, 14; status of treaties with, 11; citizenship of, 11–13, 148; no provision for naturalizing, 13; frauds on, 15–19, 133–135, 147; transfer to War Department, 18; habits of, 23–25; diversity of, 24, 25; civilization of, 12, 25, 26; schools for, 26; first school for in Oregon, 35; of Rocky Mountains, 81–86; effect of gold discoveries on, 125–127; of California, 127–129, 132, 135, 143; sign language of, 223–227; of Utah, 275–277; relative standing of Apaches, 356; slavery among, 367–373, 447, 725, 754; estimate of, at close of Rebellion, 480, 481; roads through lands of, 484, 485; torture by plains tribes; 489; Bogy's statements, 502; ignorance of suffering of, 538; helplessness of Piegans, 541; neglect of Piegans, 542; expense of subduing Modocs, 578; frontier representations of evil-doing, 694.
Inez Gonzales, capture and release of, 366.
Ingossomen Creek, fight at, 325–328.
Inmuttooyahlatlat. See Joseph.
Iron Dog, Sioux chief, escapes with band, 626; surrenders, 627.
Iturbide, revolution of, in Mexico, 30.

JACK, White River chief, leader of a faction, 690; opposes work at agency, 691; goes to Denver, 696, 697; Meeker appeals to, 698; meets Thornburgh, 699; at Milk Creek, 700.
Jackson, Andrew, advises limitation of United States boundaries, 46.
Jackson, Captain, attacks Modocs, 552, 553; exculpated by Curtis, 581.
Jackson, Helen Hunt, recommends attorneys for mission Indians, 147, 150; reports on mission Indians, 149; death of, 147 (note).
Jamajabs. See Mohaves.
Jane, Ute squaw, assists captives, 711.
Janos, massacre of Apaches at, 359; Mangas Colorado taken to, 382.
Jefferson, Thomas, estimate of Indian population, 4; originates idea of settling Pacific slope, 35, 36; favors separate government for West, 46, 47.
Jeffords, Interpreter, induces return of Apache renegades, 743.

Jemaspie, Hualapais chief, captured, 730.
Jenney, Professor, expedition to Black Hills, 588.
Jerome, D. H., member of Nez Percés commission, 646; responsibility of, 672.
Jesuits, come into Oregon, 89; controversy with Protestants, 90; meet Whitman, 93; responsibility in Whitman massacre, 108–116; suppressed in Spain, 144; establish mission of San Xavier del Bac, 155; distrust of, in Oregon, 328.
Jesus Lopez, murders an Apache, 373.
Jicarillas, Apaches, who are, 357; massacre White's party, 374, 377; part of, take refuge with Utes, 378; drunkenness of, 379; friendliness of, during rebellion, 381; fight near Poncha Pass, 680, 681.
Jim. negro boy, murder of, 262, 271; war on account of, 263–272.
John, Rogue River chief, hostilities by, 206; surrenders, 216.
Johnson, ——, murders Apaches, 361.
Johnson, White River chief, mentioned, 600; civilization of, 697; assaults Meeker, 698; brother of, shot, 704; outrages Mrs. Price, 706; surrender of, demanded, 714.
Johnson, Captain, quoted, 367.
Johnson, Nephi, leads Indians at Mountain Meadows, 293; testimony of, 318.
Johnston, Agent, quoted, 145.
Johnston, Col. A. S., commands expedition to Utah, 287; ordered to use troops as posse comitatus, 312.
Jones, Agent, report on Nez Percés, 664.
Jordan, Agent. report on Nez Percés, 665, 666.
José Rey, Chowchilla chief, mortally wounded. 133.
José Trinfan released from Apaches, 366.
Joseph, Old, Nez Percés chief, speech to Oregon troops, 101; aids Colonel Wright, 343; sketch of, 630, 631; character of 632; refuses to sell his country, 633, 634; death of, 635.
Joseph, Young, Nez Percés chief, love of native home, 23; character of, 24; name of, 635; sketch of, 636; grief of, 637; meets commission, 638, 639; objects to churches, 640; statement of his case, 642, 645; agrees to leave his country, 646; opposes fighting, 647; takes command of hostiles, 648; defeats Perry, 649; fights Howard, 650; retreats over Lolo trail, 651; defeats Gibbon, 652; runs off Howard's horses, 655; treatment of Cowan's party, 657; fights Sturgis, 657; Miles marches against, 658; surrenders, 659; sent to Indian Territory, 660; quoted, 662; sufferings of band of, 664–666; feeling against in Idaho, 667, 668; Price's statement concerning, 669; band of, returned to Lapwai, 670, 671; statement of Howard's motives, 672.
Joset, Father, meets Steptoe, 325; tries to pacify Indians, 326; accusations against, 328; puts blame on Nez Percés, 329, 330; services of, 331; quoted, 337, 338; goes to Indians as mediator, 341; reports Indians subdued, 348.
Juan José, Mimbreños chief, murder of, 361.
Juan Ortega, attacks Mescaleros, 379.
Juh, Apache chief, band of, 736; flees to Mexico, 738; goes to White Mountain reservation, 743; leaves reservation, 744; leaves renegades, 752.

KAETENA, Apache chief, offence and punishment of, 752.
Kalispels. See Pend d'Oreilles.

INDEX.

Kamiakin, Yakima chief, repudiates treaty with Stevens, 202; leads in Cascade massacre, 212; causes discontent among Spokanes, 338; flees across the mountains, 353.

Kanarrah, Pi-ede chief, at Mountain Meadow massacre, 293.

Kane, Colonel, negotiates with Mormons, 315.

Kaniache, Southern Ute chief, mentioned, 689; struck by lightning, 714.

Kanosh, Pah Vant chief, not implicated in Mountain Meadow massacre, 306, 307.

Katihotes, Yakima chief, camp of, surprised, 352.

Kautz, Colonel, opposes removals, 734; intercedes for Indians, 736.

Kaws, in Union army, 425.

Kayatana, Navaho chief, expedition against, 267, 268.

Kearny, Gen. S. W., sent to occupy New Mexico and California, 47; conquest of New Mexico, 49, 52; establishes provisional government, 52; terrifies Cheyennes and Arapahoes, 229; assumes protection of Mexicans, 256; meets Mimbreños, 365; orthography of name, 486 (*note*).

Kearny, Maj. Philip, defeats Rogue Rivers, 191; turns prisoners over to General Lane, 192; orthography of name, 486 (*note*).

Kelly, Hall J., efforts to colonize Oregon, 34, 35.

Kena. *See* Bloods.

Kendrick, Major, dealings with Navahos, 261.

Kennon, Dr. Louis, statement concerning Indian slavery, 447.

Kensler Toussaint, discovers gold in Black Hills, 587.

Kikatsa, same as Mountain Crows, 479.

Kings River farm, established, 137; Indians driven from, 138.

Kiowas, location of, 81; supposed to have originated sign language, 225.

Kirkham, Captain, quoted, 331.

Klamaths, divisions of, 190; sign for insanity, 224; slavery among, 371; treaty of 1864 with, 544; harass the Modocs, 545, 546; accused of lawlessness, 549, 559, 580; witness execution of Modocs, 582.

Klickitats, location of, 86; title to Wallamet valley, 195; conquests by, 201; power of, 202; Stevens's treaty with, 217; treaty ratified, 355; slavery among, 371.

Klingensmith, Philip, at Mountain Meadow massacre, 299; reports to Brigham Young, 300; testifies, 317.

Knapp, Agent, selects location for Modocs, 546.

Knight, Samuel, at Mountain Meadow massacre, 297; testimony of, 318.

Koolsatikara, who are, 275.

Kootenais, Stevens's treaty with, 217, 516; treaty ratified, 355; harass the Gros Ventres of the north, 510.

Krentpoos. *See* Captain Jack.

La Cañada, fight at, 70.

La Lakes, who are, 545.

Lamanites, what are, 278.

Lame Deer, Minneconjou chief, killed, 627.

Lane, Gen. Joe, first governor of Oregon, 189; marches against Rogue Rivers, 199; treats with them, 200.

Langford, —, settles on Lapwai reservation, 641.

Lapwai Mission established, 38; location of, 87.

"Laramie Loafers," who were, 484.

Larkin, T. O., announces discovery of gold in California, 121.

Larrabee, Agent, attack on, 731.

Lava Beds, described, 554; Modocs retire to, 555; troops advance into, 556; Hot Creek Indians go to, 559; Modocs offer to take for reservation, 563; fight of April 14th in, 571; fight of April 26th, 572-574; Modocs leave, 576.

Lawson, Captain, at Milk Creek, 701.

Lawyer, Nez Percés chief, Milkapsi's charge against, 330; friendship of, 331; assurances to, 333; Indian name of, 335; aids Colonel Wright, 343; asks ratification of Stevens's treaties, 354; made head-chief by Stevens, 631.

Lawyer, James, Nez Percés preacher, welcomes exiles, 671.

Leadville, mining excitement of, 675-679.

Leal, J. W., murdered by Pueblos, 65; buried at Santa Fé, 78.

Le Conte, Dr., meets Oatman family, 161; robbed by Tontos, 162.

Lee, Gen. Elliott, escapes from Taos, 65.

Leo, John D., leads Indians at Mountain Meadows, 293; betrays emigrants, 295, 296; takes part in massacre, 297; ravishes and murders girl, 298; charges Government for stolen property, 299; reports to Brigham Young, 300; quoted, 302, 312; honored by Young, 315; captured, 316; tried, 316-319; confessions of, 319; executed, 320.

Lee, Stephen, murdered by Pueblos, 62.

Left Hand, Arapahoe chief, band of, at Sand Creek, 408; not connected with Little Raven, 416; Joins Black Kettle, 419; mortally wounded, 417.

Leland, Judge, opinion as to feeling against Nez Percés, 667.

Lennon, Cyrus, killed by Apaches, 389.

Leschi, Nasqualla chief, eloquence of, 203; attacks settlements, 207.

Lewis and Clarke, expedition of, 32; sent out by Jefferson, 36; treatment of, by Nez Percés, 629.

Lindsay, Captain, expedition against Navahos, 267; bold charge of, 268.

Lindsley, Rev. A. L., recommends Nez Percés commission, 637; investigates feeling in Idaho, 667.

Lipans, who are, 358.

Little Arkansas, treaty with Cheyennes at, 437.

Little Bear, Sioux chief, on invasion of Black Hills, 590.

Little Big Horn, Custer's fight on, 607-615; number of Indians at, 617, 618; number of Indians not suspected, 619, 620, 623, 624.

Little Dog, Piegan chief, killed, 521.

Little Eagle, Piegan warrior, accused of murdering James Quail, 527.

Little Raven, Arapahoe chief, hostility of, 416; surrenders to Wynkoop, 418; sent away from Fort Lyon, 419; confused with Black Kettle's band, 430.

Little Thunder, Sioux chief, head-chief of Brulés, 233; defeated at Ash Hollow, 235.

Little Wolf, Cheyenne chief, opinion of Black Hills, 589.

Llaneros, same as Lipans, 358.

Lolo trail, Nez Percés retreat to, 650; described, 651.

Lolocksalt. *See* Slolox.

Lone Horn, Sioux chief, on invasion of Black Hills, 590.

Long Beard, Snake chief, band of, 277.

Long Sioux, who were, 591.

Looking Glass, Nez Percés chief, band of, 638; troops sent to arrest, 649; talks to soldiers, 651; killed, 652.

Lookout Station, massacre at, 438.

INDEX.   775

Lorey, Agent, reports Cheyennes discontented, 408; goes to make treaty, 444.
Lost Cabin, probable origin of story of, 587; reputed location of, 658.
Lost River, Modocs wish reservation on, 550, 551; fight at, 552, 553; objections to reservation on, 561.
Louderback, —, testimony of, 434.
Loughridge, Representative, quoted, 239; erroneous statement concerning Sand Creek, 434, 437.

MACKENZIE, COLONEL, defeats Dull Knife, 626.
Magoffin, James, services in conquest of New Mexico, 49, 50.
Mahaos, belong to Yuma nation, 156.
Mahto Iowa, Sioux chief, connection with Grattan massacre, 232; meaning of name, 232 (note); death of, 233.
Mahtotopa, character of, 24.
Man-Afraid-of-his-Horses, Ogallalla chief, opposes treaty of 1866, 482; withdraws from council, 483; makes treaty, 504; chief of Sioux police, son of, 589.
Mandans, location of, 81; supposed remnant of Madoc's Welsh colony, 81.
Mangas Colorado, Mimbreños chief, meets Kearny, 365; cause of hostility, 374; activity of, 381; killed, 382.
Manuelita, Navaho chief, made head-chief, 261; attack on, 268; cattle of, shot, 269; chief of Navaho police, 472.
Mariano Martinez, Navaho chief, makes treaty, 257; treaty repudiated, 258.
Maricopas, location of, 152; join the Pimas, 155; attacked by Yumas, 184; defeat them, 187; aid United States against Apaches, 385, 386, 389.
Mariposa battalion, services of, 133.
Marsh, Professor, charges against Red Cloud agency, 16.
Martin, Captain, defeats Apaches, 381.
Martin, Mrs., captured by Cheyennes, 412; surrendered, 429.
Martin, trumpeter, quoted, 620.
Mason, General, put in command in Arizona, 391.
Mason, Harry, whips Nez Percés Indians, 636; killed, 648.
Mattole Valley farm, established, 137; abandoned, 138; Indians murdered at, 141.
McBeth, Miss, labors of, among Nez Percés, 670.
McCleave, Captain, defeats Apaches, 383.
McComas family, massacre of, 750.
McCormick, Representative from Arizona, classifies Indians, 25.
McCulloch, Benjamin, treats with Mormons, 315.
McDougal, Captain, with Custer's expedition, 608; message to, 609.
McDougal, Governor, estimate of California Indians, 129, 130, 132.
McDowell, General, commands Department of California, 391.
McDuffie, Senator, opinion of plains, 34; opposes occupation of Oregon, 46.
McGregor, Captain, captures Hualapais, 730.
McIntyre, C. H., on Uncompahgre Park invasion, 686.
McKay, Donald, leads Warm Spring Indians, 571; accompanies Captain Thomas, 572; separated from troops, 573.
McMurdy, —, aids in Mountain Meadow massacre, 297.
McNeil, Inspector, reports on Nez Percés, 664.
Meacham, A. B., induces Captain Jack to return to reservation, 546; urges separate reservation for Modocs, 551; on Modoc Commission, 559; opposes last council, 565; proposes deception in case of treachery, 566; goes to council, 567; speech at council, 568; shot, 569; saved by Toby, 570; testifies, 580.
Medicine Cow, Sioux Chief, opinion of Dr. Burleigh, 15.
Medicine-men, murdered when unsuccessful in treatment, 105–108, 546.
Medina, Governor, objects to massacre of Apaches at Janos, 359.
Meeker, Josie, opinion as to time of plot, 703; takes refuge in milk-house, 704; captured, 705; treatment of, 706; Persune infatuated with, 712; death of, 713; statement of treatment, 714.
Meeker, Mrs., opinion as to time of plot, 703; takes refuge in milk-house, 704; wounded, 705; taken by Douglas, 706; treatment of Jane, 711; statement of treatment, 714.
Meeker, N. C., character of, 690; management of Utes, 691; complains of Utes, 696; Indians distrust, 697, 703; assaulted by Johnson, 698; applies for protection, 699; correspondence with Thornburgh, 700, 702, 703; massacre at agency, 704, 705; mutilation of, 710.
Mendocino reservation, character of, 136; cost of 137.
Meriwether, Governor, treats with Navahos, 261; dismisses Jicarillas, 377.
Merritt, Colonel, defeats Cheyennes, 625; arrives at Milk Creek, 706; advances to White River, 709; captives reach camp of, 713.
Mescaleros, Apaches, who are, 357; defeated by California troops, 378; assailed by Mexicans, 379; go to war, 381; conquered by Carleton, 383; sent to Bosque Redondo, 384; leave same, 392, 466; quarrel with Navahos, 465; Victorio settles with, 739; renegades join Victorio, 740.
Mesquite, described, 175, 176.
Messila Guard, attacks Mescaleros, 378; punished by troops, 379.
Methodist missions, first in Oregon, 37; sold to American Board, 87; none among Piegans, 536.
Mexican Boundary Commission, bury remains of Oatmans, 188; release Apache slaves, 366, 367; troubles with Mimbreños, 373, 374.
Mexican Cession, Indian titles in, extinguished, 8, 379; extent of, 27; Indians of, made citizens, 144.
Mexicans, character of, 53, 61; lead in Pueblo insurrection, 77, 78; wars with Apaches, 358–365; slavery among, 368–373; attack Mescaleros, 378, 379; supposed disloyalty of, 404; invade our reservations, 737.
Miguel, Coyotéro chief, peaceful, 719; assists troops, 731.
Miles, Col. D. S., commands in Navaho country, 262; arrives at Fort Defiance, 263; expeditions of, 265, 267, 268; explores Cañon de Chelly, 458.
Miles, Gen. N. A., defeats Sitting Bull, 626; defeats Crazy Horse, 627; marches against Nez Percés, 658; defeats them, 659; promises them return to Idaho, 660; Indians claim fulfilment of promise, 669.
Milk Creek, fight at, 700, 701, 706–709.
Milkapsi, Coeur d'Alêne chief, begins attack on Steptoe, 326; message to General Clarke, 330, 331; blamed by the Indians, 338; quoted, 342; humiliated, 352.
Miller, J. W., conduct of, in survey of Ute lands, 685.
Mills, Captain, defeats American Horse, 625.

776 INDEX.

Miltimore's train, attack on, 313.
Mimbreños, Apaches, who are, 357; treachery to, 361; meet Kearny, 365; meet Bartlett, 366; release of slaves of, 366, 367; troubles with Bartlett's party, 373, 374; hostilities by, 374, 381; refuse to be removed, 390, 391; failure of extermination policy against, 395; attempted removal to Tularosa, 726, 727; attempted removal to Arizona, 738–740; official opinions of treatment of, 741, 742; raids of, 744–747.
"Mina maska," defined, 510.
Minneconjous, Sioux, who are, 231; in Grattan massacre, 232; treaty of 1866 with, 481; in Fetterman massacre, 499; numbers and loss of, at massacre, 500; location in 1876, 591; at war, 618; defeated by Miles, 627; make peace, 628.
Minnetarees, location of, 81.
Mission Indians, converted by Franciscans, 143; citizens of Mexico, 144; stupidity of, 145; no provision for, 146; homes taken from, 147; denied all rights, 148; no title to lands, 149; attorneys employed for, 150.
Mitchell, W. C., loss of relatives at Mountain Meadows, 305; meets surviving children, 309.
Mockpeahlutah. *See* Red Cloud.
Modocs, location of, 190; meaning of name, 191; hostilities by, 192; massacre at Bloody Point, 193; attack emigrants, 200; defeated by Captain Walker, 201; slavery among, 371; character of, 543; treaty of 1864 with, 544; annoyed by Klamaths, 545; leave reservation, 546; conduct of, 549; desire separate reservation, 550; misrepresented by Odeneal, 551; attacked by Captain Jackson, 552; murder settlers, 553; go to Lava Beds, 554; troops sent against, 555; fight of January 17th, 556; conduct of whites towards, 559; commission sent to, 560; afraid to surrender, 561; causes of fear, 562, 563; Captain Jack becomes hostile, 564; preparations for last council, 565–567; the council, 568; murder of commissioners, 569–570; advance of troops, 571; battle of April 26th, 572, 573; General Davis takes command, 574; fight at dry lake, 575; leave Lava Beds, 576; capture of, 577; cost of war, 578; trial of, 580, 581; execution, 582; subsequent history, 583.
Mofras, Duflot de, estimates population California, 131.
Mogollons, Apaches, who are, 357; location of, 358; mixed with Chiricahuas, 736.
Mohaves, belong to Yuma nation, 156; names of, 157; character of, 174; tattoo Oatman girls, 175; famine among, 176; war with Cocopahs, 177; crucify Cocopah women, 178; surrender of Olive Oatman, 181–183; attack Maricopas, 184; present condition of, 187.
Mohuaches, or Muaches, Utes, who are, 277; included in Southern Utes, 681.
Moketaveto. *See* Black Kettle.
Moleles, location of, 86; treaty with, ratified, 355.
Monos. *See* Pah Utes.
Montana, gold discovered in, 477; Settlement of, 478; need of road to, 479; right to make road, 484, 485, 507; road abandoned, 508; organized, 518; lawlessness in, 521–524; state of war in, 534, 535.
Moore, Julius, killed by Utes, 709.
Mopeah, Snake chief, band of, 277.
Moquetas, Pah Ute chief, at Mountain Meadow massacre, 293.
Moquis, Pueblos, location of, 53; name of, 54; consolidation of agency of, 475.

Mora, fight at, 66.
Morgan brothers, charged with cattle-stealing, 695.
Mormons, send battalion to Mexican war, 49; winter at Pueblo, 51, 219; at Salt Lake, 81; claim to discovery of gold, 118–121; incite Oregon Indians 203, 331; furnish arms to Navahos, 266, 267; treatment of, in the East, 273; higher law of, 274, 295, 320; treatment of Indians, 277–281; disloyalty of, 281, 282; doctrine of polygamy, 283; reformation of 283, 284; blood atonement, 284, 285, 290, 298, 313; lawlessness of, 286; resist United States authorities, 287–289; treatment of Fancher's train, 282–291; attack train, 292; murder Aden, 294; treachery of, 295, 296; Mountain Meadow massacre, 297–299; divide property of emigrants, 299, 300; guilt of, 300–303; guilt exposed, 306; claim for ransoming children, 307; survivors recovered, 309, 310; slander of survivors, 311, 314; concealment of criminals, 312; crimes of, 313; terrors of, 314; receive Governor Cummings, 315; change in position of, 316; abandon Lee, 317; convict him, 318, 319; American hatred of, 320–323; sell arms to Nez Percés, 332; law concerning Indian slavery, 369, 370; pleased with the rebellion, 404; encourage Ute war, 710, 711.
Morrow, Major, pursues Apaches, 740.
Mountain Chief, Piegan chief, assaulted, 522; retaliates, 524; expedition against, 528; escapes, 529, 535.
Mountain Crows, who are, 479.
Mountain House, illicit traffic at; 523.
Mountain Meadows, description of, 291; massacre at, 295–300; date of massacre, 299; appearance after massacre, 302, 307, 308; monument erected at, 309; survivors of massacre recovered, 309, 310; heirs of victims should be compensated, 311; becomes barren, 314; trial of Lee, 316–319; results on American people, 320, 323; Lee executed at, 319.
Mountain-sheep Eaters, who are, 276.
Mowry, Lieutenant, goes in search of Oatman girls, 179.
Muckalucks, who are, 545.
Mullan, Lieutenant, opinion of Stevens's treaties, 334; urges their ratification, 354.
Mungen, Representative, criticises attack on Piegans, 532.

NACHEZ, Chiricahua chief, leaves reservation, 744; returns, 752.
Naked Horse. *See* Caballo en Pelo.
Nané, Apache chief, raid of, 744.
Nantiatish, Apache chief, revolt of, 747.
Napea, a Blackfoot divinity, 511.
Naqui naquis, Tonto chief, surrenders, 730.
Narbona, Navaho chief, killed, 257.
Nasqualias, location of, 82.
Natatotel, Tonto chief, surrenders, 730.
National Association to Promote Universal Peace, intercedes for Modocs, 581.
Navahos, location of, 82, 244; names of, 244; country of, 245; customs of, 246; industries of, 249; women of, 250–253; religion of, 253, 254; government of, 254; source of hostilities with, 255; Doniphan's expedition against, 256; Washington's expedition, 257; Sumner's expedition, 258; treaty of 1855, 261; murder of negro Jim, 262; fight at Bear Spring, 263; duplicity of, 264; Colonel Miles's expedition, 265; Hatch's expedition, 266; aided by Mormons, 267; operations against, 268; treaty of 1858, 271; name of, 358; slavery of, 447; attack on Fort Fauntleroy, 448;

INDEX. 777

Canby's campaign against, 451; Carleton's plan for, 452; operations against, 453, 454; Carson marches against, 461–463; removed to Bosque Redondo, 464; expense of subsistence there, 466; prefer their old country, 467; sufferings of, 468–471; returned to old home, 471; advance of, 472–475; present condition of, 475, 476.
Na-watk. *See* Left Hand.
Nesmith, Superintendent, opinion of Stevens's treaties, 333; changes his opinion, 354, 355.
Nevada, part of Arizona ceded to, 158.
Newby, Colonel, expedition against Navahos, 256.
New Mexico, conquest of, 49; people of, in 1846, 52, 53; Arizona set off from, 158; description of northwest part, 244, 245; losses in, by Indians, 255, 256; Apache warfare in, 356; slavery in, 368, 369, 373; put in Department of Missouri, 391; Texan invasion of, 381, 382, 402–407; troubles with Mimbreños, 738–743.
Nez Percé Joseph. *See* Joseph, Young.
Nez Percés, superiority of, 25; deputation visit St. Louis, 36; meet missionaries, 37; offer to protect Spalding, 100; protect Stevens, 203; sign for, 225; not Pueblos, 245; aid Steptoe's command, 328; blamed by Joset, 329; innocence of, 330; Mormons sell arms to, 331, 332; want Stevens's treaty ratified, 335; aid Colonel Wright, 343, 347; treaty ratified, 355; making of treaty, 516; friendliness of, 629; tribal organization of, 630, 631; country of Lower, 632; treaty of 1863, 633; Lower do not sell country, 634, 635; growth of trouble with 636, 637; effort to induce removal, 638–642; removal ordered, 645, 646; prepare to resist, 647; kill settlers, 648; defeat Perry, 649; fight Howard, 650; retreat to Montana, 651; defeat Gibbon, 652; run off Howard's horses, 655; treatment of women captives, 656; fight Sturgis, 657; Miles marches against, 658; surrender, 659; sent to Indian Territory, 660; Hayt's statement, 663; sufferings of, 664–666; feeling against in Idaho, 667, 668; Price's statement, 669; part return, 670; remainder return, 670; responsibility for, 672, 673; compared with other wrongs, 674.
"Noble red man" not wholly a myth, 24.
Nobows. *See* Sans Arcs.
Nockay-Delklinne, Apache Medicine-man, killed, 744.
Nolgee, Apache chief, flees to Mexico, 738.
Nome Cult reservation, established, 135; whites settle on, 136; massacre at, 138.
Nome Lackee reservation, established, 135; cost of, 137; abandoned, 138.
Norton, A. B., reports on Navahos, 470.

OATMAN FLAT, description of, 162, 163; Oatman family buried in, 188.
Oatman, Lorenzo, statement of, 161; attacked by Tontos, 165; escape of, 166–171; efforts to release his sisters, 179, 180; subsequent history of, 184.
Oatman, Mary, taken by Tontos, 166; fright of, 171; treatment of, 173; sold to Mohaves, 174; tattooed, 175; becomes helpless, 176; dies, 177.
Oatman, Olive, determines not to be captured, 163; taken by Tontos, 166; carried away, 171; assailed, 172; enslaved, 173; sold to Mohaves, 174; tattooed, 175; labor of, 176; terrors of, 177, 178; Mohaves try to prevent release of, 181; released, 183; subsequent history of, 184.

Oatman Royse, sketch of, 158; starts West, 159; forebodings of, 163; meets Tontos, 164; killed, 165.
Odeneal, F. B., succeeds Meacham, 551; advises placing Modocs on reservation, 552; blamed by Colonel Wheaton, 554.
Ogallallas, Sioux, who are, 231; police of, 227; in Grattan massacre, 232; treaty of 1866 with, 481; opposition to treaty, 482; efforts to conciliate, 483; in Fetterman massacre, 500; location in 1876, 591; at war, 618; make peace, 628.
Ogden, P. S., ransoms prisoners, 100; quoted, 105.
Ohhastee. *See* Little Raven.
Ojo Blanco, Mescalero chief, leaves Bosque Redondo, 392.
Ojo del Oso. *See* Bear Spring.
Okkowish. *See* Modocs.
Old Snag. Snake chief, band of, 276.
Ollacut, Nez Percé warrior, a brother of Joseph, 636; not in first hostilities, 648; killed, 659.
Oncpapas, Sioux, who are, 231; treaty of 1866 with; 481; at war, 500; location in 1876, 591; at war, 618; make peace, 628.
One Eye, Cheyenne chief, killed at Sand Creek, 417.
Oohenonpa. *See* Two Kettles.
Ord, General, policy to Apaches, 717, 718; results of, 719.
Oregon, first visitors to, 32, 33; Kelly's efforts to colonize, 34, 35; efforts of Benton and Floyd, 36; the Nez Percé messengers, 36–42; first Indian school in, 35; first missionaries, 37; early emigrants, 38; English colonization frustrated by Whitman, 38–42; Ashburton treaty, 41; boundary settled, 41–43; Greenhow's estimate of, 45; differing views of, 46, 47; Indians of, 83, 84; action of Hudson's Bay Company, 88, 89; Cayuse war, 100; Indians of, kill medicine-men, 105–108; organized as a territory, 189; Indians of southern part of, 190, 191; Indian titles in, 194; aggressions by settlers, 195, 196; behavior of Indians, 196; conduct of volunteers, 205–207, 211; removal of Governor Palmer, 208; General Harney sent to, 238; the Stevens treaties, 333, 336; slavery in, 370, 372; pay of militia of, in Modoc war, 578.
Ortiz, Lieutenant, conduct at Fort Fauntleroy, 448.
Ortiz, Tomas, leads conspiracy in New Mexico, 61.
Osages, in Confederate army, 424; in Union army, 425.
Otis, Colonel, defeats Sitting Bull, 625.
Otis, Major, investigates charges against Modocs, 549.
Otoahnacco. *See* Bull Bear.
Ott, Larry, kills Nez Percé Indian. 636.
Ouray, Ute chief, meaning of name, 683; on encroachments of whites, 684; on sale of Uncompahgré Park, 688; under pay from government, 689; stops hostilities, 706; orders surrender of women, 711; death of, 714.
Owahi, or Owhi, Yakima chief, repudiates treaty with Stevens, 202; causes discontent among Spokanes, 338; comes to Colonel Wright's camp, 352; put in irons, 353.
Owen, Agent, quoted, 342.

PACHICO, Bannock chief, band of, 276.
Pageah, Snake chief, band of, 277.
Pahsappa. *See* Black Hills.
Pah-Utes, who are, 277; in Mountain Meadow

778　INDEX.

massacre, 293, 295, 298; took no captives there, 307; captured for slaves, 369; Mormon effort to relieve, 370.
Pah Vants, said to be poisoned by Fancher's train, 290; deny they were poisoned, 306; not at Mountain Meadow massacre, 307; poison story disproved, 317.
Pal, Piegan warrior, shoots Mr. Clarke, 527.
Pala reservation, Indian title to, 147; taken by settlers, 149.
Palmer, Governor, controversy with Oregon Legislature, 208.
Palmer, Sergeant, testimony as to Sand Creek, 434, 437.
Papagos, location of, 152, 153; reservation for, 187; aid United States against Apaches, 385, 386; neglect of, 743.
Paramucka, Apache chief, killed, 389.
Parkman, Francis, quoted, 27, 585, 586.
Pawnee Killer, Sioux chief, commands hostiles, 438.
Pawnees, in Union army, 425; Cheyennes go to attack, 439, 440.
Payne, Captain, at Milk Creek, 701; explanation of pictures, 712.
Peace Policy, definition of, 19; not successful as practised, 25; neglect of Navahos under, 475, 476; tried on Modocs, 556; effect on Nez Percés, 674; defects of, 716, 717, 743.
Pease, Lieutenant, reports on Piegan surprise, 530; misrepresented, 531, 532.
Pedro, Apache chief, refuses to remove, 736.
Pelouses, location of, 86; Stevens's treaty with, 217; Steptoe marches against, 324; attack on Steptoe, 325–327; bands of, 338; fight Colonel Wright, 344; property of, destroyed, 347; punishment of, 353; treaty with, ratified, 355.
Penaltishn, Apache warrior, guides General Crook, 750.
Pend d'Oreilles, location of, 83; Stevens's treaty with, 217, 516; probable origin of name, 351, 352; treaty ratified, 355.
Penn, Captain, warns Whitman of attack, 721.
Penn, William, not only purchaser of Indian lands, 8; quoted, 250.
Peonage, what is, 368.
Perry's cavalry, capture Modocs, 577.
Perry, Colonel, sent against Nez Percés, 648; defeated, 649.
Persune, Yampa warrior, captures Josie Meeker, 705; takes her for wife, 706; infatuation of, 712; Utes amused at, 713; surrender of demanded, 714.
Petalesharro, Pawnee chief, character of, 24.
Peter, Piegan warrior, kills Mr. Clarke, 527.
"Pet Lambs," sobriquet of Colorado troops, 407.
Pfeiffer, Captain, sent through Cañon de Chelly, 461; results of expedition, 462.
Phillips, Wendell, on Indians, 23; letter to Sherman mentioned, 717.
Piah, White River chief, mentioned, 690.
Pi-Edes, Utes, at Mountain Meadow massacre, 293; sacrificed, 372.
Piegans, starvation of, 17, 538; origin of, 509; now include Blackfoot nation, 510; religion of, 511; reputation of, 512; location in 1853, 515; treat with Stevens, 516; remain peaceful, 517; rise of troubles with, 520; depredations by, 521; bad treatment of, 522; encouraged by Hudson's Bay Company, 523; conduct of whites, 524; increase of depredations, 527; Baker sent against, 528; result of expedition, 529; Indian account of fight, 530; probable truth, 531; criticism of fight, 532; result of criticism, 533; officers defend action, 534; opinions of officers, 535; neglect of, 536; sufferings of, 537; right to aid, 541; helplessness of, 542; reported depredations by, 542 (note). See also Blackfeet and Bloods.
Pigeon's ranche. See Apache Cañon.
Piñonsenay, Apache warrior, kills Rogers and Spence, 737; wounded, 738.
Pike, Lieut. Z., expedition to Red River, 29; opinion of American desert, 34.
Pike's Peak mining excitement, 241.
Pimas, location of, 152; joined by Maricopas, 155; Oatmans at village of, 160; relieve Lorenzo Oatman, 168; defeat Yumas, 187; aid United States against Apaches, 385, 386, 389.
Pinal treaty, described, 389.
Pinaleños. See Arivapas.
Pinaquana. See Washikee.
Pindah Lickoyee, Apache name for white men, 392 (note).
Pino Alto mines, settlement at, 374; attack on, 381; Fort West established near, 384.
Piopiomoxmox, Walla-Walla chief, conduct of, 206; killed, 207.
Pitkin, Governor, Jack appeals to, 697; Meeker appeals to, 698.
Pitone, Apache chief, refuses to remove, 736.
Pitt River Indians, hostilities by, 192; slavery among, 371.
Pi-Utes same as Pah-Utes, 277.
Plumbe, John, efforts for Pacific railroad, 44.
Pocatara. See White Plume.
Poemacheeah, Bannock chief, band of, 276.
Polakly Illeha. Leschi's description of, 203.
Polk, J. K., advises occupation of Oregon, 42; accepts compromise line, 43; causes occupation of New Mexico and California, 47.
Pollock, Inspector, quoted, 714.
Polotkin, Spokane chief, message to General Clarke, 341, 342; held as prisoner, 347; treats with Colonel Wright, 351, 352.
Polygamy, Mormon doctrine of, 283, 284.
Poncas, release of, 13; removal of, 21.
Poncha Pass, fight near, 680, 681; meaning of name, 680 (note).
Pony Express, how conducted, 238.
Pope, General, commands Department of Missouri, 391; memorial to, 694; Statement as to Apache war, 741, 742.
Population, Indian, in United States, 1–3; in Virginia, 4; in Kontucky, 5; in Texas and Mexican cession, 6; present increase of, 6, 7; in California, 130, 133.
Poston, C. D., buries remains of Oatman family, 188.
Pottawattamies, in Confederate army, 424.
Powder River country described, 480; Indians oppose road through, 481, 482; troops sent to, 483; right to road, 484, 485; forts built in, 486–488; hostilities by Indians, 489, 490; Fetterman massacre, 491–500; no prospectors in, 502; our claim to, surrendered, 507; abandoned, 508; Sioux title confirmed, 584, 585; Sioux refuse to sell, 589; Sioux ordered out of, 596; Sioux title released, 628.
Powell, L. W., treats with Mormons, 315.
Powell, Major, attacked by Sioux, 504; defeats them, 507.
Pratt, Captain, reforms Modocs, 583.
Price, Commissioner, recommends return of Nez Percés, 669.
Price, Gen. S., commands in New Mexico, 51; marches against Pueblos, 70; conquers them, 74–77.
Price, Mrs., at White River agency, 704; statement of, 705; treatment of, 706.
Price, Shaduck, killed by Utes, 704.

INDEX. 779

Princess Mary. *See* Queen Mary.
Prophecy of war by Joseph Smith, 281, 282.
Pueblo, Colorado, Mormons winter at, 51; settlement at, 81; in 1847, 219.
Pueblo de Taos described, 73; battle at, 74–77.
Pueblos, invasion of lands of, 11, 12; described, 53–61; origin unknown, 54; houses of, 58; join conspiracy, 61; begin insurrection, 62; massacre at Fernandez de Taos, 62–66; massacre at Arroyo Hondo, 66–69; Price marches against, 70; fight at Pueblo de Taos, 74–77; beg for mercy, 77; subsequent good behavior, 78; religious troubles, 79; object to taxation, 79 (*note*); Navahos not descended from, 245; of Zuñi assist troops, 268.

QUAIL, JAMES, murder of, 527.
Qualchian, Yakima warrior, excites discontent among Spokanes, 338; hanged, 353.
Quapaws, in Confederate army, 424.
Queen Mary, Modoc squaw, carries message for Captain Jack, 562; captured, 577.
Quelaptip, Pelouse chief, band of, 338.
Quinaielts, treaty with, ratified, 355.
Quitaniwa. *See* Foul Hand.

RAILROAD, first, to Mississippi River, 43; early proposals for Pacific, 44; proposals for Southern Pacific, 51; Cheyennes object to Kansas Pacific, 243, 408; effect of Pacific, on West, 585; effect in Leadville excitement, 676, 677.
Rain-in-the-Face, Sioux warrior, said to have killed Custer, 615; cause of hatred of Custer, 616.
Rains, Lieutenant, killed, 649.
Rains, Major, campaign against Yakimas, 204.
Randall, Captain, attack on, 649; captures Tontos, 730.
Ravalli, Father, builds Cœur d'Alêne church, 348.
Rawlins Springs, massacre at, 595.
Rawn, Captain, tries to stop Nez Percés, 651.
Red Cloud, Ogallalla chief, sketch of, 481; opposes treaty of 1866, 482; goes to war, 483; Sioux gather to, 484; attacks Fort Phil Kearney, 490, 491; not in Fetterman massacre, 500; attacks Major Powell, 504; defeated, 507; makes treaty, 507, 508; willing to sell Black Hills, 588; deposed, 626.
Red Cloud agency, fraud at, 16.
Red Horn, Piegan chief, becomes hostile, 524; camp of, attacked, 528; killed, 529.
Red Sleeves. *See* Mangas Colorado.
Reed, Autie, killed at Little Big Horn, 612.
Removal and Concentration Policy, cause of Indian wars, 19–22; unreasonable, 22, 23, 25; Spokanes object to, 335, 336, 355; Apaches object to, 390, 391; failure of, in Arizona, 395; tried with Navahos, 452, 464; evils of, 464–466; opposed by Dr. Steck, 467, 468; failure of, 468–471; tried with Modocs, 545, 546, 551, 552; Modocs object to, 568; no reason for, 642; tried on Nez Percés, 646; they go to war, 647, 648; sent to Indian Territory, 660; returned to Idaho, 670, 671; failure with Mimbreños, 726, 727; inaugurated in Arizona, 733, 734; failure with White Mountain Apaches, 735, 736; tried on Chiricahuas, 736–738; tried on Mimbreños, 738–740; official statements of results, 741, 742; effects of, 743.
Reno, Major, scouts on Rosebud River, 604; report of, 608, 609; tries to reach Custer, 609; besieged, 610; estimate of number of hostiles, 618; number of hostiles, 620; in action at same time as Custer, 621; not in fault 624.

Reservations, food at 17; of California, 135, 138, 147, 149; need of better title in Indians, 142, 150; lessened without compensation, 538, 541.
Reuben, James, Nez Percé preacher, works among exiles, 670.
Reynolds, Charley, detects Rain-in-the-Face, 616.
Reynolds, Colonel, fight with Sioux, 597; criticism of fight, 598.
Rickarees, location of, 81.
Riddle, Interpreter, warns Modoc commissioners, 565; warns Gillem, 566; goes to council, 567; pursued, 569; escapes, 570; testifies, 580.
Ridgely, ——, statement concerning Custer massacre, 621.
Riley, Lieutenant, killed at Little Big Horn, 612.
River Crows, who are, 479; Gros Ventres of the North consolidated with, 522.
Rocky Mountain Fur Company, organized, 33.
Rogers. ——, killed by Apaches, 737.
Rogue River Indians, description of, 190; hostilities by, 191; make peace, 192; kill Capt. Ben Wright, 193, 211; go to war, 196, 199; treat with General Lane, 200; massacre of, 205; fight at Big Bend, 216; go to Grande Ronde reservation, 216; treaty with, 218; slavery among, 371.
Roper, Miss, captured by Cheyennes, 412; treatment of, 429.
Roseborough, Judge, legal adviser of Modocs, 549; member of Modoc Commission, 560.
Ross, John, commands Oregon volunteers with Ben Wright, 193; commands militia in Modoc war, 562.
Ross, Representative, investigates Indian affairs in New Mexico, 470.
Russell, Green, discovers gold in Colorado, 240.
Russell, W. H., intercedes for General Harney, 237; power of, 238.

SAFFORD, GOVERNOR, on Indian affairs of Arizona in 1815, 732.
Sahaptins, location and divisions of, 86.
sah-patch, White River chief, mentioned, 690.
Sakitapix, same as Blackfoot nation, 509.
Saline River, outrages on, 439, 440.
Salmon River, discovery of mines on, 477; settlers on, killed, 647, 648.
Sanborn, J. B., member Board Peace Commissioners, 716.
Sand Creek, attack on Cheyennes and Arapahoes at, 396–401; troops at, 403; Indians at, 408; hostilities leading to, 408–411; Indians admit hostility, 411–416; proofs of hostility, 416; Indians not promised protection, 417–421; attack justified, 422; desire of officers to punish Indians, 423; feelings of loyal people, 424, 425; why women and children were killed, 426–429; Congressional report on, 430–433; misrepresentations of, 433–437; used against Chivington politically, 443; Chivington's account of, 444, 445; compared with other massacres, 446.
Sandoval, Navaho chief, accompanies Colonel Washington, 257; efforts at neutrality, 263; privileged in treaty of 1858, 271.
San Francisco, full name of, 52 (*note*).
San Juan country, mining excitement in, 682, 683.
San Pasqual reservation, title to, 147; taken by settlers, 149.
Sanpitches, who are, 277.
Sans Arcs, Sioux, who are, 231; treaty of 1866 with, 481; at war, 500; location in 1876, 591; at war, 618; make peace, 628.

780　INDEX.

Santa Anna, treatment of Texans, 27, 28.
Santa Fé, trade to, 29–31; full name of, 52 (*note*); excitement at, during Pueblo insurrection, 70.
Santa Rita del Cobré, home of Mimbreños, 357; massacre at, 361; Kearny meets Apaches near, 365; Bartlett's party at, 366; hostilities at 373, 374.
Santees, Sioux, who are, 231.
San Xavier del Bac, cathedral of, built, 155; despoiled, 743.
Sapavanari, Uncompahgré chief, accompanies surveying party, 685; quoted, 688; meaning of name, 689 (*note*); accompanies Brady, 705.
Sarap, White River chief, mentioned, 690.
Sarcillo Largo; Navaho chief, resigns office, 261; summoned to Fort Defiance, 262; reports arrest of murderer, 263, 264; attacked and defeated, 266.
Saskatchewan, meaning of, 509.
Satsika. *See* Black feet.
Saulotken. *See* Polotkin.
Saverro Aredia released from Apaches, 366.
Scalp-bounty, given by Mexican States, 360; results of, 361, 362; causes murder of our Indians, 362, 363.
Scar-faced Charlie, Modoc warrior, refuses to surrender, 553; favors war, 563; who was, 564; stands guard over Steele, 565; shoots Lieutenant Sherwood, 570; surrenders, 577; testifies, 580.
Schonchin John, Modoc warrior, favors war, 563; at council, 567; speech at council, 568; assaults Meacham, 569; surrenders, 577; arraigned, 579; tried, 580; sentenced, 581; executed, 582.
Schonchin, Modoc chief, authority of, contested by Captain Jack, 545.
Schoolcraft, H. R., estimate of land needed to support Indians, 2; estimate of population of California, 131.
Schurz, Secretary, gives time to settlers in Uncompahgré Park, 687.
Scott, Agent, report on Nez Percés, 670.
Scott, General, supports General Wool, 211; quarrels with General Harney, 236–238.
Seattle attacked by Indians, 207.
Selish. *See* Flatheads.
Semig, Dr., wounded in Lava Beds, 573, 574.
Seminoles, in Confederate army, 424.
Senecas, in Confederate army, 424.
Shacknasty Jim, Modoc warrior, at council, 567; pursues Riddle, 569; betrays Captain Jack, 576; testifies, 580.
Shampoag, treaty at 202.
Shanks, General, Joseph's argument to, 640; quoted, 647.
Shastas, include Rogue Rivers, 190; divisions of, 191; troubles with, 200; slavery among, 371.
Shavano, Tabequache chief, mentioned, 689; son of, killed, 715.
Shawawai, Yakima chief, excites discontent among Spokanes, 338.
Shawnees, in Confederate army, 424.
Shepherd's train, attack on, 313.
Sheridan, Gen. P. H., commands at Cascades, 212; in Yakima country, 217; orders to Colonel Baker, 533; quoted, 534.
Sherman, General, tests first gold in California, 121; commands Division of the Mississippi, 391; orders Cheyennes to their reservation, 440; advises extermination of Sioux, 446; treats with Navahos, 471; stops sale of arms and ammunition, 501, 502; quoted, 530; justifies Colonel Baker, 534; statement concerning Custer massacre, 617; opinion of Lolo trail, 651; report of Nez Percé war, 660; member Board Peace Commissioners, 716; Phillips's letter to, 717.
Sherwood, Lieutenant, assassination of, 570.
Shirland, Captain, captures Mangas Colorado, 382.
Shis Inday, same as Apaches, 357.
Shooters, who were, 591.
Shoshokos, who are, 276.
Shoshonees, or Snakes, location and divisions of, 83; murder emigrants, 200; sign for, 225; bands of, 275–277; aided by Mormons, 331; attack Nez Percés, 332.
Shumahiccie, Cayuse warrior, enamoured of a white girl, 99, 100.
Sibley, General, invades New Mexico, 381, 382, 403–407.
Sicangu, See Brulés
Sign language, universality of, 223; theories of, 224; tribal designations in, 225; for long distances, 226; mirrors used in, 227.
Sihasapa. *See* Blackfoot Sioux.
Sinta Gallessca. *See* Spotted Tail.
Sioux, location of, 81; war with Cheyennes, 221; sign for, 225; soldiers or police of, 227; tribal divisions of, 231; massacre Grattan's party, 232; go to war, 233; General Harney defeats, 234, 235; submission of, 236; rise of hostilities of 1864, 424, 425; hostilities of 1867, 438; acquire Powder River country, 479; treaty of 1866 with, 481; disagreement as to treaty, 482; repudiate treaty, 483; go to war, 484; depredations of, 486, 487; torture by, 489; harass Fort Phil Kearney, 490; Fetterman massacre, 491–500; misrepresentations of massacre, 501, 502; continue hostilities, 504; defeated by Major Powell, 507; burn forts, 508; rights of, under treaty of 1868, 584, 585; object to invasion of Black Hills, 589, 590; divisions of, in 1876, 591; depredations by, 593, 694; ordered to leave Powder River country, 596; Reynolds's fight with, 596–598; expedition against, 598–601; Crook's fight with, 603, 604; Custer massacre, 605–624; operations against, 625-627; treaty of 1876, 628.
Sitting Bull, Sioux chief, sketch of, 591; autobiography of, 592, 593; refuses to leave Powder River country, 596; expedition against, 598–601; Custer massacre, 605–624; operations against, 625, 626; goes to British America, 627; returns, 628.
Skinarwan, Yakima chief, assists troops, 352.
Skitsuish. *See* Cœur d'Alênes.
Skloom, Yakima chief, excites discontent among Spokanes, 338.
Slavery, women slaves of their husbands, 250; among Apaches, 367; among Mexicans, 368; Diggers enslaved, 369; Mormon law concerning, 370; in Oregon, 371; in Colorado, 372; evil effects of, 373; in New Mexico, 447; Camp Grant captives sold into, 725.
Slolox, Modoc warrior, aids at massacre of commissioners, 569; arraigned, 580; convicted, 581; sentence commuted, 582.
Slough, Colonel, leads Colorado volunteers, 404; joins Canby, 405.
Smellers, same as Arapahoes, 225.
Smith, E. P., opposes removal policy, 20.
Smith, George A., Mormon apostle, connection with Mountain Meadow massacre, 294; deposition at Lee's trail, 318.
Smith, Jack, murdered at Sand Creek, 398; attacks stage-coach, 432.
Smith, Joseph, Mormon prophet, murder of, 273; war prophecy of, 281, 282; deceit of,

283; responsibility for death of, put on Fancher train, 290.
Smith, J. Q., favors removals, 20.
Smith, J. S., at Sand Creek, 397; son of, killed, 398; testimony as to Dog Soldiers, 431; aids in treaty, 437.
Smith, Lot, destroys United States trains, 289.
Smith, Gen. P. E., quoted, 239.
Smohallie, religion of, 640.
Snake Creek, fight at, 658, 659.
Snakes, See Shoshonees.
Snyder, Mrs., suicide of, 429.
Soie, Pelouse chief, band of, 338.
Solomon's Fork, action on, 239, 240.
Sonora, policy towards Apaches, 359; pays scalp-bounty, 360, 362; results of scalp-bounty, 361; slaves sold into, 369, 726.
Southern Snakes. See Cache Valley Indians.
Southern Utes, who are, 681; mistreatment of, 682; cede San Juan country, 683; lands of, surveyed out, 685; make cession, 687; chiefs of, 688, 689; established in Colorado, 715.
Spalding, Rev. H. H., goes to Oregon as missionary, 37; located at Lapwai, 87; controversy with Jesuits, 90; escape of, 99, 110; quoted, 102; with Nez Percés, 116.
Spencer, Cascade chief, murder of family of, 212.
Spokanes, friendly before 1858, 324; menace Steptoe, 325; attack him, 326; pursue him, 327; causes of hostility uncertain, 328-333; probable cause, Stevens's treaties, 333-338; who are, 338, 339; refuse to surrender offenders, 341, 342; Colonel Wright marches against, 342, 343; defeated at Four Lakes, 344; property of, destroyed, 347; treaty with, 351, 352.
Spotted Tail, Brulé chief, murder of, 10; surrenders as a hostage, 236; sketch of, 482; Indians desert, 484; willing to sell Black Hills, 588; made head-chief, 626.
squaws. See Women.
Stanley, J. M., quoted, 371.
Stanley, J. Q. A., intercedes for Mission Indians, 148, 149.
Stanwood, Captain, ratifies Lieutenant Whitman's actions, 721.
Steamboat Frank, Modoc warrior, aids in massacre of commissioners, 569; betrays Captain Jack, 576; witness at trial, 580; becomes preacher, 583.
Steck, Dr. Matthew, treats with Mescaleros, 378; opposes Bosque Redondo reservation, 467; Carleton complains of, 468; succeeded by Felipe Delgado, 470.
Steele, Judge, legal adviser of Modocs, 549; acts as messenger to them 564; saved by Captain Jack, 565.
Steptoe, Colonel, captures Gunnison murderers, 279; expedition to Fort Colville, 324; menaced by Indians, 325; attacked, 326; fight on Ingossomen Creek, 327; retreats, 328; quoted, 333; recovery of guns abandoned by, 353.
Stevens. Gen. I. I., first governor of Washington Territory, 196; treaties of, repudiated, 202; protected by Nez Percés, 203; controversy with General Wool, 208; quoted, 215; treaties of, 217, 218; trouble over treaties, 333-336; treaties favored, 354; treaties ratified, 355; among Blackfeet, 514; makes treaties, 516; appoints head - chief of Nez Percés, 631.
Stickney, William, member Nez Percé commission, 646; responsibility of, 672.
Stockton, Commodore, aids in conquest of California, 47.

Stokes, William, arrests John D. Lee, 316.
Strong Hearts, a Sioux fraternity, 592.
Sturgis, General, attacks Nez Percés, 657; Nez Percés escape, 658.
St. Vrain, Felix, leads volunteers against Pueblos, 70; position at Pueblo de Taos, 74; services at same, 77.
Sully, General, Blackfeet offer to aid, 518; quoted, 523, 524; misrepresented by Colyer, 531, 532; opinion of Piegan hostility, 534, 535.
Sumner, Col, E. V., quoted, 236, 237, 240; sent against Cheyennes and Arapahoes, 239; defeats them, 240.
Sun dance, what is, 616 (note).
Sunflower-seed Eaters, who are, 276.
Sun River farm, provision for, 516; a humbug, 517; abandoned, 518; buildings at, burned, 521.
Susan, Ute squaw, assists captives, 711.
Sutter, John A., connection of, with gold discovery in California, 118-121.
Sweet Root. See Pachico.

TABBY, Uintah chief, mentioned, 690.
Tabequaches, Utes, who are, 271; location of, 681; arable lands of, 683; chiefs of, 689; removed to Utah, 715.
Table Rock, treaty at, 200.
Tahza, Chiricahua chief, band of, 736; consents to remove, 738.
Talsi-Gobbeth, Pi-ede chief, at Mountain Meadow massacre, 293.
Tamatabs. See Mohaves.
Tamsaky, Cayuse warrior, murders Dr. Whitman, 94; betrays the fugitives, 96; convicted and hanged, 101, 102.
Taos, settlers at, 52; massacre at, 62-66.
Tappan, Colonel, presides over Sand Creek commission, 417; treats with Navahos, 471; member Board Peace Commissioners, 716.
Taracones, same as Navahos, 358.
Tashunkah-Kokepah. See Man-Afraid-of-his-Horses.
Tatankahyotankah. See Sitting Bull.
Tatkannais, who were, 591.
Tawaitu, Cayuse chief, confers with Jesuits, 93.
Taylor, Captain, killed, 327; buried at Fort Walla-Walla, 353.
Taylor, Commissioner, conduct at Sioux treaty of 1866, 483.
Taylor, John, Mormon President, veracity of, 283; quoted, 287.
Taylor, N. G., treats with Utes, 681; member Board Peace Commissioners, 716.
Tejon reservation, character of, 136; cost of, 137; abandoned, 138.
Teller, H. M., intercedes for settlers in Uncompahgré Park, 686, 687; Meeker's letter to, 690.
Ten Eyck, Captain, sent to reinforce Fetterman, 492; finds bodies of command, 495; brings them in, 496.
Terribio, Navaho chief, captured, 268.
Terry, General, Sitting Bull's message to, 596; connection with Custer-Grant quarrel, 601; intercedes for Custer, 603; reaches Powder River, 604; instructions to Custer, 607; reaches scene of massacre, 611; mistake as to number of Sioux, 617, 618, 623; member Board Peace Commissioners, 716.
Tetons, Sioux, who are, 231; location of, 232; possible derivation of name, 516; location in 1876, 591; at war, 618; make peace, 628.
Texan invasion of New Mexico, history of, 381, 382, 403-407.

INDEX.

Texas, American settlement of, 27; annexation question, 28, 29; reputed value of, 44, 47.
Theller, Lieutenant, cut off at White Bird Cañon, 649.
Thomas, Captain, enters Lava Beds, 572; killed, 573.
Thomas, Rev. E., appointed on Modoc commission, 560; opinion as to last council, 565; refuses to deceive Indians, 566; goes to council, 567; speech at council, 568; killed, 569; body recovered, 570; indignation at murder of, 571; statement of son of, 582, 583.
Thompson, Arthur, killed by Utes, 704.
Thornburgh, Maj. T. T., investigates conduct of Utes, 692; advances to White River, 699; fight at Milk Creek, 700; killed, 701; picture on body of, 712.
Thunder Hawk, Sioux warrior, murder of, 10.
Tierra Blanco, Ute chief, attacks settlements, 680; defeated, 681.
Tilcoax, Pelouse chief, band of, 338; hostilities of, 347, 348.
Tilokaikt, Cayuse chief, meaning of name, 86; in council with Jesuits, 93; mangles Dr. Whitman's body, 96; convicted and hanged, 101, 102.
Timothy, Nez Percé chief, aids Steptoe, 328; aids Wright, 343.
Timpanagas, who are, 277.
Tinneh. See Athabascans.
Tinney, Mormon bishop, incites California Indians, 281.
Tiswin, what is, 753.
Tlickitacks. See Klickitats.
Toby Riddle, Modoc squaw, warned of treachery, 565; goes to council, 567; assaulted by Slolox, 569; saves Meacham, 570; testifies, 580.
Tomas, Pueblo chief, brutal treatment of Governor Bent, 65; shot, 78.
Tontos, Apaches, location and description of, 157, 358; rob Doctor Le Conte, 162; meet Oatman family, 164; murder them, 165; 166; carry off Oatman girls, 171, 172; treatment of captives, 173; sell girls to Mohaves, 174; subsequent history of, 187; enslaved, 369; located at Camp Verde, 730; hostiles punished, 732; removal of, 733, 734.
Toohulhulsute, Nez Percé chief, at treaty council, 638; removal from council, 646; resentment of, 647; killed, 659.
Tookarikas, who are, 275, 276.
Travis, Wes, in Ute agency cattle robbery, 695.
Triggs, Lieutenant, takes Mrs. Ewbank's deposition, 427.
Tubac, deserted, 381; reoccupied, 392.
Tucson, antiquity of, 159; effect of Apache war on, 381; recovers its population, 392, 395.
Tularosa Valley reservation, established, 726; abandoned, 727.
Tulé River, farm established, 137.
Turnwater, Oregon, settled, 190.
Tupper, Major, defeats Apaches, 747.
Turley, Simeon, character of, 67; defence of mill, 68; killed, 69.
Two Face, Sioux warrior, treatment of Mrs. Ewbanks, 428; refuses to sell her to Cheyennes, 429.
Two Kettles, Sioux, who are, 231; treaty of 1866 with, 481; at war, 500; location in 1876, 591; at war, 618; make peace, 628.
Tyler, President, favors annexation of Texas, 29.

Uintahs, Utes, location of, 690.
Umatillas, Stevens's treaty with, 217; treaty ratified, 355; removal of, recommended, 645.

Umpquas related to Athabascans, 82; hostilities by, 191; slavery among, 371.
Uncommute, Uncompahgré chief, mentioned, 689.
Uncompahgré Park, title to, in Utes, 683; reserved by treaty, 684; cut off by surveyor, 685; settled, 686; settlers remain, 687; sold by Utes, 688.
Uncompahgrés, Utes, location of, 681; arable land of, 683; chiefs of, 689; among hostiles, 705, 712; influence of peaceful portion, 714; removed to Utah, 715.
Unkpahpahs. See Oncpapas.
Upsaroka. See Crows.
Upson, Agent, treats with Blackfeet, 518.
Uré. See Ouray.
Utah, Ashley in Salt Lake Basin, 33; Harney relieved from command of expedition, 237, 238; secretary of, killed, 239; Fremont's description, 275; Indians of, 275–277; Indian troubles in, 278–281; reformation in, 283, 284; lawlessness in, 285, 286; expedition to, 287; martial law proclaimed in, 288; Fancher's train in, 289-292; Mountain Meadow massacre, 292-300; investigation of massacre, 305-310, 312–315; duty of Gentiles, 311; trial of John D. Lee, 316–319; execution of Lee, 320; situation in, 322, 323; slavery in 369, 370.
Utes, relations to Colorado settlers, 241, 242; divisions of, 277; Jicarillas take refuge with, 378; assist United States, 465; removal of, desired in Colorado, 675–680; fight near Poncha Pass, 680, 681; treaty of 1868 with, 681; objections to treaty, 682; treaty of 1872, 683; treaty not kept by United States, 684, 685; Uncompahgré Park trouble, 686–688; organization of, 689, 690; Meeker's troubles, 690, 691; charges against, 692–694; bad white neighbors, 695; refuse to surrender offenders, 696; troubles increase, 697; Meeker assaulted, 698; Thornburgh marches against, 699; fight at Milk Creek, 700, 701; conduct at the agency, 702, 703; attack on agency, 704, 705; close of hostilities, 706–710; surrender of captives, 711–713; the pictures, 712; councils with, 714; removal of, 715.

Vallé, Alexandre, quoted, 407.
Valverde, fight at, 404.
Van Buren, Martin, opposes annexation of Texas, 29; defeated, 47.
VanVliet, Captain, sent to Salt Lake City, 287; returns to army, 288.
Victor, Pend d'Oreille chief, attacked by Milkapsi, 326.
Victorio, Mimbreños chief, refuses to be removed, 739; raids of, 740; official opinions of his case, 741, 742; killed, 744.
Vincent, Cœur d'Alêne chief, talks with Steptoe, 326; recalls messengers, 328; statement to Joset, 329; charge of insult to, 330; quoted, 337; band of, 341.
Virginia City, Montana, settlement of, 478.
Voorhees, Representative, criticises attack on Piegans, 532; quoted 535, 542.

Waba Yuma. Hualapais chief, murdered, 391.
Wagoner massacre, described, 206.
Wailatpu Mission established, 38; meaning of name, 86; described, 86, 87; massacre at, 93–100; Fort Waters established at, 101; present appearance of, 102.
Wailatpus, location and divisions of, 86.
Walker, Capt. Jesse, defeats Modocs, 200, 201.
Walker, Capt. J. G., quoted, 267.
Walker, Major, expedition against Navahos, 256.

INDEX. 783

Walker, Ute chief, sacrifices at burial of, 372.
Wallammutekint Indians, who were, 630.
Walla-Walla. See Fort Walla-Walla.
Walla-Wallas, location of, 86; Stevens's treaty with, 217; treaty ratified, 355; removal of, recommended. 645.
Wallowa Valley described, 632; Nez Percés retain title to, 633–635; proposed for reservation, 637; wishes of Nez Percés for, 639, 640; Nez Percés ordered from, 646.
Walnut Creek, massacre at, 412, 444, 445.
War Bonnet, Arapahoe chief, in attack on General Blunt, 416.
War Department, should have inspection of agencies, 18.
Warm Springs Indians, aid against Modocs, 571; accompany Captain Thomas, 572; separated from troops, 573; scout in Lava Beds, 574; follow Modocs, 577.
Warner, Dr., testimony of, 467.
Warrarikas, who are, 276.
Warren, Lieutenant, attempts to enter Black Hills, 585.
Washikee, Snake chief, sketch of, 275.
Washington, Col. J. M., expedition against Navahos, 257; treaty of, not ratified, 258.
Washington Territory organized, 189; first settlement in, 190; discovery of Colville mines, 204; rise of Spokane war, 324–328; causes of war, 328–337; Indians of eastern part of, 338, 341; Wright's campaign, 341–554; Garnett's campaign, 352; ratification of treaties, 355; discovery of Salmon River mines, 477.
Watkins, Inspector, reports on Sioux, 596.
Webster, Daniel, negotiates Ashburton treaty, 41; opposes annexation of Texas, 46, 47.
Weeminuches, included in Southern Utes, 681.
Weir, Captain, attempts to reach Custer, 609.
Weir, Lieutenant, killed by Utes, 709.
Wells, D. H., commands Mormon forces, 289.
Wells, Fargo & Co., horses stolen from, 523.
Wessels, General, succeeds Carrington, 500; attempts campaign, 504.
Wheat Cañon. See Cañon del Trigo.
Wheaton, Colonel, instructions to, 552; blames Odeneal, 554; proceeds against Modocs, 555; asks reinforcements, 556.
Whipple, Captain, describes Wallowa Valley, 632; statement as to Old Joseph, 634; tells Nez Percés they must move, 637.
White Antelope, Cheyenne chief, in council, 412; quoted, 415, 416, 420, 421.
White Bird, Nez Parcé chief, band of, 638; joins hostiles, 648; escape of, 659, 660.
White Bird Cañon. fight at, 648, 649.
White Cattle. See Ganado Blanco.
White Eagles, who were. 591.
White, Elijah, appoints head-chief of Nez Percés, 631.
White Eyes, Apache name for Americans, 392.
White family, murdered by Jicarillas, 374–377.
White Knives. See Shoshokos.
White Plume, Snake chief, band of, 276; quoted, 280.
White River agency, location of, 691; massacre at, 703–706; appearance after massacre, 709, 710.
White Rivers, Utes, who were, 681; chiefs of, 690; Meeker's troubles with, 691, 697, 698; behavior of, 692–694; white neighbors of, 695; refuse to surrender offenders, 696; troops sent against 699; attack troops, 700, 701; destroy agency, 703–705; suspend hostilities, 706; removed to Utah, 715.
White Thunder, Sioux chief, murder of, 10.
White Wolf, Arapahoe warrior, warns whites, 425.

Whiteman, Agent, reports on Nez Percés, 665.
Whiting, Agent, reports on Nez Percés, 665.
Whiting, Superintendent, recommends reservations for Mission Indians, 147; quoted, 149.
Whitman, Dr. M., goes to Oregon, 37; takes first wagon, 38; rides to the States, 38, 39; secures emigration, 41, 42; mission at Wailatpu, 86, 87; controversy with Jesuits, 93; murder of, 94; accused of poisoning Indians 113; proposed monument to, 117 (note).
Whitman, Lieutenant, receives Apaches at Camp Grant, 719; reports to head-quarters, 720; action of, approved, 721; account of massacre, 722, 723; charges against, unfounded, 724.
Whitman, Silas, Nez Percé preacher, welcomes exiles, 671.
Whittaker, Captain, criticism of Reno and Benteen, 624.
Wilbur, Father, recommends removal of Nez Percés, 640.
Wilkes, Captain, estimate of population of California, 131.
Willcox, General, opinion of Victorio's treatment, 741.
William, or Whim, Modoc warrior, warns Toby, 565; testifies, 580.
Wilson, B. D., reports on Mission Indians, 146.
Winnebago reservation, lesson of, 150.
Winthrop, Congressman, opposes occupation of Oregon, 46.
Wohlpape Snakes, placed on Klamath reservation, 544.
Women, Indian, fight at Ash Hollow, 236; treatment of, 250; among Navahos, 253, 254,262; treatment by Mexicans, 368–370; generally, 372, 373; fight at Sand Creek, 398; behavior of, 426; fight at the Washita, 440; difference in, 465; torture by, 513; killed in attack on Piegans, 530, 531; criticism in Congress, 532; statements of officers, 534; treatment at Camp Grant, 721–723.
Women, white, treatment by Apaches, 367; by Mexicans, 368–370; generally, 372, 373; treatment by plains Indians, 427, 428; by Nez Percés, 656; by Utes, 706, 711, 713.
Wood. Lieutenant-colonel, opposes forcible removal of Nez Percés, 646, 672.
Wool, General, controversy with Stevens, 208; supported by General Scott, 211.
Woolsey, King S., massacres Apaches, 389.
Wright, Capt. Benjamin, defeats Modocs, 192; massacres Modocs, 193; killed, 211; effect of massacre in Modoc war, 561, 562, 564; should have been punished, 582.
Wright, Colonel, marches against Indians, 211; fight at Cascades, 212; treats with Indians, 216; sent against Spokanes and others, 342; battle at Four Lakes, 343, 344; destroys Indian supplies, 347; treats with Cœur d'Alênes, 351; treats with Spokanes 352; punishes Pelouses, 353; results of campaign, 354.
Wright, Lieutenant, killed in Lava Beds, 573.
Wyeth, N. J., expedition of, 33; quoted, 35; fight with Blackfeet, 512.
Wynkoop, Major, estimate of killed at Sand Creek, 401; sent to Cheyennes and Arapahoes, 412; concedes Little Raven hostile, 416, 418; investigates Sand Creek, 417; subsists Little Raven's Arapahoes, 418; no authority to treat, 421; statement as to Governor Evans, 422; as to Dog Soldiers, 431; Cheyennes did not surrender to, 432; at treaty of 1865, 437; reports of, 439.

XICARILLAS. See Jicarillas.

INDEX.

YAHOOSKIN SNAKES, treaty with, 544.
Yainax agency, established, 545; Modocs leave, 546.
Yakimas, location of, 86; discontent of, 202; go to war, 204; massacre by, at Cascades, 212; Colonel Wright marches against, 215; Stevens's treaty with, 217; attack Steptoe, 325; malcontents of, 338; campaign against, 352; renegades from, hung, 353; treaty ratified, 355.
Yampais, location of, 157; placed at Camp Verde, 727; hostiles brought in, 730; scheme to remove, 733; removal of, 734.
Yampas, Utes, included in White Rivers, 681.
Yanktonnais, Sioux, who are, 231; location of, 232.
Yanktons, Sioux, who are, 231; location of, 232; intimidated by hostiles, 424, 425.
Yates, Captain, killed at Little Big Horn, 612.
Yavapais. *See* Yampais.
Yellow Livers, who were, 591.
Yellow Serpent. *See* Piopiomoxmox.

Yomas, Apache warrior, saves life of Agent Larrabee, 731.
Yosemites, reputation of, 133; hostilities of, 134; beg for peace, 135.
Young, Brigham, Indian policy of, 280, 281; said to have introduced polygamy, 253; preaches blood-atonement, 285; resists United States troops, 286, 287; proclaims martial law, 288, 289; connection with Mountain Meadow massacre, 300, 301; report of, 302; accused of moving monument, 309; conceals criminals, 312; abandons Lee, 318, 319; dies, 320; visit to Oregon, 331.
Young, Ewing, brought to Oregon by Kelly, 35; estate escheats, 35; brings cattle to Oregon, 88.
Yumas, division and location of, 156; take Camp Yuma, 179; subdued, 180; massacre Gallantin's party, 362.

ZABRISKIE, JUDGE ADVOCATE, takes Mrs. Ewbanks's deposition, 427.

THE END.

Other American Indian titles offered by *Digital Scanning, Inc.*

The North American Indians
(2 Volume Set),
by George Catlin
As Published in 1903.
Volume 1:
TP: 1582182124 ($27.95)
HC: 1582182736 ($39.95)
Volume 2:
TP: 1582182132 ($27.95)
HC: 1582182744 ($39.95)

AB-SA-RA-KA The Land of Massacre,
by Margaret Carrington
As Published in 1879.
TP: 1582183821 ($19.95)
HC: 158218383X ($34.95)

Tenting on the Plains,
by Elizabeth Custer
As Published in 1887.
TP: 1582180504 ($29.95)
HC: 1582180512 ($39.95)

Following the Guidon,
by Elizabeth Custer
As Published in 1890.
TP: 1582181160 ($19.95)
HC: 1582181195 ($29.95)

The Young Reader's Catlin - My Life Among the Indians,
by George Catlin
As Published in 1909.
TP: 158218478X ($19.95)
HC: 1582184798 ($31.95)

The Man Who Married the Moon and Other Pueblo Indian Folk Stories,
by Charles F. Lummis
As Published in 1894.
TP: 1582182698 ($14.95)
HC: 1582182701 ($27.95)

The Adventures of the Ojibbeway and Ioway Indians
(2 Volume Set),
by George Catlin
As Published in 1852.
Volume 1:
TP: 1582184941 ($17.95)
HC: 158218495X ($29.95)
Volume 2:
TP: 1582184984 ($17.95)
HC: 1582184992 ($29.95)

Boots and Saddles,
by Elizabeth Custer
As Published in 1885.
TP: 1582181268 ($15.95)
HC: 1582181411 ($25.95)

The Book of the Indians of North America,
by Samuel G. Drake
As Published in 1833.
TP: 1582180946 ($21.95)
HC: 1582181322 ($34.95)

Life Among the Apaches,
by John C. Cremony
As Published in 1868.
TP: 1582183864 ($15.95)
HC: 1582183872 ($29.95)

Indian Boyhood,
by Charles A. Eastman
As Published in 1902.
TP: 1582186863 ($14.95)
HC: 1582186871 ($28.95)

King Philip's War,
by George Ellis & John Morris
As Published in 1906.
TP: 1582184305 ($19.95)
HC: 1582184313 ($33.95)

Warpath & Bivouac or Conquest of the Sioux,
by John F. Finnerty
As Published in 1890.
TP: 1582181950 ($24.95)
HC: 1582181942 ($34.95)

My Life and Experiences Among Our Hostile Indians,
by Major General O. O. Howard
As Published in 1907.
TP: 1582182604 ($27.95)
HC: 1582182612 ($39.95)

Massasoit of the Wampanoags,
by Alvin G. Weeks
As Published in 1920.
TP: 1582185921 ($14.95)
HC: 158218593X ($27.95)

Sheridan's Troopers on the Border,
by De B. Randolph Keim
As Published in 1885.
TP: 1582180601 ($17.95)
HC: 158218061X ($29.95)

Indian Heroes and Great Chieftains,
by Charles A. Eastman
As Published in 1918.
TP: 1582186006 ($13.95)
HC: 1582186014 ($26.95)

A Century of Dishonor,
by Helen Hunt Jackson
As Published in 1889.
TP: 1582182884 ($24.95)
HC: 1582182892 ($39.95)

History of King Philip,
by John Abbott
As Published in 1857.
TP: 1582183147 ($19.95)
HC: 1582183155 ($34.95)

Other American Indian titles offered by DSI (cont.):

The Story of the Indian,
by George Bird Grinnell
As Published in 1902.
TP: 1582182450 ($15.95)
HC: 1582182469 ($29.95)

Blackfoot Lodge Tales,
by George Bird Grinnell
As Published in 1892.
TP: 1582185069 ($17.95)
HC: 1582185077 ($30.95)

The Fighting Cheyennes,
by George Bird Grinnell
As Published in 1915.
TP: 1582183902 ($19.95)
HC: 1582183910 ($34.95)

From Deep Woods to Civilization,
by Charles A. Eastman
As Published in 1916.
TP: 1582186162 ($11.95)
HC: 1582186170 ($25.95)

The Last of the Great Scouts - The Life of Col. W. F. Cody (Buffalo Bill),
by Helen Cody Wetmore
As Published in 1899.
TP: 1582182019 ($19.95)
HC: 1582182000 ($27.95)

The History of Philip's War,
by Thomas Church, Esq.
As Published in 1827.
TP: 158218089X ($19.95)
HC: 1582181306 ($29.95)

The Life of Mary Jemison - The White Woman of the Genesee,
by James E. Seaver
As Published in 1880.
TP: 1582182337 ($15.95)
HC: 1582182345 ($29.95)

Indian Massacre in Minnesota: A History of the Great Massacre by the Sioux,
by Charles S. Bryant & Abel Murch
As Published in 1864.
TP: 1582184100 ($24.95)
HC: 1582184119 ($39.95)

Wigwam Evenings,
by Charles A. Eastman & Elaine Goodale Eastman
As Published in 1909.
TP: 1582186081 ($13.95)
HC: 158218609X ($26.95)

The Soul of the Indian,
by Charles A. Eastman
As Published in 1911.
TP: 1582186405 ($11.95)
HC: 1582186413 ($22.95)

Recent Indian Wars Under the Lead of Sitting Bull,
by James P. Boyd
As Published in 1891.
TP: 1582182183 ($19.95)
HC: 1582182191 ($29.95)

Life of Sitting Bull and History of the Indian War,
by W. Fletcher Johnson
As Published in 1891.
TP: 1582181985 ($27.95)
HC: 1582181977 ($39.95)

Campaigning With Crook,
by Capt. King
As Published in 1899.
TP: 1582183627 ($15.95)
HC: 1582183635 ($29.95)

Massacres of the Mountains (2 Volume Set),
by J.P. Dunn, Jr.
As Published in 1886.
Volume 1:
TP: 1582182035 ($19.95)
HC: 1582182752 ($34.95)
Volume 2:
TP: 1582182043 ($19.95)
HC: 1582182760 ($34.95)

To order any of the titles listed:

* Contact your local bookstore and order through *Ingram Books*.
* Contact the publisher directly
  (for general information or special event purchases):
   Digital Scanning, Inc.
   344 Gannett Rd., Scituate, MA 02066
   Phone: (781) 545-2100 Fax: (781) 545-4908 Toll Free in the U.S.: 888-349-4443
   email: books@digitalscanning.com
   www.digitalscanning.com

www.ingramcontent.com/pod-product-compliance
Lightning Source LLC
Chambersburg PA
CBHW030132170426
43199CB00008B/41